LETTERS

BETWEEN A

VICTORIAN SCHOOLBOY

AND

HIS FAMILY

1892-1895

LETTERS

BETWEEN A

VICTORIAN SCHOOLBOY

AND

HIS FAMILY

1892-1895

edited by DAVID LISLE CRANE

with an introduction by JULIE CRANE

with the assistance of RICHARD BLAND
(Archivist of Clifton College)

and JEAN WRANGHAM

privately printed

1999

Copies of this book may be had from the following address:
11 Springwell Avenue
North End
Durham DHI 4LY
England
or by contacting tel/fax 0191 384 7859
or on the internet at http://www.worldwidebooks.com

ISBN 0 948545 11 9

Set in Monotype Baskerville

Printed and bound by
Smith Settle, Otley, West Yorkshire

FOR

DADIE RYLANDS

a great encourager

It is an unusual pleasure to have a book dedicated to one, and it gives me particular delight to be associated with this volume of Victorian letters, both because I am aware myself of how difficult and important a thing it is to preserve and transmit the intricate texture of life in the past, and because the world brought alive again in these pages so nearly coincides in time with the world as it first came alive to me.

Dadie Rylands 1998

CONTENTS

LIST OF ILLUSTRATIONS

Original illustrations within the letter text itself

Other illustrations
(people in photographs are identified from left to right and from the back row to the front)

PREFACE

It must be very rare, if not unique, for so complete a record of a public schoolboy's experiences, emotions, trials and tribulations between the ages of fourteen and seventeen to have been preserved for posterity. It has thereby enabled the editors of this fascinating book to present a continuous, authentic narrative, reconstructed in the minutest detail, of what life was truly like for this particular boy at Clifton College a hundred years ago. What makes this collection of letters the more remarkable is the fact that not only did young Tankred Tunstall-Behrens preserve all his letters from home, but that his family equally treasured the son's replies, as well as the correspondence from his housemaster, other schoolmasters and the then headmaster of Clifton, M G Glazebrook ("the bogie").

One can recapture, for instance, the subdued excitement, mingled with apprehension, of the boy's first term, as he tries to cope with the difficult transition from prep school – the Dragon School under C C Lynam ("the skipper") – to the bewildering regime of a great public school; the mounting irritation of having to establish a *modus vivendi* with a study companion of disturbingly messy habits. Then follows the not unfamiliar experience of a trying second year, when novelty has worn off and a sense of mild disillusionment begins to creep in. Unfortunately for Tankred, by nature a very self-willed boy, whose Germanic background rendered it increasingly difficult both for him and his family to reconcile themselves to the indomitable "Englishness" of public school life and conventions, disillusionment turns into disenchantment in his final year. He accuses his housemaster of being unsympathetic and unfair; his defiance of prefectorial authority brings him into conflict with "the bogie" himself, who goes so far as to suggest to Tankred's father that all parties might be the happier if the boy were withdrawn from the school. But Tankred wins through in the end, and answers his critics by gaining a high pass into Woolwich to train for a commission in the Royal Engineers. One has to say, however, that the tone of his letters home frequently confirms the opinion of the Clifton authorities that the boy was wanting in docility, and could be tiresomely querulous and self-opinionated, despite earnest entreaties from his father to acquire the virtues of "a well adapted man".

It is not only the developing story of Tankred's career which compels one to read on ("whatever is going to happen next?"

one is constantly asking oneself). The mass of incidental detail lends so much colour, vitality and authenticity to the narrative – school food, the contents of the hampers from home, the pictures on his study wall, the treatment of medical conditions; the reaction of an adolescent away from home, sensitive to his mother's gaffe in revealing her son's Christian name on letters addressed to him at Clifton, his own assessment, in response to his father's anxious enquiries, of the extent of "vile practices" in the school. Revealing little sidelights occur from time to time in the letters from home – an interesting critique, for example, of Henry Irving's portrayal of King Lear.

David and Julie Crane and Jean Wrangham have between them accomplished a remarkable editorial achievement. To locate the complete correspondence was only the beginning of a monumental task. Then followed the tracking-down of photographs of many of the characters and places referred to in the letters. Painstaking research was necessary to identify characters and allusions, and the deciphering of handwriting (especially the father's), complicated by very idiosyncratic spelling, demanded endless patience. In short, this book is a triumph of careful scholarship and a work of absorbing interest from the first page to the last.

David Newsome

INTRODUCTION

The present edition

This sequence of 318 letters to, from and concerning Tankred Tunstall-Behrens, a schoolboy at Clifton College, Bristol (see p.280), whose home was at Newfield House, Forest Hill on the (then) Kentish border of London (see p.281), was discovered in two separate bundles (letters from and about TTB; and letters to him) among the papers of the Tunstall-Behrens family. The letters cover the period of almost exactly three years between September 1892 and August 1895, the time TTB spent at Clifton.

The text of the letters has been very lightly regularised (to ensure, for example, that the address and date are always placed first), but original spelling, punctuation, capitalisation (or lack of it) and scribal conventions have been allowed to stand; and the text has been presented typographically in a layout intended to give the reader always the impression of reading handwritten letters and not book print. Letters surviving only in draft form have been given a distinctive layout, and all editorial addition has been placed between square brackets.

The commentary consists chiefly of the Biographical Register, in which can be found details of people and animals occurring either in the letter text or the endnotes (together with a key to all abbreviated initials used in page headers of the edited text and elsewhere); and of the endnotes, which are signalled by an asterisk in the letter text.

If those who lived the lives depicted in these letters were able to read this edition of them, they would acknowledge much fact but would also be aware that what was presented here was a tiny proportion of the mass of detail that constituted their lives, and with errors, omissions, distortions of focus, tone, timing, which made out of what is presented here more a realistic novel using much that was familiar to them than a sober account of their experience of being alive in the 1890s. So be it; this is all that can be done in the way of presenting what survives of the past. What one may hope is that what is presented will be at least a sympathetic and living fiction out of these dead bones; that in some way they should live again. The past which cannot be made to live again, or which we have not time or energy to make live again, had better be abandoned, otherwise our knowledge, as T S Eliot says in *East Coker*, the second of the *Four Quartets*, is only "of dead secrets".

The letters and the writers

There is a silhouette on the title page of this book made by
Jean Wrangham from an original photograph (facing this page),
but before that we should begin with the more general
silhouette of the whole family from which these letters spring,
in the Family Tree on p.285. The Family Tree is presented
there to be read not from top to bottom but from left to
right, so that all at once we can see parents standing beside
children and grandchildren, as we trace the offspring of
marriages along the delicate lines of connection, with the sons
and daughters already grown up and married. We notice at
once Johann Behrens and his first wife, Anna Mäurer, standing
beside their married daughter, Karoline Lauterbach, with her
daughter, Christina Frauberger; and it is only the edge of the
page and the confines of this book that prevent an even wider
simultaneity. So the book has its confines and its focus; and
that focus is introduced by the silhouette on the title page.

The silhouette itself, in capturing one gesture, reveals
abruptly a central aspect of the correspondence which in the
letters themselves unfolds more slowly: the ambivalent attitude
of father and son, affectionate, challenging, proud, defiant, on
both sides. In reading the letters between Tankred and Louis
Behrens this suggestive, *positioned* arrangement between them is
a starting point, and something we can never get away from.

To light upon such a complete and self-contained
correspondence as this is a matter, largely, of luck. And yet to
say this is immediately to beg the question. For this sense of
completeness, as we know, is not the fate of all families, and is
not bestowed willy-nilly. It is too outlandish by far to say that
the Pastons, for instance, had such a sense of themselves as
almost to be looking forward to their collected and published
letters; but it is not too outlandish to assert that there are
families whose sense of themselves within a period of history
accelerates, when they put pen to paper, to an inordinate
degree, so that the archivist, coming upon them a hundred or
so years later, reads of their concerns with an astonishment at
having his particular historical preconceptions confirmed. For
this, of course, it is important that the writer is not famous, or
singular, or odd. It is his sense of an age which the archivist
wants confirmed, even as he is astonished to find it so.

That might be the case with the Pastons and their letters in
the fifteenth century. But by the nineteenth century something

Leu, Tankred: Cornwall 1892

Min, Leu: silver wedding 1902

else also has happened. Family correspondence has developed from the shadows of the Pastons, almost imperceptibly to itself, just as the novel has emerged from its tentative origins in ballad and broadsheet. So that the gentleman who takes up his pen to write to his son in 1892 has more of a consciousness of such an act than his predecessors (see, for instance, Tolley's examination of family correspondence). And with the Tunstall-Behrens family this consciousness is registering itself – beginning by summing up the age we think we know, it thence diverts our 'astonishment' into singularity of character, consciousness of self, because this poise between the general and the individual is such a driving force of their writing and our reading of the letters.

What we want from the Victorians is far from simple; and what we want from such a volume of letters as this is far from simple likewise. One of the things we want, perhaps, is what they cannot give us – their spaces: the silence between letters, the silence filled for the writers by the school holidays (when of course there is no letter writing), but for us tantalisingly suggestive. A subject of such concern for pages – a holiday in Ireland, a trip to Cornwall – so earnestly planned, so lavishly looked forward to – is suddenly over, and a new term begins with no account of the event. But here the gift of such a correspondence comes into play: so intimately do we know these people, their plans, their environs, that it is as if we have fished in the Shannon with them, and more than this, have entered that mood of friction, of disillusion, of things being not quite as they were looked forward to being, which thwarts all holidays and all families, and from which this one is by no means exempt. The letters then, carry their weight of sadness, and the affection between father and son, boy and family home, has also to be strenuously asserted and argued and sought for.

Louis (Leu) Behrens

To begin the story of the letters with the picture of Leu – the father who, in the photograph, contemplates and assesses the son – is to begin with the strangest and most oddly constituted of the correspondents, and also the figure in whom all the difficult, driving, shaping energy of the letters is contained. For it is he who is to be pleased or appeased, or appealed to. He directs the shape of the correspondence because he has created it: he it is who has decided to send Tankred to Clifton

College, and if it had been another institution, there would have been different letters; and if his decision had been for a day-school (as, for instance, it was in the case of the next son, Brian), then they would not have existed at all. So that the power of Leu is felt behind even the letters which are not addressed to him.

But his power, his weight of presence, is not just a matter of his historical Victorian paternalistic position; nor merely of the chance of his particular decision regarding his son. Behind history and chance, which shapes the very being of the correspondence, is felt the indomitable, exacting, divided personality which is shaping the character of his son.

Leu was born in Wiesbaden, which until 1866, when it was annexed by Prussia, was the capital of the Duchy of Nassau, and so it was that he witnessed at first hand the fall of an old established state into the hands of another newly arising one, and indeed it would seem that he came to England in 1871 as a result of his disgust and disillusionment with the Franco-Prussian War, by which that new state had confirmed its pre-eminence. The young Leu who lies beyond the admonitions and control of the letters to his son is a palpable presence, once his history is known, and here we have a different habitation of knowledge from Tankred, for Tankred, although he knew, one supposes, his father's history and origins, knew them in the blur of the present, and from the perspective of childhood. His father became a British subject the day before his birth.

Like many exiles, his overpowering desire was to acquire new territory – he spent his son's childhood and youth building upon and altering the house he bought at Forest Hill in 1889 (see p.281). We see, through Min's letters, one concentrated aspect of this – the building of the studio – and this change, constantly heard and seen about her, Min conveys to Tankred, partly with trepidation and more than a little mournfully – as the garden which she knew and loved was dismantled about her (see, for example, let119, 125 & 134). Min, writing to the son who, she felt, absent from home as he was, would appreciate, in his capacity as letter reader, every stroke of hammer and every unsettling movement upon the old as only those can who see with the eye of distance the dismemberments of a place they are passionately, though strangely, attached to – Min is our main insight into this focus of Leu's alterations and, somehow, this vision of a changing, quickly-shifting London.

But it was more than a house that Leu the voluntary exile

Newfield House: c1895

Leu, Min: Newfield interior c1895

Tyra: Newfield interior c1895
The wooden board above the fireplace has on it the following text in
pokerwork: Floddenfield [Edward] Thurlow [1781-1829]/ To every lovely
Lady bright,/ What can I wish but faithful Knight?/ To every faithful
Lover too,/ What can I wish but Lady true?/ And knowledge to the
studious Sage/ And pillow soft to head of age

wanted to build. His family, especially his eldest son, was to be shaped and moulded, and that was a more difficult and elusive and uncertain matter than a house, frustrating to the father, perplexing to the son: "I personally like to hear as often as possible from you, yet only when it gives *you* pleasure to write to your father, when it comes from the fulness of your heart, when you begin to feel drawn to him. Love without respect is worthless" (let111).

He concludes with a conventional reproof, but before that it is the fulness of the heart he wants to control in Tankred, and being powerless to do so is beset by melancholy: in a season of illness and death, and his son defiant, Leu is led to contemplate the meaninglessness of his vision of happiness, of kinship with his children: "The sunshine of life gets clouded, I begin almost to despair when I have to fear that the eldest, on whom I naturally depend most in assisting me in the building up of a strong & great family, & whose life I am so anxious to shape into a happy one, is akin, but not of soul...".

"The times are serious", Leu continues, and reminds Tankred of "the day of regret when no further sound passes the father's lips". Working with Leu's manipulation of Tankred's feelings towards him is an obsessive awareness of the passing of time, the silence beyond words, and the need to build up something substantial (in physical terms the collection of objects – see photographs of Newfield interior facing this page – at Forest Hill, the constant building and changing). Where Min peeps through the grating of the Ladies' Gallery in the House of Commons and enjoys the ludicrousness of an institution which sits uneasily with its propelling force (see let106), Leu is certain of the value of all monuments in an age when men fell like flies (as when do they not) – as a letter crosses, as influenza develops into complications, as men fall in war, and states that have been secure and proud through history fall, like Nassau to Prussia. But there is something in the force of such a destructive quality – death, kingdoms – which Leu wants to isolate and appropriate. He venerates the "kingdom of Prussia" (see Biog Reg under LWFB) even as he flees from it, and battle is his great motif: "if impossible then war" (let188).

Leu's naturalisation papers, coming into effect the day before Tankred's birth, seem to boast of Wiesbaden "in the kingdom of Prussia". In this assertion of the triumphant new state it is not whimsical perhaps to see the tugs of tension in Leu's character. Despairing, disillusioned though he is, he is still in awe of the triumphant new kingdom which has shaken his history and sense of his own past. The proclamation of the naturalisation papers, heralding his life in England, is boastful and mournful at the same time; and the determination to control his family, and yet the difficulties of doing so, allied with that sense of the day when no further reproaches will be heard, because the father is silent forever, informs the tone of his letters, and hedges them with his unique characteristics of successful manipulation and despair.

This despair clouds the enjoyment of his inheritance of those gifts which he wished to share with, and in some measure passed on to, his eldest son. His forbears in the old Duchy of Nassau had been prosperous and talented: his grandfather had been a locksmith in Braunschweig and his father, Johann Ernst, a master saddler and a substantial citizen of Wiesbaden (see Biog Reg under Lauterbach). In the letters which pass between Leu and Tankred laying plans for workshops and practical schemes for the holidays one senses the clink of hammer on metal and the smell of leather and stable in that far kingdom, with its guilds and busyness and assurance of its own importance which Tankred knew nothing of and which his father had left in distress before he was born. It survived, though, for Tankred and his siblings, in visits from Leu's sisters, Emma and Caro, in letters and packages from Germany, in Leu's (frustrated) determination that Tankred should speak German like a native (see let5), in odd quotations from Goethe (see let9), and in a hundred anecdotes and reminiscences which are the spaces we shall never possess.

And in the eternal, but somehow peculiarly Victorian, tragedy between father and son (in the manner of *The Way of all Flesh* or *Father and Son*; see Bibliog under Butler and Gosse), Tankred did not possess them either. At times in the letters between the two what comes across is a genuine bewilderment on the part of the son as to what his father actually *means* (see, for example, let177). And if we extend this 'meaning' beyond specific day to day details and complaints about Tankred's slipshod style (see, for example, let180, 276 & 296), into a genuine search by Tankred for what it was his father represented and wanted him to inhabit, the letters immediately open out for us so that we as readers now, with Tankred as correspondent then, are standing temporarily in the same space, with its curious, restlessly defining, aspiring but essentially elusive directions and signposts and rules and desires: "The times are serious", and Tankred, poised in a correspondence to which he is bound by distance and habit and duty and affection, is in a serious relation to them, but what is it, in the end, that his father wants him to be? At times this overpowers him completely, and because he is a boy, and beset daily by cares of a nature belonging to an institution he has not quite grasped, and aware of other cares constantly focussed by his father with an intensity he cannot understand, his response, with both his parents, is to fall into the querulous and petulant: "Although you may think you answer my questions you never do..." (let209).

The young man, Louis Wilhelm Ferdinand Behrens, that Tankred never knew, was the opposite, one imagines from his known career, of 'slipshod'. But also, it appears that no father held long sway over his developing character. Johann Ernst the master saddler died in 1856, when his son was nine and his daughter Emma was two (see Family Tree). From his father's first marriage Leu had a half-sister Caro, seven years older than himself, and his own mother and Emma's, Henriette Behrens, married again after his father's death. This complication of family relationships gives, paradoxically, two things to Leu: it both ties him up in various relationships and kinships which have to be unravelled and which cling to his identity and habits (a 'birthday list' found among his papers is an important indicator of his affections and sense of hierarchy), and at the same time it gives him – in alliance with certain other circumstances – a freedom of movement which was denied to his eldest son. His chosen exile, his being surrounded by sisters, his complicated distress at the Franco-Prussian War (he is proudly an "old soldier" in let259 & 140 as well as turning from all that Prussia represented in that war), his emergence from a fallen Duchy to make something new, all give to Leu a kind of instant and assured though complex manhood, the confidence and certainty of the exiled maker, which his son must inherit, hedged in by a history which eludes him and a father whose presence is continually felt. To find oneself the child of an exile, even a successful and substantial one, to be the second generation following upheaval, war, and change, is to live always, even more intensely than most, in the shadows of one's parents, and to carry an uneasy inheritance.

The opposite of slipshod, then, the young Leu Behrens created his own history so securely and determined upon so sure a sense of his own direction, as to know his English sponsors for some years before his settling in England, and before the setting up of his flourishing office at 71 Eastcheap, where he embarked upon the business which Tankred, with the thoughtlessness of the inheritor, was so pleased that he should be quitting (see let14), but which established the prosperity into which he was born. Some time after August 1871, when he settled in England, he began to pay court to Emily Tunstall. The circumstances of the courtship are vague, but the Tunstalls' trading business in close proximity to Eastcheap suggests that he met his future wife through his common business association with her father (see Biog Reg under Barnett), and stepped easily, in Dickensian fashion, from the bustle of the workaday world of offices and ledgers into the settled charm of the drawing room, where Emily and perhaps her two little sisters, Lilian and Mabel (about twenty years younger than she, and known in the family as "the pets"), were to be found. Emily – delicate, gentle, with literary tastes and shining with her family's affection and esteem (see Biog Reg under EFB) – was his particular object, but it is not too much to suppose that the family itself exercised its charm on the young emigré; that they had an attraction for him in his exiled state (and in any disenchantment he might have felt at the crushing Prussian victory in the Franco-Prussian War) for being French on their mother's side (see Family Tree), and for having an absent brother in British Columbia; that the talk around the Tunstall family table had about it the pleasing pulls towards both the ordinary and everyday matters of business and towards this edge of difference which distinguished them.

He married Emily in 1877, and they took up residence at Newfield. Thus it is that the Tunstall women slide from the envisaged hazy but graceful picture of their youth, towards being Grandma and Lil and Mabs, and the loving Min of Tankred's letters.

With the settling at Newfield and his naturalisation as an English subject, Leu on the birth of his first child Tankred in 1878 was moving, also, with the smooth rapidity which he had almost planned, into the shrewd and anxious assessor of his son so poignantly caught in the silhouette photograph. His stance had been worked for, but Leu had reckoned without his own innate gloom and his sense of time passing; his success, his superlative energies, lay heavily upon him. There was nothing to be done but make, and anxiously re-make, the splendours he had gained. And so it was that the house at Newfield came to be cluttered with weaponry and suits of armour which were the debris of his visionary horror, and which upset at least some visitors to the house, and were a trial to his family (see Doc App LVIII). His gift for painting was made to submit to his own grief and horror when, after his daughter's death, he painted his remaining children fixed in their affliction, outdone only in strangeness by a portrait of himself, standing at the foot of the dead girl's bed, as though he would stay and control even death, if he could. The land he bought in Cornwall comforted, but could not appease, his energies, and when he himself died in 1910 his obituaries celebrated, but could not quite locate, his oddities, the strange sense of a prodigality which had been waylaid by a certain despair (see Doc App LXI-LXVI).

Emily (Min) Behrens

The young woman who emerged from the haze of the Tunstall family picture in 1877 to be Leu Behrens' wife was not excessively young, being twenty-seven years old, and yet it was young enough, perhaps, for many of her qualities to be indistinct. She is in her early forties by the time she takes up her pen to write the first letter to Tankred at Clifton in 1892 – an established matron by Victorian standards – but in this first letter there is enough of the younger woman for us to be able to see behind it to the house which Leu Behrens visited and where the family were grouped for tea. And whereas the younger figure of Leu behind the letters can be grasped only by a sense of large historical forces and important changes working upon him, that of Min can be understood in a more accessible way, for the whole character of Min is present in these letters at different times – the young girl beloved by her brother, and the middle-aged woman writing to her son, can be caught in the same attitudes. And she had, most important for a letter-writer, qualities which no other of the correspondents could convey: a sunniness, a self-containment, and a generosity of character, together with an enjoyment of communicating her feelings in words, which must have made a letter from Min an altogether different matter, for Tankred, than was a letter from Leu. Although acknowledging the importance of those time-honoured matters, duty and obedience and education, there is something about Min with a pen in her hand which, even in the midst of crisis, is not subsumed by them. Her son, in this capacity at least, is not to be hectored, because he is of equal standing in his role as recipient of her delighted and generous response to the world in which she finds herself.

And this world, for Min, proved to be of ever-increasing excitement. As builders at Newfield clattered around her, as the younger boys were trying and entertaining by turns, as cooks came and went, until finally they settled upon one so ugly that she and Tyra were appalled in their sympathy (see let216 & 232), as her husband grew gloomy and restless, life for Min grew larger and more alluring. Min, by the time of the letters, has emerged wonderfully, triumphantly, from the hazy picture of her girlhood. She has become – winningly for this correspondence – altogether a woman of her age. She would have been happy in no other. There are a thousand causes to further and ideas to contemplate and meetings to attend. But just as she becomes suggestive of the strenuousness of the Victorian ideal, something else happens to the character of Min; she recalls this representative quality for us only fleetingly, nothing more; she is so much her own self, earnest yet delicate, serious yet humorous, that she is the perfect inhabitor of such a correspondence as this. Unlike her husband, she has strength and definition without oddity, and it is through Min, largely, that we are able to repose, in reading, upon the twin notions of a sense of an age, which we ask from history, and the delight in the sympathy of character which we have come to expect from the novel.

Min, as the beginner of the correspondence, reveals immediately two qualities which seem to characterise it, but which are in fact largely her own gifts: the quality of stability, and the possibility of movement. Min's first letter (see let1) expresses the anxiety of the unknown, but also the larger possibilities of unknowing. Her questions have about them the conscious hopelessness of one who has relinquished a child to an unknown, impenetrable world – "Have you had an exam, have you seen Mr Glazebrook – have you found some nice companions –", so that around such flung questions from the very beginning is built up a sense of how far away home is, for a boy in such a situation as Tankred's, how far away in particular are mother and sister and younger brothers – Roy and Brian wearing Tankred's discarded collars have a poignancy suggestive of those who remain behind the charmed glass of childhood, and Min's opening sentence, in its very willingness to imagine, summons the impenetrability of the barrier between that childhood and the world which Tankred as the eldest son must now inhabit, which is his father's world of duty and making anew: "We have been picturing your first Sunday

amidst fresh fields & pastures new but the only thing I
made sure of, was, that you were in that beautiful chapel in
the morning."

Min in her generosity wants to convey to Tankred a sense
of excitement and movement – hence the familiar
misquotation from Milton's *Lycidas* – but this is immediately
countered in the second half of her first sentence by a
desire to cling to a stable image – the beauty of the chapel.
To fix Tankred there – to have "made sure" of his presence
there, at a particular time – was perhaps for Min a way of
defying the knowledge which the very existence of the letters
makes apparent: that Tankred has irrevocably gone, now that
he has left for this big school (so different from the little
prep school in Oxford); gone from trips to Worthing and
outgrown collars and birthday tea with the Lambleys; gone
from the mysterious "ship called Tyra" which was perhaps of
his making; and gone from the summer which is just past
and which presaged his going and which Min's letters, for all
their dignity and family news, are grieving for.

The difficulties of Clifton were placed in a different perspective
for Min because, while acquiescing in the placing of her son in a
traditional mould, she was fascinated by progress and new ideas –
not merely about education, but about science, women's
emancipation, religion. One way out, it seems, of the gloom and
constant restlessness of Newfield was into an activity of mind and
thought which brought only light and the possibility of salutary
change. While Tankred labours under the injunctions of Mr Hall
as to the correct procedures in mathematics, Min visits the house
and grounds of a new school, Bedales, just started by Mr Badley
(see Biog Reg) "on a new system" (let20). There is nothing of the
revolutionary about Min – she does not expect such new systems
to extend to her own children; in the very same letter where she
describes to Tankred the Bedales visit, she goes on to talk of
Tyra's difficulties at Roedean in conventional terms: under her
"special teacher Miss Morris" she "is at least trying". Hers was
not the kind of temperament which rebelled against what must
be, but rather which gathered from such forces such light as there
was, to submit them to her own radiant hope. After quoting the
"Infants crying in the night" passage from Tennyson, Min writes
to Tankred in let116, "Goethe died asking for "more light" &
we are still in the same position, but the world
has moved far more rapidly in the last 50 years than ever
before & advance will I believe become more and more

rapid. Think of *Science*, the *means of progression*, the *position of women, Democracy!*"

These are banners for Min. When it is said of "the institution of Board schools" that they represent "a change as great as the Reformation", the phrase has a sound that she finds irresistibly stirring. To read of Min's enthusiasm for such matters is to know what it is like to be in the presence of an intelligent encourager of change, and so partly to know how change was wrought by just such an enabling, willing intelligence on the part of many who possessed nothing else, perhaps, but will and intelligence. To quote Mr Allen, Tom Mann, Mrs Boole, is to be, for Min, not docile but to grasp at the hope of future change. As the fog creeps down towards her study so that in the gloom of Newfield she can barely see to write (see let105), such quotations from thinkers and promoters of change shore up her hope of a larger world. And because she is a woman of order and innate happy sense, they are not fragments placed randomly; such ideas of goodness and change must unite with her own situation, her own love for her children, and, because she is the most generous of letter writers, with her poor eldest boy's narrow world at Clifton. And so it is that Tankred, in between news of Brian and Roy, and practical responses about hampers and Jaeger shirts, has all the benefits of Christo-Theosophical wisdom (see Biog Reg under George Allen and Doc App L-LI), and Mrs Boole's enlightened vision (see Doc App LII-LIII), and the excitement about Dewar's "frozen air" (let116). Sluggish and churlish and imprisoned though Tankred often is, it is through Min, if anyone, that he will be allowed to escape, back to the home he has left, and to see her figure, still neat and trim, striding out to meeting after meeting, lecture after lecture, after settling the boys with Fräulein and organizing everything with the cook; and it is through Min, if anyone, that he will be able to look beyond Clifton and its confines, toward the future she so delightedly sketches for him and which she is so certain he will enhance with his shining qualities.

It is with forbearing, with a certain just level of anxiety, that Min holds on to the idea of these qualities in her son which are being so carefully moulded by Clifton and by her husband's hopes. She does not forget, in writing of her visit to the House of Commons, to summon up a picture of the older Tankred: "I wonder if you will ever sit there, the "Honourable & Gallant Member"!" (let106) But it is only a fleeting glimpse, a nod in the direction of Leu's wishes. Where Leu might have weighed in with the qualities requisite for holding such a place, Min is satisfied with the picture itself – amused and fond, her son grown up. It is a kindly instinct in her to offer such pictures – one day you will be grown up, when you are home we will talk of such matters – for she knew well that there were difficulties enough at Clifton, and if a line from her in a letter can even momentarily ease them, then so much the better. She does not forget, then, to include Tankred in her enjoyment; but, as is the way of kindness, she will not fix him there, for her enjoyment is her own, untrammelled. On this occasion it is an outing with Mrs Beaver to hear of the Employers' Liability Bill, and as she leans forward and peers through the grating of the Ladies' Gallery to watch the proceedings below, the Min who enjoys the pomp and absurdity of an occasion, and the Min who can repeat a lesson, merge so fully that one cannot be disentangled from the other, she has so generously bequeathed what is willing and enthusiastic in her character to what her age is willing to teach: "It is a remnant of old custom, & survives as many old customs do the stage of thought & feeling which created them. You see thought & feeling go ahead of the laws before it changes them" (let106). It might be a snippet from a lecture by Mrs Boole she is quoting, or Tom Mann, but the desire for thought and feeling to dance on ahead of the laws they will change has been so welcomed by Min that the pressure of desire in the tone is all her own.

This pressure is felt in her thoughts about goodness. Change, for Min, represents an aspiration towards good – otherwise she would have nothing to do with it. And there are times when her own spontaneity troubles her, and even Mr Allen cannot reassure her. His lecture on Blake's poetry (see let66) presents her with dangers: how can we be sure that what we have chosen from instinct is after all the highest good? Should we not, after all, fall back upon duty and compulsion? Is there not something a little wayward for a mother to be voicing such enthusiasms and questionings to her eldest son who is going through such trials of character at Clifton? And so there are times when Min joins in the strenuous moral atmosphere which surrounds Tankred – "I should like you to realize (without bitter experience) the great fact that in as much as you swerve from the right in anything whatever – to that extent you are making the bed you needs must lie in. You are moulding *your own* character, which will be yours to suffer or improve to the end. If you can see that goodness is the loveliest & the best & can choose it for its own sake & for the love of it, you will yourself be the best in every way in untold measure" (let72).

It is an uneasy, sinuous compromise between the strenuous application of Victorian ideals, and the deeply personal, questing, almost psychic sense of goodness which Min was drawn to. For there, in the midst of her injunctions, is surely an echo of Fitzgerald's *Rubáiyát of Omar Khayyám* – "the loveliest & the best" (see endnote in let72). That this ethereal, lush, fin-de-siècle voguish poem can be wrenched into use for the muscular Christian notion of duty which is being placed before Tankred here, is not merely a consequence of Min's own temperament at work – it is the temperament of her age. But because Min is the most alive, in many ways, the most flexible and agile of the correspondents in this collection, it is herself mostly that is uppermost. And there is what we know of sadness in her history, too; she may perhaps be thinking, in echoing Fitzgerald, of that brother who died in New Mexico (see Biog Reg under EFB and Barnett), for whom also she herself was certainly "the loveliest & the best", if his letter to her future husband is anything to go by (see Doc App XLII-XLIII).

Min's enthusiasms, her love of life and change, her anxieties for her children, have all to be placed against a background which included the figure of Leu, who was such a creature of uncertainty to John Henry Tunstall in that letter. To perceive a Victorian woman apart from the institution of marriage which enveloped her is only possible up to a point. Min is the most lively and vibrant of letter writers, but her very vibrancy has to be gauged against the figure of Leu. Against unhappiness in marriage there was then mostly no means of radical negotiation, only a constant shifting of hope and values, so that what one is left with is a re-making into a solid picture: the portrait of Min and Leu on the occasion of their silver wedding anniversary in 1902 (facing p.xv), one's mother and father, things as they are. It is a situation, as Min might have said, "which will be yours to suffer or improve to the end".

When Min raised her head, while writing to Tankred, to gaze across the grounds of Newfield, it was to see the dismantling of a garden which she loved in order to accommodate a studio her husband insisted upon. When she emerged from her study with the letter all ready for the post, to call Tyra, or welcome Mrs Beaver, it was to confront a hall increasingly filled with armour and a strange assembly of gloomy objects. Her friends grew used to them, even as they picked their way around them into Min's study, where tea awaited them, after Mrs Boole's latest lecture had been heard, presided over by Mr Allen (see let211). But then Leu complained to Tankred that his mother was turning the hall into a public meeting room. The place was filled with earnest, chattering, philanthropic ladies, not unlike the Schlegels' house in Forster's *Howards End*. The areas of light which Min claimed in the house were centres of noisy nonsense to Leu.

And it was Leu's preferences and prejudices which must finally predominate. He might limit his dislike of her philanthropic activities to mere grumblings and a general air of displeasure, which Min was free to ignore, but she was not free to see her own young sisters in her own home until he permitted it. Some rift had arisen. Lilian and Mabel, too, apparently, had emerged from the haze of being the little sisters of Min, to become women with voices and opinions, and emerging from the stasis of that earlier picture, children and elder sister – which, after all, could not be stayed forever – they had said something, or done something, which had roused Leu's ire. The reason is shrouded in time, tucked safe beyond all scrutiny of archivist and historian. Whether it was something to do with the Barnett trouble (see Biog Reg), or some comment on the weaponry, or on Leu's business or his history is unknown. The end of the breach only is recorded in a letter from Min to Tankred, her relief obvious as she relates Leu's lordly forgiveness: "Last Sunday when Grandma was leaving your father said to her "I dont wish to see you coming alone dear Ma but ask Lil & Mabs to come & let bygones be bygones"! & on Wednesday they came with Grandma to dinner & kissed & made up & I think your dear father was very glad to see their dear bonnie faces. & now I can be happy again, which I could never be as long as our darling Lilian and Mabel were shut out from the family unity" (let49).

The matter is made more vivid, if anything, by Tankred's pleased but dismissive response: "I am so glad. It has been made up. did not I tell you it only needed time" (let51). And on he goes to demand that she answer *all* his questions, not forgetting those that he wrote "on the back of the envelope". For Tankred is so taken up with his new regime, so beleaguered by masters and boys and difficulties, so constantly running out of paper and tooth powder and stamps, that there can be nothing more trivial, to him, than this absurd matter of his aunts visiting at Newfield.

But behind such a tone lies a feeling which is also apparent throughout the letters in his attitude to his mother: and that is the idea that, in his difficult serious growth to manhood, he is growing beyond her, superseding her. Although his relationship with Leu is often tense, it is fraught with a consciousness of an authority, which must be made and shared by both of them. Partly what Clifton is about is this very forming of apparent indifference towards the delicacies and vulnerabilities of mother and aunts. Leu has "ideas" (let9) which it is Tankred's serious business to shape himself to, and collude with; Min has news of home, colour, natural anxieties, spontaneous descriptions which Tankred loves, but which he is being trained to place in a subordinate position to the matter of becoming a "thorough *Man*" (let80). The course of the correspondence depicts how interestingly, ambivalently and yearningly he is caught at a crucial point of development in this process, which it was the business, after all, of the public school system to accomplish.

Min's character is strong enough, and self-contained enough, to rise above and exist beyond such a process. In her account of the forgiveness of Lilian and Mabel, what shines through is not deference to Leu – despite a cursory obeisance towards it, largely for Tankred's benefit – but her delight in welcoming her sisters, her enjoyment in everything being well. And because she is a born letter writer it is this feeling which she can convey. Despite her immersion in the excitement of large ideas, what her letters are best at evoking is moments, gestures: one sees the old lady caught by Leu's benevolence on the very point of leaving (and thus, beyond this, to his brooding on the question all through tea); just as one sees Min herself, weary and dejected, waiting until four o' clock at "Pipes" in the hope of engaging a new cook, when finally a young woman comes in who will do, "& I think I hear her just coming into the house" (let13).

And after all, despite the robust teachings of the tradition he was enmeshed in, despite his anxieties to conform to Leu's ideal, it was also for such moments as this that the boy lived, reading the letter in the cramped study which he shared with the disorderly Irish boy. Home was suddenly evoked – briefly, vividly – his mother writing, the new cook just arriving for the first time, everything going on as it had before, as it would do until he, too, could re-enter it in the holidays. Almost unconsciously, Min's letters enable to run more gently that relentless process of mature assumption of authority which had been set in motion by Leu and Clifton. Min yields Newfield to him by the very assumption that such moments, such gestures as someone hovers in a doorway, or lingers over tea, are immediately accessible to the boy in the midst of cares away from home: "Brian told us of such a nice little dream of his – he said "I dream't that they wanted to make me a king but I said I wanted to stay with my mother so I said 'Did they make you a king all the same' No *I said* I wished to stay with *my mother*" (let13).

What Min enables by such reported anecdotes is for Tankred, the heir apparent of his father's designs, to be reconciled to his own position, and indeed throughout the correspondence his attitude towards the younger boys is a mixture of fondness and condescension. Her response to the difficulties at Clifton has about it a similar, barely conscious but sometimes hopeless tact. Her son, anxious about the rightness of the Saturday night ritual of the younger boys being forced by the older boys to fight, receives the advice from Min that he should perhaps think of it as "boxing & a training for self defence...I think if I were you, I should use my influence in the direction of getting it to be so regarded, by so regarding it yourself & when you have an adversary who is not your equal in strength, dealing gently with him" (let13).

In such a situation Min's gentleness, her wish for the good in all things, clouds her sense of the real atmosphere of that institution which she has no first-hand knowledge of, and which is shaping her son for good or ill. It is *probably* all right – especially as it takes place with boxing gloves (Min clings to the boxing gloves as a guarantee of good intentions) – and anyway, all that is needed is *re-definition* towards the good that exists, rather than any acquiescence with any aggression which may be present. The boy reading such a letter in his study may be excused for feeling a little impatient, even as he must be moved by the gentle ineptness of the advice. To imagine that a boy who has been not a month at the school will have any "influence"! To suppose that those intent on malicious enjoyment should even notice how Tunstall-Behrens is "regarding it" himself, and be prepared to base their own response upon his! If Tankred's relationship with Leu, throughout the correspondence, can be discerned as an alert, watchful, often fraught development into a partnership to uphold some typical Victorian values and ideals, then there are times when his link with Min seems to drift into sepia, and she becomes that figure of the Victorian mother with regard to her son which has become so familiar to us – remote, tender, untouched by the world.

But the vividness and self-sufficiency of her letters will not allow her to remain so for long. Whatever the troubles were which from time to time beset her, Min is exquisitely placed for us as a letter writer of the late nineteenth century. She was, after all, an intelligent woman of leisure, and she has used her intelligence and leisure generously as far as posterity is concerned. To come across her is to stumble, with delight, upon something which, although not known about previously, we always knew was rumoured of, and certainly we would be poorer had we not found it: a woman working, with perfect ease and with no self-consciousness, at the nugget of a gift which she scarcely knows she has; with a pen in her hand Min can evoke her world with a few strokes. She herself loves "atmosphere": "now do write & tell me all about yourself & that place, any little everyday thing – which to you seems trifling, would *greatly interest me*. Who shares your study, for instance – & what kind of atmosphere you are in now compared with last term -" (let156).

She herself has just given to Tankred a perfect rendering of the "atmosphere"' she is in herself. Accompanying Grandma to Norfolk, she can enjoy talking to the fishermen – she has counted 93 boats on the sea. One of the men has a boat rather like Roberts' own, and walking through the villages and along the hedgerows she takes note not only of the beauty of the place but of its orderliness, of how its idea of crop rotation was so assured that it became the "Norfolk system", and of how different this is from last year's holiday in Ireland with the disorderliness and ruin of that country. All this is given to her son, easily and with relish – reminders of last year's holiday, reminders of Roberts who was a central part of family experience and boyhood for Tankred, and not least the picture of herself, with space enough to walk out alone amidst all this newness, and enjoy comparisons with what is already felt, what she knows her son will feel again when reading; and this is mixed with her instinctive enjoyment of what is entirely of the moment: the sudden beauty of the church in the middle of the little wood, the scent of roses, the delight of sitting on the porch and hearing the birdsong mingling with the anthem within – "it was an exquisite combination". It is because we can catch Min alone, at such moments as these, as well as in her role of mother and wife, or as the enthusiastic disciple of change, that her letters yield such richness.

And then there are the times when her character seems – surprisingly, intriguingly, – to break all bounds; when we can only watch with something amounting to Leu's own appalled horror, as the fit of enthusiasm for skating with her children and their friends, in the "splendid frost" (let237) of February 1895, takes over, and Min must absolutely have skates, and must be out every day, sometimes until midnight, although her efforts cause Tyra such amusement (see let232). Indeed it is as though a kind of madness has descended on Newfield during this winter. Perhaps it was something to do with the visit of Louis Neuendorff, Leu's nephew, the son of his sister Emma. The young German kinsman, so charming and obliging, so accomplished on the French horn, must be entertained, must be impressed perhaps, and here, obligingly, was the most beautiful and picturesque winter (but also the most menacing) that could be afforded; and once sledging (see let222) had been exhausted, and skating took over, the fit for skating beset the whole family, except Leu, who wrote sagely to his eldest son at Clifton about the inadvisability of giving in to such "*Untempered* enthusiasm" (let238), and could only watch grimly as they set off wilfully – his wife and his nephew (with Louis' friend Hauerl), Tyra and Brian and Roy, Chet and Mabel – to enjoy falling about on the ice, his wife abandoning even her philanthropic schemes temporarily in order to stumble about in this unseemly fashion. Some days, for Leu, were better: then there would be music, which Min also delighted in. His nephew would play – the piano or the French horn (see let225) – and Mr Schrattenholz would be there (see let222), and the mania and nonsense of skating would settle into civility, and Leu could hope the music and the civility of the evening would calm them all, would chase the fashion and furore of exploits on the ice from their minds.

But music did not drive out sledging and skating. And Leu's worst fears were realized: on 12th February 1895 he writes to Tankred, distractedly, "Roy has influenza with pneumonia complications" (let231), and later: "My *treasures*, are *my* children if God takes them, I must submit, *he alone* knows my grief & anxiety" (let234).

Min writes – not particularly chastened – to Tankred, from the sickbed of Mabel (see let237) who has also succumbed to influenza, and has to stay on at Newfield, a nuisance, as Leu complains to Tankred, since there was so much nursing of one's own family to be done (see let238). Roy recovers; Tyra has influenza, but not badly enough to arouse great fears. The crisis is past – Louis Neuendorff's visit slides to an end amidst linseed poultices and boiled milk and barley water.

Astonishingly, Min will not let go of her "enthusiasm". After such a crisis, she can write to Tankred: "We are so sorry to have this stop put to our skating this splendid frost – which continues amazingly. We were all getting on so nicely in spite of the disrespectful way in wh. Tyra writes of my performances. I hope to go on again perhaps to-morrow" (let237).

It is not madness, perhaps. It may be that what Min has discovered is a love of physical energy, of movement, and despite everything she cannot relinquish it, cannot deny the discovery of this will for movement in herself. "This splendid frost" – it is *her* frost, special because it allowed her to slide about and stumble over and move with no inhibition. Sitting by a sickbed writing to Tankred, she insists that it "continues amazingly"; she cannot let it go.

This response to the physical continued to be felt throughout the rest of her life. If we follow her beyond the scope of the letters, we see her as a keen bicyclist, who, with her gift for recording details, kept a record, between 1896 and 1903, of all the expeditions she made (see endnote on **bicyclists** in let297). In 1912 she went up in an aeroplane – the same Min who wrote so enthusiastically to Tankred on the excitement of change. And yet not quite the same. By 1912 she was a widow; Roy had left England for Canada and then America in 1907; Tankred was often abroad; but most importantly, perhaps, Tyra had died, her death from complications following influenza in 1901 at the age of twenty preceding that of the Queen by six days. The passing of the Victorian age and the dawning of the twentieth century was ushered in for the Tunstall-Behrens family by a nearer, darker grief. The dawning of the great age of change which should have held such excitement for Min was not all that she thought it would be. The family was bereft and disintegrated. There would be no daughter visiting her with grandchildren as she had visited her mother and Mabel and Lilian; Roy's child (who bore her daughter's name; see Family Tree), born in 1918, she would never know; the only one of her other grandchildren she lived to see was Morwenna. And so it was that the relative freedom she experienced after Leu's death in 1910 became restlessness. She left Newfield (which was sold in 1912) – its darkness, its memories, the studio she had hated, the bits of garden she had loved, the room where Tyra had died – and moved from place to place, so that her remaining children hardly knew where to find her, her movements were so uncertain. She was in north London – at 72 Normandy Avenue, Barnet, an ordinary house after Newfield, and not very far from where she had lived before her marriage – when she suffered the "severe accident" which led to her death in 1923 (see Doc App LXVII), the result of some sudden enthusiastic moment, perhaps, about which her husband would have been severe.

Tankred Tunstall-Behrens

To enter Tankred's world after Min's is to confront a temperament beset by change rather than stirred by it. As Min prepares for settling Tyra at Brighton (see let1), her eldest son makes the journey to Clifton unaided. First there was the train to London Bridge, where a porter was required; then a cab to Paddington (again a porter), then the train to Bristol (another porter), another cab, until finally he arrived at Clifton – at the cost of 16/5½, duly recorded (see let7); but the cost in anxiety, the troubled imaginings of the boy summoning porters and negotiating for cabs, is recorded more obliquely. Nevertheless he is there, that figure which stands behind the Tankred of the later letters, in the tone of the early correspondence: "I am all in a continual muddle about my work, for I either dont know which room to go to or else what lesson must be done that hour, or else what master I have to go to, or what work to prepare; All is so *entirely* new & different to what I have been used to" (let7).

What first comes upon him on arrival at Clifton is necessarily relief – after the broodings of the train and the cab – at its immediacy, its ordinariness of initial welcome: "Mr Moor is *very nice indeed*...So far as I can see there is *no bullying whatever*" (let7). The disenchantment comes later, and also the falling away of the immediate fabric of welcome to reveal the hard, tough stuff of its centre – the eternal stasis of the public school picture which must mean for each individual caught within it a negotiation with externals, with seeming trivialities, with small humiliations. After the welcome by Mr Moor these begin to become apparent (see let7); to share a study with an untidy Irish boy impervious to reason is trying, but to be picked out from the mass of boys and accused of "*affectation*" regarding the spelling of one's surname is a moment of humiliating intensity not to be forgiven or forgotten: "and so he said that I was to oblige him by not write down my name as such while I was at the school & then what was worse he told me that it was only a bit of my *affectation* & this he said before all my form 18 boys. I think he *is an utter & intolerable beast*" (let7).

What is captured here by Tankred is not only the vividness of his sudden hatred for Mr Hall, but Mr Hall's own schoolmasterly speech, what must have been his actual turns of phrase – "oblige him", "as such" – in a moment of unthinking sarcasm and irritation which Tankred conveys not through irony, nor through any conscious rendering of the picture, but in the very heated recollection of the feeling of the moment, that moment when the establishment, which he had so far managed deftly, keeping it uneasily at bay, turned the full force of its power upon him.

As every schoolboy knows, bullying is about being *singled out*. It will not do forever to keep one's head down and negotiate. The time will come when one must face things. The reason, perhaps, why bullying has never been rooted out, why the public schools are so ambivalent about deterring it, is on account of this very kinship which bullying shares with fortune itself. However that may be, Mr Hall, on a September day in 1892, is caught afflicting Tankred Tunstall-Behrens on account of the oddness of his name, in idle unthinking schoolmasterly tones which he has been employing for years, and the new boy, so alert and taut and responsive, will never forgive him that. Mr Hall has in this correspondence a position which he might find satisfactory; but in spite of what else we know of him, from these letters and elsewhere (see Biog Reg) – that he was the first old boy to become a master at Clifton, the fact of his friendship with Mr Moor, and the success of his mathematical textbooks – he remains in our memory throughout the letters as Tankred's "*intolerable beast*", just as there remains Mr Moor's niceness; even though, curiously, the two seem to change places later in Tankred's feelings about them (see let138 & 275).

The matter went further than an affliction of the moment. It summoned for Tankred a recollection of that very recent occasion, just days before his journey to Clifton, when he and all his siblings had been christened in St Nicholas Cole Abbey by Mr Allen (see Biog Reg under George Allen). It had been noted in the Baptismal Register that "at parents' written request", the children were now all to be named *Tunstall-Behrens*. The vulnerable area of specialness – of not being christened shortly after birth like everyone else, of having a hyphenated, partly German name as he embarked upon the course which would turn him into an English gentleman, of having this surname attached to a Christian name which stood out as though it belonged to a German opera of tragic legend (or else to the earnest rectitude of the English novel written by the Jewish Disraeli in 1847, *Tancred, or The New Crusade*) – had been cleverly and cruelly, as it seemed to Tankred, located by Mr Hall and submitted to public scrutiny.

The matter was settled however – for the purposes of the school, if not to the satisfaction of the inner difficulties of the boy. Leu, appealed to, could write to Tankred with all the confidence and authority of the father, the maker of his son's name and fortunes: "I wrote to Mr Hall and told him that you were christened Tunstall-Behrens. The School Secretary has entered you as T-B and I have received receipt for school fees with T-B, so sign yourself Tunstall-Behrens" (let11).

This point gained, with all the confirmation of receipts and registers and fees, Leu can go on to sign himself, with an ironic humour, "Your attached pater". For he is attached to him, it is implied, doubly, by blood and by name, and by a double insistence on that name, and by a fierce affection which will, he assures the boy, rescue him from any meddling by schoolmasters such as Mr Hall in this institution which Leu has chosen to send him to, and where he is anxious that his son should both submit and shine, but which raises, for Leu, in times of difficulty, all his own edginess and ambivalence.

The place had been chosen with care. Clifton combined the gentlemanly ideals of the older public schools based on Arnold's Rugby (where Tankred had first tried for a scholarship; see Biog Reg) with an interest in science and engineering, affirmed essentially with the institution of the Military side in 1875 (see p.280). From the thriving suburb which had continued to grow around it since its opening in 1862 came day boys, sons of local traders and merchants only recently rich, and this set it apart from traditional public schools, as did its willingness to make special arrangements for Jewish boys (whom Tankred looks out for, slightly uneasily, and does not find, in let7). Viewed from outside, it might have seemed the ideal place for the son of a well-to-do, but uneasily-placed, German merchant, intent on an English notion of things for his children, but also having in his bones a yearning for making things with his hands, for seeing things actually work, for the best machinery (see let115), which would often be from Germany now, and in his memory a picture of a thriving, working craftsman father and grandfather in far away, lost Wiesbaden.

From the inside, where Tankred was placed, it necessarily looked different: "Nothing is at all better than it was before, I cant stand this place for anything, let alone that I always feel so bilious & sick here, there is hardly a day that I do not feel sick & bilious, I cant make it out, it is most unbearable..." (let96).

This Tankred writes at the beginning of the autumn term of his second year at the school. The gloom he expresses can only be part of the complexity of feelings which beset him. The gloom, one feels sure, is partly Clifton but partly it is the influence of Newfield, which he has just left and to which his Sunday letters find their way, picking a path through all the tensions, memories, conversations of the holidays just past before they light on home, with anxiety and obsessive visuality and love: on the round tin box in the right hand top drawer of the chest of drawers where there is a pearl-handled pocket knife, forgotten in all the busyness of leaving and now remembered as urgently needing repair; on fruit which "I suppose it is no longer possible to have" (let96); on the arrival of bog oaks and the ordering of rods (see let104); and on the prospect of Roberts' visit at Christmas in his naval reserve clothes (see let112). All these things Tankred's letters create and relish and battle with, and amidst the strenuousness of doing so his health fails, he is sick and bilious, his concentration lapses and he cannot work. The letters are full of tension at the beginning of the term until his feelings settle, his health recovers somewhat, and some kind of equilibrium between school and home is arrived at.

This is the term during which sickness afflicts many of the friends of the family at Newfield, and when the sense of death and time passing combines unhappily, for Leu, with the intransigence and hauteur of his eldest son (see let111): it is the term of Aunt Eliza's visit (see let100-6), and grandmother's illness (see let105 & 110), and worries about Tyra's schooling (see let111). Tankred is affected by these things, but what seems always uppermost in his mind is the importance of retaining vividly in place – both in his own mind and in actuality – those who work at making things or performing physical tasks, those who represent for him movement and energy, and the possibility of things being made or physically organised in the future. Pattinson, Roberts, are the subjects of his most anxious and determined enquiries. These people represent a kind of independence, through their skill, as well as a promise of continuity and shared enthusiasms with his father. The thought that work and measurement and the arrival of twine (see, for example, let12, 14, 19 & 33) was still going on at Newfield was essential.

They represent also, perhaps, an energy quite different from the rigorous academic and sporting/military regime (see endnote on **Corps** in let3) of Clifton. Tankred does his best to move out of his sets (see let96). Nothing could be more laudable than his dejection at his house's misfortune in football, where instead of being "cock house" they were "miserably licked" (let108). And yet still, like an anchor, there is Roberts with his boats and Pattinson in his workshop, back at work again after his illness (see let96; the illness soon to prove fatal, however), and the silence and integrity and self-containment of their work by contrast with the hectic congratulatory or condemnatory quality of school sports is something to cling to. And yet no one could suggest that such sporting energies are reprehensible – far from it. One must move through them in order to attain to the other, perhaps. So the boy ponders, moved by enthusiasms he does not wholly feel, and longing, in his need to have fixed in his mind the stasis and certainty of home, for detail, for a minuteness which verges on a passion. One careless moment with the picture he holds of Newfield, it seems, and it could come toppling down. And because what holds Newfield in place for Tankred is the letters, there are times when the letters themselves become objects of great fragility, their ordering of the utmost consequence. The questions they contain are not the throw-away queries of the moment, common to the rhetoric of letters; they are things Tankred desperately needs to know, things he must have the answer to. To have the answers safe serves the two purposes of satisfying the day-to-day difficulties of public school life, and reassuring him as to the detail of that intransigent picture of home which he holds forever before him, and from which, after Tyra's return from Roedean, only he was exiled.

This need was not always recognized by his parents. Immersed in adult cares – Leu afflicted by a sense of the suddenness of death (see let111), Min nursing Mrs Beaver and Boss (see let110), with the little boy at other times romping noisily through the house – they sometimes miss the desperation of Tankred's letters, and only the hectoring quality of their demands registers in reply: "Now I must say a composition to a father like: by commencing "I cant see why you should want me to write to you in person always if I want to know anything which concerns you in person, as I cant write two letters. I wish you would write & let me know how it is to be arranged. do answer my question in my *last* letter (to his mother)" I consider lacking the very rudiments of respect. Don't you think so too?" (let111)

This remonstrance plunges Tankred into an appalled submissiveness which cheers Leu up considerably and gives him cause to congratulate his son on winning "an important battle". "I congratulate you", writes the disillusioned survivor of the Franco-Prussian War, "upon the victory. I take it that your head has gained therewith supremacy over the body & its passion, a most, if not the most important, development in man...I hail in you the second generation, who I can feel now, has entered the manly path, to carry out the further building of the family, a son who will ripen into a man, who will not allow either head or heart to run away with himself..." (let115).

Leu was premature in his congratulations. The physical restrictions of Clifton hourly afflicted Tankred: fastidious by nature, the scarcity of bath water and the restrictions as to types of soap (see let7) merged into his resentment about mathematics and stamps. To have difficulties and misunderstandings about the actual direction to mother or father of the letters themselves was just too much. Even at his most contrite he has to make this clear: "You know it always gives me pleasure to write to either of you, but there is really a difficulty about it, if I write to you indiscriminately I forget to which I have asked which questions & it all turns unsatisfactory. Dont you feel it the same if I address my letter to mother as if to you? because if you do it is all right & I will write to you alternately & then I shall know where I am" (let112).

Leu's suggestion – that Tankred should discriminate between *kinds of subject* in writing to his parents (see let115) – leaves the problem unresolved, and one of the intriguing things throughout the correspondence is the idea that Tankred never entirely got it settled 'where he was', and that the letters remain from his point of view both intensely important and unsatisfactory and indiscriminate. It would be difficult, after all, for a boy even of Tankred's orderly habits to maintain a correspondence with his father which dealt with "the inner man, your future, the building up of your manhood, the morals of man & his connection with the outer world" (let115) and keep for his letters to his mother such matters as queries about Tyra and the boys and instructions as to hampers. It was not to be done; but the very existence of the difficulty gives an interesting insight into the way this Victorian family was being urged to the very edge of some new organic definition of itself as a family; the formal, almost courtly quality of Leu, and the more instinctive, warm response of Min becomes a distinction which Tankred, away from them both, is becoming impatient with. At home he might acquiesce unthinkingly in such distinctions; at a distance, in difficulties, never entirely happy, he wants a warmer, firmer attention from them both.

Most vexing of all to Tankred are those spaces in the letters which his parents, wilfully as it often seems to him, refuse to fill. His eternal cry – 'why do you not answer my questions?' – is more than a demand for specific answers on practical subjects. It is a *cri de coeur*, and means, on a more desperate level, *where are you?* After his first holidays from Clifton, which one gathers were rather strained (Min talks in retrospect of organizing things in future so as to avoid "all unnecessary disaster & friction"; let39), the first letters of the new term, January 1893, begin with the taint of this strain upon them. Tankred is belligerent, Min is irritated – "you do not adopt a kind or *fitting* tone", she complains (let44) – and then, as though repenting of her own tone to a child who is, after all, away from home and not quite well, she writes again, two days later, to tell him how the work on his bedroom at home is getting on, and to advise him to wear his thick coat when he gets out of the swimming bath (see let45); only to have the letter countered immediately by Tankred's letter to her, in high dudgeon at being so taken to task, and unrepentant (see let46).

But despite the unsatisfactory holidays, Tankred meticulously notes the dates for the next holidays in his first letter of this term (see let40), nor does all his belligerence and all his sparring with Min prevent us from gathering from his letters a pervading sense of longing for home, an acute summoning up of the picture of Newfield: what does his room look like now, don't on any account put Tyra's box in a hot room (see let46) – the activities and concerns of the holidays must be stayed, kept centrally significant, must not dwindle or die during his absence – and this most hectoring of letters ends with a wretched *plea* for letters. Despite everything, they are his "only real pleasure".

By temperament, perhaps, Tankred was not suited to enjoy the peculiar pleasures and sadnesses of being the absent one. By nature practical, and at an age to be insecure, there was nothing of benefit to be derived from surveying home from afar. The privilege of having things slightly blurred by distance was not to his taste. In his insistence on facts he anticipates at times our own reader's sense of not knowing, our quite differently orientated need to know: "Why do you say *poor* dear Mrs Beaver?" (let21) he asks, alert to the omission of news; and thus he prompts Min's reply, which does half of the work of the editor here – "why dear boy I must have told you that our dear friend Hugh Beaver is no more, he died in S. Africa on Aug 29th of inflammation of the lungs" (let23); although Tankred's further worry upon the subject – how he got inflammation of the lungs (see let24) – Min's letters decline to satisfy, the answer fruitless perhaps. His mother's vagueness at conveying information of such moment even as this – her being "under the impression" (let23) that she had told him about it – only feeds Tankred's neurotic distrust of the reliability of her letters as regards *facts*. "It must have been very nice to hear Tom Mann" (let48), he comments, after a letter from Min which has rather run away with itself on the subject of the London poor (see let47); but "You say you have answered all my questions. I think you make a mistake."

What makes his mother most vivid and lovable – her enthusiasms, her energies and instinctive affections – are what, perhaps, discompose him most, even as they most attract him. His own enthusiasms were more tapered, more hesitant. When Professor Boys gave his lecture to the school on "Quartz Fibres", one cannot make out Min's son from the rest, to gather from the dutiful, rather heavy report he gives of it (see let27).

Part of the interest of the correspondence lies in the sense we have of this boy being in a state of transition: the crucial years of fourteen to seventeen are caught, are held, and yet in another way they are not caught at all, they are as supple and intangible as the glance the boy gives to his father in the silhouette photograph. Tankred Tunstall-Behrens, listening to Professor Boys' lecture, rubbing shoulders with boys whom he may not care much for but must, for his own sake, tolerate, is preparing, as he listens, for the letter he will write home. This letter will be correct as regards facts, for the boy is a lover of facts, and he is conscious of duty, and so his concentration is focussed. But with what a difference in energy are the two concentrations, mother's and son's! Min, too, reports faithfully what she has heard, but her rendering is touched always by her liberating delight, so that, lesson though it is, it becomes her own. Tankred's lessons are harder, with more import; Woolwich looms ahead of him, he must learn dutifully, and not disgrace himself: "The Staff & diplomatic Service must be ever before your eyes", as Leu tells him later (let80). At a certain circumscribed hour, a day or two after the lecture, it must be reported to Newfield; there is no room for enthusiasm: "Last Wednesday we had a lecture by profess. Boys On the way they can find out the heat any thing gives out in fact with his instrument he could tell the heat given out by any star in the heavens & he showed us how if a candle was lighted at the other end of Big School, it would alter the position of a machine..." (let27). "The way they can find out" – the "they" is a give-away; knowledge has not touched his life yet, or at least not transformed it, and the stars in the heavens move him about as much as the other end of Big School.

What is made almost palpable through Tankred's letters is the relentless grip of an institution, working upon a constitution which only partly wants to succumb to it. He has a sense of the huge advantages of doing so – the glory of one's house winning at football (see let204), the easy gradation of progress through one's sets, the beautiful simplicity of the public school outer picture – Newbolt's poem, in fact, and Min's idea of the chapel (see endnote on **chapel** in let1) – at the same time as having a fierce independence, a sense of what must be kept secret in order to have any space at all. The occasion of Aunt Eliza's visit to Bristol presents Tankred with a difficulty not on account of the visit itself, but in the form in which it presents itself in the letters: on no account can Min's letter requesting the visit be shown to Mr Moor. A separate letter must be written, dealing specifically with Aunt Eliza, with no allusions to Tankred's health, umbrellas, or doings at Newfield (see let100), and with no room for the possibility of Aunt Eliza visiting Tankred's house at school. "In your letter there is no part I can show Moor which does not contain something I dont want him to see...It is useless & I dont want to tell him anything about my health & in the other I dont want him to have the chance of making me see her here" (let101).

The "exact facsimile" which Tankred insists that Min sends of a letter which he himself writes, using her phraseology, is one which contains nothing but the plain facts of the matter, with no room for the fluctuations of Min's thoughts and anxieties: "You will realize dear boy that it is exceedingly kind of your great Aunt to take the trouble of coming on purpose to see you & I know you will give her a cordial reception & thank her for coming" (let101).

In the smooth translation of her worries into this modified sentence Min might have sighed in relief as to Tankred's manner of receiving Aunt Eliza. He knows what is owing to aunts and can deal deftly with them; but housemasters are a different matter and need more careful managing.

But if Tankred's letters give a sense of the power of an institution, they give also the sense of the fragility of terms and sets and teams, as terms slide to an end, are suddenly over. No other measurement of time, perhaps, yields such a sense of both intensity and transience. At the end of Tankred's first term, the last few letters have a feeling of this: "There is no news this week, & besides it is so near the holidays that most things can wait till next tuesday week" (let36).

Amazingly, things can suddenly wait, the time has come when conversation will soon supersede letters, the significance of the term, whose actual moments as they passed were of such overwhelming importance, begins to blur into the glow of the holidays. Things must be packed up and the boots must be tipped (see let36), and there is *King Lear* with Mr Lynam (see let35), putting the school report in its place. Mr Lynam, in fact, seems to put all difficulties in their proper place. As light and bright as his name, his few letters always usher in sense and movement and genuine affection. Mr Lynam, the headmaster from the prep school where Tankred shone, seems formed to belong to the holidays, and in his presence Tankred is always an easily shining creature. Whenever Lynam appears there is an alleviation of anxiety. He knows the system so well he can afford to be dismissive about it: "The idea is that scholars are likely to be cocky & think themselves great swells & so they must go down a peg!" (let38)

Thus he breezily reassures Min as to Tankred's report; and then in the same breath, "I am looking forward to meeting Tankred at the Lyceum at 5 minutes before the advertised time of performance of King Lear – We shall easily meet in the entrance Hall – The Doctor is to meet us there too..." (let38). Plays must be watched, friends must meet, Mr Lynam seems to imply, despite the foolish doggedness of institutions.

And Mr.Lynam also is the writer of that letter (see let2) which heralds Tankred's life at Clifton, and is such an unusual letter for a schoolmaster to write about a pupil, and which strikes Min, too, with its generosity (see let13). Such is Tankred's "strength of character" and "keen sense of justice" (let2), writes Lynam to Mr Behrens on Tankred's entering Clifton, that he was "a difficult study for a young headmaster" (see Biog Reg under CCL), and it is clear that the man waiting in the Lyceum theatre for the boy he thinks of as a friend on equal terms has had his times of difficulty with Tankred while he was under his care at Oxford: "we have had many a row! some his fault & some no doubt mine" – and also that throughout these difficulties Lynam has held on to some quality in Tankred which must be recognized and given space to, even within the 'rows' themselves. "I have never known him tell a lie", he writes, and the statement is of interest on two counts: we remember it later when, in Mr Moor's letters to his father about Tankred's unsatisfactory behaviour, he seems to have become in Moor's eyes an unhappy, shifting, self-justifying creature (see let142 & 144); and secondly, it suggests that by making such a statement Lynam was alluding to a quality in Tankred which is only partially explained by the conventional public school virtue of telling the truth at all times (see Potter, p.19). Tankred's truth telling, perhaps, was a more real and a more vulnerable virtue than this, and one which Lynam wants to protect him from. With his more experienced eyes, Lynam perhaps had a sense that when this real and rather strenuous virtue comes up against the structured and fictionalised ideal of 'truth' which belongs to a noble institution it is never a happy collision. For the real has a habit of sniffing out the pretence in the fabric of the other, and speaking out against it with an unguarded impatience:

"It is perfectly sickening too to be in the house he is such a suspicious old devil, he suspects one of goodness knows what without any reason except that he dislikes you & what is more tries to blacken ones character to others by it, Besides he is such a hypocrite, he pretends to be on the best of terms & then talks of one behind ones back, & if you go for him about it he retracts it as much as he can & makes rotten reasons which anyone can see through..." (let138).

Thus Tankred writes of the housemaster who was *"very nice indeed"* (let7) eighteen months before, to the relief of the boy arriving at Clifton for the first time. He is, of course, becoming used to the routine, not so noticeably frightened by the school's outer structure, he is immersed in its ways. He is also a year older, and he is bored. "He seems to think barging a very bad crime, at the same time there are many worse things, a little healthy bunting surely can do no harm, & if that were the worst thing that was done, the school might think itself well off" (let138).

Such a statement is enough to set off all the alarm bells in parents and schoolmasters, especially parents who are far away and have recently heard such dreadful stories about public schools; but surely not Clifton? (see let134 & 135) What "worse things" might the school think itself very well off without? "Will you please give me your definitions of "barging" & "bunting" (let140), writes Leu anxiously, but it would, of course, depend on his own experiences and his own sexual alertness as to whether he was reassured by the answer: "Barging or Bunting consists of making any unnecessary row by generally kicking up a row by fighting (friendlily) & wrestling & scuffling about" (let141).

Leu wrote to Mr Moor; and received a letter back (see let138A & 142 and Doc App VII) which shows that Tankred was a "difficult study" for his masters at Clifton, too, but somehow – whether it is his increase in years and inflexibility, or the largeness and inflexibility of the school itself, after the relative freedom of Mr Lynam's more relaxed regime at Oxford – somehow at this juncture he seems a study more exasperating for his elders than intriguing, and for all his qualities, which Mr Moor and even Mr Hall never deny, it looks as though what we are witnessing is what has happened throughout the whole course of the public school's history, recounted in autobiography after autobiography – the misfortune of a noble and well-meaning institution failing a sensitive temperament.

But Tankred revives. He is "eccentric", complains Mr Hall, and will not follow models even when they are placed directly in front of him – and "boys of his age who are learning the elements of their subject cannot afford to be eccentric" (let145). But for all this accusation of eccentricity his character is direct, and there is not enough of strangeness or fearfulness in his make-up to make him cower at this point. Occasionally he is overcome by a sudden eruptive failure of nerve – as Leu explains to Mr Hall "he works himself into despair & apparently loses control over himself" (let146), but the loss of control is temporary and partial, perhaps, for in the crucial and apparently arbitrary decision which Nature seems always to be making at this age, Tankred seems even at his most unhappy and hedged-in to be destined for strength: we can see it in the manner in which he re-assures his parents about the "vile practices" (let135) prevalent in public schools, which they have recently heard the reports of. Suddenly the boy seems older than his parents, knowing more than they do, clear-eyed and clear-headed, willing to make use of language they can accept: one knows the sets to avoid; everything else is negotiation: "*all* Public schools are morally *weak* to a more or less degree" (let138).

This first crisis of Tankred's occurs at the end of the Easter term of 1894. At the beginning of the summer term he seems to settle down, his report is better and he is congratulated by Leu (see let162); he works so assiduously his trousers are worn through the seat (see let163). Meanwhile at Newfield there are tensions between his parents, so much so that it becomes a question whether they will attend Commemoration at Clifton (see let164). Min's holiday with her mother in Norfolk, extended a week beyond her planned time (see let156), refreshes her considerably, and on her return she is met so kindly by her husband with Tyra and Lilian that everything for a while seems better. But not for long: she cannot help speaking enthusiastically about the "franchise question" (let164; five months later it has become the "franchise vampyre" – let208), and Leu cannot curb his impatience. The intense moments of pleasure in Norfolk, where, alone and unencumbered, she had sat and listened to the birdsong in the sunshine outside the suddenly discovered church in the middle of the wood (see let156), quickly faded in the gloom of Newfield. And besides, her husband and eldest son's enthusiasms – their longing to go to Cornwall – she could not join with (see let156 & 293), for Cornwall is a county, a kingdom almost, which reacts differently on different temperaments, and Min had discovered a strange aversion to it. She could sense that they were set upon appropriating it, setting part of it up for their own, far from London, far from friends and talk and questions of interest, and Min could not bear the thought of Newfield being thus extended into a far-flung province which would be for her exile, where the talk was all of boats and fishermen and mussels, much as she relished these things – strangely, perversely – when she was alone.

And so Tankred, the recipient of his father's tart comments upon his mother's difficult ways, hovers uncertainly at Clifton, and does not know what to do about booking a room at the hotel (see let163). "Do go all *the same* by yourself, I will be with you in spirit", writes his "loving & unfortunate" father (let164).

All is well, however – at least temporarily, and the next thing we hear of Commemoration is a letter from Leu announcing his and Min's safe arrival home (see let165). The term ends with an exchange of letters between Tankred and Leu dwelling with a shared worry on the holiday in Cornwall and pheasants and the musselman.

As Tankred grows nearer to his sixteenth birthday and his entrance to Woolwich, the picture seems to shift slightly, the possibilities of relationship between father and son which were latent in the silhouette photograph are realised into adult amity, a move towards equality: it is Leu and Tankred, with joint enthusiasm, who long for the holiday in Cornwall (see let167 & 168) – none of Tankred's enquiries about this or about pheasants or guns are treated by Leu with anything other than a steady sense of their importance (see let170), despite his busyness and despite Tankred's gaffe about Mrs Gard (see let176), where boyish enthusiasm leads him into the danger of losing some manly sense of honour. Tankred is reprimanded for this, and he is reprimanded, more than once, for his lack of attention to *style* (see let180), but increasingly as the letters proceed there is a sense of Leu, although still the anxious nurturer and maker of his son's character, being repaid by an eldest son who is in the process of becoming everything he intended and more: indeed it is the *more* which is at times perhaps disconcerting for Leu and which stands out in those few letters where it appears, startling in their self-possession and confident assessment: on the subject of Roy being beaten by his father for his waywardness Tankred is disapproving, but even his disapproval is hedged with the knowledge that his father was in difficulties. He is concerned, dignified, and falls into an assessment of his own childhood and relationship with Leu which signifies that already his boyhood is almost over: "I am sure I shall be better for having been brought up as I have without force & being treated as a sensible being & though it may have made me more unruly & more trouble to you for a time yet I am sure I shall turn out the better for it; I think I have arrived at a stage now when I can truly appreciate it, & make the true use of it" (let213).

And so it is that Leu confides more and more of his impatience with Min's activities to Tankred – the meetings she loves to organize are a trivial fashion, he complains (see let211), and like all fashions will pass away. Fashion he cannot tolerate, perhaps because fashion is a parody of that change which brings down kingdoms and removes one's friends forever, and which we must all one day endure – "Nature does not permit taking liberties, punishment follows" (let238). Fashion, in its devotion to the ephemeral and to constant change, is a fatal mimicry of Providence, and Leu in his appalled and gloomy recognition of the ways of Providence can do nothing about meetings and fads for skating except retire to his studio, his Tusculum (see let211), and beseech his children to change into dry clothes, and lure his nephew Louis Neuendorff to cease skating and play the French horn instead, and wish Mabel would go home (see let225 & 238).

But if fashion is something to be avoided, style is another matter: without good style there is no building (just as, if *Tankred* wants skates, he must have really good ones that will outlast a momentary enthusiasm; see let230), and Leu, at least in one suddenly evoked picture of Min's, is a master builder, striding about the garden he is re-ordering almost in the manner of the driving and driven energy of Ibsen's Halvard Solness, who also builds on his wife's garden (see let134). Or so it seems to Min, who loved the garden as it was and who was living through a season where the fashionableness of Ibsen suggested such a picture. But for Leu, style – like tactics in battle (see let140) – and behind style that shaping moral force that guided it – could make or break situations, kingdoms, individuals, and examination successes, and he feared that lack of proper attention to it (and complaints about Tankred's style are all over the reports in Doc App I-XV) could be the downfall of his son in his mathematical work, and also in his life more generally. Tankred must approach his life as a master craftsman might, taking no delight in extravagant show (see let211), but rather in good, sturdy, and in this following passage almost Johnsonian, competence: "It is an entirely mistaken idea of yours, that plain words must necessarily be rude. No Sir, our language is so pliable that the most unmistakable meaning should be expressed in refined form. *Make yourself therefore the master of language*" (let63).

It is Tankred's most difficult effort: the truthfulness and love of justice and fair dealing which Mr Lynam recognized, which Leu cherished, were qualities so strongly held in a temperament which tended towards the impetuous and fiery, that they would on occasion override all considerations of 'style' altogether, and lead Tankred into heated and dangerous antagonism with the authorities at Clifton. He is "querulous &

critical" (let267) as he nears his seventeenth birthday, "systematically insolent" (let271), and regarded by the VIth form as "the only dangerous boy in the house" (let271). "Boys' lives are made up of small incidents" (let273), writes Mr Glazebrook, the maker of all these observations, who as headmaster and therefore responsible for the style and moral fabric of the entire establishment, was of course responsible for such "small incidents" being treated as "of very great importance" (let273) by the boys themselves.

When his nerve fails, as it does in his final year at Clifton in this violent row with the VIth formers in his house, as the Woolwich entrance examination looms nearer, it is Tankred's style – in manner, in writing essays, in speech towards those in authority above him – which betrays him. Tankred's nerve fails, but it is also the nerve of a whole establishment which we sense being tested at this season of Tankred's second crisis; the influenza which sweeps the whole country at the time of the great frost, and which attacks Mabel and Tyra and Roy at Newfield, visits Clifton and claims the life of the much loved, gifted and amiable Mr Moor (see let251). The readjustment to which an establishment is always subject in times of illness and which can be to the child who has not succumbed a time of relief or lightness, as adult anxieties are no longer focussed upon him (Tankred declares he feels "all the better for the extra sleep" (let239), as the daily regime of early waking is necessarily relaxed during the epidemic), is followed by a time of exhausted and bewildered grief; behind Mr Hall's dignified dealings with Leu regarding his son we see a man mourning an old friend (see let260).

The time passes, however; Mr Moor's death is assimilated, sadly, into the knowledge Clifton has of itself and into the consciousness of his friends, and the impatience which Mr Glazebrook and Mr Hall feel for Louis Behrens and his at times strangely wayward and forceful son (see let271) passes too. The boy will remain at Clifton, after all; indeed, if he will but contain that waywardness and that occasional rashness of temper under pressure he will do the establishment credit (see let271 & 279). There are examinations to prepare for and no more time must be lost.

At Newfield spring and summer progresses and Leu is laid up with rheumatism (see let291). Min has all the enjoyments of a new piano and Lilian is engaged to a Mr Burdett who is kind and rather old and "belongs to one of the oldest if not the oldest firm of Solicitors in Grays Inn" (let289), although it is

Mabel, perversely, who looks "blooming" (let297). A summer holiday in Cornwall awaits them, in Mrs Gard's cottage despite Leu's dignified stand (see let293), and Min looks forward to bicycling when she is there (see let297). When Tankred arrives there his future will be decided, for the letters end – suddenly, triumphantly – with his success in the examination for Woolwich, announced to us in the delighted response of Spall (see let307) and Miss Etheridge (see let306) and Mr Lynam (see let308), and having around it the silent, glowing satisfaction of Leu.

<u>Tyra and the boys</u>

For Tankred, immersed in the cares of Clifton, his sister Tyra (two years younger than he) and his younger brothers Brian and Roy (respectively seven and nine years younger than he) were fixed points of stability and delight, the two little boys, ordinarily named as the elder two were strangely named, and separated by two years as Tyra and Tankred were, forming almost a distinct family of children. The few letters from Tyra, Brian and Roy – scattered throughout the correspondence – are received by us now, as they were received by Tankred then, with a happy lightness of response: for these children have no duties, no responsibilities, they do not need to pack up hampers and – perhaps what is the freest thing about them – they do not have to answer any questions. They can neglect to write for months on end and not be subject to the slightest reproof; they can forget Tankred's birthday and he doesn't mind (see let180). Their letters when they come can be scrappy and hastily written and even at times boastful of their idleness (see let99) and still – for these very reasons perhaps – have around them the unchanging sense of a guaranteed affection on both sides. The boys because of their youth and Tyra because of her sex are safe from Tankred's irritability or distress. When Tankred thinks of them it is of their being settled at Newfield, with the occasional absence from it – and to think also of Mr Edwards and Fräulein and the Owsleys.

This is not to say that Tankred's younger siblings were an indistinguishable blur: the boys, Brian and Roy, spring out from the letters with their own separate colours of character, and causing the eyes of their parents, one gathers, to fix differently upon each of them. When regarding Brian, Leu was complacent and happy; for Brian, it seemed, blossomed under his 'ideas', seemed shaped to fit them, and gave "no trouble" even in the matter of illness – he obligingly did not catch influenza in the post-skating crisis in which Roy's health was such a cause of anxiety: "Brian keeps uncannily well & is getting stronger every day, going his own way, pleasant & no trouble to any one, working by himself & absolutely happy which is a blessing, – In him there appears to be the artist or scientist -" (let238).

There were, of course, occasional lapses: with childish mischievousness and hauteur, Brian manages inadvertently to secure the abrupt departure of the young gardener, Luke (see let216). But despite this – which was a cause of great concern not only to Brian himself (see let222) but to the family, and had an impact upon its domestic structure – it was Roy's misdeeds which were more worrying, because Roy of all the children was the one whose imagination seemed to range outside that structure, so rigidly made and maintained. If Brian's easiness enables Leu to view with satisfaction a future artist or scientist, then on looking at Roy – far more anxiously and fearfully – he can see nothing but the daily difficulties of the here and now, and potential trouble for the future. To mould Roy was a matter of challenging and at times physically chastising (see let65 & 212) a temperament beset by sudden inexplicable energies, many of which were beyond Leu's understanding. "I have got a flute and I shall play it in Ireland when I ride on the donkey", writes Roy (a quite different kind of artist) to Tankred (let89), when the talk all around him is of fishing rights and shooting and home rule (see let86 & 87). Such a sentence – childish, scrawled out hastily to his brother though it is – argues a self-containment and a mental picture of his own self which reaches beyond Newfield and packing cases and family plans. It is a vision of himself existing beyond what "Father says" (let89); and Leu sensed, one feels, this slippery, wandering self-containment of Roy. It goes hand in hand with a certain nervous agitation (see let203) and a wiry physical frailty (see let137 & 262) and mere forgetfulness: it is Roy who is prone to illness and who tumbles into holes left by the workmen (see let119).

Tankred's thoughts about his brothers carry this knowledge of their differing temperaments, but because he is not their father, it does not weigh heavily upon him. And in his thoughts of Tyra there was yet more occasion for lightness, for her character encourages cheer. Tyra's four terms at Roedean were unsuccessful, and – for the duration of this correspondence at least – she was thereafter under Mr Edwards' tutelage at home, and most of her few letters are from there, sitting at Min's side (see let297). Tankred supposes – rather heavily and wrongly – that she will be upset at being fetched home from Brighton (see let112 and endnote on **sports** in let95) – but it is a bright-eyed, light-stepped Tyra whom one imagines sending messages via Min (see let116 & 226) and enjoying her new bedroom (see let136) and settling importantly to examinations with Mr Edwards, than which, writes Min, "no scholarship exam could be more silent orderly & methodical" (let130).

Leu's own anxiety and ambition for his children seems to have been disarmed by this very sunniness of disposition which was Tyra's. She has for him, one imagines, the essential joyousness of Min without Min's tendency to lavish her energies upon ideals which Leu found questionable or tiresome. When Leu explains to Tankred his own ideal of his children's future character, the idea of Tyra's being "a good woman" (let115) is tagged onto the end of his aspiration in a way which frees rather than confines her: her future goodness is hazy yet certain, for she is tractable and amiable, and has none of the waywardness of Roy, or the sullen irritability of Tankred. Whereas the re-arrangement of Tankred's bedroom becomes an area of negotiation and disagreement, bringing the idea of Tankred's attitude towards extravagance, frugality, excess, luxury and his future aptitude for the life of a soldier under scrutiny (see let50 & 52), the only thing that is apparent in Tyra's response to her own room is her simple and direct pleasure in it (see let136), so that she does not come under any scrutiny at all. In this way, although one might imagine that the only daughter might be the most entrapped within the letters, Tyra flies free of them, in the way that only the most genuinely sanguine people can fly free of complications.

While Tankred struggles at Clifton, Tyra, who dislikes Brighton, is free to leave, though retaining from it much that could be salvaged of pleasure (so that she looks forward to the mid-term holiday visit for old girls; see let299), and is allowed to study at home with Mr Edwards. No reader of these letters, with the evidence of Tyra's atrocious spelling before him, can believe that Leu *really* thought there was the remotest chance of Tyra going to Girton (see let115). She is no blue-stocking, and Leu, despite his avowed aspirations for her, is glad of it: "I for one do not like a girl to be away from home, my notion is that a girl's place is by the side of her mother" (let115), and so Leu's 'notions' concerning Tyra, swaying between the picture of the girl at home with her mother and his vision of a young woman at Girton, settle nowhere except in the here and now of the letters, and in the affection he feels for her. It is noticeable that to Tyra's unsuitability for Roedean there is attached no idea of blame, nor is there any great focussed intensity which accumulates around her character in the process of removing her – nothing like the furore there would have been had Tankred actually in the event been removed from Clifton (see let271). The question of where to put Tyra is a problem for Leu, and a decision will have to be made, but it is a problem outside the figure of Tyra herself. Likewise with her health: her "strain", for which a consultation with the doctor Lichtenberg is required, visits a physique and constitution "so well made & physically perfect" (let216), as does anaemia and an accompanying "tendency to lounge" (let222). But anaemia, strain and lounging are not qualities one thinks of in thinking of Tyra: unlike a long line of Victorian heroines, she is not a dangerously moping, introspective, novel-reading girl (not like Alice in Gissing's *Demos*, for instance) who has to be lured back to health and the real world. Her reading, when she does it at all (and one of the objects of taking her out of Roedean, one senses, was to try to encourage Tyra to *read*), is undertaken with the same good humour and willingness to please and be pleased with which she does everything else. Her family are kindly and fond of her, and her world is large enough for her capacities, and so she has no incentive to escape through books. She is not a changeling reader, then, but a homecoming reader, happily finding a route through the books she reads back to the world which suggested them, confirming the affections with which she set out: Mr Edwards lent it to her, and because "The wreck of the golden fleece" "was a prize belonging to one of his boys" (let136) she can enter his school of St Bartholomew's at the corner of Kirkdale and Sydenham Park (just near Newfield) more securely, one imagines, than she can enter the world of whatever story the book told; or it is Tankred's book, and she knows he will not mind her lending it out (see let136).

The affection which is apparent between Tyra and Tankred is an alluring, and at times tantalizing evidence of the kind of life which existed behind the letters. This life is summoned up, briefly but vividly, by Tyra's energetic affection, and yet is allowed to escape by her essential laziness. Between "I have got such heaps to tell you" (let207) and "I realy cant think of any thing to say" (let196) lies the pulsating life of a hundred conversations between brother and sister which we can never catch because she who might have shed light on them is never quite at ease with a pen in her hand; there is goodwill and a desire to communicate, but also some reluctance and a self-conscious notion that her spelling was bad and her handwriting was improving, and also that her education generally was a matter of some concern. Perhaps Tyra's happiest mode of correspondence with her brother was to send a few words under cover of someone else's letter, or with a gift which she had made herself – a "pin cussion" (let185) or a book "with *gold* letters in it" (let116), promised but too difficult to do as she had wished (see let116A).

But as time goes on, and under the care of Mr Edwards – surely the most patient and gifted of teachers, like his shadowy counterpart at Clifton, Mr Hall's temporary substitute (see let241 & 245) – Tyra's style improves, her letters grow longer and less constrained, and at times attain almost to the naturalness of Min's. In what is probably her best letter (see let232), written at the height of the skating passion, Tyra summons for Tankred a picture of a home taken over by pure enjoyment of a passing season, and the excitement of a fire on the other side of the railway, and the discomfort of having no water, so that "Mable feels like a pie already with a crust out side". And through Tyra's eyes, Mabel, and Min herself, become different people. Mabel is not the nuisance she is for Leu, with whom in the past there has been difficulty (see let49), but the very young aunt who is almost a cousin, and between whom and Tyra there is perfect amity and equality; and Min is subjected to Tyra's mirth and thus becomes less stately, less serious than the mother enjoining Tankred to achieve his best qualities – "You know mother does look so very funny bundling about on the ice, she makes me split." And behind this letter, too, of course, lies Leu's and Tankred's anxiety about Roy, around which the light irresponsible high spirits of Tyra are allowed to roam: "Dr Warry came to day to see Roy & says he has been having Influenza & has Pneumonia mother will tell you all about it." – "I presume Tyra has not been told how bad he is", writes Tankred to Leu (let235), "She does not seem to realise it in her letter of last night." Around such a statement – as about the comments upon the desirability of her leaving Roedean – there is not the slightest suggestion of severity. A space is made for Tyra in the family to be lighthearted and happy, to rescue sparrows (see let169), to take care of dogs and kittens (see let122, 136 & 297), and to enjoy her music lessons (see let262); and Leu's larger system – his wish for her to be educated, good, and dutiful, as well as somehow morally *elevated* – can shape itself around her, and there is no doubt that the shape of her character will yield to it.

"I wish it was already the holidays", writes Tyra (let207), but in this wish we cannot concur, for if the holidays mean for her the actual presence of her brother and the enjoyment of his company, they mean for us that both Tyra and her brother fade beyond a bourne where we cannot reach them, and it is only in Tyra's most thoughtless scribblings that part of that silence is revealed: "What is your school like this term I hope it is nicer than usual" (let185). Tyra, who had not enjoyed Roedean, was a sympathetic listener, one imagines, to Tankred's troubles at Clifton, and what she heard would have been of a different order from that related to his parents, for to Tyra Tankred can speak without constraint and without any fear of being judged or scolded; just as Tyra in her letters to Tankred is direct in her opinions and her likes and dislikes – "Mr Perks & his Miss Jones came yesterday Fräulein & I do not like her atall" (let196).

And just as Tyra's letters reveal a hint of the conversations between brother and sister which we can never quite grasp, so they give us – slightly, suddenly, with only half a mind on the job – more than a passing glance at the colour and movement of life at Newfield: Edith Owsley's wedding presents (see let196), the delicate *tableau* of the vine tree on the dining table (see let199), the gradual change of the garden from chaos back to order and the child hurrying back from tea at Mrs Beaver's to be just in time for her late afternoon lesson with Mr Edwards (see let129) – are all vividly evoked by the girl who did not think of herself as a letter writer and who was happiest with the kind of interchange to be achieved with her brother actually in the room with her, or romping about the desecrated, precarious garden (see let119 & 130).

The history which lay behind the Tunstall-Behrens children, so much a matter of hard work and investigation for an editor now, was made up of knowledge which they took for granted. Leu, in leaving his native country, made instantly for all his then unborn children a certain quality of inherited strangeness which was eventually, perhaps, to prompt Roy's departure from England into another voluntary exile, and which made for some of Tankred's difficulties at Clifton. His children carried their father's inheritance in lighter ways, too – not only in the unEnglish names of the two elder siblings, but in the anecdotes, parcels, visits: of Louis Neuendorff, for instance, in 1895, which gives a sense of the ease with which the family incorporated its German relations, of whatever generation. The young man's obliging acquiescence in the skating interlude, and his abrupt desertion of the "slide" which is the occasion of reproof from Tankred (see let222 & 223), argues an informality and ease and acceptance amongst his cousins, as does his obliging way with his scent when Min comments frankly upon it (see let222).

Tyra was in the midst of this perfect acquiescence: cousins from Germany were as much a settled matter of her existence as the Owsleys, or her friends Maud Mellor and Marjorie Monkhouse. And it is not too fanciful to suggest that it was a gift from Germany which brought into being what became the most suggestive image of Tyra. Some time shortly before her twelfth birthday in 1892, during the summer before Tankred's first term at Clifton, and her own at Roedean, a parcel arrived at Newfield, addressed to Tyra, from her cousin Tina Frauberger. On Tyra's opening it, the family saw amid its contents a tiny implement in the shape of a boat (see endnote on the **"ship called Tyra"** in let1), and Tyra and Min, at least, saw with delight what it was: a shuttle for the working of that intricate and delicate art called 'tatting', which was for Tyra perhaps a fleeting enthusiasm, but which for cousin Tina was one form of the lacework that was her life's work. She had only that summer written an article on the revival of the art of tatting, and was certainly by 1894 the principal of the school of fine embroidery in Düsseldorf, where she was to remain for the rest of her long working life.

Min and Tyra were not the only ones who fell upon the gift with delight. Roy and Brian, too, saw its possibilities, and occasionally, when the shuttle was not in use, they would beg to be allowed to devise their own games with it, its shape suggesting many nautical adventures and imaginings. But tatting was Tyra's latest enthusiasm, inspired by cousin Tina, and the shuttle was often in use. Besides, it was fragile, and so Tankred, who loved working with his hands, and liked to please his little brothers, made them a small model boat in imitation of Tyra's shuttle.

There was a linguistic delight about it; for "Tyra's shuttle" could be translated from English into German, as "das Tyraschiffchen", which could become, when re-translated, "the ship called Tyra". And so the model boat made by Tankred was named "the ship called Tyra", with a linguistic happiness which seemed to encompass what was most closely related and most affectionate in the two languages, and to suit the to-ing and fro-ing between Germany and England, in letters, in family news, in birthday tokens, which was the origin of the gift. What takes Leu some trouble and formality to achieve in the matter of his children's surname, has been instantly and naturally arrived at by the sweep of an image.

The ship called Tyra almost launches this correspondence, for it is mentioned by Min in her first letter to Tankred as having to be left at home while she travels to Brighton with Tyra and the boys. Some few years later, after Tyra's death, father and brothers had a real boat commemorating their sister, a 13ft St Ives built 'punt' made specially for them, and in Cornwall still, long after Tyra's death now, long after lace-tatting has faded from fashion again, and Tina Frauberger's career as principal of her embroidery school is over, there survives fragmentarily the old boat called Tyra, bigger than Tyra's shuttle, or that boat made by Tankred for his brothers, but holding in its history both chance and linguistic shapeliness, the sudden domestic enthusiasms of the moment and the affections which must endure.

DAS WERKZEUG

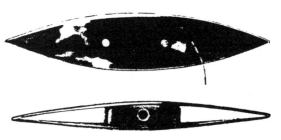

Das Schiffchen. (Natürliche Größe.)

Acknowledgements

An edition of this kind, involving so many different kinds of information, cannot be even imperfectly completed without the help of very many people knowledgeable in ways the editor is not; and we who have made this book have a great many debts to acknowledge.

The project could not have been contemplated without the ready enthusiasm of Michael and Romi Tunstall-Behrens and the generous co-operation and help of the living generations of the Tunstall-Behrens family, especially Morwenna and Kenneth Till, Hilary Tunstall-Behrens, Charles Turner, Robert Burdett and Peter Tunstall-Behrens; without the silent help of Mary (Joy) Behrens; or without the ready encouragement of Gerald Blake of the Department of Geography and Joan Kenworthy, Principal of St Mary's College, in the University of Durham.

Our first source of archival help has been from Clifton College, as is clear on the title page, and no less vital has been the help of John Coulter of the Lewisham Archives for local information about Forest Hill. For the German research almost everything useful that has been done has been with the help of two old friends, Monika Lacher of the Großbritannien-Zentrum at Humboldt-Universität in Berlin and Patrick von Richthofen. The German research has reached the Kirchengemeindeamt of the Evangelische Gesamtgemeinde Wiesbaden and the Stadtarchiv of the Landeshauptstadt Wiesbaden who have been courteous and ready in response to difficult questions.

More focussed help has been abundantly offered: by Ruth Escritt of the Dragon School, Mrs Lesley Raymond of Roedean, Miss Elizabeth Bushnell of St Leonard's, Mr J P Campling of St Bartholomew's School; by the archivists of Bedales, Cheltenham, Dulwich, Malvern, Manchester Grammar School, Marlborough, Repton, Rugby, and Wellington; by Barbara Dennis of the Victorian Studies Department in the University of Wales at Lampeter, the Revd Paul Spurgeon at Lower Nidderdale in Yorkshire, the Revd Peter Nickols-Rawle at Breague in Cornwall, Mr John Lobb, Anne Thomson, Josslyn Gore-Booth, Charles Colquhoun, Anthea Morrison, David Fuller, Gregory Crane, Margaret Crane, Suzie Boddy, Marie-Anne Fillaudeau, Norman Burgess, David Maynard of James Purdey & Sons, Kate Bishop of the Wellcome Trust, Anne-Laure Fillaudeau, John Dennis, Gerhardt Wiesend, M le Maire at Banneville la Campagne, Calvados, France, Alastair Massie of the National Army Museum, Michael Geach of the

Truro Diocesan Library; and also by the archivists of a number of Cambridge colleges: Christ's, Clare, Emmanuel, King's; and of a number of Oxford colleges, besides the University Archives: Balliol, Christ Church, Corpus, Hertford, Magdalen, New College, Pembroke, Queen's, St Edmund Hall, St John's; and of University College, London. The Cornwall Family History Society, the London Metropolitan Archives, the Manuscript Section of the Guildhall Library, the Jaeger head office and press office, the City of Westminster Archives, the Royal Geographical Society, the Geological Society, the Office for National Statistics and the Public Record Office have also been most generous with their help.

Mary Qualter of Galway County Library and Tony Storan of Limerick County Library led us through the thickets of Irish research with unfailing kindness and patience and Deanna Pettus of the Lindsay, California, branch of the Tulare County Library did the same for the USA. The Bodleian Library and the British Library (to whom thanks are due for permission to reproduce the preface of George Allen's *Things to Come*: BL shelfmark 4372 ee 26) have been places of constant resort and the Universitätsbibliothek in Stuttgart and the University of London Library have readily answered tricky questions.

Castle Print of Richmond in Yorkshire have helped us at many crucial moments in the making of this book, and especially in the preparatory stages of the production of the dust jacket. Two very old friends and colleagues, Tom Craik and Derek Todd, have helped enormously by their enthusiastic response to the whole project and by their eagle eye, as has Mandy Green. It is perhaps the intimate circumstances, of friends and family, out of which an enterprise like this arises that are in the end the vital and incalculable help to acknowledge. Our two daughters, Kate and Nell, have lived with this book almost as much as we, and have courteously and thoughtfully picked their way round the work it has involved.

Roy, Tankred, Brian: boat called Tyra c1901

Min, C C Lynam, Tyra, Brian, Roy, Tankred: Cornwall 1892

C C Lynam, Tyra, Roy, Brian, Leu: Cornwall 1892

SELECT BIBLIOGRAPHY

A Boolean Anthology: selected writings of Mary Boole on mathematical education, ed D G Tahta, publ by the Assoc of Teachers of Mathematics, 1972

"A Chat about Clifton College", by a Clifton boy [in School house, to sit the Woolwich exam in 1893], *Chums* [a magazine for boys; see Robertson Davies, *The Merry Heart*, London (ISBN 0 14 02.7586 X), 1998 (first publ 1996), p.11 & 258-9], vol 1, no 7 (Oct 1892), pp.102-3 (cited as *Chat about Clifton*)

Adams, Jad. *A History of Kings and Princes Garth and Forest Hill*, London (ISBN 0 9520590 0 2), 1993

Adburgham, Alison. *Shopping in Style: London from the Restoration to Edwardian elegance*, London: Thames & Hudson, 1979 (cited as Adburgham)

Allen, George William. *"Things to Come" being essays towards a fuller appreciation of the Christian idea*, London: Elliot Stock, 1892

Beckson, Karl. *London in the 1890s*, London (ISBN 0 393 033 97 X), 1993 (first publ 1992; cited as Beckson)

Bence-Jones, Mark. *A Guide to Irish Country Houses*, London (ISBN 0 09 468750 1), 1988 (cited as Bence-Jones)

Burke's Irish Family Records

Butler, Samuel. *The Way of all Flesh*, 1903

Chadwick, Owen. *The Victorian Church*, vol 2, London (ISBN 7136 1020 4), 1970 (cited as Chadwick, vol 2)

Cicero, Marcus Tullius. *de Oratore* (Book I), translated into English with an introduction by E N P Moor, London: Methuen & Co, 1892 (preface dated Clifton, Jan 1892)

Crane, Denis (i.e. Walter Thomas Cranfield). *The Life-story of Sir Robert W Perks*, London: Robert Culley, 1909

Descriptive Account of Norwood, Forest Hill, Dulwich and District, London: Robinson, Son & Pike, 1893

Dictionary of National Biography (cited as DNB)

Flower, Margaret. *The Development of Forest Hill between 1801 and 1910*, (typescript lodged at Lewisham Local Studies and Archives, London SE13 6LG), ?1976

Frauberger, Tina. *Handbuch der Spitzenkunde*, Leipzig, 1894

Frauberger, Tina. *Handbuch der Schiffchenspitze*, vol 1, Düsseldorf, 1914; vol 2, Düsseldorf, 1921

Gosse, Edmund William. *Father and Son*, 1907

Grosskurth, Phyllis. *John Addington Symonds*, London: Longmans, 1964 (cited as Grosskurth)

Jackson, Holbrook. *The Eighteen Nineties*, 1913 (new ed with an introduction by Malcolm Bradbury), London (ISBN 0 09 173159 3), 1988 (cited as Holbrook Jackson)

Later Victorian Britain 1867-1900, ed T R Gourvish and Alan O'Day, London (ISBN 0 333 42495 6), 1988

Newsome, David. *The Victorian World Picture*, London (ISBN 0 7195 5630 9), 1997 (cited as Newsome)

Nolan, Frederick W. *The Life and Death of John Henry Tunstall*, Albuquerque: Univ of New Mexico Press, 1965 (cited as Nolan)

Potter, Jeremy. *Headmaster: the Life of John Percival, Radical Autocrat*, London (ISBN 0 09 478200 8), 1998 (cited as Potter)

Pullen, Doris E. *Forest Hill*, London (ISBN 0 9504171 1 4), 1979 (repr 1981)

Sturt, George. *The Wheelwright's Shop*, Cambridge, 1923 (repr 1993; ISBN 0 521 44772 0)

The Cliftonian (magazine of Clifton College)

The Draconian (magazine of the Dragon School)

The Sydenham, Forest Hill and Catford Directory 1894, London, Forest Hill: Victoria Printing Works, 118 Stanstead Road, [Forest Hill], 1894

The Victorians, ed Laurence Lerner, London (ISBN 0 416 56220 5), 1978 (cited as *The Victorians*)

Tolley, Christopher. *Domestic Biography: the Legacy of Evangelicism in Four Nineteenth-Century Families*, Oxford (ISBN 0 19 820651 8), 1997 (cited as Tolley)

Winterbottom, Derek. *Henry Newbolt and the Spirit of Clifton*, Bristol (ISBN 0 948265 80 9), 1986

Winterbottom, Derek. *Clifton after Percival: a Public School in the Twentieth Century*, Bristol (ISBN 1 872971 80 6), 1990 (cited as Winterbottom, *Clifton*)

Roy, Tyra, Brian: Cornwall 1892

Clifton Chapel: 1887

1   Sunday night Sept 18th 92

My Darling Boy

We have been picturing your first Sunday* amidst fresh
fields & pastures new* but the only thing I made sure of,
was, that you were in that beautiful chapel* in the morning.
I am longing to hear from you as many details as possible.
Tyra is reckoning on her birthday tomorrow. Ethel & Violet
Lambley are coming & as we* intend going to Worthing on
Tuesday I shall be very busy. I thought I could take Tyra
with us & send her to Brighton* on Friday from there. I
trust it will turn out well for all! Brian and Roy have taken
to wearing your discarded collars & really look charming in
them so quaint & old fashioned & the broad white band
sets off their dear little faces. They would like to take the
"ship called Tyra"* but I cannot undertake such a
responsibility without your help!

Our address will be 3 Windsor Terrace, Worthing. I wonder
all kinds of things about you. Have you had an exam, have
you seen Mr Glazebrook – have you found some nice
companions – don't forget to tell me every thing – it is ¼
to 11pm so I suppose you are in bed – and will begin work
in ernest tomorrow. God bless you my Precious. We all send
no end of love especially yr loving Mother
                    Min

2   School House, Crick Road, Oxford*

19.ix.92

My dear Mr Behrens,

I have just received a very jolly keepsake* from Tankred & a
very kind letter from him. I have written to thank him for it
but I cannot help writing to tell you how much I shall miss
him. A boy of his strength of character & keen sense of justice
was a difficult study for a young headmaster, especially coming

as a first boarder – & I fear that in many cases my treatment of him may not have been judicious – He has been in many ways a useful tonic to me, keeping me up to a higher standard than I shd have otherwise attained to – I know how much more he respected example than precept & often I have felt that his keen sense of justice has reacted upon me & made me more impartial than I might have been without the feeling of his criticism – we have had many a row! some his fault & some no doubt mine but I hope & believe that we shall always be friends,* perhaps all the better friends for knowing each other so well – I have never known him tell a lie & have always trusted him – I have always had a very great respect for him as well as affection &, more than any other boy I have ever had under my charge, shall I watch with anxious interest his future – with kindest regards to Mrs Behrens,
Believe me,
Yours respectfully,
C.C.Lynam

3   M = Moors House,* Clifton

Sept 21st Wednesday. 1892

My Dear Father

I am getting all right.

I will write again directly I have found out all about evrything & have a good long time to write you a really long letter & that will be probably on Sunday. I am only writing now to know, as it is compulsory to join the fives courts whether you like it or not, whether you would rather send me 5£* a term for 5 terms to be a life member or pay 1£ in the bill this term & have it finished with altogether.* Please answer *all questions directly*, I also want to know whether you would rather I join the gymnasium or the Rifle & Engineering Corps.* The expense is about the same & whether I should learn Boxing or fencing or Both. So now Good bye dear father from
your loving Son
Tankred.

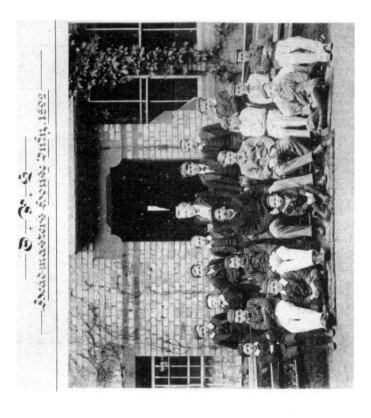

Headmasters House July, 1893

C C Lynam (centre), Tankred (right of CCL)

Tankred is very smartly dressed; an anonymous writer in The Draconian in 1923 says that as a boy at the Dragon School he "prayed nightly" among other things for "a suit of 'dittos' buckled at the knee, as smart as that worn by 'Tinker' Behrens."

M G Glazebrook

4   [22.9.1892]*

Dear Father

Mr Hall Headmaster of the Military side* wants me to learn Science instead of German & is writing all Particulars. When you write to him Please write Plainly bye the way I should rather like to join the Rifle corps *than* the Gymnasium

In haste

Tankred

5   [23.9.1892]*

My dear Son,

Be a life member & tell me whether I shall send you cheque for £1.* – Join the Rifle & Engineering Corps.

Learn *both* Boxing & fencing, provided it can be conveniently managed so that it does not interfere with your other studies. I am obliged to Mr Hall for his letter, to which I shall reply shortly. Chemistry can be but useful to you & once begun, I am sure *you* will take a *deep* interest in it. Yet the language must *not* be neglected for reasons you know. German you ought to speak like your mother tongue.* You have a sound basis already which wants brushing up. Mr Glazebrook held with me that you ought to prepare for exams in it, pray *confer with him*, he said there was a splendid master for German* at Clifton. It is impossible for me at the moment to judge whether there is room & time for extra-lessons, without knowing your table of lessons.

But you promised me a *long* letter next Sunday which will probably tell me all. I am only writing this in a hurry being pinched for time. In my next I will enlarge on the different items we have to consider *wisely*.

Pray tell me what made you choose Woolwich* in preference to Sandhurst?
with my best wishes for your welfare & good shake of hands
Ever your loving pater* Leu

3

24.9.1892: 6 (TTB to LWFB)

6   [24.9.1892]*

My dear Father,

I made a mistake as to the price in the Rifle Corps. I am
sending you the list of payments.* if any thing on this
would make you alter your mind, please write & tell me. if
not let me know as *soon as ever* you can that you still wish
me to join. As far as I recollect I never said any thing
about Sandhurst, for I only wish to go to Woolwich, I may
have answered this question wrongly as I could not read it.
in Haste from your loving
Son Tankred

7   M = Moor's House, Clifton College, Bristol

Sept. 25. Sunday. 1892

My Dear Mother & Father

I write mother & Father because I dont think "Parents"
sounds nice it sounds so stiff. This morning we generally do
work from 10-11. But our form master Mr Spense hurt his
leg some time ago & so cant walk very well & so we do
work at his house, & today the room in his house which
we work in could not be used so we got off work & so I
have an hour extra time for writing this letter. I have been
longing all the week to write this letter, but Partly because
I had no time before & partly because I had to wait till I
knew something about the place I had to wait till today. I
am all in a continual muddle about my work, for I either
dont know which room to go to or else what lesson must
be done that hour, or else what master I have to go to, or
what work to prepare; All is so *entirely* new & different to
what I have been used to. Of course at present it is an
awful muddle not knowing whether to do Chemistry &
Physics or German, for my part I should like *very much*
to do both but I dont know how it is to be done. I
regret very much not *being able to do greek*. When I know

what I have to do each hour I will send you a copy of my
routine & then you can see what hours I do each thing. But
now I will tell you what hours we work & play Evry day.
On Sunday we get up at a quarter past eight then house
prayers & breakfast. Then we have school from 10-11 &
chapel from 11-12.15. dinner at 1.30. Then nothing till Chapel
at 4-5.15. Mr Glazebrook preaches. Then sometimes a lecture
at 8.P.M in the big Hall at the College. On a week day we
get up at 6.30. Prayers. 7. Preparation 7-8. Breakfast. 8.
Prayers for the whole school & call over 8.45. School 9-11 &
11.15-12.15. Dinner 1.30. Preparation 2-3. School 4-6. tea 6.
Preparation 7.15-9.15. Supper 9.30. Prayers 9.40. Bed 10. That
is lights out. on Half Holidays That is Thursday & Saturday
we work from 11.15-1.15 & then nothing till preparation from
7.15-9.15. So we have house Prayers evryday in the morning
evening, Something is read out of the Psalms & then two or
three Prayers, & we have School prayers once a day at
8.45-8.50. I think it has on the whole rather a good effect
on the Boys but I cant really judge as yet. We have roll
call at our House at 7.AM. 1.30PM. at 6.10PM. and at
9.40.PM. & School roll call & prayers from 8.45-8.50. In
the after noon we have tea in our Studies, they supply tea,
sugar, milk, bread, Butter, but other from that we get
nothing for tea so for that we have to rely on our
Hampers each boy is allowed to bring a Hamper & have
one sent as well. Dont send a Hamper till I ask for it. We
get very good food here, at any rate it is all good & fresh,
no resurrection pie.*   For Breakfast we get tea and Coffee,
Bread, Butter, & either Fish, Ham, Tongue, Sausages or
stewed Kidneys & bacon, or eggs. For dinner we get, Veil,
beef, Mutton that is saddle of mouton, Potatoes, & cabbage
or beans, gravey. all of these things mind you are all really
good. For tea I have explained, for Supper we each get
bread and milk, or Cocoa, & Biscuits or bread & Butter.
By the way we some times get Porridge in the morning for
Breakfast. Mr Moor is *very nice indeed*. We have a very fair
house library. So far as I can see there is *no bullying whatever*.
Evrybody has to fag, his 1st term, so I have to fag a little
& a little only such as tidy the library 8 times this term, &
a few other odd things, but next term as I am in the
Middle 5th* Modern Side I shall not have to fag at all. I
have heard *scarcely any* bad language of any sort here, that
is to say one or two strong words but no Smutty words.*

I expect I shall join the rifle & Engineering Corps here. They do drill from 6.30-7.15 on Tuesday & Friday evenings. You have to Gymn at least twice a week. either from 12.15-1.15 or 2.30-3 or 3-4. That is to say evrybody is obliged to join the workshop (only carpentry I believe with Lathe) Gymnasium or the rifle corps. I received you letter & Postcard all right Dear Mother. And I have also received dear Fathers letter. Please write to dear Tyra and tell her I am so sorry I did not write to her on her birthday & sent her no Present, But I really had no time whatever. I hope the dear little Boys are getting better. They really looked very poorly. Please write again soon.

I have an Irishman* in my Study with me, by the way we all have Studies here in some there are 4 Boys some 3, some 2, & some 1, there is only one boy, this Irishman, besides myself in our Study; this Boy, has no Idea whatever of order & never puts any thing away which He takes out of the Cupboard & consequently our Study is always in a state of disorder which nearly drives me mad with Him, any reproach you give him about this continued disorder he gets angry & sulks, the disorder would not be so bad if our Study was larger only it is so small* that unless evrything is in its proper place there is no room whatever to do anything. I dont like him at all But one must put up with it I suppose it might be worse. On Sunday in the afternoon we usualy go a walk on the downs,* at least I did last Sunday, we were attacked by half a dozen lads who threw stones at us. The other day one of my master's asked me whether my name was the same as my fathers So I explained that you wished me to join my mother's and father's name & that that was my name,* and so he said that I was to oblige him by not write* down my name as such while I was at the school & then what was worse he told me that it was only a bit of my *affectation* & this he said before all my form* 18 boys. I think he *is an utter & intolerable beast*. Please will you tell me what to do in this matter This master was Mr Hall who wrote to you. If you think proper you might tell him that that is my name though please dont allude to what I have told you.

Please tell me whether Roberts has sent Those Lines & Twine* yet, – if he has ask Pattinson whether he has wound the lines on the reels I made last holidays which are in your bedroom,

C H Spence

H S Hall

J Polack

E Pellissier

C W A Tait

E C Plant

W W Vaughan

if Pattinson has not tell him to stretch & wind them as soon as he can. Please put the twine with my netting in the top of the clothes cupboard in my bedroom taking care not to move anything that is already there. Dear mother let me know when you are going back home* & then I can write for some things to decorate my Study with & a Hamper, because I cant write to you now for these things as you could not manage it when you were away from Home. There is still another thing I dont like at all here. That is we none of us have any hot baths* to wash in what we have in place of this, is that we bathe in the baths twice a week.

it is no good writing to ask if I could have a bath once a week. *So Please dont do it.* I was not allowed to use the soap you gave me we all *Have* to use a sort of carbolic soap. When we are once in our Dormitory there is no ragging talking or anything of the kind. There are 28 boys* in my class and 14 or 13 boys in my Dormitory & 48 boys in our House. I cant see any Jews he* though & I know there are a good many.* It cost me 16/5 to come here as I will show you.

	s.	d.
to London Bridge*	0	6
Porter	0	2
Cab to Paddington	2	8
Porter	0	3
Fare to Bristol	9	11½
Porter	0	3
Cab	2	8
	16	5½

Now I brought back 2/6 to include fare home. So that leaves me 13/- Pocket money. Please adhere *to all my instructions, at least till you have written to me about any of my instructions which you think are not necessary & have received an answer back to your letter from me.* Please write a long letter and tell me all about Worthing, Tyra, Yourself & the boys. Dear Father I hope you wont mind me sending this to Mother *1st* as I cant write this letter again as it is too long to do that with, & sending it to mother 1st Saves the extra 1d.* Evry Half holiday we Play football from 3.15-4.30 about. This of course is compulsory. any day we may go into Clifton* to get anything we want any time we can find before 4.P.M. of course there are lots of places which are out of Bounds But we can go into most parts of Clifton & any where on the downs but not down by the river or across the river. I am going to enquire about boxing & fencing, & also find out about learning the violin & how to answer a thing or two in Fathers letter of yesterday.

You need not send a Cheque for 1£ as that will be put in the bill.* It is I think not the thing to do for me to go to Mr Glazebrook about it* if you wish you ought to write to him about it yourself. I really dont know my self whether there is time for extra lessons or no I expect it could be managed if you were to write to Mr Glazebrook about it. But think of him and trouble him as little as you can, as of course he has many other things to think of so he ought only to be written to on the most important matters. They have a sort of institution here of Evry Saturday evening, the Bigger boys *make* the smaller Boys fight (with boxing gloves) which, though I dont mind it my self, I think is rather Barbarous because I dont think anyone should be forced to fight, it is of course quite a legal thing in this way the head boy* of the house & the House master allow it. Excuse me saying I would send this letter to mother 1st but on 2nd thoughts I really must send it to father 1st as there are one or 2 items which I wish him to know before he writes to Mr Hall. Dear Father directly you Have thoroughly read the letter Please send it immediately to mother & ask her to send it back to You to be filed without fail.

I dare say Mr Edwards would like to know that Mr Hall teaches me Maths, but he makes the lessons intolerable & if it does not alter soon somehow, I shall begin *really* to *hate* Maths *altogether*. He growls at my style *not of writing* but of putting down my sums with a very few words, I know it is not quite right how I do them.

We Do Conversational french & German, & Geometrical Drawing.

Dear mother Please write on the proper paper father gave you so that I can file it. We had no exam our forms were judged from the Scholarship* work as is quite proper I think. I have

not seen Mr Glazebrook to speak to once, you see if he
went into making personal friends of all the boys in the
school it would take up all his Time being the Headmaster
he has to behave like a King to his subjects. I have found
some rather nice boys & three or four beasts in some ways.
I find a new boy at a public school cannot begin work in
real earnest as you can perhaps see from the begging* of my
letter. but as I have never been taught any Style he cant
expect me to know it all at once. So to end up I think I
can safely say my 1st experiences of Clifton are very nice
on the whole. So with love to all Good bye Dear Mother &
Dear Father

From your loving Son Tankred

8   Sept. 25. Sunday 1892

Dear Mother

I have sent a letter to father & told him to send it on to
you *as soon as he can*. So Dont Think I have forgotten you
quite. you will see in the letter why I sent it to father 1st.

So good bye Dear Mother in
haste your loving Son Tankred

Please send me 10 more 1d. Stamps.

when you write to Tyra tell her Plainly & exactly how to
adress any letters* to me she wants to send.

9   26.IX.92

My dear Boy,

Just a few lines touching upon the most necessary & to thank
you for your long letter of the 25th – I shall amplify matters
shortly in fact before very long I hope to be able to devote
most of my time* to your, your sister & brothers education.

26.9.1892: 9 (LWFB to TTB)

Your *good mother* I expect home shortly on acct* of change in our home ministry,* so I leave letters for her here. Remain calm, everything will be attended to –

To *Mr Hall* I have written & told him besides other things to take you with his Chemistry class. We must manage *the German* somehow. I wish to come down & make Mr Hall's acquaintance & then we will at the same time discuss the question of German. In the mean time find out the German master. I could perhaps see him at the same time?

<u>Engineering Corps</u>   It means
    £3. 3. 0   for 3 classes at 21/-
       6. 6   Gaiters & gloves
       7. 6   new tunic & trousers   £3. 17. 0 per annum.
of course the £3 & pounds all add up. *Believing in you* that you will do your best in your studies & follow my advice, I made up my mind to save these extras on my self & let you join nevertheless. Get *new* tunic & trousers.

What I asked you was: *Why* did you choose Woolwich in preference to Sandhurst?*

And now go on fearless, use all your abilities. Whatever work you do, let it be sound & thorough. Never despair, act wisely & collected.

Try & get out of the muddle. Address yourself to Mr Moore, who is surely ready with his advice & direction when such are wanted. Choose the right moment & right words & you will not go amiss.

Be kind to your Irish colleague. One must improve one another so teach *him* the *importance* of order, explain to him the *waste* of time *disorder is*. Instill with him Goethe's words:
    Gebraucht der Zeit, sie geht
    so schnell von hinnen,
    doch Ordnung lehrt noch
    Zeit gewinnen.*
[Use the time, it passes/ by so quickly,/ yet order teaches us/ to gain more time] In later life he will perhaps be grateful to you.

Greek, you must *not* forget. Keep it somehow afloat. I *don't* want you to forget it, as I *require* you to know it for my ideas. That point we will settle too when I come down.

And now one word re hating perhaps Mathematics. Such an idea is *absolutely* wrong. Mathematics are your force,* you must persevere & you will achieve success. don't you believe you are acquiring knowledge for Mr Hall. No No. It is you whom you benefit. It requires men to overcome difficulties. You find such, very well – overcome them & the more difficulties which may be or are horrid, you overcome, the happier in your mind you will be later on. There is nothing so disagreable from which one cannot extract *some good.*

As ever your loving

pater Leu

Roberts sent Pilchards & wrote abt twine &c &c

10   [27.9.1892]*

Dear Father

I am only writing a hurried scribble to thank you for your nice letter & to ask one rather important question which I asked you in my last letter the answer of which I could not gather from your letter. I will write again soon and answer all your letter but I have not time now. *Please tell me as soon as you possibly can am I to go on signing myself.*

Tunstall-Behrens

it seems to me it must be *now or never* with it. Did you mention it in your letter to Mr Hall
In haste your most loving Son

Tankred

P.S. Dont forget to send some more stamps at once as I am using my last one for this letter.

11   29.IX.92

My dear Tankred,

I wrote to Mr Hall and told him that you were christened Tunstall-Behrens.*   The School Secretary* has entered you as T-B and I have received receipt for school fees with T-B, so sign yourself Tunstall-Behrens.

Mr Hall is now of opinion that you go on with your German for the present & we decide about Chemistry when I come down to Clifton, which will probably be next week. I shall let you know day before.

Enclosed 2/- in stamps.

Love from us all
Your attached pater
Leu

12   Clifton College

Oct 2. 1892

My Dear Mother & Father

I hope you are quite well & the boys at the same time. This is the one thing which I look forward to during the week, having time to write to you. Thanks much for your letter which I am just going to answer. I wish mother would write me the letter which she promised it is a long time coming. I think I will wait a little to ask for anything I think I will wait till father has been down to see me as he says he will be coming down shortly. Dear Father I dont quite know what you mean by "Giving up most of your time to our education, before long." I cant express my gratitude & thanks enough for your *so* Kindly allowing me to join the Engineering corps here. I quite appreciate your statement that 3£ here & there very soon mount up; this sentence may be rather stiff but I dont know how to express my feelings otherwise in a letter. I chose Woolwich in preference to Sandhurst because Woolwich is the

Engineering academy & Sandhurst is for the officers in Ordinary regements only besides I thought you wanted me to go to Woolwich. I really dont know how I can keep up Greek here Though I very much want to as I have only 2 or 3 hours a week in which there is nothing-compulsory to do that is to say they are play hours. I think you must have misunderstood my meaning about the Mathematics, I merely meant that he made the lesson so exceedingly dissagreable, As to "Acquiring Knowledge for Mr Hall" I really dont know how you gathered *That* from my letter. I really cant abide him he is so dissagreable. Would you please tell me what Roberts said about the Lines & twine I could not read that in your letter? How many pilchards Did Roberts send, did they arrive fresh & not Bruised? How did you dispose of them? did you grill any on a grid Iron? did you try to marinate any? Do you know yet, for certain whether Roberts is coming for Christmas or what date he will arrive? I belong to the Choir here, & next Thursday the Choir are going to a place called Brockley* in Drags* That will be awfuly nice. I like this place pretty well, for I cant say I really like it for several reason, nor can I say I dont like it, in fact I cant quite express how I feel towards it. Next time you write please answer my *last* letter in ful, also this one. There is really no more news just now, So Good bye

dear mother & father from your loving Son Tankred

13 Newfield*

Monday Oct. 3rd 92. 9.30.p.m

My Precious Boy

I cannot tell you the pleasure your letters are to us, you tell us so nicely about everything & it is delightful to know all the time almost exactly what you are about. I am very glad that your report is on the whole so satisfactory, that there is no fagging, no ragging in the bedrooms & that the food is so good & also that you like your housemaster which is a very great point. What you say with reference to the Mathematics lessons may wear off. Mr Lynam told us that on principle they were always rather down on scholars *at first* so don't be in the least discouraged by it. you said quite the right thing about the name it is always a proper and sufficient answer to say you do a thing because your parents wish it. Your father wrote to Mr Hall & I had already informed the Secretary. so that the cheque to the bankers came back with the correct name upon it. there only remains to inform Glazebrook & I have waited in case there should be anything else to say at the same time not to trouble him twice. I agree with you about the "compulsory" fighting. but as it is done *with gloves* I suppose it may be regarded as boxing & a training for self defence. – anyway if you have to do it I suppose you only treat it as practice for boxing – I think if I were you, I should use my influence in the direction of getting it to be so regarded, by so regarding it yourself & when you have an adversary who is not your equal in strength, dealing gently with him. You will understand the difference I mean in the *spirit* of the thing, between boxing or real fighting.

I think with regard to extra lessons or Greek you must feel your way & settle down *this* term. everything is so entirely new & different from your past experience & you need not be surprised if you cannot quite express what you feel about it all, but nevertheless – do not be weary of trying to express it as you proceed for we shall never be tired of listening. I have been very much gratified by a very kind letter of Mr Lynams to your father,* in which he spoke very frankly of the great trust & confidence he had always felt in you, recognizing your love of justice & speaking of the great interest with which he would follow your career – He began by saying he had received a very nice kind letter & keepsake from you. I think you hit on the very thing to give him most pleasure. (It was rather fortunate his own watch had met with an accident!) I tell you this about Mr Lynam because I know you have often felt as if he did not like you or appreciate your efforts in the right direction & I think it is only fair that you should know it. he said you had had many a fight often your fault but no doubt often his which I think most generous from a master.

The pilchards came when *I was away* unfortunately – carriage

3.10.1892: 13 (EFB to TTB)

6/6 – I should think in quantity – the big red earthenware bowl in the kitchen full. Some were cooked as they should have been *at first* on the grid – but some have been put into a sort of pickle which Sophie calls marinated – vinegar laurel* leaves onions mustard &c – which will be ready in a fortnight the others have been – as *I think* too much salted – partly unsalted & fried like herrings they were good but too salt – Your father told Roberts to send you some but I think that was a mistake so pray write to him *if you think* so & countermand them.

How do you get on with the singing in the choir? do not sing at the top of your voice because it only wears it out & carries no farther & when your voice *begins* breaking (which may not be for a long time) you will have to leave off for a time –

I should have written to you before dearest but the cook I had engaged for Oct 1st cried off. so as soon as I had taken Tyra to Brighton* on the 27th I came home & proceeded to hunt about for a substitute. I spent weary hours at an office – "Pipes" a kind of mart for employers & employed until four o'clock without success when one likely young woman came in. I found she was cook at Val Prinsep's a well known artist so I went next day for her character & engaged her & I think I hear her just coming into the house – Agnes has come back in her old place & Sarah is to be parlour maid – so I hope for the best. You know these changes of ministry involve great trouble & time & having caught a cold in addition I felt on Sunday so sadly that I actually stayed in bed until 5 o'clock.p.m. The weather was raw & chilly & I felt I was out of harms way – but it is the first time since I have been married that I did such a thing.

It grieves me to leave my sweet little boys alone with Fräulein Wehrmeister at Worthing* though the people at the lodgings are as nice as they can be & I believe they are safe & very happy – They go for walks on the downs which they call *Bergen** & hunt about for traces of wolves & robbers! on the beach they build very nice things with bricks & stones with sand for mortar & as some mischievous person undid it every time they wrote up "trespassers will be *prosecuted*" to keep them off. alas! in vain! I read about the Queens dolls to them in which they were much interested & in the pictures particu-

15

larly of one dressed like a celebrated dancer Taglioni – & Roy has taken to calling himself Taglioni-lumpi in his comic little way. I don't know if he really understood that lumpi was a lump & Taglioni a dancer, but one might think so. Brian told us of such a nice little dream of his – he said "I dream't that they wanted to make me a king but I said I wanted to stay with my mother so I said 'Did they make you a king all the same' No *I said* I wished to stay with *my mother* (I dont know if I told you this before)

I hope to go back to them sometime this week, but I hardly know how to manage it. Dear Tyra did enjoy her week with me at Worthing sleeping with me every night & looked all the better for it. That cold of hers was most unfortunate –

God bless you my precious. I feel he does *greatly* & will. With our united love & hugs. Your fond mother
Min

14   Clifton College

Sunday 8th* Oct 1892

My Dear Mother & Father

I hope you are quite well. You cant think what pleasure it gave me to see you* on Friday though I am very sorry I could only see you for so short a time. Thank you so much for the fruit. I will send back the Pall Mall* next week & see about the books for Father. I am so glad he is going to leave off buissiness. It will be such a treat to have him at home all day, the house & workshops will I feel shure will progress much faster, I hope your room* is finished now, did you send Dear Tyra any fruit. I beleive I am going to play in the House 2nd fifteen at Football. Dear Father please send me as soon as you can the etching & other things you were going to send me & describe if you can how to put them up so as to look nice. It really will be *a pleasure* to come home next holidays to have

father at home & not always away in the city, we can do
so many things together then. There is really no news to
tell you but I will write a longer letter next week when I
know there will be some more news, I wish there was some
more news but there is not. So Good bye dear Mother &
Father from your loving son Tankred.

P.S. Thanks so much for the Papers they arrived this
morning. When you write please leave about 1¾ inches
margin because it is rather awkward to file your letters so
that they will be readable.

Please send a paper basket among other things, mind a
small one. This Thursday if it is fine we are going (that is
the choir) out an expedition though I dont quite know
where to* you will hear all about it next Sunday. And if it
could be managed I wish you would let Pattinson make me
a deck chair about 2 feet wide I suppose you know what I
mean, I dont want a small one but on the other hand
rather a big one. Please let me know when my twine
arrives from Roberts. What did Dr Wharry write to you
after his visit* you have not told me yet. Next Thursday
week, we go to Malvern* for the Public School field day
that will be very jolly too. we have been two runs that is
sort of Paper chases instead of Football, I dont like them
very much. Next term we must try and arrange for Music
& Boxing.

15   Clifton College

Sunday. Oct. 16. 92

My Dear Mother & Father,

I hope you are quite well. Please do answer my last letter
soon. You have not written now for more than a week, Is
mother at home. Please look at   F.W.Putzgers.
                    Historischer Schul-Atlas
                            zur
            alten, *mittleren* und neuen Geschichte
            Verlag von Velhagen & Klasnig. 1891.
                                Leipzig

& see if it is not worth adding to our collection of Atlases. It has some maps in it which we have not got in any of our Atlases. My German grammar is

A German Accidence
for the use of Schools.
By
J.W.J.Vecqueray
assistant master at Rugby School
London. Longmans, Green & Co.
New Edition

I will send you the pall Mall directly.

I have no other German books except a translation book which I shall not use any more soon.

When my room is being arranged please dont forget to put 2 hooks in the wall for my hammock. If you look in my box with my book's up stairs at the top of the house you will find a thin mauve or grey "Livy" please send it as soon as you can. The light in our Study is awful we used to have at home a sort of thing to attack* to an ordinary gas bracket and so bring the light lower down, it had a green shad, I believe it is now in the store room & we dont use it now so if you could send it amongst other things it would be very useful. Have you yet informed Mr Glazebrook about my name being hyphened together. Please mother let me know how many jaeger* shirts you sent me with & with how many long jaeger underdraws. Please send me a brush & bottle of Tanin* to paint my throat with. Last Thursday I went with the Choir Expedition we drove for about 2 Hrs.* to a place called Brockley coon.* it is a deep wooded valley about 1½ miles long. & about 300 yds wide, thickly wooded with Limestone Cliffs it is very pretty we stayed here & took our tea with us and then came back at about 6.P.M. Next Thursday there is our field day. We & Malvern's artillery have to hold the Suspension bridge* till four o'clock against Marlborough & Cheltenham.

No more news now so good bye dear Mother
& Father from your loving Son Tankred.

JAEGER'S
Sanitary Woollen Ladies' Outer-clothing.

In ordering by measure, a good fit can be guaranteed if the necessary measurements are furnished according to directions, or a still better plan is to send a well-fitting garment as a model.

The woollen stuffs, which are microscopically tested for adulteration with vegetable fibre, can be supplied by the yard, and samples can be inspected.

Each garment (Jacket, Mantle, &c.), which is made in strict conformity with Dr. G. Jaeger's directions, bears the registered Trade Mark.

Jackets, Mantles, &c., of fine stocking-nette stuffs are made in various sizes and shades, and are closed in double-breasted form, according to Dr. Jaeger's Sanitary Woollen System.

Dr. G. Jaeger's Sanitary Woollen Dress, made of Pure Sheep's Wool.

DR. JAEGER'S
SANITARY WOOLLEN UNDERCLOTHING
FOR LADIES AND CHILDREN
IS KEPT IN STOCK BY
MISS SARAH FRANKS,
23, MORTIMER STREET, BERNERS STREET, W.,
At the prices quoted in this catalogue.

Miss FRANKS also undertakes orders for garments of special construction under Dr. Jaeger's system.

Jaeger advertisement: 1884

Boy's study at Clifton: c1900

16   [18.10.1892]*

My dear Tankred,

I had sent your letter of the 8th to Worthing, from where your good mother will return with the boys next Tuesday. *Pall Mall* you need *not* return, possess another one.

re decoration of your room. Pray give me a sketch of the room & I will do the needful. I gave it too flighty a look when I came to see you, but I am afraid some of those flimsy ornaments on the walls will have to go.

deck chair I do not quite realize what you mean, do you mean something like this? I think it will be more to advantage to buy it because Pattinson's time is expensive. However I will see to this, paper basket, etchings &c as well as to the hooks for your hammock.

the twine from Roberts arrived last night.

Livy I forwarded this morning, regarding the gas elongation I wrote to mother about, because I cannot find it.

Dr Wharry's report & jaeger-inventory I leave to the mother too, personally knowing nothing about it! *Tanin* & brush go by to nights post

Hyphen I have not informed Mr Glazebrook yet, shall do so next opportunity.

I send this via Worthing

the german Atlas I am going to look at; the german grammar I shall buy.

I noticed that you left 2 useful atlas *at home.* Why? you know we have duplicates & I *wish* you to have *always* these Atlas *at hand* to *study them!* As much as I could make out there is very little geography* at Clifton? You have a *turn* for geography which I was *very* glad of, *don't* let it sleep, but study & *improve* on it, it is so very useful, an Engineer as well as a soldier *should* know it *well.* I never save in books if they are for the advance of knowledge & learning. Keep therefore geography on in your leisure hours. I shall *probably* buy you a german atlas for study.

The collection of books is divided into 4 sections
and **I**   for type – print
and **II**   for binding
and **III**   books of reference
and **IV**   books for learning

I feel that I have not yet answered your *long nice* letter 3 weeks ago, I shall do so one of these evenings.

Keep well & happy, take a delight in knowledge & stick to earnest work, whereby you will give great pleasure to your pater who loves you dearly

Leu

17   3 Windsor Terrace, Worthing

Oct. 19th. 92

My Dear Blesséd

Your dear father has forwarded me your last letter & his *reply,* which I enclose. I believe that gas *elongator is* in the store room & that if it is not found sooner I shall find it on my return home – on the 25th.

I intended when we sent subscription for the chapel to *Glazebrook* then to tell him about the name. Don't you think it would confirm it to make the subscription in your name T.Tunstall-Behrens. I think it would.

Wharry did not write *to me.* I really think there was not anything to say, he *said* that you were all right – also that of course if one were a cowboy & *thought* of nothing but exercise and fresh air all ones days, one's physique might perhaps be more perfect. As that is out of the question one must make the best of mind & soul & body. The strength & purity of the *spirit* are *the thing*, for that is *You* & will keep the body right & the mind free to work & develope to the utmost. The *Spirit is the* spark of God in us & draws its strength & life & inspiration & power from the love of Him – Try to *realize* it, for it is the mainspring & yet so very simple.

We shall picture the "holding of the bridge" on Thursday. It is a delightful idea. Will *you* take part? *do tell us all about it.* I have not your clothes list here but I remember *2* long Jaeger pants – & will refer when I am home again.

Since I have been here I have had such a cold that I am afraid I have not yet personally profitted by the change but I have had quite a treat of *reading* & have read some curious things. I will write more later my precious Boy.
We are always loving & doting upon you – your fond Mother
Min

18 21.X.92

My dear Boy,

Salt – Hensel says – forms the red globules in the blood –

I have been thinking that if you tried to take salt with your meals, which you have not done hitherto, you might be rosier & in better health? Some I know say salt is unnecessary pointing to the savages who never take salt with their meat &c. yet there is this to be said the savages have a great deal more exercise thereby contributing to the assimilation of food, which you have not. I remember having had an aversion of salt as a youngster & was in consequence no doubt pale. I submit this to you because I think the son should profit by the father's experience. Bite *well*, masticate that is another half of the battle won! I want you strong in body & mind! don't forget to gargle *every* night *before* going to bed with *salt* water that

& tanin will soon set your throat in order.

In love your pater Leu

[addition in EFB's hand] Just what your mother has always told you. Love & hugs from her. Min. Worthing.

19   Clifton, MR. H*

[23.10.1892]*

My Dear Mother & Father

I hope you are quite well. Please dont send that gas elongator till I ask for some other things. Dont send the subscription for the Chapel in my name. how much are you going to give. Bye the way, last week we had to pay 5/- subscription to the Bristol boys clubs* whatever they may be so I expect you to pay me back, but instead of sending me 5/- I will send you 5/- shortly & then you can put 10/- in the bank for me. Dont forget to let me know about the pants & shirts. the deck chair is like this –

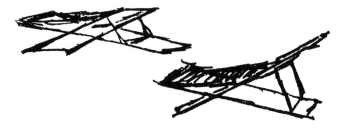

it costs about 3/6 if you sent the money I could get one here. the drawing was on the spur of the moment so excuse such a bad one. Please tell me what Roberts sent *exactly*. how many lines & how many balls of Twine. I left the atlases at home because I did not know whether we would use them here or not, I shall take them next term it is not worth sending them. thanks for the Livy & Tanin which arrived promptly. The Tanin has done me a lot of good I use it every night. I will eat plenty of salt & see if it does me good. Last thursday was our field day there was our corps 100 strong on one side &

23.10.1892: 19 (TTB to EFB/LWFB)

the Malvern Artillery who had two 16 pounder field guns & 2. 9 pounder field guns too they were on our side & on the other side about 300, composed of Malvern's infantry force & Marlborough & Cheltenham.

We are supposed to be foreigners who have advanced & taken the suspension bridge before the troops could advance from Gloucester, but when the English (Marlborough, Cheltenham, Malvern) advance they come in too strong a force & we (Clifton & Artillery) are the rear guard to Keep the bridge free till 4.P.M. when our army would have retreated over the bridge. So that we really had to cover the retreat of our army because the Enemy (English) came in too strong a force. Now you can see from the map [see following page] our 1st position just in front of of that cross road by the waterworks & an advance guard, on that slight rise with the copse, with a canon. Now in the 1st attack the enemy were not successful, & they were driven back. then as the Field day had to continue we were ordered to retreat the two guns retreating to the second position as marked on the map, and then the enemy beat us back & we were not able to stand. the Points at the end of each arrow show the position each column was in at 4.P.M. I with the advanced recruit detatchment. Being a recruit of course I did not do much but next term when we go to Aldershot* I shall not be a recruit. We (recruits) go to drill on Mondays, Wednesdays, & Fridays. Next term we build bridges in the big baths & make fortifications in the Close (the field behind the college). I dont know what to do, I can't get on with my work try how I will, I get sworn at all round by all the masters in whose form I am, whether I work or not. I have worked as hard as I can under the surrounding circumstances & I dont seem to be able to get on with my work, I wish I knew what to do. Now I am going to ask for some grub it will be rather a lot but remember it has to last till the end of term so dont be astounded. I write now as I know Mother is coming home for good next Tuesday. 6 pots (of ordinary size) of jam not jam which has had oil to preserve it.
a small Dutch cheese (round) of about 3lb
a *small* ham all ready cooked for eating like the 1st one we had from that shop in our road*
4 galley pots* of *home* made potted beef. *if you know exactly*

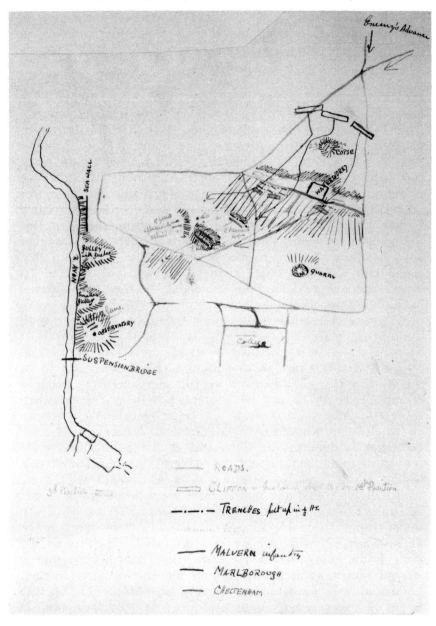

23.10.1892: 19 (TTB to EFB/LWFB)

what I mean, & how to make it. if you dont know how to make it send the equivalent in bought potted meat.
3. *small* tins of sardines.
2 *small* cakes, you know what I like.
& send a little honey in the comb & some nice biscuits
& 2 cakes of menier* chocolate & some good cocoa
& 3 tins of preserved milk you know what I mean.

I know this is a lot, it is to last 2 of us for tea & sometimes for breakfast for 9 weeks so send the things at your discretion. *Please send some maté tea**

So good bye dear Mother & Father from

your loving Son

Tankred

Excuse such a fright of a sketch the door is opposite the window. the room is 11ft 6in high, there is only 2ft between the window & wall

there is a wall 6ft wide & 11½ft high here then on the left hand side of the picture there would be a wall at the right angles which is also 6ft wide. then on the wall opposite the window there is the door & a plain book case which cover all the wall to a height of 5ft 9 leaving about 5ft 9in uncovered. this is the best I can do in such a short time if it is altogether useless let me know & I will try again

[See additional letter 19A on p.271-2]

20   Newfield

Oct. 29th 92

My precious Boy

Five shillings safely received. Your last letter* is not before me. I have read it once. Your account of the holding of the bridge was very interesting to us. I will try to send you a hamper next week. You really do ask for a great many things! When you say "for two" do you mean for yourself & the boy who shares your study or how do you arrange those things? Your father will write about the lamp. but there are such very *cheap* lamps giving first-rate light with a shade that I think it is not worth *sending* anything. You should make a round of the studies & compare the lamps, for light & cheapness.

Mr Allen asked me for your address & said he would like to *write to you* which is most kind of him.

Mrs Stapley asked very kindly after you & said she thought you were so much like me!

With regard to your lessons my precious I can only recommend infinite *patience* & pains! Make it a subject of prayer declare to yourself that you *Have the power & the light* to grasp each subject. Do so at night *& also* before you prepare, & before you go to your lessons – Do not be discouraged or depressed & in the holidays you can confide your difficulties to Mr Edwards. I feel it cannot do otherwise than come right & you know Mr Lynam said they were always extra severe with scholars at first. How long are the Xmas holidays?

Poor dear Mrs Beaver has reached England and we intend to go to see her this or to-morrow afternoon.

I heard such an interesting lecture on the "Symphalmograph". This is an instrument made by setting two pendulums swinging at right angles to one another & united by two arms which control at their meeting place a *point* which records the vibrations. I send you two specimens of the record. They vary infinitely according to the length of the pendulums & their relation to one another. The two specimens I send are to our eye harmonious but some are or seem to us inharmonious, just as in music we have concords & discords; possibly we might become accustomed to the inharmonies of the symphalmograph as we have done to so great an extent to the musical discords. The comparison of the two sciences is very interesting.

Please return the drawings!!

Our boys find it rather hard to return to their lessons after so long a holiday as you may imagine.

God Bless you my Precious. I was going to conclude but I must tell you that I went to Haywards Heath from Worthing to see Mrs Willans & a school "Bedales"* just going to be started on a new system by a Mr Baddeley – I only saw the house & grounds which are both beautiful we can talk of the system when you are at home. I also went to see Tyra – I first had a chat with Miss Lawrence & Tyra's special teacher Miss Morris – They seem to say she has made a start this term, & I can see she is at least trying. I saw the fencing lesson & then took her & the Lambleys & Betty Holt for a drive & to tea at the "Creameries" – which they all seemed to enjoy. I wished I could do it oftener. Tyra sends her love to you & would enjoy a letter from you. No end of love from your fond mother

Min

21   Clifton College, Moor's House

Oct. 31. 92

My Dear Mother & Father

Please answer my last letter* in full. Please send Van Houtens cocoa a big tin. When I say for two I mean it is to last two for teas to the end of term, we don't give one tin especially for one & another especially for the other we just each use the one that is open. that is me and the boy who shares my study. Mind I most want the Incandescent burner as in last letter, you know what I mean I suppose.

The Xmas holidays begin on Dec. 20, & go on for about 4 weeks 3 days, not less, I have written to Roberts not to forget to come to see us at Xmas I want to know if he could come on Dec 20, as far as you are concerned, & travel from Bristol with me.

Why do you say *poor* dear Mrs Beaver? Explain & let me know all about Mr Beaver too. I wish I could Keep those drawings & get some more different like Mr Allens & frame them. We are having a most exciting house match.* Our House has got 10 points to the School House's 10 points in 1hr 20min & in the next 1hr & 20min which was on a diffrent day to the last the School House got 3 Points & we 6 Points so that is their 13 Points to our 16. The Game is who ever gets the 27 Points at football first. this only applies to House Matches not to other Games. Our House has been on the whole since the school began the best house at Games, I am Glad I have come to the best House in the school for games & grub. I do hope father will leave off work before the holidays it will be so jolly, and the workshops* & all other things will get on so very fast. no more news now so good bye dear mother & father
From your loving Son
Tankred

22   Clifton

Nov 1 92

My Dear Mother

I expect you have not heard about Mr Roberts' very bad illness, I am so greeved about, not only because he is bad, but that after having had a *very* bad mackerel season he should be cut short in the Pilchard season & so have practicaly earnt nothing all the year besides the expense of the doctor. I enclose the letter I received so you shall know all I know about it. I do hope he will be able to come to town at Christmas & that he will get quite as well again as he was before & not get like poor Mr Tucker.
So good bye dear Mother
from your loving Son
Tankred

Please send some more stamps

23   Newfield

November 4th. 92

My Darling Boy.

Pray do not be disappointed at the non arrival *this* week of your Hamper. The things want so much collecting & cannot be sent of course in batches.

"Poor Mrs Beaver" – why dear boy I must have told you that our dear friend Hugh Beaver is no more, he died in S. Africa on Aug 29th of inflammation of the lungs. I heard of it while at Worthing & am under the impression that I told you of it. The two little boys are very nice. Hugh (our godson) & Guy, 2yr & 1yr old, & a third* anticipated about Xmas. It is so very sad! They have gone to Mrs Beaver's mother* at Eyrecourt Castle* in Ireland.

6.11.1892: 24 (TTB to EFB/LWFB)

I am so sorry about Roberts. We received your ½ term report. did you see it? I think you will soon feel your way & get on. of course everything is new & the system is naturally less in leading strings than at Mr Lynam's & you must get accustomed to it – you see how important the writing* is – fatal to you I mean. You must see it yourself.

I have just received from Hoare* £4. 8. o royalties on my patent!* which you will be glad to hear tho' it *is so little*.
I will try to write more later

God Bless

Your loving Mother

Min

Wish you had heard Mrs Boole yesterday on the relation between intuition & intellect.

24   Clifton College

Nov. 6th. 92

My Dear Mother & Father,

Why dont you write to me father?

Please make haste & see about that incandescent burner, the light in my study is *frightful*, And it hurts my eyes *frightfully* & makes them ache till I dont know what to do, in the 1st place the light flickers & is so awfuly dull so I hope you wont neglect thinking about it sharp. It does grieve me so about poor Mr Beaver, he was such a nice fellow, how did he get inflammation of the lungs. I did not see my half term report. I am glad you received the 4£ 8/- it looks more promising. You did not tell me about poor Mr Beaver before. Please write on the right paper, & *please answer my last letter in full.*

There is really no more news, will write again soon; – Please

Min's patent "Omnidress"

Brian, Min: Newfield 1892

see that dear Father writes to me. So good Bye dear
Mother & Father

from your loving Son

Tankred

25   Newfield

Nov. 10th 92

Darling Boy!

The lamp we bought yesterday is a beautiful one & cost
13/-. I think it was very good of your father to get such a
nice one. The metal part only requires rubbing up with a
leather – *no whitening* or anything of that sort – It will burn
any kind of oil but the best & least smelly is white water
kerosene which is only the petroleum extra filtered & I dare
say extra dear. I hope to send off your Hamper to-morrow
Friday – you must buy a quart bottle of the oil for the
lamp. I feel a lamp is better for you in every way than gas
as it does not vitiate the atmosphere. The only doubt I
have is as to your being permitted to use it – in that case
take great care of the lamp & bring it home. Keep it very
clean. I will send a leather & old tooth brush for brushing
out the perforations *gently!* A thousand greetings my precious
from your loving & fond mother

Min

More anon.

26   Newfield

Nov. 11th 92

My Dear Boy,

I am very sorry to have to defer the sending of your hamper

31

until tomorrow Saturday so that you will not receive it before Monday or Tuesday. I thought the box had a padlock or that one could easily be had & as your father wishes to put handles on the box & give you a better padlock I cannot have it until tonight. I feel it is really an insult* to Mr Moor to send you such a hamper, when he supplies you so liberally with everything you can require & I must confess I look upon it as a great extravagance in as much as it is not *needful* & the money spent some other way would be more profitable. Still darling I have great pleasure in giving you pleasure – I remember a hamper was a pleasure to me in my school days & one is glad to have something to give away – I know you are. I have sent you what you asked for. You will tell me what the potted meat is like? eat it *first.* I thought my present cook* would not make it very well so I bought a little. I hope you will enjoy all the other things & that they will arrive in good condition.

I took the two boys & Fräulein to see the Lord Mayors show at Meadows shop* (the picture shop). It was such a pleasure to them & they were so sweet. There were about three hours of waiting which I rather dreaded but they were quite amused watching the crowds & talking to some other little folks, telling us what was going on & which we could not see.

I will let you know in time whether it will do for Roberts to come on the 20th of December. How unfortunate his being so ill! Four *balls* of string & one hank have come.

Dr Wharry sent us a magnificent salmon from Roxburgh, N.B.* weighing nearly 12lbs. I suppose of his catching. So different to the salmon which reaches one in the usual round about way.

You know I had to take 2£ out of your banking account & put in your 5/- & another 5/-, so I simply took out 30/-.

I have now paid back & made all the other accounts right with that & what I had for my patent.

Mr Allen asked me yesterday for your address to write to you. He also asked if he should see Tyra when he came here on the

25th & asked if she had dyed any melon seeds. I think it is so kind of such a man to bear all these little things in his remembrance. I hope you will feel like writing him a nice natural little letter in reply just as you would to me.

Dear, Precious I think of you every day many times in all the pauses & trust you a* progressing, learning by every little failure "rising on stepping stones of your dead self to better things" as Tennyson so beautifully expresses it* –
A thousand loves from your fond
mother Min

1/- in stamps enclosed.

27   Clifton College, Bristol

[12.11.1892]*

My Dear Mother & Father,

I received the lamp yesterday all safe, it is an awfuly good one. thanks so much for it. I dont see that the hamper is not needed, for if I did not have it I should have nothing but bread & butter for tea always & should have to go from dinner to 8 A.M. the next morning with ony a ½ a small basin of bread & milk & a little bread & butter which is not enough considering we get up at 6.30 & go to bed at 10.P.M. Please tell me how many lines Roberts sent I dont quite understand from what you said. There ought to be 4. Lines. Are there that number, that is what I paid for. has pattinson wound them on the reels I made for them? *Dear Father why dont you write? Do let me have a nice long letter.* Last Wednesday we had a lecture* by profess. Boys On the way they can find out the heat any thing gives out in fact with his instrument he could tell the heat given out by any star in the heavens & he showed us how if a candle was lighted at the other end of Big School, it would alter the position of a machine, for this machine you have to use the thinnest fibre or twine you can get but now they make

a very thin string of crystal which is about 10 times thinner than our hair. no more news now will write again soon, So good bye dear Mother & Father from your loving Son
                              Tankred

28   Sunday 3.p.m. Nov. 13th 92

My Darling Boy,

The key to the lock of your box is <u>"Great"</u> I hope the box & the letter will reach you simultaneously for it would be tantalizing to have the box & not know how to open it.*

There is one thing I omitted to enclose & that is a Jaeger shirt, which I think you must be short of, but as it was not re-marked with the others I cannot quite make it out – perhaps it was too small & left out intentionally. If you want it. I will post it?

I was so happy to finally get the box off, that I forgot to write to you by yesterdays post as I intended. & I expected Fraser & Alexis & Amy Chitty to dinner – & cook ran a whole needle right into her hand so I was diverted from my intention. Dr Parnell had to take the needle out.

It has been lovely this morning in the garden & the bees were buzzing away & making the most of the sunshine outside the hives.

I wonder if you are just writing to us or taking a country walk? You have not told us much of the neighbourhood yet, which must be lovely.

Our two dear boys have colds & are not so robust as I could wish to see them. They are always very busy & industrious & find more things to do than time to do them in.

I enjoy my little study & it is so snug & comfortable that every one likes to congregate in it.

34

No other big work is proceeding every thing is at a stand still waiting to decide how to support the ceiling in the old library, on account of the weight of the books overhead. So I don't think you will see much finished indoors by Xmas, but there is a great change & improvement up the garden.

I hope to have a nice long letter from you to-morrow – don't forget that everything is news to us which seems to you most tame & every day. I think it will be best to take decorations for your study back *after* the holidays. If you can bring home with you the empty pots & biscuit tins – conveniently – please do. Love & hugs & thoughts & greetings from yr fond mother.

Min

29   Clifton College, Bristol

[20.11.1892]*

My Dear Mother & father,

I hope you are quite well. *Father why dont you write*?!!!!!!!
I have asked about three times & I wish to know why you dont write; I dont want the Jaeger shirt thank you. I must really thank you awfuly for the *most beautiful* hamper really I never expected such a magnificent hamper, the cakes are beautiful, I dont wonder you thought it extravagent the lamp is a lovely one it gives as* splendid light I cant thank *you* enough for the Lamp & hamper. One of the boys in our house got his cap* the other day that is to say he plays for the 1st 15 at football so all the house is jubilant. About the neighbour hood I will tell you when I come home, Good only 4 more weeks. I will write you a good long letter soon only I 1st want you (Father) to send me a nice letter which you owe me. no more news at Present. So Good bye dear Mother & Father from your loving Son

Tankred

30   Newfield

Nov. 22nd 92

My Darling Boy

I am so happy that you were delighted with your hamper & that the lamp is really a success. I wondered afterwards how you would carve the ham & open the sardines.

Your dear father has only not written because he has been busy.

A letter of mine to Mr Lynam has been waiting about two months for his (to post together). To-night we have tickets for "King Lear"* so I suppose it won't be written to-day.

Mr Perks was here from Saturday to Monday & seemed to really enjoy it, on Saturday I met him at the Schubert concert at the Palace* & on Sunday afternoon he took the two small boys to tea at Grandmother's. he said they entertained him all the time.

Your father is going to write to Roberts to cheer him up & hope he will come at Xmas but really I doubt if he will be able to do so.

You must consider the holidays what you want to do for the best either for German or with Edwards or music; five weeks though a good holiday is soon gone. Try to spot what the difficulties over your work are which block the way – because they *must* be got over by hook or by crook.

Of course the writing is an impediment. by the bye – fully takes two ls – awfully, beautifully &c. extrav*a*gant (*not* extrav*e*gant) You know I do not mind your mistakes a bit but I think I had better tell you of them in future. *Find a rule* for the *doubling of consonants at the ends* of words in English – there must be one, & *I* only know by sight.
We all send you our dear love particularly your fond mother
Min

27.11.1892: 31 (TTB to LWFB/EFB)

31   Clifton

Sunday Nov. 27th 92

My Dear Father & Mother.

Do tell me about King Lear. *Is father going to be free from business by Christmas?* I am Glad Father's going to write to Roberts, If he does come at Christmas* we will see that he is *properly* looked after, after his illness, *wont we?* Please do tell *me how many fishing lines Roberts sent,* you never told me; I have so many things to tell you which are too long to tell you in a letter, but as there are only 3 more weeks to the holidays I think they can easily wait. Last Friday we had a very nice concert I am sending you the Programme. Dear *Father did you receive that small packet* safely?* Please let me know. Do write a little more frequently.

I dont know any rule for the doubling of consonanants except that full takes a single "l" in compounds & adding the final "y" it doubles. No more news just at present. Thanks for your letter to day.* So Good bye Dear Mother & Father

From your loving Son
Tankred

32   Newfield

Sunday Nov. 27th 92

My Precious Boy,

You often say I might write to you by the way, under difficulties, I mean with everyone talking around & so I will. Dear Grandma has been here which has been a rare treat to me (Lilian & Mabel are out visiting) Our dear boys have had such a happy home day. There is a new Chippendale cupboard made of the niche in the little hall – with some glass doors taken out of an old house pulled down in London (Ward found them) & the boys helped to fetch the musical instruments to pack into them & tried to play the pan pipes, bag pipes, reeds, horns &c

&c – I could see you & Tyra – in my minds eye doing the same thing some seven years ago. Roy afterwards rejoiced in a story from his father & Brian enjoyed odd folks* with me. We found a box of your juvenile tools in the old library which they are very delighted with.

I hope you are answering my last letter to-day.

Thinking you might like to see the account of Gladstones visit to Oxford I saved it for you & enclose.

We went to see "King Lear" on Tuesday & saw Mr & Mrs Gladstone & party in a box. The play is of course most interesting but Irving represents Lear as mad *from the beginning*. His performance & conception is wonderful, but that seems to me a mistake.

The work in the house proceeds slowly, the old library ceiling not being up yet – little odd things & preparations are being made. I am sorry I shall have to change cooks again – it really is a burden.

I hope you are feeling well & fit in all respects my precious. The holidays are very near now & we shall be so glad to see you. With love & hugs always
Your fond Mother
Min

33   [28.11.1892]*

Dear Mother

Please dont Put Tankred on my letters I thought I asked you before, & you have just done it.* Received your Letter. Please answer my Questions. *Did Father receive my little parcel about a week or so ago, for a birthday present.* Thanks for the letter.

You seem not to understand about the lines From Roberts. *Were There.*

4.12.1892: 34 (ENPM to LWFB)

4 Fishing lines white in colour
and did Pattinson wind them on the reels
I made last holidays?
& also were there 4 balls of Twine in all weighing 2lbs?
Please attend to this

in haste from your
loving Son Tankred

34   34 College Road, Clifton College, Clifton, Bristol

Dec. 4. 92

Dear Mr Behrens

I have had a talk with your boy & I think, so far as I can
see, there is nothing the matter beyond what a little time
and patience will rectify. He is quite young for his form for
one thing, and for another he seems rather untrained in
methods of working – for example, he finds great difficulty
in taking notes of what he is taught in form, and he tells
me he has never been used to doing so. His methods of
working too in mathematics do not seem to give Mr Hall
satisfaction. He also finds great difficulty in his French and
German – he seems never to have had any sufficient
grounding in the grammar of the languages – and he finds
the drill he has to go through here very irksome – Thus I
fear several things have combined to make him dissatisfied
with himself and to dishearten him – also – and I hope
you will not think me unkind for saying this – I fear he's
had rather too good opinion of his own attainments, and it
has been a little painful to him finding his own level. He is
really too good a fellow for this to affect him long but I
expect it has had a depressing influence on him. I hope
next term when the strangeness will have worn off and he
will know more what is expected of him, he will get along
all right. *I am quite sure* that he is a boy who will make his
mark before long – if he is treated judiciously and meets
with kindness and encouragement.

I must apologise for not having returned some pamphlets Mrs
Behrens lent me – they *shall* be returned but I have had no

time to look at them as yet. I fear I am a hardened anti-antivivisectionist, and so long as the antivivisectionists continue to eat butcher's meat and do not enter on a crusade against all hunting & shooting & fishing of animals for purposes of mere sport, I cannot quite believe in the genuineness of their outcry against scientific vivisection for the purposes of research and the diminution of human suffering. I believe the Marquis of Worcester who hunts six times a week is a great ally of Miss Cobbe's! With our united kind regards to Mrs Behrens & yourself

Yours very sincerely
E.N.P.Moor

35   [7.12.1892]*

Dear Mother,

Mr Lynam has asked me to meet him in town on the 23rd & go to "King Lear" with him. May I go? & also can you give him a bed for the night, Please let me know these things by return, Please write soon.

Tankred

36   Clifton College, Bristol

Sunday Dec 11th 92

My Dear Father & Mother

Why dont you write? why dont you tell me – for the 3rd time – whether you ever received my little parcel to Father for a Birthday present. We come home next tuesday week. Do write & answer my questions in my last letters. There is no news this week, & besides it is so near the holidays that most things can wait till next tuesday week. Please send 4/6 before next Sunday to tip the 2 boot's* here – every one does it & I have not got the money to pay it with as I have only Kept 17/6 for travelling money. Dont forget it will you. No more news.

So good bye dear mother & father from your loving Son
Tankred.

[See additional letter 36A on p.272]

37   Newfield

Dec. 16th 1892

My Darling Boy,

Pray thank Mrs Moor for her kind note. I am so sorry you should be unwell & that it should just interfere with the exam. I trust you will be well by the 19th & 20th & that the holidays & rest will just set you up. I happen to have a Postal Order for seven & six & as I don't like you to have no margin for emergencies I send it instead of the 4/6 you ask for. I consider that 2/- & 2/6 from each boarder to the two bootboys who are paid by their master is *really* too much – a collection of 1/- from each boarder for each boots would be ample & just – but I merely say it as a criticism & not for you individually to act upon at present.

Your 4 balls of string & the lines weigh together 3¼lbs – I believe I have answered all your questions but if not you will so soon be here that we can leave everything until then. I hear Mr Allen wrote to you. My love to you dear boy – How glad we shall *all* be to see you Your loving mother
Min

38   School House, Crick Road, Oxford

22.xii.92

My dear Mrs Behrens,

It gave me the greatest pleasure to read the kind letters which

you & Mr Behrens wrote to me – I am sure I most
heartily reciprocate your friendliness – I enclose Tankred's
midterm report – it is I assure you better than most boys
(especially scholars) get during first term – The idea is that
scholars are likely to be cocky & think themselves great
swells & so they must go down a peg!   I am looking
forward to meeting Tankred at the Lyceum* at 5 minutes
before the advertised time of performance of King Lear –
We shall easily meet in the entrance Hall – The Doctor* is
to meet us there too – He is spending the night at a
friend's in Town – but I shall have the pleasure of
accompanying Tankred to Forest Hill & seeing you all I
hope.

Believe me
Very sincerely yours
C.C.Lynam

NEW TERM BEGINS

39   Newfield

Jan 21st 93

My Dear Boy,

Enclosed is the note I made at the time with reference to
your account – so that must be what I owe you 8/- must
it not?

I hope you found a pleasant companion for the journey
down & are looking more cheerfully to the term before you!

I have spent to-day in putting everything in order. Your
father came home to lunch. The *Genth* case* is down for
Monday so we *hope* it will come off.

No news since you left. It is all much the same only very
quiet. We must make our arrangements at the beginning of
the next holidays to avoid all unnecessary disaster &
friction, to enable us to enjoy both the holidays & one
another more.

You appreciate *organization* & its advantages & will I know enter into the spirit of what I say. A thousand loves from your fond mother

Min

40   Clifton College

23.I.92*

Dearest Mother,

Do write & tell me whether Father has done the *burning* on Tyra's box* & whether she likes it or not. Take care of my *leather work please* till next holidays. Our next holidays begin on the *11th of April to the 5th* of May. Do tell me all about the case in *detail*. I received your letter, I think that must be right but you know afterwards the *Cardigan* came to less than we thought it would so I think perhaps you would be right in putting 10/- in. Please square up the new acct. Unfortunately two of my *jam pots* in my hamper were smashed to atoms & the reflector of my lamp very badly dinted. So now good bye dearest mother from your loving Son

Tankred.

P.S. *Please send some stamps by return*

Have my glasses* from Hulbe* come yet.

41   34 College Rd, Clifton

29.I.93

My Dearest Mother & Father,

Mother why dont you write & answer my questions. & send those stamps instead of neglecting me for a week. I am afraid since you have not yet sent me any stamps that I shall have to send this letter without one too. Father wrote to me as if he had not seen that letter from me which I sent to you, it seems funny. Please answer my questions in my last letter conscienciously as I cant always write a duplicate of all my letters to see whether you do or not. Is my room finished yet. I have been awfully poorly this week I was in bed all thursday & have not gone into school again yet; I had a bad cold & slight chill. I* awfully done up, you know I have come to the conclusion that the measles made me anemic & that is why since then I never felt really well, I wish I could cure it. do write soon. I will write again soon but there is no more news dear Father & Mother from your loving Son Tankred.

42   Newfield

Monday Jan 30 1893

My Dear Boy

You will be glad to hear that your father came off with flying colours in the *G.** case last Friday. I am very thankful. It remains to be seen if the amount will be forthcoming – You did not say with whom you *share your study* this term? Your expenses inclusive of pocket money come to £5. 2. 3 – *so nearly covered by your Xmas present!* which is very satisfactory! I enclose a few stamps but think when you have none by you – you could *buy one* & not put me to the double tax* on receipt of the letter!

We expect Mr Allen to-night to dinner. On Wednesday we intend going with Grandma to *Romford* to see her houses* there. Write soon dear Boy & tell me how it is this term! Yr fond mother
                                        Min.

43   Clifton College

31.I.93

Dear Mother

I do wish you would write a decent letter. You keep me
waiting a week & then you only write a few words & dont
even answer my questions in my last letter. Do please write
a decent letter *this week* & answer all my questions. Please
send me by return with a letter a blue *"Somerville's 1st french
reader"*,* I think it must be on the bottom shelf of the
bookcase in the nursery anyway somewhere on that book
shelf. what do you mean by my *present nearly covering the
expenses*, you must take it out of £8. 10/- allowance which
is due from Father & put the balance together with 5/-
which I paid as school subscriptions which instead of
sending to you I want put in the bank. What do you mean
by Grandma's houses at Romford. Please tell me Also how
much I shall have now in my bank altogether.
So good bye from your loving Son
Tankred.

44   Newfield

Feb. 2nd 93

My Dear Tankred,

In writing to your mother you do not adopt a kind or
fitting tone, which grieves her both for her own & your
sake.

You have sent me three letters dated Jan. 23rd 29th & 31st
respectively.
In reply to your questions in rotation
The *burning* of Tyra's box is not begun
Of course I will take care of your leather work

I think your father wrote* about the Genth case how it was
won. Well now Genth is trying to appeal & by any ruse to
put off paying.

You know I will do the best I can about paying in that former balance in your account. I will let you know what I do. Your actual acct stands £12. 13. o & I owe the balance of this being about £3. o. o as well as the smaller balance of last term. I *meant* your father's present about covered what you have had to spend so that as a matter of fact this terms £8. 10. o would be nearly intact.

It was most vexing about the jam pots & must have made an awful mess.

You must *never* send letters *unstamped*. You have money & it is quite unpardonable

I am most grieved that you are unwell but it may be only the change of air & a kind of reaction after the holidays, do not think that you are still aenemic from the measles, because *I* think you are much better & stronger now; be careful as to your diet. Get the doctor not to give you port wine as I think it very undesirable. I enclose some iron for you to take a small dose of every day for some time when you are out of the doctors hands. If you are not well I daresay he will *put off* your joining in the *runs** which are trying to you.

I send your *comforter** (add it to your list also the *shirt* you should have had from *Hope* of Cheapside*). I send you *two french books* as the *Somerville* is a *writer* not a reader.

Grandma has two houses at Romford that is all, we have deferred going to review them until next week.

Dear Tyra has also had a bad cold & been in bed like you!

Mr Allen dined here on Monday coming early in the afternoon & entertaining our small boys most kindly both that afternoon & all the next morning with tricks & tales! I think it is exceedingly kind of such a man!

On Tuesday was the Kroekers dance we did not intend to go but they pressed us so much that I went by myself as your dear father would not. Grandma has been here for a day or two, – & I am very busy as usual, – I expect a new cook on

Monday & I do not know scarcely how to prepare for her seeing that Roberts is so blind & leaves everything so imperfect. To-night I intend attending Mrs Booles lecture at Mr Allens & taking tea with her first.

Although you complain that your questions are unanswered you do not think of yourself replying – you have not yet told me what *study* you have nor *with whom you share it*??

I suppose your place in the school is still exactly the same??

I suppose being unwell you have not yet been able to see whether your lessons with Mr Hall are easier to you??

I send you my love & blessing & pray that God may guide you in all things every moment of your life as I know he will. Never omit to pray to him earnestly yourself – pray *earnestly* because "Prayers without thoughts never to Heaven go".*

Write me a nice letter at the next opportunity – Your loving mother
Min.

45   [4.2.1893]*

My Dear Boy,

I did not tell you how your room was getting on. The furniture is in, the curtains up – new washing set, sponge basket &c & yesterday your father & Pattinson spent a long afternoon in lining the two side walls with prints, those which were in the hall beside. Chas XII, Columbus, & the brazen serpent* which is over the bed (I am sorry that one is behind you) I have advertized the stone columns for sale or exchange hoping to get rid of them. Dont forget to use vaseline or hippacea* until the soreness you complained of is quite gone. *tell me how you are!* Was it the swimming bath which gave you the chill – you ought to wear your thick coat *when you come out of the bath.* Love from us all especially yr. loving mother
Min

46   Clifton College

6.II.93

My Dearest mother,

I should like to know what my not befitting tone was, besides you must remember that you had not written to me for more than a week, I do wish you would write regularly once a week so that I might receive it always on Sunday morning. Do please hurry Father up about doing the box, Has he finished preparations for the Bloiler case* yet? when is the case to be heard? Father told me he had won the case but told me no details, so I wish you would tell me all about it in your next letter. You see now you have the balance of about 3£ to pay in, also if you can the balance of 10/- & also 8/- which I paid out of my pocket money for school subscriptions & which I want you to pay into my bank. It was annoying about the jam, also I told you at the time that unless the potted meat was properly covered with butter it would go mouldy which most of it has done which is such a waste. As to sending letters unstamped if you dont send any stamps as you often have not I have sometimes had to ask you for weeks running for stamps before getting them so I resorted to sending them unstamped as a last resort to rouse you from your state of deafness to my entreaties. I still think I must be ænœmic still because I feel it. Thanks very much for the Iron & the book* which are alright, would you please send me my (Green) Public School revised Latin Grammar, by Kennedy by return. Thanks for the Shirt which has been received.

Have* enquired of Mr Allen about my scales yet? Have you received. I share a study with a fellow called Irvine an awful ass I cant bear him, I could not get a study with the fellow I wanted to. My place in the School is still the same. I was bottom of my form this week I cant get up I dont know what to do, however I am going to try jolly hard this week, I do want to get up if I cant I shall have to give it up in despair. I find they* are somewhat easier in the Euclid only (of course) though I dont notice it much they must have done me a good deal of good. Have doors been put to my pigeon holes & a lock? – What does the room look like? does it look nice? is

there a carpet in it & what sort is it? do the prints look nice? I am feeling better though I never seem to feel quite well. No the baths did not give me the cold as I had not been there before. Have you removed all my belongings to my room yet? My books & Chemical bottles, dynamo etc. do put them all there as soon as possible & dont put Tyra's box in a hot room so as not to give it a chance of warping before I can put on the two locks next holidays.
So good bye dearest Mother from your loving Son

Tankred

Do write soon please, it is really the only real pleasure I have in the week is to receive my home letters.

47   Newfield

Feb. 11th 93

My Dear Boy

I hope this will reach you to-morrow morning to wish you a happy Sunday & a good week to follow. No despair! Nil desperandum!* You know it is better to be bottom of the middle fifth* than top of the lower & if you are rather young for the class, you must remember it & not be discouraged but work away with a will, & you are sure to succeed. Let me know how you got on this week. The things from the office are not here yet but otherwise I think your room is finished. The pictures look very nice. *West's Brazen Serpent* is above your head. I would have preferred that you should have had it to look at when you were in bed. over the wash stand are Columbus & *lick licking licked!* (you know the 3 dogs from the office – & over the chest of drawers the "waiting for the attack" which was in the yellow room. On the floor are the two rugs which were there before & I believe the old bear skin is coming. Those old fashioned wooden (kitchen) chairs & the fender fr. my bedroom. The clock case between the fireplace & cupboard has no clock in it yet – over doors & cupboard are shelves & one has ornaments upon it. All the bottles are on the mantelpiece until the bookcase comes & then I will put in all the books for you.

Mr Allen asked very kindly after you on Thursday. I stayed at Mrs Stapleys to high tea after a lecture by *Tom Mann* about the poor of London. He is a working engineer by trade & of course is really one of the poor himself. He says the great trouble of the working classes is the intermittent character of their employment in many trades, that those who begin their married life with the best intentions, when work falls off & they have got through their reserve fund (if they had any) & pawned everything pawnable to buy food *then* the wife is driven to associate with all the other women to devize means of getting food somehow they meet at the public house to discuss their plans & make their arrangements & so habits of drink & bad company are formed which are the ruin of so many.

They have now since 8 years an association* for supplying all the things they want to buy good & at a fair price rather like the stores* & they also try to produce these things under fair conditions for those who produce them – fair wages & hours & healthy workshops &c – by this means gradually withdrawing the work from sweaters &c &c – & this they are extending gradually & constantly as the association grows & their means increase.

In the evening there was a conference to form a "Social reform Union" for 3 London parishes the object of which is to enforce whatever good laws exist for sanitary & other arrangements for the good of the poor – which are too often at present a dead letter, because not known or understood by those concerned & the management of such departments understaffed.

I think it is such a duty for those who understand these things & have some leisure to look after their poorer brethren & help to make the conditions of their existence such that they may be healthy both in body & mind. Think of a dwelling for 16 families with *one* W.C. in it!

13.2.1893: 48 (TTB to EFB/LWFB)

Tom Mann is a very earnest advocate of the movement to give women equal opportunities with men in everything particularly in making their wants known to parliament by direct representation.

Mrs Etheridge is going to post this & I am afraid she will be off – God bless you my precious – I have answered all your questions. We all send our love. Brian & Lumpi who are as still as mice waiting for me to read to them with hugs Your loving mother

Min

48   34 College Rd, Clifton, Bristol

13/2/93

My Dearest Mother & Father

Thanks for the letter I received on Sunday morning. I have been getting on better this week I think but I shant know till next Saturday or Monday. I dont at all appreciate the 3 old rugs, for without a nice carpet the place wont be fit to sit in, However nice the rest may be I shall never like to go & sit in it. Please put the bottles safely in the book case & all my other things too till I come home, however dont move any of the things which are on the top in my cupboard already. It must have been very nice to hear Tom Mann. You say you have answered all my questions. I think you make a mistake. You dont say whether you have got the new tray for the broken one Houghton* 89 High Holborn sent? You dont tell me whether you have received my scales from Mr Allen? You dont say whether my three looking glasses from Hulbe have come yet? Do you think you will be able to let me have your store cupboard for my dark room you could retain the top *two shelves at least* for your own use to put away things you would not want to use much. I am going to send you 5/- more to put in my bank. So that will be 10/- altogether I have practicaly sent you this term to put in extra to my bank.

Do write & advise about Roberts' subscription what am I to do since the Canon does not write? *Please send some more stamps.*

Please see to sending me a block of the paper. & *Please what does it cost??*

thanks for the Latin grammar. You Dont tell me anything about the forthcoming *Bloiler case?*
No more news so good Bye Dear Mother & Father
From your loving
Son Tankred.

49   Newfield

Feb. 17th

My Darling Boy,

Yr. 5/- recd. this morning. I am most anxious to tell you what I know will give you great pleasure & happiness. Last Sunday when Grandma was leaving your father said to her "I dont wish to see you coming alone dear Ma but ask Lil & Mabs to come & let bygones be bygones"!* & on Wednesday they came with Grandma to dinner & kissed & made up & I think your dear father was very glad to see their dear bonnie faces. & now I can be happy again, which I could never be as long as our darling Lilian & Mabel were shut out from the family unity. I know you will rejoice too my precious. I will answer your letter to-day or tomorrow. A thousand loves from your fond mother
Min

[See additional letter 49A on pp.272-3]

50   Feb. 19th

My Darling Boy

This comes wishing you a happy Sunday. I can't see your last

Lilian Burdett (née Tunstall)

Mabel Tunstall

letter to answer questions. I have just written to Mr Allen about the scales. Houghtons I have not yet been to. I think it all nonsense what you say about a carpet in yr room. & from a soldier too! A sanded floor & a camp bed is all you should think of asking for! really you make me laf! Your father gave Roy & Brian a tool basket* to-day – & they are *so* happy to have a *real* carpenter's tool basket! they think they are the *happiest* boys that ever were – happier even than Tankred for he had no tool basket! I feel so happy now about Lilian & Mabel & I know they are glad, Grandma is glad, *you* are glad & so is Tyra so we must all thank God on this Blesséd Sunday – I hope to have a letter from you on Monday we all love you no end. Yr fond mother.

Min

51   34 College Rd, Clifton, Bristol

19/2/93

Dear Mother,

I hope you are quite well. I am so glad. It has been made up. did not I tell you it only needed time; Had you spoken about it to father Since I came back to school. Do try & find my letter & then go carefully through it & answer all my questions as they are all very important & also those questions on the back of the envelope.* No I really shall not be able to enjoy my room without a carpet, it wont be comfortable to sit in ever, it will always seem so very cold & being a cold room will always be too cold to sit in for preference, I know from experience before when there were only those rugs it was always a nasty cold room, what would father's study be like without a carpet? why it would be a wretched place; However I hope I shall get a carpet in it soon, when you have been persuaded.

My Bank acct should stand now when all has been paid in as follows –

£.	s.	d.	
12	13	0	after present of 5£ had been paid in
		10	Saved this term from pocket money & remitted to you to be paid in
		8	balance of last terms allowance
	3	7 9	balance of this terms allowance
Total	16	18 9	

Then if you dont object to giving me a present of 1/3 it would then be 17£ I have, if you cant give it me I shall save up the amount & send it to you so that anyhow I shall have 17£ in the bank.

No more news now till I hear from you which I hope will not be later than Wednesday.
So good bye Dear Mother from
your loving Son
Tankred

Dont forget to send me stamps at once, a most Important Item.

52   Newfield

Feb. 21st 93

My Precious Boy,

In reply to your letter of the 13th. Questions! I have not yet exchanged *rubber tray*. Have written about scales. Your three *looking glasses* have arrived. If you like to write two notes to Mrs Lynam & Miss Bagallay I will send them on for you.

I think I shall be unable to let you have my store cupboard for a dark room & your father says that his damp recorder registers absolutely no damp – in the dark cupboard you began arranging & that if you do not want it he is going to *use it himself!!*

You can't do anything at present about Roberts' subscription. No news of the Bleuler case.

You left the first 6 numbers of "Progress"* in your writing case

Your watch can so very easily have the hand replaced by any local jeweller or clock maker – that it is not worth sending.

Paper & stamps enclosed. I will send you a copy of your account when it is settled. The glasses have to be deducted.

With regard to the carpet – if there is one of course you are welcome to it – but what you say about the cold & discomfort is truly absurd. The room is free from all draught now – has a stained & varnished floor & looks most comfortable with the three rugs – but if it had absolutely no covering & the clean stained floor I personally should think it quite comfortable enough for *me* & I should like you to entertain more simple views with regard to personal comfort than you do. It is very well to have taste & to cultivate it even & even to gratify it if you have the means but it is most important to realize the difference between necessaries & *luxuries* & to be *entirely independent* of the *latter*. I consider as it is, that your room from its position is the quietest the most retired & therefore the very nicest room in the whole house without any exception.

Have you taken the iron? and are you better? Have you taken any runs?

Mr Sharman was here the other day & sent his love to you! How are you getting on with German? climbing out of that class?* Pray notice Tyra's handwriting. It is really capital. I do wish yours were bolder. I am glad you wrote to her. No more news at present my dear Boy, but eternal love & blessings from
Your loving Mother
Min

53   Feb. 24th 93

My Dear Boy,

Mr Allen gave me yesterday from his man quite a new & complete box of scales & also the little book of his poems for you which he intended bringing to you at Christmas. You will see in the last page some mottoes written expressly for you. I think it so very kind of him. The last one is very true & means if you do not see it at a glance much the same as the injunction which I think was Christs – to be "in the world but not of the world"* –

Mr Allen gave a most interesting lecture yesterday on the works of Thomas *Lake Harris* – in which he said incidentally that the test of our Christianity was if it made us better than we were, if it removed the barbarism of the heart – if the churches bring practical help* to man – if it brings to a nation all things necessary to a nation – to a trade all things necessary for that trade – special remedies for special needs, if it rescues the womanhood in each craft &c &c – if not it has lost its vitality. God Bless my dear school boy & give him strength for all *his* needs! for whether we are small or great we need it just the same. We must not do good or refrain from evil, because we are forced or repressed but because we see the beauty of goodness – because we see it is better & we prefer it. For instance we require no law no pledge to make us sober – we prefer it. *You* know the pleasures & advantages of knowledge, or some of them, & so you sacrifice willingly your immediate inclination to gain it & so on. We all send our love particularly yr. fond mother.
Min

Write a little note of thanks to Mr Allen.

54   [26.2.1893]*

My Dearest mother & father

I hope you are quite well.

26.2.1893: 54 (TTB to EFB/LWFB)

Do please see after Houghton as soon as you possibly can or else they wont give you a new one. they will say that you broke it & that it was not broken in the post. Do tell Tyra her looking glass has come, I will write two notes for Mrs Lynam & Miss B. soon & then you can send them on; Please tell me what sort of a note I should write to them? I wish I could have your store cupboard as I feel shure there must be damp there; what is fathers damp recorder like? Where did he stand it in the dark room? Let him stand it on the floor & then see. What does he intend to use it for? Why cant I do anything for Roberts, How can I let it Slide for such a long time. How do you mean no news about the Bleuler case? When is it to be heard? Has father finished working the case? How is he likely to come off in it? What is Gent doing? has he paid yet? Can I write to father yet is he free from the *city* yet? Have the things come from the office yet? I dont like my watch to be mended by the watchmaker here he is too bad I shall send it home soon to be generaly cleaned as well by Tyler.* One of the boys wants a block of paper like mine with lines on it do let me have it as soon as you can & tell me what price to charge him for it. When the glasses have been deducted from my account it ought to be 16£ exactly left in the bank. As to the room I want it, you must understand, as a place to sit comfortably, not a place where you always feel shivering and cold to the marrow however I shall see what I actually think when I come home.

I am a bit better but not the thing yet. Yes I always run now. Do let me know Sharman's adress please?

I have got out of the Jew's* set in German & am climbing out of the next already. What are the new scales like are they as good as my old ones? have they got glass pans? how many weights are there with them & are there any very small ones. How much is there to pay for them? What is Mr Allens adress? What are we going to do next holidays? as Mr Lynam has asked me to go with him & I have not accepted yet as I dont know what the family are going to do.
No more news in haste your loving son.
Tankred.

55   1.III.93

Dear Mother,

What shall I do, I have worn the elbow of my coat through & have nothing to wear while it goes to be mended, so I have had to fall to that low pitch of borrowing somebody else's coat; Now it wont look very well to wear on Sunday when it is mended. Do you think Dore could satisfactorily make me a new coat & waistcoat without measuring me & send it or not. let me know 1st* what you think. In your last letter you did not answer all my questions of my last letter but one. Do get it & answer them please? What is a good thing for chillblanes? It is horrid, I have never had any before & now of all things they have *covered* my *fingers* (not even toes). I dont want any hamper this term but I want you to send me 5/- instead, as the other fellow* brought back no grub & cant get his grub box yet so I have nothing to eat, so I want 5/- to subsist on till then. Only mind it is *instead of my hamper.* & is cheaper than sending me a hamper, so please send it as soon as possible as I am on the verge of Starvation. So good bye dearest Mother
from your loving Son
Tankred

56   Newfield

Thursday March 2nd

My Dear Boy

Enclosed five shillings for grub – I think it would be a mistake to have a coat made by Dore or anyone without measurement as you must have grown since the last was made – If you can't hold out until the Holidays I see no alternative but to have one made at Clifton – dont be rash however. –

Try rubbing your chilblains with hippacea before going to bed, on the hands you cannot put anything which stains..
In haste yr fond mother
Min

Miss Bagguley: c1890

The Lost Behrens.

A ship that's lost its bearings
Will oft strike on a rock.
A man that's lost his bearings
Is said to run amock.

A bike without its bearings
Can surely never run
A firm without its Behrens
An earth without a sun.

So give us back our Behrens lost
Turn night once more to day
Un Behrens'd been we barely bear
Our Behrens being away.

Anon poem upon Leu leaving his office

57   Newfield

Mar. 11th 93

My Darling Boy

No letter of yours came to rejoice our hearts this week, but we had your mid-term report* – you will be glad to hear that against mathematics was "much improved except in style" I think that under the circumstances very encouraging. Although I could not answer your *many* questions at once I promptly sent you 5/- to *save you from starvation!* Mr Allen dined here last night & left after lunch to-day. I showed him the dark room you began arranging & he said tho' small it would do – with the sink fitted up & by having a good curtain to the outer door the inner door might be open for air – It seems not to be damp, of course the sink would have to be put in.

We expect to hear about the Bleuler case in two or three weeks – The second edition* of the Genth case is to be some time after Easter.

You may assuredly write to your father, who is always at home now & very busy trying to get everything finished & in order. The things from the office have not yet come. Your bank acct is as you say.

Percy V. Sharman Esq., 223 Gipsy Hill Road Norwood London S.E. I have not yet had a bill of the scales. the Rev Geo. Allen, 33 Bloomsbury Sq.

As the holidays are not at Easter & your father thinks he may be required in town for the Genth case after Easter, & you & Tyra do not need more change than being at home in the short holidays we do not intend going to Cornwall these holidays. I think it will be very pleasant for you if you can join Mr Lynam for a few days on the sea – *do not you.*

I have noted what you say about Roberts subscrip & *paper block* & scales & will reply later. so do not say I omit to answer your questions. Not knowing exactly how you feel to-

wards Mrs Lynam & Miss Baggalay I cannot write so *truly* consequently not so well as you. Be kind & gracious but natural & sincere – Do not write what I have written – or say you gave trouble if you never did – but if you did it is graceful & proper to allude to it. let me see your draft.
I want you to have this tomorrow so adieu my precious

Love from us all
Yr fond Mother Min

58   34 College Rd, Clifton, Bristol

[12.3.1893]*

My Dear mother & Father

I hope you are quite well. Today The Rifle corps had a church parade, & we all went to St Mary Redcliffe's church* to church in Bristol. It is a lovely church I dont know whether you have ever seen it it is perpendicular architecture & on the top inside has those sort of carvings* like we have on the ceiling in the Morning room & all the church is painted I dont mean all over but in the right places, for instance these carvings on the roof are painted gold. the ground plan would be something like this.

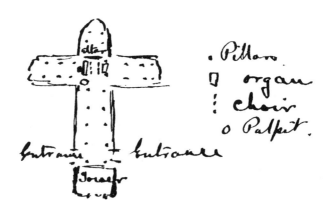

18.3.1893: 59 (RTB to TTB)

It has a very good choir & a very nice sounding organ. I
wish you would write more often especially Father, Thanks
so much for the chillblane cure & the 5/- which were so
prompt in arrival. Do tell me what the Damp recorder is
like? also where you stood it in the dark room? And if I
dont use it what do you intend using it for? Did you ask
Mr Allen about the damp? Do tell me what the new scales
are like? & whether they have returned the old weights &
how many weights there are.

Dont forget to tell me what I can still do about Roberts &
the stingy Canon? Pray do try & have the things from
Roberts before I come home as I must put my room
straight next holidays. I cant put it off holidays after
holidays its no good. Also dear mother if you dont see
about Houghtons tray soon they wont give you another, It
is now past half-term & there are only 4 weeks more term
& you have not seen about it yet as far as I know, Also
have you collected all my things & books etc from around
the house & put them in my room so that they are all
there then ready for me when I come home, collected. No
more news now so god* bye Dear Father & Mother
from your loving Son
Tankred

Please send me some stamps soon as mine are all gone.

[See additional letter 58A on p.273]

59   Newfield-House, Forest-Hill

d. 18. März 93

Lieber Tankred!

Heut will ich dir eine Geschichte erzählen: Ein Bauer lag unter
einen Eichenbaum und sagte: "Wenn ich der liebe Gott wäre,
ich hätte auf diesen schönen Baum große Kürbisse wachsen
lassen." Da fiel ein Eichel auf seine Nase, daß sie blutete. "O
weh!" rief er "Wäre das ein Kürbis gewesen, hätte er mein

ganzes Gesicht zermalmt." Er merkte, daß der liebe Gott doch klüger ist und war zufrieden.

Es grüßt dich dein
dich liebender Bruder Roy.

[18th March 93// Dear Tankred,// Today I want to tell you a story. A farmer lay beneath an oak tree and said: "If I were the good God I would have made big pumpkins grow on this beautiful tree." Just then an acorn fell on his nose and made it bleed. "O my goodness!" he cried, "If this had been a pumpkin it would have smashed in my whole face." He noted that the good God is wiser after all and was contented.// Greetings from your// loving brother Roy]

60   Newfield

20.III.93

My dear Boy,

I have asked Siegle* to forward the African Map direct to you at Clifton, I presume however he has to order it from Germany first. Let me know when it reaches you. –

In your february report* there is a remark: "I hope he is getting on better this term. I think he fails from want of patience & temper, and is apt to blame others rather than himself when he does not succeed" which deserves reflection from your side. the remark is well meant & being true as I experienced myself, should bestir you to follow my often given advice viz learn to master yourself first & in investigating matters commence by seeing whether the fault does not lie with yourself. Instead of impatience, plod away & conquer instead of being angered. You doubtless realize by now that I wish nothing but the best for you & my desire is to make a happy being out of you. I therefore hope you will follow your pater. I am glad to see you soon & hope we two have a jolly time together

Ever your loving
Leu

62

Big School, Clifton, set out for a lecture

Long Penpole

24.3.1893: 61 (CCL to EFB)

61   School House, Crick Road, Oxford

24.iii.93

Dear Mrs Behrens,

Thank you for your letter & enclosure – I will bear it in mind if the opportunity for recommendation occurs –

I had the pleasure of seeing Tankred yesterday morning – I was up in Bristol on business and he breakfasted with me – I thought him very much grown & informed generally – I start on my cruise next Friday & hope to wire to him my whereabouts on the 11th or 12th April & then he can come & join us or not as he feels inclined –
With kind regards to you & Mr Behrens & hoping the latter is going to take a good holiday
Believe me
Very sincerely yours
C.C.Lynam

62   34 College Rd, Clifton, Bristol

[26.3.1893]*

My dear mother & father

Thanks for the 5/- so promptly sent which I believe I thanked you for before,* but you dont answer any of my questions or write the letter you promised to do. The map of Africa has already arrived thanks very much for it. You never write now or answer my questions or send the stamps which are most necessary to letter writing, You seem all to be sleeping or departed. Last week in the Short penpole* (a race of 8 miles across country) one boy* in our house came in within 5 minutes of the 1st boy* the race is for boys under 16. In the long penpole we had the 4th & 6th boys* in & the race is about 13 miles for all over 16. So we did very well, however I wish you would write & send some stamps & answer all the questions you have left unanswered. – Here are a *few* of the most important

Have my things come from the office yet if not do see that they come before I come home on the 11th of April?

Have you collected all my belongings to my room yet, do please see that this is also done before I come back?

Have you seen about Houghtons tray, do please do so before I return? Also about the block & stamps I asked for

Is Tyra's desk burnt yet & is it taken out of the heat & damp where it cant warp?

You know it is sickening these things hang on from time to time and it does not seem to dawn on you before I have asked the same thing half a dozen times separately that I mean what I say. I dont wish to seem disrespectful, since I always feel sorry for it afterwards; But really this is of such frequent occurence that this is how it appears to me and you know one cant say things in letters like one can in plain words without being rude so I wish you would try & attend to it once & for all. I always try to be regular in writing, & answer your questions; and with the exception of the last week or two I think I have written to you, almost without one failing, evry week ever since I was at school away from home which is nearly 7 years now.
So good bye dear mother & father from your loving son
Tankred.

63   Newfield House

30.III.93

My dear Tankred,

It is an entirely mistaken idea of yours, that plain words must

necessarily be rude. No Sir, our language is so pliable that the most unmistakable meaning should be expressed in refined form. *Make yourself therefore the master of language.* As a rule I attend to letters addressed to me even to my children,* as far as they concern important points, *vide**
Map of Africa, because I expect the same, besides being time saving. A few years more & we shall understand one another probably better. As soon as I am free from business entangles, I shall write regularly to you as promised & then at length.
Enclosed stamps

Your loving pater
Leu

64   34 College Rd, Clifton

1.4.93

My Dear mother,

I am sending you Mr Lynam's letter,* I should like to go very much but, I have so many things I want to do before we go away in the summer that unless I work in real earnest all these holidays I shant be able to get them finished, so I dont see how I can accept? do you? I am going to write out a list of the things I want to do these holidays before I come home so you will be able to see what I want to get done & what will actualy be done in the end.

Could you come & meet me at paddington* on the 10th & then we could go & do any shopping we wanted to do & perhaps go & see Grandma? I suppose about 11 o'clock to 12. would be the most convenient time to meet me.

Half past ten would be too early would it not? Besides if you write & tell me you will come & meet me at about 11 or 12 to meet a train which I believe leaves Bristol at about 9. I shall not have to get up as early to go by the special train,* which I hate. Look & see what fast train there is that leaves Bristol at about 9. & see what time it gets to paddington & then simply write & say you are going to be at the station at that time to meet me & then I can show it to Moor & he will have to let me come by the later train. Please let me know an answer by Friday. I am so glad the holidays are so near I am thoroughly sick of the term & the place. No more news now so good bye Dear Mother from your loving Son

Tankred

65   Newfield

Ap. 3rd 93

My Darling Boy!

I am very glad your house has done so well in the races!

With regard to your questions, you know I am happy to answer them & when I write I very often, almost always, take up your last letter & answer every one – as you will see by referring to my letters. I think dear boy – you are over anxious about all these things; you know that I am glad if I am able to fulfil your reasonable wishes & that whether I say it or not I am surely endeavouring to do so – Very needful things I do at once & you should feel that the others are safe in my hands & not worry either yourself or me –

The day after you left I collected *everything of yours* I could find & placed it in your room.

The *Houghton tray* I have now changed without any difficulty on their part

I cannot hurry the *things* from the *office* as they do not depend on me – & it is doubtful if they will be here before the 11th. We can see about a *block* in the holidays. I have none myself.

I enclose a few stamps

Tyra's desk is not yet burnt in – & is safely where you left it.

3.4.1893: 65 (EFB to TTB)

I had not sent the *old* weights so we have the old & the new – I believe the new scales are like the old.

I am glad you wrote to Mr Allen, I believe it pleased him. He came here last Monday & brought his friend Mr Bush of *Schropshire* who is so clever in many ways electricity chemistry &c &c – I am sure you would enjoy talking to him.

On Saturday I took Brian & Roy to Mr Allens to be photographed – They sat several times once without their jackets & shoes & stockings with sponge & towels – to be called "the order of the bath".

Roy got into sad disgrace today by poking a stick through the old window at the back of the hall – It was very naughty of him & he was severely punished. He felt it very much & I hope he will give up doing such things, for remonstrances have hitherto made no impression. Your father put his damp recorder on one of the shelves of your dark room. It is a round thing with little perforations letting in the air which tells upon a fine hair spring in the centre & moves a needle resting on the spring. I have not seen it myself. *Tell me what you would like to do about accepting Mr Lynams invitation?*

We will talk over what to do for Roberts when you are here, he has not been fishing for six months!

Our garden is getting into delightful order now thanks to your fathers recent supervision & work – & it is just now one mass of blossom, the pink wall trees are just going off & the plums & pears & cherries make a white vista from my study window (with the boys union jack waving in their midst) truly beautiful to behold. I suppose the apples will be in bloom to greet you when you come but I regret you cannot see it now with us in its silver glory.

Grandma Lilian & Mabel are spending a fortnight in Wales at *Llandudno*. What a lovely Easter it has been, I never remember such an one. How unlike the snow of last year at Bessy's Cove* – I need not say how we are looking forward to seeing you & dear Tyra. Tyra thinks she will perhaps be in the drilling eight – she & Maud Mellor are the only girls who can

67

swing quite round the *horse!** I shall be so glad for you to put our boys up to boxing again, for it has rather dropped of late. They are always so busy with really useful work – *hepeling** as you used to do.

Make a list of those things which you think need doing – so that we can at once on your return set about them – Tyra is only due on the 14th & perhaps the Lambleys* will come too these holidays – as their parents are not home yet & Miss Badams has gone to Canada.
Our fond love to you my darling boy. God bless & keep you – Your loving mother

Min

NEW TERM BEGINS

[See additional letter 65A on p.273]

66   May 14th 93

My Dear Boy,

I thought I should have heard from you on Monday or Tuesday last & wonder how it was you did not write last Sunday. I shall try to write to you every Sunday. Last Sunday afternoon I took Brian & Roy to hear Mr Allens telling of Cinderella in St Nicholas Cole Abbey* – They enjoyed it very much. He said the three (2 bad & 1 good) so often mentioned by fairy tales represented the body & spirit – The two first being of no use without or compared to the one & goodness of the third.

Mr Hughes lunched with us to-day & in the afternoon Mr & Mrs Lambley came & stayed to dinner, they think of staying in the country while Mr Lambley is here, that is, until the end of July & taking a governess to teach Ethel & Violet who I suppose find it very quiet & rather miss their school life.*

On Wednesday your father went to see Pattinson who is going on much about the same – not yet having undergone the operation.

Brown's house hall: early C20

Mrs Boole: portrait by LWFB 1898

21.5.1893: 67 (EFB to TTB)

Mr Hall wrote that he would not recommend your taking *chemistry* & German & so you would continue German & take it for the entrance exam at Woolwich in accordance with our wishes (if only one subject could be taken by you).

Do write to me at length, how you find it this term & how you get on. There will be much quite new to you on the Military Side.

I saw Mrs Boole on Thursday at the C.T.* I am so sorry we missed her lecture I am sure it would have greatly interested us. Mr Allens lecture was on William Blake's poetry – "The marriage of Heaven & Hell" &c – There is to be a Blake society for the study of his poetry – One of the points which struck me was. That he says, goodness to be goodness must be spontaneous – for the love of it, because we like it best – (not from *duty*). *I* think that; that voluntary, of choice goodness is the highest ideal, but I feel that until we know the true beauty & preferableness of goodness so as to do it for its own sake we must be compelled – or compell ourselves to work in what we know to be the right way, as a mould for the higher nature to grow in. It is not as though evil thoughts & evil deeds had no results both for ourselves & others & did not make the bed we have to lie in. I should like to talk to you more about this some other time but think about it in meanwhile. Of course if we realized the full beauty of goodness we could never be otherwise than wise & good – If we knew how horrible a burn is we would not put our fingers in the fire or near it but I think we should save children who know no better from burning themselves. God bless you my dear boy. It is too late to write more to-night.

Your fond & loving mother
Min

67   Newfield

May 21st 93*

My Dear Boy,

I am looking forward hopefully to a letter from you to-morrow morning, which I have been picturing you writing today. I have been reading to the boys the illustrated books out of the rat trap* much to their delight. Luke said he was going to see Pattinson to-day so I hope he will – as we were prevented going last week & when we heard, he had not yet undergone his operation. We hope to go to see him next Wednesday. I wrote to Mr Lynam to tell him how very uncertain it is what we shall do in the holidays & asking him to make his arrangements for the holidays independently of you.

Mrs Bell has asked us & Lil & Mabs to go to them on the 31st & see the Derby.* It is very kind of them & I daresay it will be a pleasant party.

May 22nd Monday. So disappointed at not hearing from you to-day. This Whit Monday has really been the most perfect day. the weather simply heavenly. I was enjoying it so much when I discovered to my great regret that our cherished birds nest had been robbed of its fledglings by Luke & Spall (with your fathers consent I must admit). I cannot say how disappointed & sorry & mortified I am. It was so perfectly idyllic to have birds building overhead & to think they could not be safe with us, is horrible.

The end of the garden with the new fowl house looks so very nice – neat & picturesque burnt red clay ballast on the ground the little shed in the further corner well gravelled – & the raised kennel as a roosting place. nice hurdles round about 5ft high. I am only afraid they will fly over into the garden.

Our raven is getting many white feathers. I enclose a cutting of an important incident in Sir Hope Grants life which you will like to see.

I expect Caro & Emma on a visit soon. I expect a new cook on Friday – Sarah is going on the 16th of June – I am going to try Agnes in her place & have a new housemaid.

May 23rd Dearest Boy I thought I should have heard from you to-day!

Mr & Mrs Walter Wright were here, the former very ill indeed – Beri-Beri again which is a kind of dropsy.

Your father wishes me to go now for a nocturnal tramp
with him so I shall post these stray words to you my dear
Boy with fondest love

fr yr mother
Min

68   Newfield

May 27th 93

My Dear Boy,

I cannot imagine how I should be three weeks without a
line from my first born son! If you were ill in body I
should hear from Mrs Moor.

Pray write to me to-morrow dearest boy – You have so
much to tell me which I am longing to hear –

Pattinson on Wednesday had caught a cold which swelled
his face up & retarded his operation. He had been so well
that he begged to be allowed to get up & help the others
& then caught this unlucky cold. It seems likely to be a
very long case. In the summer holidays Mr Lynam is going
cruising to *Skye* & says cannot we go there too? The Genth
case may come on in a fortnight for which the counsels
fees are due again.

What did you do at school at Whitsuntide. Now mind I
expect to hear on *Monday* Love & kisses from your fond &
neglected

Mother Min

69   Newfield

June 11th 93

My Dear Boy.

I hope that as you do not write it is a sign that you feel happy

& arc well in every respect. You know *I* feel *much happier if I have news from you.* This is such another glorious Sunday & I am writing in the garden. Mr Hämert & Mr Perks are here. The latter we brought home with us last night from Chislehurst where your father & I Fräulein & the boys spent the whole day – The morning on the Common & after lunch at Mr Perks a good walk through fields & woods & strawberry plantations. Such a change & rest it was. We intended going in the evening to a soirée to meet *Stepniak* & the friends of Russian Freedom – but we got home too late & met Mr Blackwell on the way coming to see us – so we had a quiet evening & ramble. I was very glad for I felt very tired.

Tyra was 2nd in her class of 12 – & 8.6 out of 10. & the last two weeks 4th & 6th so you see she is improving – she says she is also reading now that she only goes* with Marjorie & another big girl.

Brian & Roy did enjoy the day with us at Chislehurst so much – particularly riding on the box to & from Bickley station. In the next holidays Fräulein Wehrmeister is going to serve at the German Hospital* & I am going to have a French lady – in hopes that the boys will learn French again & you will pick it up. I expect Caro and Emma at the end of the month on a visit. On Tuesday the Wharrys & a party to lunch – Altogether I am exceedingly busy – I wish I had a letter from you my dearest boy – every day I expect it & every day I am disappointed – *June 11th* to-day – *so 36 days!* I really cannot think how it is you do not write at all? I wonder so much how you get on upon the military side, & what exams you will have to go in for in July & *when* it is to be? *Tell me that!* Dr Webb spent a night here lately – he is getting on famously – a niece & nephew of Mr Bells were here lately, Captain & Mrs Hall and they asked us to go & spend the day with them at Aldershot when you next had a field day there – so you must let me know when it is – I suppose *next* term? They are very nice people – Now my dear boy God bless & keep you – write to us. I send you my eternal love. always yr fond Mother – Min

Fräulein in hospital uniform: 1893

Marjorie Monkhouse: Roedean c1893

R J Morich: 1892

70   34 College Rd, Clifton

11/6/93. Sunday

My Dear mother & father

This is the first real opportunity I have had of writing to you with the exception of the 1st week when there was no news, so I will begin & answer your questions in order. I am enclosing a *routine** which will show you what work I do & where; & please notice I have nearly 3hrs work evry evening & only 2hrs set apart to do it in so it fills my time up all the more as I have to use odd times to do work in. I am in the Middle 5th Military that is in 5.y.* Then you must know that that has not much to do with it as we only do divinity in form & evrything else in separate sets. I am in the

> 2d set for Maths. under Mr Stevens.
> 3d set for German under Mr Morich the head German master (& German) in the school.
> 3d set for Latin still under Mr Spence
> 4th set for French under Mrs Morich.

I never seem to get on in Maths now in fact I do* know as much Maths as I did when I 1st came here, I am still doing, Combinations, Permutations, & Binomial Theorem, which I have been doing evry term since I have been here, In Euclid I am doing the 3d & 4th books. In Trigonometry I am beginning Logarithms & the solution of Δs with Logs as if they were new I have so utterly forggoten them although I knew them fairly last year, it is simply disgusting going back so in Maths; I do no Arithmetic, & that is about all maths I do. In Latin I do Livy & Horace & Vergil for construing; you might show this & The routine to Mr Edwards or tell him about it as he wanted to know. I have no chance of a scol.* I am sure; however that will not stop me trying my best you may be sure. Please see if you can find *6* of my Progress at home because I have the other six here & I want to have all twelve bound as they are getting valuable & are no more to be had, by the bye the next subscription wants paying in now for it.? Do tell me all about poor Pattinson.

Do you know yet what we are going to do in the Summer Holidays? If father & Mr Edwards are coming to see me they had better come on the 23d & 24th of June as we have two whole holidays* & I could be with them all the time. How are the two law suits* getting on? I appreciated your paper cuttings which you sent me. What do you mean by Pattinson's case being a very long one, How long will it probably last. Our cricket (School) Eleven* has been very successful this year Having* a good beating to every team we have played except one, Our House eleven has unfortunately been beaten badly except the last match. no more news just now I will write again as soon as I can so good bye dear father & mother from your loving Son

Tankred

71   34 College Rd, Clifton, Bristol

18/6/93. Sunday

My dear Mother

How is it I have not heard from you since I wrote; or have you not yet received the letter which I posted the 1st thing on Monday morning Last. Thanks for my shoes which are a little large but is better than being a little to Small. How is Pattinson? You must not think it extravagant of me but I want 4/- to get two books second hand. then you generally send me 7/6 for fruit in the summer term & Then I either want a hamper or 13/-, If you think it cheaper to send me a hamper please let me know & I will tell you what I want in it, but I should think it would be cheaper to send me the money. however in any case do send me the 11/6 as soon as possible & as I am utterly penniless. & Please send that 5/- to the Draconian* for me if you have not already done it.

The Exam* is on the 27th 28th & 29th of this month & worse luck on the 29th I might otherwise have gone to Marlborough* for a field day which is rather rot. You know I sent a book to the librarian at Oxford* which cost 3/6, did I pay for it out of my allowance or did I pay it out of that 10/- I gave you, be-

cause if I paid it out of my allowance you still have 8/-
of mine after you have sent the 5/- to the Draconian.
Please send me the money soon as I cant possibly do
without it. Last thursday, we played* Trinity college Oxford
& gave them a beating, we have only been beaten once this
year. Do tell me about the two Law suits, & whether any
thing is being settled for the summer holidays. We have
been having frightfuly hot weather* here yesterday it was
69° in the shade at 7 in the morning or 85°, in the shade
at midday. I rather wish I had brought my camera with me
but I dare say I shall do so another Summer term. It is
much hotter here than it ever was at Oxford. Are father &
Mr Edwards thinking of coming down to see me on the
23d & 24th or not I believe I told you we had two whole
holidays then so if he was coming it would be best for him
to come then. Are we going to have much fruit this year in
the garden or is it too dry? There is really so very little
news it is hard to know what to say. we do so much the
same things from day to day that if I were to tell you all
we do it would be the same in every letter. We dont seem
to do any arithmetic on the Military side & now I am
going in for the Exam I dont know what I shall do not
having done any for so long. Did Mr Lynam write &
answer you after you had written to him or not? There is
really absolutely nothing more to tell you about So good
bye dear mother & father from your loving Son Tankred.

Please send me a packet of envelopes.

72   June 20th 93

My Darling Boy

We were so thankful to hear from you at *last!* & very glad
to have your list of duties. Your time is certainly well filled
up. I showed it to Mr Edwards as you asked me to do & he
thinks you are going on quite in the right direction. He says
you are in the next form to the top on the military side &
that they are sure not to ignore arithmetic eventually.

This is not an answer to your first letter but to the last of Sunday June 18th. With regard to money as you know I have 13/- of yours 5/- of which is for the Draconian as you said. I did not pay anything out of it. I will enclose 11/6 in this letter – the 4/- for books & 7/6 to do as you like with.

What makes you fix on 13/- (or a hamper) for.

The 2nd trial of the Genth case is due to take place to-morrow Wednesday & before that your father seems disinclined to decide anything at all – either about coming to see you or the Summer holidays – so I cant tell you about the 23rd or 24th but I will try to write to you to-morrow night. I am going if nothing prevents to-morrow to take the boys & go with Mrs Wharry & her little girl Olive to see a flower competition at the botanical gardens Regents Park – rather a trial in the heat. the Duchess of Teck & Princess May are to give the prizes & I daresay our boys will like to remember it. Our thermometer in the sun at 8 a.m yesterday registered 90°! *Much* cooler to-day & no sun but no rain. Would *you* like to come home for two whole days holiday & might & could you? (if your father does not wish to go to Clifton) – Or do you enjoy more some excursions with the other boys? Send me word by return. I have not asked your father if he would be agreeable to it – but I shall be glad to know in time so as to consider it with him.

Pattinson has not been operated yet & is very well considering but weak. he comes to see us occassionally. I fear the drought for the first crops – hundreds fall off – & everything is parched in spite of the watering & a new fire engine which father boys & gardener* all enjoy pumping.

I shall think of you specially on the examination days & try to help you. We expect Caro & Emma early next week. We have taken a few very nice photos amidst a good many poor ones. I recommend you not to be anxious about your exam. You have not been especially coached for it but you cannot have done a years work without progressing & if you have lost in some things you must have gained in others. – I know you will do your level best – if possible try to be rested before hand – & not cramming to the last & God Bless you my precious boy. I feel He will bless you, & I need not be anxious about you &

yet there are often things I would like to say to you. I should like you to realize (without bitter experience) the great fact that in as much as you swerve from the right in anything whatever – to that extent you are making the bed you needs must lie in. You are moulding *your own* character, which will be yours to suffer or improve to the end. If you can see that goodness is the loveliest & the best* & can choose it for its own sake & for the love of it, you will yourself be the best in every way in untold measure.

Your fond & loving Mother
Min

73   Clifton, Bristol

22/6/93

My Dear Mother

thanks so much for the money & letter. I am afraid I could not come home for the two days though I should like to very much. I dont know why I said 13/- instead of a hamper but I should like the equivalent of a hamper *without the carriage* If I do not have one so do let me know which you would prefer, & then if you prefer to send me a hamper, I would tell you what I want, & if not let me know what the equivalent is. What do you mean by Pattinson comes to see you, surely he is not allowed out of the Hospital & when is he likely to undergo operation.

Then you seem to have still 8/- of mine after you have paid the Draconian (do, do it soon)

In haste your Loving Son
Tankred

74   26.VI.93

My dear Boy,

I was very glad to have seen you.* We timed matters; punctually half past nine I entered the hall.

re dark room, just one word

I propose putting the sink in the *broken* corner. do you want the water tap at a *certain* height? how high? I remember you had a rose, but I cannot find it.

God bless you old fellow, go on *fearless* with the exam & send me only a word re dark room & exam when the latter affords you time

Always your loving
pater Leu

The Canon cannot let us have the Haven before 15 Sept which is too late, unless we can make other arrangements, shall book us for Ireland

75 34 College Rd, Clifton, Bristol

29/6/93

My Dearest father.

You see I am writing the moment the exam is over as you ask. I am sending you my time table & the papers; & the Cliftonian. I am also sending The last *six* Progresses & I want you to have them bound nicely with the *other six* which mother will know where to find & when they are bound put them in my book case. We come back on the 1st of August. It was rot not being able to go to Marlboro' today because of the Exam. I hope Mr Edwards enjoyed his short stay here, I was *so* glad to see you, it was nice your coming.

I would like the *Sink* now as I draw it. Then where I have put lines so ≡ let there be a board – sloping onto the Sink – so that we can stand wet dishes etc. on it & the water will run into the Sink. Then let the rose stand in the centre at the back of the Sink as in drawing, & let its base (the

rose's!) stand level with the top of the Sink you will easily see how it works, & you will find it either in the cupboard or the book case in my room. let the Sink be of a convenient height to work at & also the (shelves) or rather the table should be where shelves are marked, let the table be firm & substantial and let it be covered with *one* piece of oilcloth for preference. And above all see that *not even one infinitesimal speck of light can get in anywhere.* There ought preferably to be shelves as well as the table they might be up the wall in a position similar to those two rotten ones I once put up. but let it all be firm & solid. For the window, I would either use a piece of ruby glass or cover it with special ruby paper. about the artificial light that will be necessary we can talk next holidays, but of course electric light* would be better, as it gives no heat, in such a small place.

How do you propose to find out a place to stay at in Galway. I hope there will be some fishing & shooting, I should thing* there would be, besides sea fishing there might be trout & Salmon fishing in such a place as Galway & I hope it will be as wild as possible. So now good bye Dearest father from your loving Son Tankred.

P.S. Dont have the rose connected with the main because it wont do to be restricted to certain hours* in the day only when we can have water, so let it be connected with some pipes indoors, & placed so that in winter time it wont be frozen wont you?

76   1.VII.93

My dearest Boy,

I thank you for your letter of the 29th which gave me great pleasure. As *you* will be at home for a few days, before we go for our holidays, I think it best to confine myself to the exclusion of the light in the room, the water arrangements can be done in a forenoon & as I think the Sink will have to be placed differently in order to economize room, we may discuss that on the spot.

3.7.1893: 77 (TTB's telegram)

Enclosed I return cheque for your signature, as it is otherwise no good; pray write, *there & that which I pencilled,* & return.

Mrs Beaver has written informing me of a house with garden 3 reception rooms 4 bedrooms, nursery &c &c horse & trap, donkey cart & donkey & *two* boats at Banaghcr (2 miles from her house Eyrecourt castle) on the Shannon, Galway. Possibly we can make arrangements & enjoy ourselves if the weather remains propitious. With much love Your pater

Leu

[addition in EFB's hand] I was so glad to hear all about you from your Father & Mr Edwards who both enjoyed their visit immensely. I should have enjoyed coming too but on the whole I thought it would be as well not this time –

77   Alma Vale, Bristol

JY. 3. 93

Telegram to: Behrens Newfield Hall Forest Hill Kent

Have got a 50£ scholarship* Behrens

78   Newfield House

July 3rd 93

My own darling Boy,

How glad I am! How heartily I do congratulate you! & how Thankful I feel to the Almighty. You see dearest you have felt unnecessarily discouraged & it is as Mr Lynam said – if you had only gone in for the exams at the end of each term (when you were unfortunately laid up) you would have known better where you were, & *not* felt discouraged. Really my blesséd, I feel so very happy about it & you. I expect you feel quite relieved now the exam is over & so well over. From your marked papers* we thought you must have done well.

Eyrecourt Castle

Tyra, Brian, Roy, Tankred: Ireland 1893

Caro Lauterbach

Emma Neuendorff

6.7.1893: 79 (TTB to LWFB)

Caro & Emma arrived on Thursday night – we went to meet them at the station* & since then I have been very busy. I have taken Emma about with me to the Band of Union* & to-day to a play "12th Night" acted in Mrs Baller's beautiful garden on Clapham Common. I am corresponding with Mrs Beaver about a place on the Shannon river in Galway two miles from Eyrecourt Castle for the holidays* – it is inland but there are nice excursions, boating & fishing – a pony & donkey trap garden cow &c – but I fear one cannot take it for only one month with option of extension & I do not like to be responsible for two months rent if we do not care about it or if it pours with rain.

You must make a list of what you know you want – so that we can at once get it on your return & lose no time so that if we wish we can stay away all the holidays.

God Bless you my Precious Boy as indeed he does & will. You cannot know how your mother loves you but I am sure it must nevertheless do you good & make you happy. Your fond mother

Min

79   34 College Rd, Clifton

[6.7.1893]*

My dearest Father

Have you received the cheque again yet? Have you received the progresses & perused the list of old Cliftonian officers* yet? I want to know. Mr Edwards very kindly I thought wrote & congratulated me & So did Mr Lynam so I shall write to them presently. You will find out I hope from Mrs Beaver all about the fishing & shooting there.

Dont forget we come Home on Aug 1st next tuesday, three weeks. Hurrah!!! We have a whole holiday to day Thursday for the Royal Wedding.* I think I told Mother that I have had a very bad attack of diahorrea but it is all right now & I shall go into School again on Friday. So now good bye from your loving Son Tankred.

80   9.VII.93

My Dearest Boy,

Your telegram gave me great pleasure since it must be an encouragement to you. Go on steadily, do firm & solid work, remain modest but self-reliant, thus you will lay the foundation to a thorough *Man*. Regard the scholarship principally from the point of honour. You have now the first foothold on the ladder to success, rise on it, rendering good service to your Country & giving joy to yours* by upholding our name as one of *free & strong* citizens. Such are your father's wishes & he has no doubt to lead you to happiness if you follow his advice. The Staff* & diplomatic Service must be ever before your eyes. In Russian & Persian* you will have to *score*, as engineer you must be first, not forgetting an allround education.

Progress is in the binder's hands. The Cliftonian & cheque came to hand. Truly that is a bold array of officers, I trust you will swell the list as one of which Clifton will ever be proud.

You know your two aunts are staying with us, that is the reason why I did not write before.

We settled so far to go to Banagher on the 2nd or 3rd of August. I want very much first to have *you* all 3 days *with me here*, in order to settle our tackle & dark room. I suppose it is scarcely possible for you to be here before the 1st of August evening? Besides I have such a lot of things to settle re house &c &c before we leave, so that I have my hands full up. I mean to enjoy myself thoroughly *this time* with my first born. Bathing we do in the Shannon. I presume the river must be at Banagher pretty strong since the lady's husband & son or daughter of which former we rent the house were drowned in the river. Mr Edwards just called & I hope you* will manage to be a fortnight with us. I propose that we three make our excursions to the sea with the knapsack. Prepare to get every thing regarding yourself ready in the least possible time. – A hearty shake of hands from

Your loving pater

Leu

81   36 Sussex Sq, Brighton

[9.7.1893]*

Darling Tankred

Thank you somuch for your letter I am so glad about your scholarship. We brake up on July 27th. How nice it will be if we can go to Ireland. I cannot swim atall well yet I can only swim a very little.

We are soon going to begin our exams.
from your loving sis
Tyra

82   Newfield

11.VII.93

My dear old Boy,

Enclosed letter from Tyra* & one from Roberts I suppose.

I know what lively interest you take in the small Boys. Brian is busily engaged in developing architectural propensities, he is building dykes &c &c now. the small man* is as funny a one as ever, when he learnt of your scholarship he said "I am going to Lynams, I shall take my scholarship too". If God preserves his splendid physic I daresay he will easily – But one thing worth recording & why I really write is – You know his fight with the naughtyness. Well I had to call him to order the other day & asking him why he did not behave better he replied with one of his inimitable looks: "father you see I turn over so many new leaves, but – unfortunately there are always ink spots on it".

It is a great joy to me to have you & the two small boys, I long to see you all thoro' men, every one of you has his points & I want to see the 3 brothers *well knit* together, they must stand like a rock, the protectors of their country & family.

It is just 11 p m I am saying good night to you & take this to the post.

fondest greetings from your mother & pater

Your Leu

83   34 College Rd, Clifton

[12.7.1893]*

My Dear Father

Thanks so much for your letters. Why does mother not write??

We shall indeed want a day or two to settle everything. I shall be home I hope by 3.30.P.M. not later on Aug 1st to arrive earlier is I am afraid impossible.

I am so glad you will be able really to enjoy yourself this time. I hope Mr Edwards will be able to come I am writing down in a book everything I shall want to get done personally & everything re. tackle *etc.* of ours which I can think of so as to be able to know exactly what we have to get done when I arrive home. Have you found out from Mrs Beaver about the *Salmon* fishing whether we *can get any or not* & about *the Shooting.*

It was a letter from Roberts, I enclose it & want to know from you how to act? Let us act promptly. So now good bye dear Father for the present in haste

your loving Son Tankred

Please send me ½ a dozen stamps as I have run out.

84   14.VII.93

Dearest Boy

I see you write in haste. I think one ought never to be in haste?.

84

16.7.1893: 85 (TTB to LWFB)

Enclosure* answers most of the questions. I hope Edwards & Perks will be with us at Banagher. You cannot ask them before for a contribution for Roberts. Write to Roberts "Sorry too that we cannot be down this year. We are off to Ireland. I asked you abt the Archdeacon, because I wrote to him at the time that I had the promise from father & friends to make up for your illness & loss by a subscription & I wanted him to head the list. You did not reply to my enquiry, nor did the Archdeacon answer. I had to go back to College & so I hope now when I get home to look up my friends & father for collection, to which I shall add my mite, which results I mean to send you from Ireland."

Mother has been occupied with a party which she is going to have to morrow (a garden party) to which she expects *60* people. I daresay that accounts for her not writing so frequently. Whilst they are having their garden party, I shall go to town* & perhaps look around for our equipment. Keep well, God bless

Your loving pater

Leu

[addition in EFB's hand] My Dear Boy, Though I did not write to you at once I sent your questions to Mrs Beaver as you will see. I have much to do besides the *party* as father calls it – correspondence about Banagher – to study what we shall want – *many* things & how to get them ready & there in the next fortnight. besides having Caro & Emma here – Fräulein's away. I love & think of you & I hope we shall have happy Holidays together. all bent on the happiness of the others self foregetting!

85   34 College Road, Clifton, Bristol

[16.7.1893]*

My dear Father

I have been reading about Salmon & Trout fishing since I knew

85

nothing about it, so as to know all about getting our tackle ready & how to manage it when we get there. So now I know a good deal about it at least enough to know what tackle to have I believe the fishing is very good there, at least I have heard so from other people, I am looking forward to the holidays are not you. What I really wanted to know more than anything else was, & do let us find out before we go there as it is very important.

(1) Is it necessary to obtain permission from anybody to fish in the Shannon & adjoining streams or can any body fish in the Shannon & other Streams? because you know on some rivers the right of fishing belongs to someone & it is necessary to get permission from them before you have a right to fish at all in them.

(2) Shall we be able to get permission to get the shooting in some parts or how does that stand!

You see this is very important since if we dont know these two things we might be taking fishing tackle & guns & then find we could not get leave to fish or to shoot so do find out.
I will write again soon so good bye from your loving Son Tankred.

86 Newfield House, Forest Hill, Kent

17.VII.93

My Dear Boy,

Mrs Beaver will be here to morrow, when I shall put your two questions before her. So you will hear later. You know I want to go with you Perks & Edwards with the knapsack thro' the country to study home rule* for myself, I wish to sleep in the huts with them to learn all about it.

I notice that none of your letters are dated, pray do *that for the future* & don't forget it, dates fix periods & to ascertain periods we require dates.

It is customary to thank the person for the smallest service. When I refer to this, it is not from the point of fault-finding, it is the mere desire to see you in every way if possible perfect. I remind you that: "Noblesse oblige"   Of course you received my stamps?
Your loving pater
Leu

87   Newfield House, Forest Hill, Kent

18.VII.93

My dear Boy,

Mrs Beaver was just here & waited in vain for your mother, who went to town at 10 this morning on "wild women's"* Committee Meeting & had not returned by 5.30 p m when she left. I am afraid your mother must be developing a disease. Last night she went to gathering to see the women return from Chigago.* She went at 7 p m & returned at midnight. –

However I asked Mrs Beaver re your questions –

Q.1 No permission to fish in the Shannon is necessary

Q.2 Her Brother* will be able to get us some permission for shooting.
Your loving pater
Leu

88   Newfield House, Forest Hill, Kent

[23.7.1893]*

My dear Tankred

I wish you many happy returns of your birthday Miss Etheridge and I are so glad that you have doubled your scholarship* I hope when I go to school I shall get one too. When we go to Ireland Father is going to take us all into one of the Irish cabins, and we are going to sleep a night there, if the people will take us in. Wont it be fun when we go to Ireland?

From your loving brother
Brian

89 Newfield House, Forest Hill, Kent

[23.7.1893]*

My dear Tankred

I wish you many happy returns of the day. I shall be so glad to see you in the holidays. We look at the workmen* and crawl through a little air hole.

I have got a flute and I shall play it in Ireland when I ride on the donkey. When I go to the Cabin I shall tie my knapsack round my wrist. We shall have two boats on the river Father says.

From your loving brother
Roy

90 Newfield

July 23rd 93

My Precious Firstborn.

On the eve of the fifteenth anniversary of your birthday I write to wish you many happy returns of the day – & Gods blessing upon your every thought, word & deed now & ever. What changes since your real birthday in 1878 & how well I remember it & the dear little creature who weighed 8¾ pounds

88

& brought such a load of love with him & filled my heart with joy! The love has not changed only grown with his growth, but the little creature has, & realized in the time *many* of his mothers fond wishes & prayers. The prayers & wishes will always follow him, that he may love truth above all things & seek & find it & that he may make the utmost of talents committed to him. I cannot express a millionth part of what I feel my darling boy but perhaps you can feel it in your heart. The tailor Hoare sent me a guinea as the 10% royalty* on the sale of *two* dresses!!! but such as it is I propose dividing it between you four dear children that you may each for once in your lives have a birthday present of your mothers own earning. You can buy some little thing with it which you like to have & keep. I do not *send* the postal order as we expect you so very soon –

I wished so much to have written to you yesterday before post time but we were in town all day. We went to Libertys* in the morning for a "corot" (a Japanese bronze fire receptical) for the fireplace in the Japanese room & elsewhere in the afternoon.

We are all looking forward to the holiday excursion & being together & we must see how happy we can make one another. God bless you my own precious, a fond hug from yr loving mother

Min

91   Newfield

July 25th

My Blesséd Boy,

When your father read my last letter to you he reminded me that my statement with regard to my earnings was not strictly true because it can only be called "earnings" if it is a profit on the outlay & this is not so as I have never been able to repay him what he laid out on the patent. I mention this that I may not create any false impression, but I intend dividing the guinea among you all the same.

I am busy preparing for Banagher & I hope we shall get off on the evening of the 3rd of August. I have to order stores pack linen & many things which we shall not find there. We all send you our dearest love & hugs particularly your fond mother

Min

92   27.VII.93

My dear Boy,

I thought of you on your birthday, in fact I had written you a long letter which, for reasons to be explained perhaps at another occasion, I did not post. I kept this letter however & although you did not hear from me on "your day" you must have felt your fathers good wishes surrounding you, in fact as they always do, special days or otherwise. To make a thorough well adapted man of you, is one of my tasks. It won't now be long before I see you, then we can talk more about it.

doubtless you heard of the Notice from the War Office re Prelim Exam.

I am writing to Mr Hall by the same post & would like you to confer *with him* on the subject *before* you leave. The *last* exam on the *old* system is on the 13th of Sept. You know what the old system consists of, the new we don't. You are 1 year younger in 93* than Sept 94 & that may count for something. I have my own opinion on the subject, which I withhold until I have yours & Mr Hall's.

With much love
your pater Leu

93   Newfield House, Forest Hill, Kent

29.VII.93

My dear Boy,

Mr Hall's idea agrees with mine *not* to go for the Sept 93 exam. My personal view was not to avail oneself of an exam simply to push through, but rather to make for a stiffer one in a straight way.

Enclosed cuttings re Army exam in the House.

drop me a line at once when* you arrive at Paddington. If you could come before 3.30 & say *be at London Bridge** by 2 p.m or *1 p m,* I would meet you at *London Bridge* & we might do half a days shopping in town to save time – If you cannot come before *latest 2 p m** to London Bridge it is no use. I will then wait for you at home.

I am glad to see you so soon again.
Your loving pater
Leu

94   34 College Rd, Clifton

[30.7.1893]*

My dear Father,

I shall arrive at Paddington at 2.45. & so shall probably be able to get to London Bridge by 3.30. In your last two letters you adressed me
T. Behrens
instead of Tunstall Behrens
So dont forget another time.

I am looking forward to the Holidays. So good bye dear Father from your loving Son Tankred

NEW TERM BEGINS

95   Oct. 7th 93

My Precious Boy,

It grieves me not to hear from you & not yet myself to have written to you. After leaving you at Paddington I went on to Grandmothers to dine & sleep, returning next day home. I spent some days in putting things in order & then as Tina & her husband* did not come & Grandma & Mabel were at Folkestone & I felt a little rest would do me good – I went down to them for a few days (fine). It was very delightful. The place is charming on the top of the cliff with a nice walk & grass in front of the houses & at the foot of the cliff a beautiful road winding through trees & gardens to Sandgate. The breezes were fresh and bracing, such a contrast to Ireland. I walked as much as possible, in the morning to Sandgate in the afternoon in the opposite direction to a place called the warren, a kind of landslip on the cliff road to Dover – It seemed so curious to meet so many people every where after the solitude in Galway. On the Sunday a friend of Nita Cox, Rex Earle a very nice young man who is one of the masters at a school in Dover came to see us – he had been for several years at the Elliott Bank school in Forest Hill & knew Chet Owsley of course very well. He also knew something of the Dulwich preparatory school. I think it would not be a bad plan to send Brian & Roy first to Elliott Bank as it is a good school & nearer home – if we decide upon a day school for them.*

I have thought very much about our talks as to your immediate future my dear Boy & you know that I have nothing nearer at heart than your welfare and I feel sure that under the circumstances what you suggested* would *not* be for the best. I am quite sure dear, so pray be satisfied.

I am very much distracted to do for the best for Tyra. I have been to the High School at Sydenham & it seems that by coming home & going there she would miss nearly all the gymnastics & *all* the sports.* Truly a pity!

15.10.1893: 96 (TTB to EFB)

To-day I went with your father to Lobbs,* to lunch at the winter garden* & then to the Arts & Crafts exhibition.* The glass industry is the most remarkable quite exquisite & equal in its way to the Venetian. Most of the other things if at all nice were so fabulously dear as to put them quite out of competition with the german work for instance. Burne Jones & Walter Crane & Morris were the main designers & there were some beautiful tapestries & other things of their designing.

I expect Aunt Eliza on the 11th for a few days. Mrs Walker stayed here from Monday to Wednesday & Mrs Wharry spent Thursday afternoon here, so you see I have been very much taken up – but I hope soon to write again & soon to *hear from you.* It is the least I expect that you should write to me *every Sunday.*

I hope you are fortunate for your study companion this term – & pray tell me if anything else is better than before.

Washing well would be a great thing *every night,* but I daresay you are lazy about it as you are at home only at school you go to bed earlier & it should therefore be easier to you. If I do not hear from you on Monday – write by return – You will be glad to hear Pattinson is at work again.

With Love & hugs. Always your fond
Mother Min

96   34 College Rd, Clifton

Sunday 15. Oct. 93

My Dear Mother.

Has Mrs Etheridge been able to take the boys every day* after all? When is Mrs Beaver coming to see you? I was pretty fortunate in my study companions* but they might have been better. As to washing I am not at all lazy about it, the fact is one cant wash at night. Nothing is at all better than it was before, I cant stand this place for anything, let alone that I always feel so bilious & sick here, there is hardly a day that I do not feel sick & bilious, I cant make it out, it is most unbearable, however I am going in for all the exercise I cant* possibly get even if I cut some work for it, & see what that will do for my complaint, for as it is now I can never do any real work. I brought back no writing paper, stamps or envelopes, so do please send me some stamps, & envelopes & also 8 pairs of stockings as you sent me back without any, you need not tell the tailor* to send my great coat till I write for it as I dont want it at present, you know I had my umbrella recovered last holidays well you know I have had it bagged for good & all & cant find it anywhere. I suppose it is no longer possible to have the fruit, so as I did not write promptly dont go to any trouble to send it me as if it cant be easily sent now I shan't expect it. I gave my pearl handled pocket knife to you I think, if not to father, if he cant find it it may be in that round tin box in my right hand top draw of my chest of draws, do see that the very best blades are put into them, & see that the handles are not cracked when they come back. I am glad Pattinson is back at work, has he to go to the hospital any more? I am going to write regularly every week now perhaps twice a week, so I do wish you would write to me twice a week do do it. I am now in the bottom division of the top set in the school on the military side in Maths, in the Second set of Latin & the 3rd in French & German so I got out of 3 of my sets.* So good bye dear Mother from your loving Son

Tankred

P.S. do send some ordinary notepaper as well too. Has the money been sent to Roberts, do send me a letter to copy to send to him with the money if it has not already been sent.

97   Newfield

Oct. 16th. 93

My Dear Boy

You don't know how sorry I am not to hear from you. I am

William Roberts

Gilbert

just sending ten pounds to Roberts for you with enclosed
words. If you wish to write to him yourself, pray do so. I
am asking for Gilberts right name & address to send him
5/- – tell me what pipes you wish sent at the same time –
also if *you* would like a hamper *of fruit. I asked you before.**
Love & hugs from your loving though neglected
Mother Min

98   Newfield House, Forest Hill

Oct 21st /93

Dearest Tankred

Please send me the nib* you said you would give me for
my maps. Mother has told me you have hurt yourself at
foot ball. I am so sorry I hope you will soon be better.
Roy is a great nuiense* & he does not allow us to write
our letters quietly. Is'nt he lucky he has half a holiday on
Wednesday & a whole holiday on saturday.*

I have just got "barbielous schmerzen"* & I cannot eat any
fruit. Fraulein has been trying to sleap & Roy has been
making such a noise so she got up so angry that she
rushed out & shovled him into the garden.
from your loving brother
Brian

99   [21.10.1893]*

My dearest Tankred

I am sorry that I have not written to you before but I
have been so lazy & I hope I will not be so lazy any
more. I hope you always do your lessons nicely & I hope
you are quite well & happy. You are a very nice Tankred
but you must write to me.
From your loving Roy

100 Newfield

Oct. 22nd 93

My Dear Boy,

I enclose Roberts' letter. I hope you liked what I said to him & that it expressed your wishes. I have not yet sent 5/- to *Gilbert* because I thought perhaps you wished me to send pipes at the same time so *let me know?* I have not yet drawn your 5£ from the P. Office because the 26th Oct is the date for making up the book & I thought I would have that done & interest reckoned & then draw – I could not possibly *yet* attend to gloves & mufflers.

I shall soon send you some pears – not *quite* ripe that they may travel well & be eaten by degrees. You must tell me if you feel better now for taking more exercise – it is the very thing I would recommend you & not to bolt your food or eat sweets. The food you have is doubtless all right, plain & good. Notice if anything in particular disagrees with you & avoid it.

I sent *no* stockings because you said you needed *none* this term.

I suppose you received yr. gt coat safely.

Pattinson has to call still at the Hospital & his face is still bound up & not quite strong yet but in health he is a renewed creature & in food partakes of everything like other people. I am very glad you have moved up in three sets which shows I think that you do do *some* real work so do not feel discouraged although I like you to feel as I do, & I know you do feel, you would like to do your *very best.*

Aunt Eliza spent about a week with us which was very pleasant & I wished you & Tyra had been there to see her. She wished it very much herself & would like to *come to* see you at Mr Moors as she is staying at 7 *Great George St. Park St. Bristol.* You will realize dear Boy that it is exceedingly kind of your *great Aunt* to wish to take the trouble of coming *on purpose*

Brown's house: front view

Aunt Eliza Andrieu: 1899

to see you & I know you will without needing to be reminded give her a very cordial reception & thank her for coming. *Write at once* to her & tell her what day & at what hour is best for her to call if she is so kind & then look out for her so that she does not wait, & make it all pleasant. You remember you liked her very much & she is very kind.

It has occurred to me that you might like to arrange to meet her in the first class waiting room of the Bristol Railway Station – if that is *nearer to her address* & *you* had *permission* to go *there*. I merely suggest this in case *you* felt freer at an outside place. If you ask her to do this, you must say *either* "as it is nearer to her" or "if she does not mind" & when you see her you must feel quite at home with her like with Grandma – To Mr Moor you must say that your great Aunt Madame Andrieu is staying at Bristol & wishes to see you – you may give him the enclosed note* *if you please*.

I will try to send fruit paper & stockings tomorrow by goods train.

I hope you may yet find your umbrella. I think your monogram was burnt in. Mrs Beaver & Boss are here since last Tuesday – he is very good & much less trouble here than at Eyrecourt. Of course he is more at home with us & has no one to trouble him. our boys are very nice to him particularly Brian. They spend all their spare minutes in the workshop making a cart – on old wheels – which they do remarkably well – but two being of bad wood collapsed & each one is better than the last. Miss Etheridge continues to come every day.

I hope you are *writing to me* this pouring wet Sunday *or to your father* who I know would like to hear from you & might perhaps go down to see you – (he mentioned it lately which makes me say so more particularly). My blesséd Boy I only wish I could take your difficulties upon me & bear them for you – but we each have our tasks to bear & our experience to gain & must all of us the youngest & least as the eldest & the greatest bear ourselves manfully & bravely & indomitably in the path before us, choose what we believe to be the path of duty – It is never easy, but it is easier than to shirk ones duty & as you say at football, the misfortunes happen to those who are

23.10.1893: 101 (TTB to EFB)

not playing up – I know you will *play up** my dear boy without my enjoining it upon you.

Your father calls to me to tell you that the stuffed birds from Dublin are not here yet – God bless you my precious. *Write at once to Aunt Eliza* Andrieu. No end of love from your fond mother

Min

101   34 College Rd, Clifton

Monday Oct. 23. 93

Dear Mother,

Thanks so much for your letter. I will write a long letter later as I have no time now. How long is Aunt Eliza Staying in Bristol? I wish you had told me of it before as now I cant possibly I think see her before Thursday.

In your letters* there is no part I can show Moor which does not contain something I dont want him to see. As in his note.* It is useless & I dont want to tell him anything about my health & in the other I dont want him to have the chance of making me see her here. So do write the exact facsimile of the following letter by return to show him. I shall receive it if you write by return by tuesday Evening or Wednesday morning which is heaps of time since Wednesday afternoon is the *very* 1st chance I have of seeing her

[TTB's model letter] Dear Tankred, Your Aunt Eliza is coming to Bristol expressly to see you. She is staying at 7 Great George St. Park St. Bristol. You will realize dear boy that it is exceedingly kind of your great Aunt to take the trouble of coming on purpose to see you & I know you will give her a cordial reception & thank her for coming. Write to her & tell her what day & what hour is best for you to go to see her in Bristol. Your Fond Mother. [model letter ends]

24.10.1893: 102 (EFB to TTB)

Please write all other things on another sheet so as I shant have to show them to Moor. Why cant I go & see her where she is staying? do let me know by return with the letter whether I may write & tell her that I shall come to see her at her house. I am writing now to tell her *I cant possibly** her till Wednesday afternoon, so I will write & arrange it finally when I have received your letter.

102 Oct 24th 93

My Dear Boy,

Aunt Eliza is staying at Mrs Barnett's a cousin of ours – as I do not visit them, I think it undesirable for *you* to call there – there is no other reason but the family division* & nothing personal in it. So write & arrange to meet Aunt Eliza *either* at the waiting room (1st class) of the Bristol railway station or any other place that you think is better. I suggested that Aunt Eliza should take you for a drive – but you are really better able to make an arrangement than I – knowing the place –

A picture gallery, museum, or place of amusement in Bristol would be very suitable.

If any of the Barnetts came *there* with Aunt Eliza there is no objection to your treating them with the same courtesy with which you would treat anyone else, on the contrary! – Only it is not the thing for me to *send you* to a house at which I do not myself visit.

I believe you will arrange it very nicely – When you go, have some money in your pocket in case there is anything to pay.

I did not send your parcel *yesterday.*
Fond love from your Mother
Min

[EFB's copy of TTB's model letter] Newfield Oct. 24th 93 Dear Tankred, Your Aunt Eliza is coming to see you; she is staying at 7 Gt. George St. Park St. Bristol. You will realize dear boy that it is most kind of your great aunt to take the trouble to come expressly to see you & I know you will give her a cordial reception & thank her for coming. Write & tell her what day & at what hour you can best go to see her in Bristol. Your fond Mother [copy letter ends]

103 Oct. 30. 93

My Dear Boy,

I should have liked to have heard from you this morning – you said you would write to me you know. Aunt Eliza told me she spent an hour with you in the Zoological Gardens* – Do tell me all about it. Boss is getting very fond of Brian – but has not yet taken Roy into his affection – How did you like your hamper. We think the Bishops thumb pears delicious – & they should be just right if you eat the ripest first. We find there is a space left square & deep under the lawn near the mulberry tree lined with stone flags, it was a cistern – & it is being arranged to keep food in. also another well nr the little oaks.
Yr fond mother Min.

stamps enclosed 1/-

104   34 College Rd, Clifton, Bristol

Oct. 32.* 93

My Dear Mother.

How did the bog oak turn out, did the other bog oak arrive, or has it not come yet, I mean the other 2 trees. Has Father sent the feathers to manning yet, & the wood for the rods. Is

Mr Eyre coming next Christmas for certain. Last week I was top of my Form though how I did it I dont know, I got 200 marks more than I did the week before; But unless I put on 30 more marks still this week, I dont suppose I shall be top again. You know when one is top one has to take a list of the order & marks of the form for the week to the bogie, so when I went to him, he said I was "very promising" which was a great deal for the bogie to say. I play now for the 1st house fifteen last house match forward & this one half, so on the whole I am not getting on so badly as far as that goes. But I still feel bilious which is very wretched. Though I think my biliousness is gradualy getting less by having more exercise. If I was father by the way I would not send the wood to Manning to have the rods made as I have a catalogue of Enrights Castleconnell* who is the crack maker of that kind of rods & his are much cheaper & would probably be vastly better. so we might put that & the feathers off till next holidays. I received the progresses all right. Have you received yours they wrote to me for your adress as they had lost it. Do keep the stick for me at home thanks very much for it. I received the hamper all right, the pears are very good when they are riper. thanks for the stamps you sent. I thought Father was going to give Roberts 3£ as well & then I thought you were going to send me a letter to copy to send to Roberts so that *I* might write to him. However it is over now & does not much matter but why did Father send nothing. Do send Gilbert all the pipes that are not already smashed* & a *reasonable* amount of different tobaccos Father will know what to send but do try & sent* the fingerless gloves & scarfs knit in grey or white wool as it is just now they want them.

Thanks for the coat which is all right I have not yet found the umbrella. Do let me hear of the birds as soon as they arrive. How is Father's Studio* in the garden getting on. I had rather a jolly time with Aunt Eliza, though I felt rather nervous at 1st, she gave me 10/- before she went. We had a very pleasant time. *Please send some toothpowder by return.* Thanks for the Stamps. Have you seen to the knives. The Stylographic pen may be found in my Norfolk suit somewhere. There is no more news now so good bye
Dear mother from your loving Son
Tankred

P.S. One of my boots rubs my right foot & makes it awfuly sore I believe I shall have a corn so do send me something to cure it.

105   Nov. 4th 93. Saturday

My Darling Boy,

If your boot pinches – *have it stretched* at a bootmakers! See that your sock has no seam or darn pressing on the spot or select a *thinner pair of socks* if possible –

Enclosed toothpowder – I do not see your stylographic pen – I have both your knives –

Pattinson had one – to reblade – & is now again in the hospital – I fear he has to undergo a second edition of bone scraping & that it may be a long affair but I have not heard from him.

Such a fog is rolling down over our garden that I can scarcely see.

Your father considered it would be spoiling Roberts to send him more.

Dear Boy! I am so glad you were top of your form & your report is very good. Do you find the work in any way easier on the military side – & *what is the difference* – as you have been moved *on* I suppose the work must be more difficult – or at least more advanced?

I am *very* glad you feel better with more exercise & I attribute the improved result of your work to your feeling in consequence better in health –

When you say you play for 1st house 15 – do you mean that you are in the 1st 15 at football in the whole school?

10.11.1893: 106 (EFB to TTB)

I *should* start *advertizing* in the school for lost articles (your umbrella) – a town crier or something – 6d. reward – "Lost – such an article who ever shall bring the same will receive the above". – – Perhaps a reward is demoralizing for a school so dont do that – but contrive some system of getting things back & checking the common property business to some extent.

I am glad you enjoyed Aunt Elizas visit, she seemed pleased herself.

Who is the "bogie"

Dear grandma has been very sadly indeed laid up with inflammation of the st* but I am thankful that she is mending now – I shall ask your father to write to you about Progress, Manning, oak, rod &c. God bless you my precious.

Always your fond mother Min

106   Newfield

Nov. 10th 93

My Dear Boy

If you write to your Father & *ask him those questions* he will write to you & be glad to hear – so do so at once. I have had the enclosed from Tyra some time but mislaid it.

W.G.G.*Purnell wrote to me from Wellington (he left Malvern because his housemaster* died) asking me for stamps – as swaps. I saw Aunt Eliza at mothers on her way back to Paris & she seemed very pleased to have seen you – Dear Grandma seems to be better, she was up in an armchair in the dining room. I have not much to say today dear Boy but I think you like to have a greeting from your mother.

You must tell me how you get on in your class – now you have once been top perhaps you will again! On Wednesday Mrs Beaver & I went to the ladies Gallery House of Commons from 12 to 5.30 p,m. & heard the debate on the Employers Liability Bill.*

103

Mr Perks gave the tickets – it was very interesting to us the procedure – & it was surprising to hear them discussing whether it should be discussed in Committee or in the House – after all these centuries they have not yet decided which is best. I wonder if you will ever sit there, the "Honourable & Gallant Member"! Some of them speak very badly one is quite surprized. I was glad to hear Balfour a most polished speaker & one of our best men. – The ladies gallery is a very stuffy little place,* & one looks down thro' a gothic grating, & what with the great effort to hear it makes one quite giddy. It is a remnant of old custom, & survives as many old customs do the stage of thought & feeling which created them. You see thought & feeling go ahead of the laws before it changes them.

I have a lovely basket of roses on the table from the garden & two brugmancias. Brian fetches me to dinner & sends his love to you & asks you to send post marks.*

Yr loving mother Min

107 [12.11.1893]*

My dear Father,

I cant see why you should want me to write to you in person always if I want to know anything which concerns you in person, as I cant write two letters. I wish you would write & tell me how it is to be arranged. Do answer my question in my last letter. How is Pattinson. What did Moor put in my report I want to know? The work on the M&E* is certainly harder & there is more of it than anywhere else. Of course the work is more advanced the higher you get. The 1st house 15 means the 1st 15 in our House who play against the other houses. The bogie is Glazebrook I thought you knew that. We would have been cock house (that is the house that beats all the rest at Footer) only we played so badly in the last match that we lost it & have no more chance it is sickening for it was not as though we couldn't but we literally chucked away the match. So good bye dear Father

From your loving Son Tankred.

108   34 College Rd, Clifton

Nov. 22. 93. Wednesday

My Dear Father,

Why have I had no letter from you this week, you are generally so prompt in writing. There is very little news this week. I consider we (that is our house) have been very unsuccessful unfortunately this year. We ought to have been cock house, but our forwards threw all our chances away by playing so badly in our match with the only other house who had a chance against us, & so instead of winning as we certainly ought to have done we were miserably licked. We play house matches every fine Tuesday afternoon & if not then of* Thursday afternoons. Yesterday afternoon we had four of our best men away & so were not calculated to have beaten our opposing house, & though we ought to have beaten them it was badly managed & we lost so now instead of being cock house we are left second with two other houses whom we beat, it is awfuly sickening when we ought to have won. This year the system of house matches has been altered much to our disgust, for each match is settled in one afternoon by the house who gets the most points, whereas before to win one had to get 27 points & so sometimes the match went on for three days.* And that is where our house scored; for we were never known to have been beaten in a 3 days match, & so we should most probably have been cock house this year. *Do ask mother whether she has seen about send* Roberts the things.* So good bye dear Father from your loving Son

Tankred.

109   34 College Rd, Clifton

Sunday Nov 26. 93

My dear Father

How is it you have not written yet or mother either you usualy write so regularly & promptly. what is the matter with you?

You know last year we asked Roberts to come up for Christmas but he could not come so dont you think we ought to ask him to come up this christmas, as we practicaly at the time asked him to come the next Christmas when we heard he could not come then. I wish you would ask him it would be so nice. How is Pattinson? do tell me. there is really no news at present but I will try to write again during the week. So good bye dear Father
From your loving Son
Tankred.

[See additional letter 109A on p.274]

110   Newfield

Dec 5th 93

My Dear Boy!

Mrs Beaver & little Hugh left us yesterday & I think their presence must account for my not writing to you, it may seem an inadequate reason but I can assure you that the constant presence of a mother & a child, the former quite full of her personal plans & arrangements, filled up every little gap from morning until night. Of course we are very anxious to help her all we could & can. I spent quite three whole days over a sale for her, which took place in Perry Vale;* one day inspecting the things – one day in buying them & one in collecting. we spent about £70 & laid it out very well in just the very things she wanted.

Part of the time Boss was unwell & shut up the whole time in the spare room, for we feared he had whooping cough – & Mrs Beaver was laid up with very bad headaches. Your father was laid up a few days with something like influenza,* a very bad chill caught planting fruit trees one day & increased by persisting nevertheless in doing the same thing next day. Fräulein was also laid up for two days with something of the same kind. You can picture that all the nursing & arranging takes up a great deal of time attention & thought.

In addition your dear grandmother has been very ill for three weeks in bed. we were most anxious about her & I went as often as I could to see her though not so often as I would have liked as I have only one dear mother. I dont know what I shall do when I lose her. I trust she is really better & getting stronger & that she will be quite well again, but inflammation of the bowels* may be a very dangerous thing.

Another thing which militated against my writing as much as I otherwise would is that we have lately sat in my little study & the table & writing materials are often monopolized by some one else. Yesterday your birds arrived from Ireland & are I think very nice (charge 14/6).* Yesterday I saw Mr Allen & his very young wife perhaps they will call here to-day. When do your holidays begin & end?

We have been greatly saddened by the death of Dr Webb we heard he had inflammation of the lungs. your father wrote to him, & the next day about mid-day he passed quietly away – aged forty – with apparently such a good & useful future before him & such good health & strength. it only shows that we should all be ready to be called away, & work while it is day for the night cometh when no man can work.* I trust you are well my darling boy & making good progress in every way & finding the satisfaction which good work brings. I feel you can hardly appreciate what it is to begin life, as you can, with every opportunity of arming yourself for whatever lies before you in the future, by discovering what faculties you possess & developing them. It makes me wish I were in dear Tyras shoes or yours – but the past can never be recalled. One can never realize that too much, as a reason for making the most of the present, our best possession!

I shall be so glad to see you dear. Have you any plans of what you would like to do in the holidays? If you have, write & tell me about them. God bless & keep you with dearest love.

Always your fond mother Min

Miss Barlow was here all the afternoon & prevented my posting this – She has learn't for a year with Mr Edwards & has enjoyed & profitted tremendously by his very excellent teaching.

111   Newfield House, Forest Hill, Kent

11.XII.93

My dear Boy,

I possess four of your letters to which I only now reply. Of course there is, or rather should be a reason for everything. What I want, of which I informed you before, is to be, as a father on the most intimate, loving yet respected terms with my sons. I wish to be their best friend in life & aim at being loved & respected by them. Now I must say a composition to a father like: by commencing "I cant see why you should want me to write to you in person always if I want to know anything which concerns you in person, as I cant write two letters. I wish you would write & let me know how it is to be arranged. do answer my question in my *last* letter (to his mother)"* I consider lacking the very rudiments of respect. Don't you think so too?

I personally like to hear as often as possible from you, yet only when it gives *you* pleasure to write to your father, when it comes from the fulness of your heart, when you begin to feel drawn to him. Love without respect is worthless. As there are things which interest more a mother & others more a father, I suggest that the son divides his letters accordingly & pleases both. What do you think.

Sickness seems to be everywhere just now. I had just written to Dr Webb & crossing with my letter came his death. Mr Pattenhausen senior is very seriously ill, and Mr Pattenhausen has been laid up. Mr Perks was laid up for a fortnight & just now I received a card from his housekeeper informing me that he is down now with influenza fever 104°.

When birthdays remind you of advancing years, when death around us emphasizes the comparatively short span of a human life, grief comes over me when I feel one or any of my sons a stranger to his father. The sunshine of life gets clouded, I begin almost to despair when I have to fear that the eldest, on whom I naturally depend most in assisting me in the building up of a strong & great family, & whose life I am so anxious

Henry John Webb,

B.Sc., Ph.D.,

Principal Aspatria Agricultural College,

Born May 7th, 1853,

Died 28th November, 1893,

Life is real! Life is earnest
And the grave is not its goal;
Dust thou art, to dust returning
Was not spoken of the soul.

Herbert Thomas (see Doc App LXIV-LXVI)

to shape into a happy one, is akin, but not of soul. The times are serious & require all the nerve of a whole family if they wish to remain such. I shall battle, I will hope that the day of regret when no further sound passes the father's lips, will never come upon you.

As to the bogie that was one of your dear mothers enquiries *not* mine.

Enclosed you find references to Roberts, read my letter, add the necessary & post it.

What about confirmation, there is a paper* from Clifton requesting communication before 25th January if such is desired next March. I should like to hear from you on the subject.

Mother is doing her best for Roberts' things. the woman who attends to it has sickness in the house & so the things won't be ready before next week. I vote that Roberts takes them with him on his return. You might ask Roberts to bring the necessary twine for our salmon net, I mean the one which broke in Ireland.

the work at home is disgustingly slow & sickening as well in doors as out of the house. Pattinson is no better & for other reasons I think I have to calculate without him. Spall is sick at home today. Added to all this the days are short & work thereby curtailed. But for all that I keep at it & reckon upon success & victory after all.

Tyra, we have determined to come home for good. I don't know whether you know it already. Pray don't write to her about,* as she does not know it & we don't wish her to.

I look forward to your bringing home a happy disposition in which I shall rejoice to see you again.
                    Your loving father
                                    Leu

the 2 Birds came home. I don't think they were good enough specimens. they cost 17/-

14.12.1893: 112 (TTB to LWFB)

112   34 College Rd, Clifton, Bristol

Thursday. 14/12./93

My Dear Father

Nothing ever has or ever will pain me more than the thought that I have hurt the feelings of either of my parents, I know I have done it very often, but I hope you will entirely overlook & forgive the past for which nobody could be more sorry than I, but it cannot be undone. Up till now I dont think I have ever really said I was sorry for what I had done, because there was always that obstinacy inside me which said "dont give in" & I could not get over it. It has always been my inmost wish to please both of you you implicitly* but I have not been able to subdue myself sufficiently to carry that wish out. However If we two ever spend another unhappy day together I am determined it shant be my fault. You dont say why you delayed so long in writing. I am very sorry I forgot to write to you on your birthday & wish you "many happy returns of the day" so I will do it now. You know it always gives me pleasure to write to either of you, but there is really a difficulty about it, if I write to you indiscriminately I forget to which I have asked which questions & it all turns unsatisfactory. Dont you feel it the same if I address my letter to mother as if to you?. because if you do it is all right & I will write to you alternately & then I shall know where I am.

I come home on the 22nd a Friday shall I tell Roberts to come by the 11.15.AM. from Marazion* which gets to Paddington about 8.P.M. on Saturday 23rd. Also shall I tell him to bring his naval reserve clothes as he looks so much better in those than in his best Sunday go to meeting clothes. Please drop me a line or a card by return so that I can send off the letter.

As to confirmation dont you think we might consult about that in the Holidays. I think with you that Roberts might take the things back with him. I won't forget to ask him about the twine. How long will Pattinson be disabled now, has he been operated on again?   what are the other reasons why you will have to calculate without him? How disappointed Tyra will be not to go back to school. I have been in bed since Monday with a feverish cold again in the Exams, & they are my only chance I think of getting out of my form, because I always pull up in the Exams. isnt it a nuisance.

So goodbye dear Father from your loving Son

Tankred

P.S. I will answer mothers letter tomorrow, I ought to have written to her before. Thanks for those cuttings which interested me very much. Is it your wish to have Roberts with us? I mean does it give you pleasure?

113 Newfield

15/XII/93

My dear Boy,

I was very sorry to hear you too are not well. doubly disagreeable as again it happens at the exam. I presume you wrote to Roberts? I thought you would pick perhaps Roberts up at Bristol? of course I don't know when you break up at school. Spall is now ill for a week –

Let me hear from you.

Always your loving father

Leu

114 [16.12.1893]*

My Dear Father

I dont understand your note at all. had you received my letter when you wrote it. I have not written to Roberts yet. I cant see how I could pick him up here unless he were to travel up at night which would be very disagreeable for him in the winter time. Will the other arrangement do. Do write & answer my questions I asked you about him and I will write to him or else it will be leaving it too late I thought I told you in my letter we came home on Friday 22nd did I not? Do let me have a card from you before it is too late.

ever your loving Son
Tankred.

115   Newfield House, Forest Hill, Kent

Sunday 17.XII.93

Dear Son of mine,

You have won an important battle & I rejoice for your sake over it, I congratulate you upon the victory. I take it that your head has gained therewith supremacy over the body & its passion, a most, if not the most important, development in man. with such a foundation you may now go on fighting fearlessly – To conquer at all we have first to conquer ourselves. You want to know why I delayed writing so long? Because I wished the wounds to heal first & the love for you had to obliterate all dark spots first. Everything past shall be & is forgotten, I hail in you the second generation, who I can feel now, has entered the manly path, to carry out the further building of the family, a son who will ripen into a man, who will not allow either head or heart to run away with himself, but who will marshall head to go with heart, & heart to go with head hand in hand! I thank you for your birthday wishes. I hope to be allowed to see you, Tyra & the 2 Boys grown up as happy men & a good woman, strong, loving & united in yourselves, then I shall feel that my life has not been quite in vain. And hence Avanti! [forward]

Regarding your letters to your mother & myself I believe I suggested already that you divide matters relating to certain things between us, thereby avoiding unsatisfactory results either way. There are points like concerning the inner man, your future, the building up of your manhood, the morals of man & his connection with the outer world, which I should like to discuss with you. About the confirmation we will then consult during the holidays.

I am very glad you thought of having Roberts here during Xmas, we promised him London & I am glad to see him, in *his naval reserve*, which is quite the thing. If you pick him up at Bristol you save yourself going the next day to Paddington; however do as you like best either bring him with you or let him follow. In case of need wire* to him & let me know *what* you arranged. Mr Edwards & myself thought of going to Paddington.

Pattinson has been dismissed from the hospital, on the declaration that they could do no more for him. I fear from that, that his necrosis* is fatal & so I can no further reckon on him.

Tyra's school question became so far a deciding one, since she is now thirteen & if she is ever to go to Girton* she will have to buckle to. I think the arrangement we arrived at can be but beneficial to Tyra. Mr Edwards will coach her for a year & then we thought of sending her perhaps to St Andrews* in Scotland. I must say here that I for one do not like a girl to be away from home,* my notion is that a girl's place is by the side of her mother, but we shall see; we will have a year to consider. the only unsatisfactory part are her gyms & games; I don't like her to lose those, but time will advise us, I daresay when she is once home. At Brighton* she had the latter but nothing of teaching so to say & then that abominable influence of those little jewesses, which I abhor!

Your illness during exams is very disagreeable, we must see whether you cannot get through some other means with another form.

I long to see you home for the holidays. I think I have found the lathe of the age, it is dear, very dear but an exquisite invention, when we decide upon one, we will have to save up for some time.

I bought a fine drilling machine, you will see some alterations

in the workshop. We must save more time, do more work &
have better tools, a thing Pattinson was always averse to.*

Much love from your dear mother & your loving father
Leu

[addition in RTB's & BTB's hands with bracketed notes
from LWFB]   Love from Roy. (Roy)
                    Love from Brian. (Brian)
                    Kisses from all the family. (Roy)
                    Hurrah from the boys! (Brian)

NEW TERM BEGINS

116   Newfield

Jan 25th 94

My Darling Boy,

I have not forgotten you as your lights are turned out these
two nights & I think it will be a great source of pleasure
& inspiration to us. You cannot think how I try to learn &
absorb everything which can make me a more able &
better mother to my children. You know we are *all* of us
as Tennyson says but
                    "Infants crying in the night
                    Infants crying for the light
                    & with no language but a cry"!*

Goethe died asking for "more light"* & we are still in the
same position, but the world has moved far more rapidly in
the last 50 years than ever before & advance will I believe
become more & more rapid. Think of *Science*, the *means of
progression*,* the *position of women, Democracy!*

You cannot realize what progress those four headings represent,
but you may just think of them, bear them in mind &
find out that they mean a complete revolution – One thing
alone, the institution of Board schools* – someone has truly

said it means a change as great as the Reformation. The wonderful way in which natural laws have unfolded themselves – evolution electricity telephone* &c &c – is simply stupendous – did you hear of Dewars "frozen air"* the other day?

I forgot to pay the 4/- into your acct for the auntie's present. but will do so – & if you will write out a statement of your acct with your father including the 25/- travelling I will see that the dressing gown is struck off. Tyra seems to be shaking down to the arrangements for her lessons &c very nicely & I think it will be very good for her to have some intelligent companionship instead of only children like herself. You know Mr Lynam was exceedingly nice in educating his boys – beyond lessons I mean – in general knowledge which was a great advantage to you.

Tyra seems to enjoy reading now – so I hope that will be a help to her. How many stockings did you take?
"   "   trowsers   "   "   "
& do you need bathing drawers.

God Bless you my dear Son. Pray try to extract from the whole of your environment all the profit physically morally & spiritually that you can both by examples & warnings & most of all in self conquest – that is the stuff your future self will be made of. I hope I may help you all a mother can & any way my love will always surround you.

Your loving Mother
Min

Tyra wishes to hear when your term ends for the book she is making (with *gold* letters in it!)

[See additional letters 116A and 116B on pp.274-5]

117   34 College Rd, Clifton

26.I.94

Dearest Tyra.

I enclose a printed thing with the dates of the end of term on.

When you have looked at it do give it to father to keep as it will tell him all about the rest of the holidays this year.

Do see that the enclosed letter to Roberts, goes *just* after my oilers* are sent off if they have not already been sent. But if they have already been sent do send the letter at once. I will write again soon. So good bye dear Tyra from
your loving brother
Tankred.

118   34 College Rd, Clifton

26 Jan 94

My dearest mother,

Do send me a pot of Hippacea & a small bottle of Podopholin* & 24 penny stamps. I got into the right study by good luck but I ought not to have gone by so late a train however it did not matter.* I did not get out of my form, but I think I would have if I had been there for the Exams. It is rot! Do tell Mr Edwards that we began "Analytical Conics" to day. I will tell you more about my work later as also everything else. Dont forget to send me what I asked for. So good bye dear mother from your loving Son
Tankred

[See additional letter 118A on pp.275-6]

119   Newfield

Feb. 4th 94*

My Darling Boy.

It seems a long time since any of us heard from you & we shall be very glad of your news! The excavation for the studio is going on apace – & your father has had the happy thought of saving the carting of the clay by wheeling it all to the foot of the second Lansdowne lawn* & thus lengthening it to nearly as far as the table, levelling where the table is, so making a second little platform & then asphalting under the table to keep our tootsies dry. The District overseer* is so baffled to find the building is more than 30 feet from any other building which makes it free of his fees.

Roy had such a tumble into the hole left by the work people, to-day, to the detriment of his nose & eyebrow. Your father has been working away at the pruning & the trees look splendid. Almost in bloom in the orchard house – I hope we may have such a spring as last year – It is quite springlike already – I expect grandma to-morrow & Mrs Boole on Tuesday to stay until Wednesday & I suppose some one else on Thursday & Friday & perhaps go to see "The Transgressor"* at the Court Theatre on Saturday (if we get tickets) with your father & Mr Edwards. Spall is not better, but not worse for working – Mr Pattenhausen is here & we are all talking in my study so I get on badly & I am now going to be Bademeister* to Tyra.

Thursday – My dear Boy. Sorry these lines were not posted. I see Tyra says I take no exercise* but I intend to consult a medical woman Dr Scharlieb in a few days after which I hope to be free to take as much exercise as I like of which I will not fail to inform you. Dear Granny is here, she came on Monday to see Rook & is still not free from him. We are looking out for a letter from you every post. With love from each & all of us
Your loving Mother
Min

120   34 College Rd, Clifton

7.2.94

My dear Mother.

I dont know, I dont seem able to get on a bit. I was 6th in

my form last week when I ought to be top or 2d. I can*
understand a word of my Analytical Conics & am very
hazy about my Dynamics so I feel thoroughly disgusted with
my self. Then about Arithmetic we do a one hours exercise
per. week, & I can't do them a bit, the others are not
much good either but that is no consolation to me. If
father had not debited me for the one guinea dressing
gown I should have been exactly square up to now. Why
do none of you write I have had now only a letter from
you one from Tyra & one from Roy. I am sending home
3/6 for you to put in the bank for me. And some
newspaper cuttings which I want you to give Father to put
in the 2d *drawer* from the left in my pigeon hole cupboard
where there are some cuttings already. I will send them in
two envelopes both to be put in the same drawer. As to the
travelling money I always have had & thought it was not
counted in our acct. so I did not count it but if father
wishes to begin & count it I should then owe him 25/- it
being understood that he pays for the dressing gown.

I took 4 pairs of stockings I think didn't Tyra tell you. I
dont need any bathing drawers thank you as I have a pair
here already if I want them. I have had such a lot of work
to do lately that I have really had no time to do anything
else. So good bye dear Mother from your loving
Son Tankred.

121   34 College Rd, Clifton

10.II.94

My Dear Father

Thank you for your last very interesting cuttings. It seems very
funny that you should not write to me; it seems as though
you meant not to write till I had written first to you. We go
to Aldershot for our field day early in March I believe the
14th however I will write again soon & let you know the
exact date; I do hope you will avail yourself of Capt. Hall's
invitation* & come down for the field day. Do tell me what is

happening about that horrid law suit?* Shall I write to Hulbe & ask him the price of the purse* or shall I tell him to make one if it is not over a certain price. Do write me a letter for me to copy & if necessary will you send the old purse to him as a copy? As to the knife my chum here still wants one so I feel I ought to get one for him, so if I send you Zeiser's* last letter do write me a letter of which to send him a copy; of course I must apologise for not having writen for so long. Last night we had a lecture from a master of Cheltenham, Mr Hitchens, on coal & coal mines.* I have heard him lecture before at Mr Lynam's. First he began by showing us a few views with a magic lantern of a coal mine taken from photos taken by him by magnesium light which were very nice. Then he began to explain about the coal strata, how there was always a bed of clay underneath the coal which used to be the soil the trees grew in & how on the top there was always sandstone or other strata which told us how the land had sunk & the sea bed covered it for a period. Then he showed us fossils which have been found where the print of rain drops in the sand have been left us & the print of the foot of an animal which was just like the print of a mans hand & so they called it the Cairotherion* or the beast with the man's hand, He showed us the tooth it had which was quite different from any teeth now; Then he showed us all with the magic lantern, the fossilized fishes of the time. Then he said there were no birds at that time but there were fishes & scorpions nearly like ours & beetles probably butterflies then he spoke of the trees there were tree ferns like those now in New Zealand, & south of caws* like this form all cupped shaped & the tree which was the biggest grew to 100 feet some times called the lepidodendron a sort of giant moss some thing like this

whose descendent now is only the little "club moss" which grows here only an inch or two high.

Then he gave us a few experiments with small explosions of coal gas & air, for he explained that fire damp, was only the hydrogen which had not been able to escape from the wood when it was being changed into coal, & was only explosive when mixed with air. So It was very interesting. I do hope you have allowed spall to thoroughly clean the guns. Do put some napthaline* in our fishing creel amongst the tackle or the moth will get to the flies & eat them all up. Do let my little rifle & the little repeating rifle go to Blanch's* & be thoroughly cleaned so that in the future they will shoot straight. Next holidays if we dont go away I hope to put all our tackle guns etc in thorough order & make a nice case for them & also to put up our dark room, – By the way what about Eastman's.* For it seems a pity that all our nice guns & tackle should go to irremediable rot just for a few shillings worth of labour of cleaning by Spall & the gun makers & our own time & trouble, does it not?

So now good bye dearest Father

from your most affectionate son

Tankred.

P.S. there is going to be a class for "Topography & Fortification" to be taught by some officer who knows it well so Mr Hall says, however it is not quite certain yet. I suppose you dont mind me joining it.

122   Newfield House, Forest Hill

[11.2.1894]*

Dearest Tankred

Thank you so much for your letter, we thought it so sweet of you to write to us all. The little boys were so delighted with their letters. I always help them every Sunday with their letters to you.

They are going to try to write to you alternately every sunday.

we have just got a sweet little dog called "Juno"* & it is very well trained it is an Irish terreier & of a redish brown colour.

The fungus was growing all under the hall floor & rotting all the wood.

The studio is being built & is getting on very well.

I am going to a little party with mother at the Woods tomorrow at half past seven, it is very lucky it is just after my lessons.*

The boys & I are already longing to see you again. Do you know we get our bread from a steam bakerie* now it is very much nicer.

I have finished "Charlie Lucken"* I liked it very much. I dont quite know what to read now.

Roy was so pleased that you said you would get him some Licorise, but I think he ought to pay for it, dont you?

There is realy no more to say
from your ever loving sis
Tyra

123   Newfield House, Forest Hill

[11.2.1894]*

Dearest Tankred

Thank you very much for your nice letter. Smith has come & I think you'll like him very much. We do work in the workshop a little but father says we must not get in Smiths way. Spall is at work again now. We do play about in garden but as there is so much clay about now we get our shoes very dirty so Fräuline dose not like us to go to much in the garden without her. I supose you know the studio has been begun to

be built. We think it will be finished in April. I am very
sorry that I did not write last sun day as it was my week
to write but Ethel & Violet were there & I wanted to stay
with them. Good night Tranked* dear
from your loving brother
Brian

124   Newfield House, Forest Hill

[11.2.1894]*

Dearest Tankred

The stove is a little sprit lamp which mother had, which
your old nurse youst to use when you were little. Thank
you very much about the licorice. Please will you write to
me soon? Did Tyra tell you about the fungus in the hall?
Pattie gave us some more choclates for the clock & at the
same time she gave us an Xmas card each mine was a cat
consert & Brian's was a nigger consert. We must go to bed
now so good bye dear Tankred.
from your loving brother Roy.

125   Newfield

Feb. 11th 94

My Dear Boy,

We were *each* & *all* of us rejoiced to hear from you, & each
over our separate letters.* Patty is here & we are all sitting in
my little study. I have a slight headache & do not feel much
like writing but I must tell you of my visit to Mrs Scharlieb.
M.D. yesterday you will be glad to know, the result was very
satisfactory. there is so far nothing seriously wrong. I have a

Ethel Lambley: (on reverse)
"Lims best love to Tibs"

Patty Pattenhausen

Brown's house; rear view

little thing to wear which is not inconvenient & is preventive so there is nothing to prevent my taking as much exercise as I like which is a great comfort. I also went afterwards to see Mrs Willans who now lives near Regents Park. I saw the youngest boy* – who just missed getting into Sandhurst lately & is going in again in June. The other two boys already have commissions one in India, one in Ireland, both in the same regiment.* Mrs Willans lent me a book about the army & preparation for it which I think will be very interesting to us. I will pay in your 3/6. your father said he had debited you with the dressing gown – but there were many little things not debited to you – such as boat repairs & so forth. This afternoon Fräulein was out & the boys wrote to you by themselves as you will perceive. it gave them great pleasure. The new little dog is so far well trained & keeps to heel, but he is chained near the potting house – & there are so many people in the garden I think he will be quite spoilt. The new studio is rising in the place you know & will soon block the prospect from this window. I trust it will be a great source of pleasure from the interior & that much good work will be done in it. It is impossible to enjoy the garden while the works are proceeding but it is supposed to be finished in three months!

Your Grandmother has been with us all the week until yesterday – in attendance on Rook who I am sorry to say has been very unsuccessful.

It is very very troublesome & such an impediment to the taking of necessary nourishment. I liked to hear about Mr Hitchins lecture.

It is now 5 minutes to ten & Tyra is in bed & calling me – we are both most punctual at ten o'clock & we picture you in your little bed with the lights just out & hope you also remember.
God Bless you Dearest no end of love from your loving Mother
Min

I note your troubles with regard to Mathematics & will write of them later.

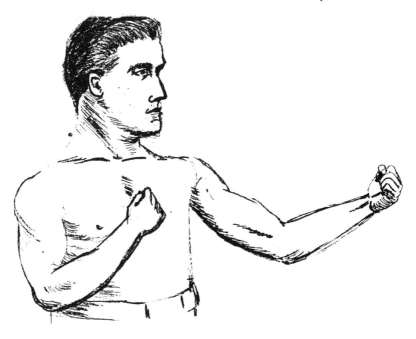

126   [16.2.1894]*

Dear Father

Why dont you write? I want besides to know about joining
that class. Do write soon.

Tankred.

127   34 College Rd, Clifton

19.ii.94

My Dear Father

do write to me. also if you dont send me some stamps
there will be no more letters home as I have neither *stamps*
nore *money* at all, & I had to get some one to *give* me the
stamp to send this home.

I cant think why you dont write. I have no more time to
write more now so good
                        bye dear Father from your
                                loving Son Tankred.

128   22 feb 94

My dear Boy,

I am *extremely busy*, shall write in the next few days. Was
very pleased with your drawings. Enclosed 9d. stamps.
                        Your loving father
                                Leu

129   Newfield House, Forest Hill

[22.2.1894]*

Dearest Tankred

I am so very sorry not to have written before but we went
to Mrs Beavers on Sunday to Xenia's Birthday Party, we
saw General* there & he asked after you, you know his
school has broken up on acount of scarlet fever.

I am reading "Two thousand years ago"* now & I like it very much.

Mr Edwards is going to give me a little exam tomorrow. The studio is making good progress & they are begining to put on the roof now, but the inside is not duge out yet & made flat. All the clay which came out of the new vine house at the top of the garden and all the clay out of the inside of the studio is being put on the lawn.

we have at least got one private place in the garden now that is where the table is where the tree was blown down.

The studio is so funny father has used up all the bits of stone he had & it is all put in the wall, there* also some little old windows built into the wall & a seat of stone is going to be put out side.

I feed the fowls nearly every day & the little black game hen eats out of my hand. I also get Juno's biskets ready. on Wednesday I went to tea at Mrs Beavers only just got in in time for Mr Edwards*

with love from your ever
affectionate sis Tyra.

130   Newfield

Feb. 23rd 1894 6.40.p.m

My Darling Boy,

Tyra is in the midst of her 1st examination with Mr Edwards – A most solemn occasion I can assure you – no scholarship exam could be more silent orderly & methodical. It is quite wonderful to see Tyras papers & exercises how neat & well written they are. & I am in hopes that our present plan is going to be very satisfactory indeed – of course the work she is doing is very primitive indeed – but it is only the beginning – she is learning to learn. I wish that you had early acquired that order & a good handwriting.

23.2.1894: 130 (EFB to TTB)

This little room of Tyra's seems so pleasant & easy – such a jolly outlook over the garden. The Garden – by the way – I dont know if I shall get to like it later. It seems to me so spoilt. First the view from my study – gone entirely – closed now by the studio & the banks of (clay at present) which lengthen the upper lawn to the table (nearly) & make two more flat terraces – the last bank reaching the apple & pear tree nearest the house (Lansdowne side). The studio will of course look better when finished – aged – & grown over – but being perpendicular & *horizontal* on such a steep incline, from above it looks most comical – as though the roof sloped from front to back. When the trees are green it will be a little modified, but there is now no wandering up that once long & pleasant slope or running down it.

How is* dear Boy – that when I sent you nine stamps – (since when not nine letters have you written) & you send me 3/6 to put in the bank (which I did with the 4/- more), you say you have not a stamp & not a 1d. – It is not the right thing for you to be penniless – I do not know how you can get on without any money – & not seem miserly. Do explain it to me.

Mrs Beaver is now at Colbrae* with her children. She came over this morning with Boss & Guy – who is so much improved – Boss has quite gone back in his temper & manners since he left here – but is grown & advanced. Xenia came too & a young friend Beatrice Earle. they all had lunch with us – quite a party – Would you like me to send you anything dear Boy. I mean *grub!* I hope you remember us when your lights are turned out we always do. Twice I was out & then Tyra did it alone.

In a conversation (overheard by Fräulein) between Brian & Roy – Roy said "do you know why concerts are so called" – Brian "no" Roy "Why you know the Queen had a husband who was called Concert,* well he died & ever since there have been concerts." They are both in such a way because when alone for ½ an hour lately they upset the paint in the workshop – & are now forbidden *ever* to go in there – alas & alack for nails & glue & all the luxuries!

Since you left, our three maids took to quarrelling so much that I am obliged to let our nice cook go – & McColby being well again is coming back, she is a nice woman but I doubt she is not strong enough for a permanence. However – the young & strong are not permanent – so I take her.

I know you will be glad to hear that I feel all the better for my visit to Dr Scharlieb – You see if one thing is out of place it disarranges the others & I think I can perceive a distinct difference for the better, for which I am most thankful.

Dinner &c – after which your father & Mr Edwards went to Mr Barlows – I had a nap – put Tyra to bed & now say good night & God Bless my absent dear. With love & hugs. Always your fond Mother
                                                    Min

131   34 College Rd, Clifton

25.II.94

My Dear Mother.

As a matter of fact I dont think there are many little items not payed for as I payed more than I ought to for the big things in a lump thinking what would about pay for all, & besides I would not have got the dressing gown at all had I not thought it was a present. However I suppose now it must remain, but in the future as I see it is no good being lenient & neither side counting odd sixpences or so in the final acct I shall deal to the last farthing in every thing & have a strict understanding before hand as to who is to pay for what. How is there no long slope now has the path been altered into terraces & steps too? I think I must have sent nearly nine letters *home* perhaps not all to you, but of course I write others as well to Roberts, Manning, Jumma, *etc* you dont seem to realise that. Neither have I a stamp nor a penny, some times I get the whole or part of my weekly pocket money, 1s. & that just saves me. I dont know exactly how I manage but I just can somehow. What I want you to do in the way of grub is to send me the *equivalent* of a *proper* hamper in money, & then I can get what I like here & it saves the carriage & trouble of packing etc. I think that derivation of the word "Concert" was very cute of Roy. Are not the Boys ever going to be allowed in the workshop again? I am daily expecting a letter from Father which he has promised to send in the next few days. So now good bye Dear mother from your loving Son

Tankred

132   Mar. 3rd 94

My Dear Boy.

Do not regard this as an apology for a letter. I should have sent you stamps but I understood from your father that he had done so. I understand *now* that he has not yet done so – I just enclose 3/6 towards the hamper. I will send you 6/6 more (but it is not necessary you should have it all at once) – If you do buy food, pray buy good wholesome things – not trash – of which latter I hardly suspect you capable. (the Postal orders are those you sent me but it is all the same). Our dear love to you – if I can write more to-night I will. Your loving Mother

Min

133   34 College Rd, Clifton

[5.3.1894]*

My Dear Mother

Thanks for your card & the money, Do write me a letter soon, & send me some *tooth powder* as I have used the last all up & have no more left at all now. Do ask father to write. Last Friday we had a lecture on central Africa,* there were some good lantern slides but the lecture I thought was rot. There is

no more to say now so good bye from your loving Son
Tankred

I will write a longer letter in a day or two.

134   Newfield

Mar 11th 94

My Darling Boy

I know you think you hear very little from your only
mother, & that her thoughts if not expressed on paper &
sent through the post are not of much use to you – Well
in reply I can only say she is always thinking & always
doing something or other for the best, & she hopes that
both her doing & thinking will be of use to her children
sooner or later in Gods Providence. I certainly heard
something the other day which gives me some anxiety. No
allusion was made to Clifton, but of the *dreadful* evil* going
on in Public schools generally, quite unspeakable! And
Marlborough boasted of being better than the others *because*
(& that is the worst of it) *because* the boys are *always* under
surveillance! no cubicles! no private studies! – as though
English public school boys were not as a rule gentlemen, &
could not be trusted! Now my dear Boy I devoutly hope
Clifton is not like that & that the boys there *are* to be
trusted! If they are not, I trust & pray that, if there were
only one trustworthy boy amongst them his name would be
Tankred Tunstall-Behrens. No one is too young to know
that sin of all kinds brings its inevitable & fatal punishment
to the sinner – & not to the sinner only but to the third &
fourth generation. Individuals are not alone, nor can they
do anything which affects themselves only, each deed – nay
each word, is cast into eternity, like a stone into an endless
sea on which the rippling circles never cease to form &
have no shore to break upon – If you think of it you will
see how profoundly true it is of all things small & great –

11.3.1894: 134 (EFB to TTB)

Now I have often told you how great a power *one* individual has for good – however young the individual, however small the voice – *one persistent voice & example for good* has the greatest power, for he has the Almighty & the unseen Hosts upon his side & the wicked hide their faces & are ashamed – I do not speak figuratively it is the plain & simple fact. Of course there is much evil in the world but we are not told to shun it, but to keep one'self "unspotted from the world"* to be "in it but not of it".

I do not say this in any mistrust of you my dear Boy, God forbid! You know I have always trusted you. *You said you had been sent from home too young* to resist evil by yourself – Well you are still young compared to many at Clifton but I firmly believe you are old enough & strong enough to resist whatever you know to be wrong or unwise, few know it better & it is for those who know to lead & not to be led or driven or goaded.

Tyra has two nice little friends here to-day from the dancing class Violet & Lucy Cambridge, they are partly vegetarians which seems to suit them very well.

It is a sunny afternoon. The building still proceeds. A man is hammering at the studio wall. Your father lives in the garden as though he were a master builder.* I shall be so glad if it is ever quite finished, so that we may enjoy our garden in peace. I quite look forward to Sundays when the garden is free from all those workmen! I like to go up with the children before even the gardener* comes. When do your holidays commence dear? I hope they will be satisfactory. Think *first* what it is *best to* do – & set about it – don't expect too much of the holidays & be satisfied when they close. Try to enjoy the simple feel of being with those you love as they enjoy being with you. I think the mistake is, to *expect too much*, something super human – a kind of external Heaven on earth, when Heaven is *within us*. God in us, His love in us, radiating on those around & to the exclusion of all else. I cannot treat of selfishness in such a connection for it is *incompatible*. Our small boys are such dears. I cannot recall any of their frequent funny remarks. Just now Roy added to our prayers "Pray God help dear Fräulein to do her English lessons". –

11.3.1894: 135 (LWFB to TTB)

I dont think I told you – One day he was exceedingly naughty & Fräulein was telling him of his rudeness & naughtiness – so he said "Do you think Tankred is *a very nice* boy?" Fräulein "Yes." "Well Tankred does it & I like to be exactly like Tankred"! So I had to explain to him that he must distinguish between bad & good & only imitate the good. I wish you could have heard it all & seen how what the admired & beloved big brother does, sinks into their hearts. There were the ripples!!

We have not settled about Tyras music yet, so she only does theory* with Mr Edwards. He is pleased with her progress so far. I am very busy as usual. We always remember you at 10.p.m & trust you remember us. It is not the only time I devote to you. God bless you my Precious. Think of all I say & write soon to your fond Mother.

Min

135   Newfield House, Forest Hill, Kent

11.III.94

My dear Son,

Your letters of the 10 & 19th as P C of 16th all of february came duly in my possession. I was particularly delighted with your efforts in drawing, persevere, draw what *you see* & form your own style for representation, it is sure to afford you many a pleasure. Dont worry abt analytical *conics for the present*. It might be bad faring* were it now in 1895,* but you have a year before you & I reckon that in that time you will master it with ease. Do *all* you can in *Arithmetic*. How do you fare in *other* subjects *outside* Mathematics? Mr Edwards would like to know *what* Text Book, if any, you use for *Analytical* Geometry?

I think in perusing the position between father & son, you won't find it funny that the son, who left his father's house for school after his holidays should *first* write to his father & not the father to the son? Think over it!

132

Clifton College: watercolour by Henry Barraud (1811–1874)

Hulbe's emporium

11.3.1894: 135 (LWFB to TTB)

We are at the 11th of March today, if you let me know when you are at Aldershot I will undertake to be there with your mother & see Capt Hall.

My law-suit with Bleuler is deferred to April now.

You had better write to Hulbe "Georg Hulbe 43-47 Linden Straße St Georg Hamburg" & ask him first what he would *charge you* for a purse, as you had to see whether *your* budget permitted *you the expense.* The knife I sent you in the meantime. Your description of your lectures gave me great pleasure, continue to do so, for whatever concerns you interests me.

from Eastman's I had no satisfaction, their system is that of bribery evidently & it behoves one to warn *others* of taking a Kodak.* I have sent to Munich for lenses now.

I quite agree to what you say abt our guns & tackle, but I have so much on my hands just now,* (& I daresay the children have already sufficiently reported to you what I am doing) that I must nolens volens* leave all that until you come home for your holidays to take that part in hand.

The class of Topography & fortification I *like you to join.*

The other day I received your report,* again there is a complaint about the *style* of your work. You should *not* fall behind & *always* remember that style is counted in your exam. Remember all you do is for yourself & *not* as so frequently *erroneously* imagined by youth for their masters!

Another remark in your report rather distresses me. It says: "I have had to speak very seriously to him about the lines he is taking in the house. He lets himself be led."* As a man, as a soldier, as a leader of men, it is *imperative* that *you* should lead *others*, & never be led! It won't do! Remember to judge, you must put yourself into the position of Mr Moor, you should *assist him* in the good name of the house & be above incitement or guile. The distaste you occasionally ventilated against those boarders, surely cannot apply to any practised vice? – I cannot imagine vile practices at Clifton? Whatever there is, I wish you to open out to your father & confide in him. I suppose it is but imaginary domestic discomforts & those you are bound *to battle down,* appeal to reason & *contribute* towards the good understanding between your house master & his other boys. On reflection, I am convinced you will agree with me. Anyhow I should like to have a clear description from you of what is going on & whether as I hope every thing *is morally* clean?

What scholarship are you making for this year? The wilson?* Let me hear soon from you
Your affectionate
father Leu

136   Newfield House

March Friday 16th 1894

Dearest Tankred

I wish I had been able to go down to Clifton* with mother the other day. Do you know that poor old Rex was ill in the night & was found dead on the following morning, we also have a new little pup an Irish terrior he is sweet & is called Jove he is four weeks old.

I hope you do not mind I lent "two thousand years ago" I am going there to dinner & tea & will bring it back tomorrow.

Brian has not been very well he was very sick the other day but is all right today. My room is lovely now I have got curtains & the nursery table. I am afraid the boys have not done as they planned in the way of writing every week. I have just read such a lovely book that Mr Edwards lent me it was a prize belonging to one of his boys called, "The wreck of the golden fleece",* I feal quite lost with out a book now as I have finished it. There is no more to say so with heaps of love & longing to see you again from your loving sis
Tyra.

137   Newfield

Mar. 16th 94 Friday

My Dear Boy,

We had such a delightful day on Wednesday. Although we only made up our minds to go to Aldershot* at the last moment every thing went well & turned out for the best. The Halls were most kind, Mrs Hall meeting us at the station & driving us up to her house; we were stopped on the road by the 6th Warwickshires & Capt Hall leading his men, an interruption rather resented by their spirited poney. We were very glad of breakfast & a fire, for our maids contrived to put *our* breakfast on the table, just too late for us to partake of it & we were rather nipped* on the journey down. We had a comfortable carriage & enjoyed a pleasant drive to the scene of action where we found ourselves just in the centre with the general & his staff & heard the command given – to keep the height & keep a good retreat open & then as you approached we retired before the retreating Warwickshires – had it been a real action we should certainly have been bespattered with blood – Then as I told you we saw the march past from just opposite to where your corps was stationed after which we drove to the station to find out where & when we might find the Cliftonians & this gave us time to lunch with the Halls, & the rest you know. I need not say how glad I was to spy your right eye behind another boys cap, followed by the left one & the rest of your dear *phiz* & to see you well & jolly after the days exertions. I can't think why you didn't all of you open your capes – for it was very cold & many of you must have caught cold, now just tell me whether they did or not! (catch cold) I did, though I was wrapped up. It was a good long day from 5.30.a.m to us – & must have been the same to you & the keen fresh air was quite intoxicating. I feel as though I should like a succession of such days of fresh air & exercise & country scenes. I am looking forward to hearing from you both a reply to my last letter & your personal experiences of the review.

Tyra is having her lessons. Such nice lessons as I think, & makes me wish I had had our Egouadya as Roy calls him.

18.3.1894: 138 (TTB to LWFB)

Yesterday Fräulein being out I spent with the boys. Brian had had a bilious attack & it was very grateful to him to have me & they both enjoyed my giving them their bath – Roy seems so springy & athletic he ought to be famous at sports. Captain Hall's opinion is that boys can't be sent too early to school & when I said *you* went at eight, he said "Ah he'll be all right then!" I trust that all things will work together for your good my precious! You must cultivate the faculty for turning all things to good in some way. evil as a warning, good as an example. all as experience & matter for reflection. Tyra would so have liked to have seen the manoeuvres. I am sending a letter she wrote some days ago.* She gave it me & I meant to write at the same time & could not until now. God Bless you Darling. No end of love from your fond Mother

Min

138   34 College Rd, Clifton

18./3./94*

My Dear Father,

I was so pleased you came to Aldershot, though I wish I had seen you before,* why did you not come & see me before just before we were getting into the train as there was about an hour before in which I had nothing to do. Do write & tell me exactly what you thought of the field day, Did you see me individualy march past, as I want to know whether I held myself up or not? But do write & tell me how we compared in smartness etc with other schools. By the way what was the price of that knife as the boy wants to have it & pay for it. As to the Analytical conics, I am already getting on better, as I understand it better & can do problems if I have the formulæ before me but I dont know my formulæ. Mr Edwards will be able to understand it I dare say. We use C.Smith's Conic sections. Macmillan & Co. dated revised edition 1892. As to the arithmetic we have done about 21. questions this term & this is all we have done & the results have not been good either. I am not very good in French I am worst in it of all subjects I think, but I get on all right with my master* & he thinks I am working satisfactorily. But in German I have got into a new set this term & though I was easily top of my last set I cant get a mark* in this set, I think it must have something to do with the master,* as I have been a term under the same master for french & a term for German before this term & never have I been able to get one in any of his sets. It seems to me that though I should by rights write to you first, yet there should be no hard & fast rule by which if I cant write you should feel it doing the wrong thing to write first, surely there should be no such feeling between father & son. Dont you think I ought to write to Zizer,* & not leave his last letter unanswered. if so do write me a short german letter, apologising for not having written when he had taken the trouble for me & having asked me to write & select one of the two knifes drawn. I am making another small drawing to send you but I have so little time & have not yet quite finished it.

I suppose you have put about Eastman's in the papers. If you will coincide with me when I come home & help me, I will work with a will & put every thing in order. I want to know whether you would mind me exchanging my little rifle & 15/- for a gun in splendid condition (muzzle loader) by John Manton the crack maker of the begining of the centuary it shoots well, – & as I can trust my chum not to do me. It is the boy who is going to have that knife. If you dont want me to do this, I will buy it altogether. However I must think of my budget.

We must also arange our darkroom next Holidays. About the style of my work, well I shall do my best. About my report I too am most disgusted as it* all a lie, as I will prove to you anon. Well in the middle of the term I was reading out some lines a boy had to do for a sixth and he like a fool instead of writing down what I dictated,* without my knowing it put in some rot, to cheek the sixth. Well he finished the lines & gave them up; So when he had given them to the sixth who was in his study, the sixth went out, so I said let us have a joke to fool the sixth, & find the lines & hide them in his study & he will think they have been taken by someone to show up on some future occasion. Well you see it just happened that the sixth had looked through these lines & seen what the boy had written & when it came out that I had hidden them, of course having hidden the lines as much as said that I had known what had been written, when I did not know, So it was an unlucky coincidence, so I explained the matter to the sixth & got 250 lines to write (Well the boys in the fifth form have certain privileges.)* This row was told to the head of the house* who must of misunderstood it altogether & so he accused* of telling lies & being an accomplice of the boy who wrote the lines & took my fifth power* away, which as you must see was all wrong. However if I had wanted to make a row about it & have what was fair done, it would only have got the other fellow in a worse row, so I took what I got & said nothing although it was so unfair. Well this got to Moors ears. Well then at half term I went in to see my report before it was sent home & saw the quoted sentence. So I went out & said nothing but thought what was the best thing to do as I couldnt under any circumstances allow these *abominable* lies to go unrefuted, for there is no other word for them. I ought to have said that before this he had taken an opportunity to jaw me, His idea seems to be the* you are led by whomever you go about with at all so that is no criterion, at least when he jawed me he said well you go about with so & so a good deal & barge* (but that is my nature & if anything I instigate it) & so you are led by the nose by them. I proved to him that I had not barged this term so all he could do was to allude to my barging last term & make that an excuse. Well after seeing my report, I came to the conclusion to go to him & ask him what he meant by it so I went. And told him I was going to write to you about it & as it was a little indefinite, I asked him what he meant by it. He referred to his jaw & to the row I had had about my fifth power about which he did not understand a word as I told him, however he said if I wanted to say any more about it we must rake up the whole matter again, but I was not going to do this because of the other fellow. Then he said that I ought to have taken all he put in the report* heart, but I said I didnt see that as what he had put was all wrong & as there was a right & wrong side to every question I should write to you & put it in the right light. Besides then he said he knew what was ryght & practically told me I was telling lies. Besides I dont see how by catching a glimpse of me only now & again he can expect to know what he professes. In fact he couldnt tell me that I had barged this term, in fact he had not reason at all – except that row, of which he evidently did not understand a word. –

18.3.1894: 138 (TTB to LWFB)

He seemed to think that if one is accused falsely one is to take the accusation to heart & that it is the wrong think* to refute it; But one of his arguments was you did not refute the accusation abt your fifth power so I must take it that it was just. A few nights after this he called me up & tried to butter it over, However that was not much good. If this is not lucid, I cant make it more so in a letter but will explain it further in the holidays.

It is perfectly sickening too to be in the house he is such a suspicious old devil, he suspects one of goodness knows what without any reason except that he dislikes you & what is more tries to blacken ones character to others by it, Besides he is such a hypocrite, he pretends to be on the best of terms & then talks of one behind ones back, & if you go for him about it he retracts it as much as he can & makes rotten reasons which anyone can see through, & then tries to finish you by saying practicaly that what he says is bound to be right & you are telling lies & are impertinent & self concious, for denying & disproving his confounded accusations.

Besides this in my last row with him I have deliberately caught him telling lies to get out of what he had said before. And I think if I can get the other two or three boys to come we will go to him in a bunch & catch him to his face. I am not afraid of the old beast, he can send me to the Head if he likes for making a fuss about it, but I have the right on my side so I dont care. Unfortunately he has chosen the wrong time to do all this as this term I have been very quiet in the house & not bunted* at all & so the sixth stuck up for me, the other night the head of the house went to him for something or other so the first thing Moor said to him was "Isn't Behrens a great nuisance in the House". So he said "not in the least", rather a snub for Moor. Then Moor tries to go for me because I had a good character from Mr Lynam, which said I had strength of character, so he tried to make out because I bunted with other fellows last term that it was being led by them & showed weakness of character, In fact he hates me as he shows in every way. He seems to think barging a very bad crime, at the same time there are many worse things, a little healthy bunting surely can do no harm, & if that were the worst thing that was done, the school might think itself well off. About this other row I have had with him; He drew all his reasons, from one day having seen me, when with someone else, who wanted* give something back to a boy in another study, just put my head in the study & go away with this other boy when he had given it back, I remember seeing him at the time. the other day one of the boys out of that study went to him to get some imposition paper & so Moor jawed him for his work, and asked if *I* ever went into their study & when he said "no" Moor didn't seem to beleive him & made him promise again, so hearing this I went & asked him what he meant by picking me out in this way for every thing that went wrong, so he got out of it by saying that he had mentioned my name *casualy* if you please, amongst the names of the two fellows in the next study, whom I rather like, & Moor said then that he never accused me of making a row there & that he had never mentioned barging; So afterwards I went again to the fellow who told me about it to see if he was sure about what he told me & he was. Now there was absolutely no reason for him telling me a lie, so I beleive it was quite true. What is one to do with such a man one cant get on equal terms with him. It is simply a loathsome hole this what I hate most is, (i) Every body is always suspected capable of doing any thing. (ii) people like Moor are always prowling about trying to get some one in a row & (iii) Moor's word is held worth anything, you can easily see that moor does not *beleive* one word you say. This is the same to a more or less degree in all the houses. Then in form it is simply loathsome some of the masters thank goodness only one who has any thing to do with me is like it, looking about every where all the time to catch some one cheating as though no one could be trusted, & always suspecting it is simply horrid to do work under such a man. I expect you will be getting weary of this long letter all grumbles you may say but it is quite true nevertheless.

You say you wish me to open out & confide in you, well I will but mind whatever I tell you is not expected to go beyond your ears, & if it does anyway not with my name *attatched* to it. What I am going to say, shall be said & I wont say any more about it, what I mean to say is that suppose you told moor or anyone else & they got hold of me & tried to pump me I shant tell them any thing, to you only will I say anything about it. First of all I dont know who told you or what you

heard about Marlborough. You must know that *all* Public schools are morally *weak* to a more or less degree. And it was just because I happened to know that Winchester was worse than a good many other schools, that since I had to be a boarder, I did not want to go there, that is also the reason I always thought & will think that it is better to be a day boy as one is less affected by it. It is impossible not to hear talk of this kind & it is even more impossible to remonstrate with it because in that case, one would be promptly cut by every body & in fact one could not stay at all without being utterly miserable if ever cut. It is evident that masters know as well as we do what goes on & they do what they can to stop it but they never will be able to stop it. Of course every one knows the worst sets & one need not have any thing to do with them, but If you wanted to have nothing to do with any one except those who were really "pi"* ones acquaintance would be limited to a *very few*. There is no more to say now, so goodbye dear Father from your loving Son
Tankred

[See additional letter 138A on p.276]

139 School House, Crick Road, Oxford

28.iii.94

My dear Tankred,

When do you break up? Game for a cruise this Easter? I leave Liverpool for Stornoway in a steamer about 5th or 6th of April & mean to cruise about N. of Scotland – Vassall will be with me but Church I am sorry to say is off to British Columbia to farm. I shall be delighted to give you a berth if you can come – for a week or 2 or 3 as you please –

We* had a grand picnic & expedition to Dorchester* on Friday – sausages &c – Do you see anything of Macfadyen? I hope he is getting on well – Jumma is farming in Isle of Man. Do you ever hear from him? How are the maths getting on?
Best love old chap
Yours ever C.C.Lynam

141

140   Newfield House, Forest Hill, Kent

30 March 94

My dear Son,

I was very pleased to receive your long letter of the 18th, postmark Clifton *27th*. Before I go into answering the different items, let me draw your attention to:

	individually	*knives*	*beginning*	*century*
	individually	*knives*	*beginning*	*century*
and *not*	individualy	knifes	begining	centuary
	thing	*practically*	*casually*	*believe*
and *not*	think	practicaly	casualy	beleive
	attached			
and *not*	attatched			

In an exam, mistakes with the above, will detract from Conic Sections. In order to save yourself much disappointment give the matter thought before it is too late. The foundation must be sound & for this reason I decide that *these* holidays you will do *Arithmetic* with Mr Edwards. 21 questions this term is a farce when it should have been 21 questions *per day* or the very least every 2 days. Bring your *German* Books with you, we could have a go for it. Who is your German Master? Please give me *his* name by *return*.

I too regretted that I could but find you the last moment at Aldershot, but no one could tell me at 3 o'clock where the Cliftonians were, when I asked. You might have lunched with us at Capt Hall's (of the 6th Warwickshire fusilier reg.)

The field day was highly interesting. Glorious as it may be to be with the victors, of course you remember that a well timed, strategic retreat requires equally good generalship & possesses its glory. – When you are at home & give me the ordre de bataille & dispositions we will then go into the tactics. As to the march past, none of the schools shone except the Cambridge bicycle-corps which I am told is composed of older fellows. There was a great lack in bearing & smartness throughout the schools. The worst figure, the boy-officers cut, with back up, belly out, knees asunder, about this form, most ludicrous!   the passing line instead of coming straight past the   standard came like this   or worse   Teach   your boys first bearing   then

Leu before the Franco-Prussian War

E N P M*oor*

proper marching by themselves, then in small groups & then in company form.. When approaching the first flag you may arrive in semicircle, ⟨ then the officer should give the command eyes right, ⟨ permits the semicircle then to straighten to the left, the legs from that moment must come at a tempo, like *one* step shot out of a gun & by the time you reach the saluting point the line should be as straight as a die.

It was impossible to discover you in the ranks. If I were you I would not rest until the Cliftonians earned the reputation of the crack regiment. Time spent in barging & bunting might be better & *advantageously* employed in this wholesome & manly exercise. The knife I made you a present of – Muzzle loaders unless of exquisite workmanship in stock & barrel & of artistic merit sell now always very cheaply. I should say your little rifle and the knife in exchange for the gun described, should be fair. Certainly write to Mr Zeiser "I.I.Zeiser junior Esq Nürnberg" you might have done so before & be able to write in German by yourself. I should say somewhat like this "werther Herr Zeiser Vergeben Sie mir, wann ich Ihnen erst heute für Ihre Güte & Gefälligkeit danke. Vater hat mir nämlich inzwischen ein Messer geschenkt & da ich mit meinem Budget haushälterisch vorgehen muß, so habe ich von einem Kauf vorerst abgesehen. Ich danke aber nichtsdestoweniger herzlich. Recht freundliche Grüße an frau Zeiser & Sie von Ihrem T.T.B. Clifton College.*

There are as you know state laws & social laws both of which should be observed. I may as capt or col at one time or another carry any private's gun, but that does not entitle the private to come & ask the Capt or Col to carry his gun – In the same way I may, doubtless have, & will write to you first, but it appears to me not appropriate for the son to say: "It seems as if you won't write to me first until I have written &c"

As to going away for our holidays, I have so far fixed on the summertime. The feeling existing between you & Moor is undesirable. You say barging & bunting is *your* nature & if any thing you instigate it, although the school considers it a crime? Will you please give me your definitions of "barging" & "bunting".

30.3.1894: 140 (LWFB to TTB)

Surely you have self command & won't take refuge under your nature? I feel convinced you would never in your life deviate from truth. I grant you, that a good joke with discretion is doing no harm, only on the other hand house orders *should* be obeyed & if I take to refuting there should be no exceptions in which Mr Moor is right. You ought to realize that a masters task is not all honey, you should assist in alleviating his burden & if, as you yourself say, the masters do their best as they are bound, to eradicate weak morality, by which they *must needs* exercise surveillance, you should not construe such unfairly. It is quite right that you do not bring a school-fellow into a row, but supposing *you* had been that school-fellow & seen the consequences you brought upon the other fellow, *then* I *expect from you* that you would manfully enter the arena & declare *before every one* that the fault is yours & yours alone, for which you will not permit another to suffer. Is that just & right or not? Never be a coward, neither physically, nor mentally! I take it from what you mentioned that the immorality only extends *to talk & not to acts*, am I right in this my presumption? I appreciate your remarks on Winchester & day boys, yet even amongst the latter, filthy talk, I am afraid, is not altogether avoided. Associating however, when you know it is not "pi" for reasons of fear to be cut by every body & possibly stand alone, would not be, in fact never was my style. I don't say act the horror-stricken-sanctimonious beast, no, simply avoid such society & when you come in contact with it remonstrate kindly that you have no pleasure in it, that if they care for you, they better leave such talk to when you are not there. Introduce a *healthy* atmosphere, be the leaven, rise to be future man! worthy of your country in every respect. What I have done in my school & youth days, you can do too – I had plenty of friends, some dearly attached, differing on the same point, yet never was there any smutty talk in my presence, because they knew I was not the man for that. Yet although I strongly disagreed there, they loved & seeked* me. Lay the foundation to a noble simple life, free from conceit & vanity, aspire above all to be first & foremost a man!

Write soon to Your loving
father Leu

When coming home, you will work with a will & heart, you are my man!

3.4.1894: 141 (TTB to LWFB)

141   34 College Rd, Clifton

3.4.94

Dear Father,

The reason of the letter being posted so late was that it took some time to write. "Knifes" "thing" & "attatched" must have been slips, my German master is Mr Morich the Head German master. Barging or Bunting consists of making any unnecessary row by generally kicking up a row by fighting (friendlily) & wrestling & scuffling about. I will explain about this & Moor when I come home. I quite agree with you that the mutual feeling between Moor & me is undesirable in fact it is simply loathsome to be in his house at all. And every one feels as I do on the subject. As to the other question you asked me, It does extend further than words. Anyone in the whole school from highest to lowest cannot help hearing of birchings & expulsions & what they are for. In the second place *everyone under Moor* is liable to suspicion & if a master suspects anyone he asks questions which show very plainly that he knows of the existence of it beyond words. The length to which it goes can never be known for although you cannot help knowing of what goes on if you have any thing to do with the higher fellows in the house, of course one has not any opportunity of judging as to the length to which it is carried on. However all this can better be explained when I come home.

So now good bye Dear Father from
your loving Son Tankred.

142   Clifton College, Clifton, Bristol

April. 6. 94

Dear Mr Behrens

I fear you will think I have been somewhat dilatory in answering your letter, but I was unwilling to answer in a hurry.

6.4.1894: 142 (ENPM to LWFB)

It is I fear undeniable that your son & I have been seriously at odds this term. I have had to speak to him more or less seriously more than once, and he has not taken it well. It is not with myself only that he has fallen out – you will see from his report which will reach you in a day or two that both Mr Hall and Mr Stevens are seriously dissatisfied with him. Yesterday he came to me for imposition paper to do 150 lines set by his German master for doing other work while in his German set – a very serious offence – and today I hear from his Latin tutor* that he has done an examination paper in Livy so badly that he must do it over again as a punishment. Also the VIth form have sent him up to me on one occasion for not doing an imposition set him by one of them. This is not a satisfactory record. As to his truthfulness I am not aware that I have accused him of untruthfulness – but this I admit, that when he is corrected he is so full of excuses that it becomes necessary to point out to him, as I have on more than one occasion, that *some* of his reasons are not valid, and are even trivial. I admit this also that his manner of self-justification is such that it sometimes provokes me by bordering on the insolent. I will only mention one instance. I showed him his last report before I sent it to you, & told him what I referred to, in a way which I may say I should not have taken the trouble to do to an ordinary boy, and shortly afterwards he came to my study & asked me what he was to say to you in explanation of his report. I think you will admit that this was slightly provoking. As to the barrier existing between us to which you refer, as I am not conscious of having set one up, I can hardly be expected to remove it. And I must plainly say both to you & him that until his whole attitude undergoes a change in the direction of more docility & patience under reproof, there is little chance of his making the best of his career here. There is much ability in the boy and a great deal that is good and excellent – no one is more conscious of it and grateful for it than I am, but he is very self-willed and self-righteous, and is too ready to take reproof as an insult. I am quite ready to be on the old terms with him as soon as ever he likes, but any advance from me to him in his present mood would only encourage him in what I consider his chief defect and do no permanent good to him.
[unsigned but in ENPM's hand]

143   [7.4.1894]*

[draft letter from LWFB written on letter 142] dr Mr Moor,
Your letter of the 6th was unfinished & unsigned; you have
evidently been interrupted? I am for the strongest discipline,
punishment if deserved but with strict justice, which
demands that the condemned should be heard. My boy says
that you practically accused him of telling lies. Now if I
asked you to remove *this* impression – (having ensured that
is no "advance"?) Reprove him by all means as much as
you think he deserves, punish him likewise but don't make
him think you consider him a liar when *you cannot prove* it.
You err very much if you believe that parental feelings
mislead me into enamourment with a boys thoughtless
notions or disobedience, I reprimanded him *before* your letter
came. Your remark "and I must plainly say both to you &
him &c &c" you will admit on reflection, is totally uncalled
for

144   34 College Road, Clifton

April. 9/94

Dear Mr Behrens

I am sorry my letter was unsigned – Could you send me
the 2nd sheet & then I can sign it and tell you whether it
is also unfinished. There were *two* sheets – the second of
which was written on one side only, as far as I remember.

I have had an interview with your boy and asked whether I
have accused him of lying. He refers to one occasion on which
I did not accept his excuses – & this apparently he interprets as
an accusation of lying. he says there were other occasions, but
he can't remember them. I do not think I need say more –
However I have asked him to try & refresh his memory before
post time & will let you know. He has just been in again and
the other instance he brings is that I disputed his statement that
it took him longer to dress and longer to write 100 lines than
the great majority of boys. He seems as far as I can see

to imagine that this also amounts to an accusation of lying – there are other occasions but he has not "such a prodigious memory as other boys" and cannot remember them he says. And it seems quite impossible to bring him to reason. I am very sorry – I hoped by giving him an opportunity of bringing me to book to clear away the clouds. I am very sorry that the remark of mine which you quote annoyed you and must ask you to accept my apologies.

I enclose your boy's school report* which will show you that others are equally tired of his habit of self-justification..
Yours very truly
E.N.P.Moor

145　9 The Avenue, Clifton

April 11th 1894

Dear Sir

I have had it in my mind to write to you for some little time, but I have been very busy & I was anxious not to trouble you needlessly.

I expect you will find from yr son's report that he has not been so steady over his work lately as he used to be, & from remarks made to me by other masters I do not see how his last report can possibly be wholly satisfactory. Though I am not yr son's form master* he does more work with me than with any one else, & I think it wd be unfair to you if I allowed the holidays to pass without pointing out that for some few weeks past there has been a most marked falling off in yr son's work, & there seems to be creeping over him an attitude of opposition that makes him most difficult to teach.

About a fortnight or three weeks ago, I was extremely displeased at some of his work & took him to task severely for it. Instead of taking my criticisms & strictures in the spirit in which they were meant he made matters worse by making excuses, & trying to defend what was one of the worst pieces

148

of mathematical work ever submitted to me. He took up such an attitude of indocility then that I told him it wd become necessary for me to write to you unless there was some change next term. Unfortunately the work of the past fortnight has not corrected the unfavourable impression I had formed but has rather increased it, & I sincerely hope that before another term begins yr parental advice may convince him of the folly of trying to take a line of his own in defiance of all the teaching & warning he gets from me. It is difficult to explain matters in a letter without making it very lengthy, but I may say there are certain recognised canons of good style, & "good form" in mathematical work – without appreciating these fundamental principles of style & method a boy may become a clever manipulator of symbols, but he cannot become a *Mathematician* in any real sense. Moreover, in working for a competitive exam it is of the utmost importance that good methods which conduce to accuracy & pace, shd be enforced.

After more than twenty years' experience I find it necessary to insist on certain things, & equally necessary to reject as intolerable certain other things. Again & again this term after explaining some new method, & enforcing a particular application of it, I have found yr boy *alone of the whole class* utterly ignoring my advice & sending up less satisfactory methods of his own. Even when there is a model worked out in his textbook for his imitation, & he is doing examples *exactly similar to those in the book*, he has often produced & sent up some extremely inferior solution of his own, utterly ignoring what all others in the class have appreciated & applied. What can I call this strange behaviour. Eccentric, it certainly is; but boys of his age who are learning the elements of their subject cannot afford to be eccentric. It is most suicidal, & most difficult to deal with, & the result of this term's work, as shewn by the exam, exhibits an unsatisfactory state of things. While others who have worked in the same class & had exactly the same teaching, have laid a good foundation for further work, yr son's knowledge seems to be unsound & chaotic & I fear until he unlearns some of his self-taught methods solid progress is impossible. Once more; in a certain class of examples there is a clumsy unscientific method which may be called "the refuge of the destitute" & shd never be tolerated by any one who aspires to become a mathematician. In the recent exam yr son (alone of all the class) adopted this method almost in every instance where it was possible. Perhaps he thinks that I am needlessly particular & full of fads. Let that be as it may, as long as he is in my hands he must put up with my "fads", for I certainly cannot allow his usual mode of working to go on unchecked during the remainder of his time under me as a Woolwich pupil. I may add that I shewed some of yr son's work to Mr Stevens in the recent exam. Mr Stevens' sole remark was brief but to the point. "Horrible" was his only comment, & I venture to say it wd have been endorsed by all my mathematical colleagues.*

I have dwelt at length on some peculiarities in mathematical work which have come prominently under my notice, but I regard these things rather as a symptom of *a state of mind* which gives me some uneasiness. Yr boy has considerable ability, but he is at present untrained, & at his age it is foolish in the last degree for him to set his opinion against that of men who learnt their subject, & had even taught it successfully before he was born. I happen to know that mine was not the only subject in this exam in which yr son's work was disappointing, &, without having any certain information on the matter, I am inclined to think that there must be some general cause for the recent falling off in steadiness & industry.

You might, for example, find out what sort of companions he associates with. This is a point on which his House-master Mr Moor might have something to say. It does not lie strictly within my province, but I am not unobservant, & I am disposed to think that in his House yr boy does not associate with those who are strenuous & conspicuous for industry & respect for discipline & school rules.

I hope you will forgive me for troubling you at such length. I have written in great haste among interruptions, as I am just starting for my holidays. If you can write to me before we begin work again I shall be found at

Sea View
Southerndown
Nr Bridgend, Glamorganshire
Yrs sincerely
H.S.Hall

146 4.5.94

[draft letter from LWFB to HSH] dr Mr Hall. I can but thank you most sincerely for your letter of the 11 April. I need hardly say, that the boy's ways cause me great grief & that I absolutely agree with & endorse what you say. being out of my sight at Clifton, I would deem it a great favour if you would exercise your hand over him, for from communication with him you are about the only one he cares for, reveres & esteems. Enforce a kind but firm hand over him & if he then won't alter, he will have to bend or break I have advised him sufficiently Industry strict respect for discipline, & rules are indispensable! He has great anxiety abt Woolwich, & feeling unhappy in his house partly because I think he cannot find the time there for study as he ought, he works himself into despair & apparently loses control over himself. In no way do I wish to put this forward as mitigation, I mention it merely as an observation made. – I waited until today to reply, not wishing to disturb your holiday. If you could spare a moment during the term to inform me how the boy is getting on I should feel grateful. Believe me, dear Mr Hall, Very sincerely.

147 May 5th 1894

[postscript from HSH to LWFB written on a copy of a printed circular letter* of 28.4.1894]

P.S. Many thanks for yr letter received this morning. You may rely upon my doing all I can to help yr boy on in every way. There is really no reason why he shd be despondent about himself – he is well started for his age, but he must learn to be *docile* or we shall be pulling different ways.

With regard to this German & Chemistry question,* as far as getting *into* Woolwich is concerned, there is really nothing to choose. *At* Woolwich the Chemistry people *may* have the advantage, but to what extent I cannot say. My circular letter is merely to inform parents, not to alarm them for I don't think there is any real cause for alarm. In yr boy's case the arguments for & against Chemistry are very evenly balanced. Probably German wd land him a little higher *at Entrance*, but we have the after course to think of. Please reply at once. Excuse haste – I am very busy. Shall be pleased to write again shortly & say how yr boy goes on.

148   Newfield House, Forest Hill, Kent

5.V.94

My dear Boy,

I have made you a present of the apparent steel* hand blunderbuss & put it in your cupboard in your room. Last night cousin Bella & her fiancé Mr Jones, a civil engineer, came to dinner. I was sorry you could not be here & hear Mr Jones express his regret at never having had the good fortune or chance like you viz to make for the Royal Engineers. He considers it worth the endurance of any burden & trouble to have such an opportunity offered to one by the parent. A life of hard work has convinced him & could he but have a chance now, he would give half his life. He is one of many who gained experience & paid for it. You know my idea & wish; *I* want *you* to *profit* from the experience of elders & keep *your* experience-powder dry for *further* researches. So pray execute my wishes *gladly* with a will, still better with enthusiasm! Find happiness in your work & think of the glorious trees & fruit I produced by the grafts. I hope to hear good news from you!

With love. Your affectionate
father Leu

6.5.1894: 149 (LWFB to HSH)

149   [6.5.1894]*

[draft letter from LWFB to HSH in reply to letter 147] dr Mr Hall, It seems to me as far as my boy is concerned he falls short of the needful 5 terms? I think he can do no better than continue his German under all circumstances. If you could see your way to let him take Chemistry *besides* as a *reward* for docility I am sure he would take to it with love as he does to mechanics at home. In my opinion he ought to do more athletics, exercise will enable him to take more work as relaxation & if properly planned would keep him out of barging & bunting

150   [8.5.1894]*

L.W.F.Behrens Esq*

Received your letter all right. Please tell Tyra I will write & answer her post card in full in a day or so. Please let me know when Dr Bücher replies. also let me have the letter from the man about the mussels when it comes. Also tell me *as soon* as the old second hand book spinster writes about that book if she does. I wrote to a man* to send the prices of the fancy pheasant's eggs, if you feel inclined to have a sitting & hatch them yourself. I will tell you which are the best for feathers. if not I will write & ask that boy I know if he has any to spare. anyway write & let me know. Tankred

151   Newfield House, Forest Hill, Kent

11.V.94

My dear Boy,

Dr Bücher asks what you want his regular* for, he can send forward a Kilo for 5/- &c. – I shall reply in your name that is to say from you. The mussel-man has so far not written neither the spinster bookseller. The latter has neither sense nor sentiment; & money is her parole.* Enclosed the letter from Macarthey I daresay you can do much better otherwise I should prefer a golden pheasant cock to breed from with game hens, or even try a sitting of pheasants eggs. – I hope you are well & delighting in your studies. I asked Mr Hall to see whether he could not manage to let you have Chemistry *extra* (besides German) as a *reward* if you did well otherwise, feeling sure that it will be most *rivetting to you*, the way I know you. Best wishes from

your loving pater
Leu

152   34 College Rd, Clifton

Sat. 12. May. 94

My Dear Father

Your letter is very hard to read I am sending you it to send it back & tell me what the words underlined are. as regards Dr Bücher if that is 5/- a Kilo do let him send me a kilo to try as one would use it very slowly, a little going a long way. I cant read the word underlined but I suppose it is "Rugal"* It is stuff for restoring rusty things to their original form provided the rust has not flaked of if this is what he tells you the price for do let us have some.

Do ask mother to drop the mussel man a card in my name & ask him if he ever recieved my letter if he did not I enclose a list of the questions which I want mother to write again to him as she did in the last letter. Ask her to be very careful to keep the copy I send her. In case we cant* get the book from the spinster would you give her the price for it. I believe it is cheap at this price, of course we would have it on approval first. As to the pheasants I am sending you some other advertisements. of course, we would want the golden & coloured pheasants only for their feathers. I will write again

154

soon but do send me some stamps as this is my last
so good bye dear Father
from your loving
Tankred

We have two Holidays on Commemoration, 22 & 23 Fri. &
Sat in June are you Coming down

153   Easthill House, Mundesley, North Walsham, Norfolk

May 19th 94

My Dear Boy.

If you write to me here it will be a great pleasure to me
to hear from you. Dear Grandma needed a change very
much & so did I. so we came here yesterday together.

It is a most breezy bracing place – flat sands – dry when
the tide is out – washing the foot of low cliffs on which it
constantly encroaches. I can only see three boats drawn up
on the beach & so far I have gathered that lines are put
out for soles – nets for herrings & also crab pots are also
put out. This is five miles from North Walsham, to & from
which runs one daily omnibus now & two in July. The
church is a part of an old ruin covered in in the beginning
of this century. I only wish I could send you some of this
invigorating North Sea air – you would be a different
being. I feel myself so much better in it – no heaviness or
limpness. It would be a grand thing for Clifton Coll. if
they were here – but it is no use to say such a thing – it
is only a reflection of mine. We have a fire here & sit in
warm cloaks in our breezy apartment – rather a change
from tea in the garden at Newfield – which looked most
smiling as I left it on Friday & the rhododendrons just
coming into Bloom & here the lilacs are still in full flower
– I gave those school books of yours to your father to send
you – before I left. I do not know how many days I shall
stay will write again soon am off to post this myself – My
love to and prayers for you my dear Boy Always your
loving mother
Min

154   Newfield House, Forest Hill, Kent

19 V 94

My dear Boy,

Just a line to send you some stamps. I intend writing to you to-night exhaustively. I forward books & chain at same time. Spall claimed from me 11d. & 6d. on your a/c which I paid, for forwarding of gun etc eg "Some of those odd 6d. & Shillings", I suppose it is allright –
                                   Affectionately your
                                             father Leu

155   Newfield House, Forest Hill, Kent

23.V.94

My dear Boy,

Your letter of the 12th did *not* contain the mussel-questions. Nevertheless I handed your letter to your mother. whether she has written to the mussel-man I cannot say. she is gone with your grandmother to Mundesley. When time permits I will have a wooden press made for Tyra, the copying press is too heavy & unsuitable* piece of machinery for the purpose –

So far from the Canon no answer. If we cannot have his house during your holidays, I don't see how we two can go there.* Enclosure from Roberts came today. As your mother takes her holidays with her mother & wishes the children & fräulein to go to Mundesley after her return, it really becomes simply a question concerning Tyra, you & myself as to holidays. One can spend them at home, there will be plenty ready & plenty to do for enjoyment either way. For Iceland it is too late, there we ought to go in June. The Rhine is open to us, yet my budget for this year does not include travelling on the Continent for 3 & I must say I don't like dear Tyra to be done out of her holidays & we two going alone even if we roughed

23.5.1894: 155 (LWFB to TTB)

it. Verrons! Kommt Zeit, Kommt Rath. [We'll see! With time comes counsel] I feel inclined to come to Clifton for Commemoration, tell me the *last time* for applying for *tickets*, if I come I may perhaps bring Mr Edwards.

Pheasants. What I would like, must be golden sort, a cock & a hen bird, *not* related. Unfortunately I know no one keeping or rearing pheasants; to rear from 2 different sittings is too cumbersome & unprofitable. Can you tell me *where* you put the *african* maps? You had 2 & I gave you "several" *detail* maps from african companies –

The other day I saw with Burger the heating & welding of Iron in water by electricity. I enclose you a detailed description which will be of interest to you. It is clear to me that the 20th Century belongs to Electricity; for nobody can yet see the far reaching consequences of this invention. Why the Smithy of the future might, so to say, be conducted in a drawing room & sunken costly ironclads* they will be lifted; we heat weld, bolt & hammer with water, repair the leak, if necessary put a new steel armour on her, all with ease & comfort! And i Mathematics and 2 Languages and 3 Engineering, comprising electrical engineering & Knowledge of Chemistry, a future ought to be secured!

I am anxious to hear from you how you are getting on now. Inform me as to your work & doing. Everything interests me concerning you, in order to insure your success in life. Do take physical exercise, drill or games, you will work all the freer mentally. Do your best in everything you undertake, work for the sake of the matter, remember that you don't work for your masters, but for yourself; be one who confers lustre upon his country, not on whom the country confers lustre. Best wishes from
your loving father
Leu

156   East Hill House, Mundesley, N.Walsham

May 30th 94

My Dear Boy,

I have been longing for a letter from you ever since I came here & am still hoping for it each time the Post comes in. The air here & everything suits both dear Grandma & me so well that we thought it a pity to leave so soon. we hope to stay yet another week. It was so rough until yesterday that no boats put out but yesterday I saw two boatmen drawing in a boat rather like Roberts' boat so I waited for them to come up the cliff & had a talk with one of them – a very nice fellow – he said he worked with his brother – & there was only one other pair who got their living by fishing in Mundesley – he had just been to see his crab pots after the storm & had lost 6 – they cost 6/- each (without their labour) & are partly of iron not like the Cornish pots –

He goes out herring fishing in the Autumn, they go up about to Aberdeen & then follow the fish southwards. The French have much larger boats & heavier gear & catch about 10 to our one – Is that not foolish of us? I mean, not to improve our boats & gear – that is so – but I can scarcely credit it! I asked him what he would charge to do for us what Roberts does – & he is going to think about it. He said "not much" they had "no charge & were always satisfied with what the visitors gave them". I counted 93 boats in sight on the sea – larger than fishing boats, all at one time suddenly – & he said they were traders – who had put into some port during the Storm & went on now the calm set in, they were all going northward mostly with three masts, & in the front three little gib* sails.

You cannot think how much benefit I feel from this thorough change & how much I needed it. It is just what you would wish for me I know. I have taken several good tramps by myself (as grannie cannot walk far) in different directions.

The neighbourhood is very pretty I think, long winding country roads & lanes between flowering hedgerows – most picturesque snug villages – dotted about near to one another –

the ground well tilled. I read that farming is well understood, that by bringing up the marl they improved the sandy soil – & the crop rotation (obviating the fallow year) was first introduced here & called the Norfolk system.* What a contrast such a countryside to poor ould Ireland with its disorderly or ruined cottages & farms.

The sea encroaches here & there are only three breakwaters which I was surprized to see cost £430 to place though merely of wood. I wish we could have a few tramps here together. On Sunday afternoon found myself at a pretty church in the midst of a little wood – & walking round it smelling some lovely roses climbing up the walls – I heard a murmuring sound through the open window & found the service going on. – so I sat down in the porch & looked out on the trees & sky smelt the fragrance of the wallflowers & heard the birds singing without & the anthems sung within the church – it was an exquisite combination.

Now dear old boy – I am telling you all of myself & this place – now do write & tell me all about yourself & that place, any little everyday thing – which to you seems trifling, would *greatly interest me.* Who shares your study, for instance – & what kind of atmosphere you are in now compared with last term – God bless you my dear boy now & for ever. Love & hugs from your fond mother
                    Min.

I do not know if there is any reply from the Canon – After this rest, I would feel more equal myself for a visit to Bessy's Cove.

157   Newfield

31 V 94

My dear Boy,

I wait to hear from you – The enclosed should interest you. The Germans have less bounce but more head –

4.6.1894: 158 (TTB to LWFB)

The dark room is splendidly finished.
Your loving father
    Leu

158   34 College Rd, Clifton

June 4. 94

My Dear Father

I hope you are quite well. I am sorry I have not written before but I have had really no time. If the Canon has not written why not write to him again perhaps he never recieved your letter at all. Do Try & get the house I do so want to go. Thanks for the parcel, stamps, & cuttings & newspaper. I hope you are getting the stuff from Dr Bucher. As to the Pheasants, Surely in the cutting I sent you, you could find what you wanted. The money you gave Spall is all right. I will write in detail as soon as I can possibly find time.
                    Your loving Son
                        Tankred.

159   Newfield House

7.V.94

My dear Boy

from your letter of the 4th I see you are allright in health and trust doing well at studies?

Your mother is coming home to night, so we shall see what to do abt the Canon – & let you know. – Dr Bücher is sending the stuff with advice as to application.

With your next letter, I await your reply as to the diff questions, which you will not overlook.
                    Best wishes from your
                        attached father Leu

8.6.1894: 160 (LWFB to TTB)

No letter yet from your Mussel-man don't know if your mother wrote

160　8 VI 94

My dear Son,

Mrs Moor has asked us for the Commemoration & we mean to go. It will be for you to secure in time a decent bed room for your mother & self at the Hotel I was at before with Mr Edwards, I believe the Royal?* I shall let you know before, when we are coming, perhaps we may turn up a day before & have a look at the surrounding country.

Your mother, I must say dear,* arrived last night in first class health & look. I am very pleased to say she is happy which is certainly very pleasing news for you too. Enclosure re some fishing Services would appear a gold mine to a reader who believes it tale quale*

Kind greetings from your
father Leu

161　Newfield

Friday June 8th

My Dear Boy

I have just read your dear Fathers letter. He received me very kindly with Tyra & Lilian at Liverpool St Station last night which made me happy & gives me some hopes of a good time coming. I say this because I know you will be glad I have asked him to send you a cheque for one pound. I am glad for you to buy good grub but not to waste it on anything which does you no manner of good.

At the Hotel you must say your parents are coming for commemoration & you want a nice bedroom for them – the invitation to us is from the ladies of Clifton College for the Reception in the Council Room* on June 22nd at 8.30.p.m –

Acquaint yourself thoroughly with everything that is to be done there before & after – so that we may have a very nice & profitable visit – We might come a day or two or three before & make some excursions either with or without you

> yr loving mother Min.

Steadily & well with the cheque which you must endorse by writing your name on the back.

162 15 VI 94

My dear Boy

This morning I received your report.* I am glad it is better & I don't wish to withhold from you your mother & your father's joy thereat. It is a ray of sunshine, it gives me hope to see yet the fondest idea of my life carried out, viz to see you a happy man, strongly rooted in humanity's greatest nobility, sound Knowledge, a square heart for humanity, unfettered by sentimentality or false ambition, free from all vanity, taking our creator & his laws for our support! So an improving dear Son of mine, file off the inaccuracies of style, let us have a clean surface, a clean platform, such must be the foundation of real wealth. What you learn, you learn for yourself & I rejoice at the accumulation of such fortune! With a manly embrace

> your loving father
> Leu

163   34 College Rd

17.6.94

My dear Father,

Thanks very much for the 1£ & the letters to hand. I have
not yet ordered a room at the Hotel as I dont know when
you are coming. When you come please bring some tooth
powder as mine is already exhausted, if there are a pair of
mocassins my size at home, that is a little smaller than yours,
do bring them & if not do write to America for some as
mine are in holes, then get me some (2 or 3) black silk ties,
not satin, you know what I mean, usable on both sides &
about so ========================= broad. Then
if there is time let Batzer* make me a pair of light, *quiet*
trousers, a little larger than the last he made for me, I think
he can do that all right, but he can surely do it before you
come if he makes haste, but any way I want you to see that
they are all right before they are sent to me, I have only
one pair of trousers my others are worn through the seat, I
know I am bothering you a great deal but I hope you will
be able to do it. The African maps are on the left hand top
shelf in my book-case with the other atlases. We can talk the
other things over when you come down, I am making a list
of them not to forget them. So good bye ever your loving
Son Tankred

164   19.VI.94

My dear Boy

Tyra & I chose a pair of trousers for you like the attached
pattern. Batzer will send you the trousers tomorrow afternoon
so that you receive them on Thursday morning. Enclosed a
tie, another one I leave here. I wish *you particularly* to *attend*
the Commemoration this year, whether *we come or not*, mind!
The franchise question* has anew overcast the sunny sky I
thought at last arrived, so our coming, as many other things

have become questionable.* Do go all *the same* by yourself, I
will be with you in spirit
Your loving & unfortunate
father Leu

165   Newfield House, Forest Hill, Kent

25/VI 94

My dear Boy,

we reached home safely. Enclosed letter from* Roberts, read
& post it, making such additions as you might like. with
love
your father
Leu

[addition in EFB's hand] Tyra was enchanted with your
present, she thinks it lovely – we both send you our love &
a *screuge!*

166   The College, Clifton. Secretary's Office

29th June 1894

Dear Sir

I have the pleasure to inform you that I have today handed
to your son a cheque for £50 being the year's payment of
the Scholarship* gained by him at Midsummer last.
I am
Dear Sir
Yours faithfully
W.D.L.Macpherson.Secretary

W D L Macpherson

E J Barff

A E Hillard

G W C Hutchinson

O Siepmann   *E H C Smith*

G H Wollaston
(portrait presented 1899)

167   34 College Rd, Clifton

July 10.* 94

Dearest father

I cant find any questions in your back letters to answer yet.
1 = What about Bessy's Cove? 2 = Has mother written to
the mussel-man? 3 = Have all the guns returned from the
gun makers. 4 = Has Smith made my Taxidermy box, &
had the knives ground. Has he done the other little things
I asked him to do for me. If we cant go to the Cove,
what are we going to do in the holidays. We come back
exactly three weeks today. I have not forgotten about the
plant. I am sending you some cuttings which may interest
you, & the Cheque.
                    ever your loving Son Tankred.

168   10.VII.94

My dear Boy,

We have no news from you – Perhaps we shall manage
Bessy's Cove yet somehow.

Don't you forget to bring home my letters to show *you which*
questions you left *un*answered.

Why don't you send the cheque? the College informed me
they had handed *it to you*. Write!
                    Your loving father
                              Leu

169   Newfield

July 10th 94

My Dear Boy

We cannot think what is becoming of you as you do not write.

I should like to know when your exam is or was! We are comparatively very quiet here as the boys are still at Mundesley they enjoy it very much, & write us nice letters in English & German. Roy wrote in german last time & Fräulein said he was so annoyed because he intended writing in English to find he had written in German. We are still corresponding about Bessy's Cove but I am afraid if we do get Harry's Cottage it will be in a poor state. neglected & anyhow. I have just written to Baxter about the mussel seed – written the questions on separate paper, leaving room for the answers – and asked him to return it filled up by his manager

Spall & Smith are moving the studio furniture into the new studio to-day – collected from different parts of the house – I have not seen it yet but am afraid it will be rather full – however it is a step in the right direction!

The holidays are very near now. One always seems hurrying from one thing to another. I enclose five shillings for you dear. do not spend it on anything *un*wholesome – Tyra is I think beginning to progress. She has usually a hospital – we now have a sparrow rescued from the cat & a starling (in the parrot cage) which I picked up on Sunday morning early in the glass studio.* It seemed exhausted – I picked it up myself, though I did not like the sensation. I am afraid it will not get on very well. Pray do not let your 50£ cheque lie about or be lost. Love & kisses dear Boy from
Your fond Mother
Min

have you been to the Owens again Perks was pleased you went & we called*

170   Newfield

11 July 94

My dear old Boy,

Your lines of yesterday (evidently predated?) came in my possession the 9th evening with accompanying cheque. When

Vine house: Newfield

Capt Harry Richards

12.7.1894: 171 (HR to EFB)

you bring my letters I shall show you the questions. We are in correspondence abt Harry's cottage, I suppose we would have to furnish it from Truro. Mother, I fancy wrote to the Musselman. The guns are all at home, I did not get the cartridge filler, if we want it, we can have it at a moment's notice. Smith has not been able to do the odd things for you, but don't let that bother you, it will be all right. If we do not manage Bessy's Cove, rest content, we mean to make the best of it in some other shape. What I fear is the awful bustle when we go, & all is to be got ready in a day or two. I rely upon your undertaking my share. I am anxiously waiting for the plants.

Pheasants, I do not wish to pay as much as 15/- for a cock or anything like it. I was waiting to see whether you got some from your friends. don't the Owens keep pheasants?
Your loving father
Leu

171   Bessy's Cove

12th July/94

To Mrs Behrens – Madam,

In reply to your letter of today – respecting Cliff Cottage, Mr Nighton informs me that he intends keeping it solely.
Thanking you, I am Madam
Yours respectfully
H.Richards

172   34 College Rd, Clifton

July 13th 94

My Dear Father

I hope you have not forgotten those papers you were going to find for Mr Hall.

13.7.1894: 173 (LWFB to TTB)

I enclose the name of that plant* & am probably going to be given some seed, it comes from the Caucasus. Do let me know directly you know if we can have Harry's cottage as then I will at once write to Roberts about our tackle. My July Progress has not yet come, have you renewed the subscription. No the letter you received was posted at 8.30 am Monday morning the 9th.* I wont forget to bring the file home.

I want Stoneham* to get me all the parts of the following book that are out & to go on sending the parts to Newfield as they come out.

Published monthly 1/-
The Royal Natural History
Edited by R.Laydekker. BA. FGS. FZS.
Published by Fredrick Warne & Co
Chandos House, Bedford St, Strand

You pay for it now, I will give you the money when I come home. Make haste & get it or the parts already out will become dearer.

The owens do not keep pheasants. As for *Golden Pheasants* you wont get any cheaper if so cheap except from a Bankrupt. However I will write to my friend about them.

When I sent you the other advertisement about Pheasants, I sent it because it was from a man at Croydon* whom we could at any time go & see. I think I sent you it did I not? I will write to mother as soon as I can in the mean time dont forget to ask her to hurry up the Musselman. Ever your loving

Son Tankred.

Please send 6 stamps. This is my last.

173   Newfield

13 VII 94

My dear Boy

Read the enclosed.* I am truly sorry – what we are going to

do I cannot say yet. If we look up other places we shall not get our sea fishing. What do you say of trying Sennen?* write

Your father
Leu

174   [14.7.1894]* Saturday, 8.45.AM

L.F.W.Behrens Esq*

Why should we "cut off our noses". Could we not make a last bid for Mrs Gards at the cove. At Sennen we should get very little boating, you know the Major's went there. Scilly would be much better than that. The idea of having a cornish boat or yacht would be nice but would only do for you and me. I cant think of any other place besides these in the united kingdom. The Continent seems the only place to look for some other place for spending our holidays.

Will write longer on Sunday [unsigned but in TTB's hand].

175   Saturday. 14 July

L.W.F.Behrens Esq*

I have seen Mr Wollaston about the plant. He says he had better cut a bit off his big plant in the autumn after the holidays & then give it me So will get it alright, he also asked me to take you to see him when you come down when he will gladly give you bits of any plants you like as you take an interest in gardening, he is a botanist & naturalist in general & so he has a good many other rare plants in his garden.

Tankred.

176   Newfield House, Forest Hill, Kent

16.VII.94

My dear Boy,

I had truly forgotten the papers for Mr Hall & thank you for your reminder, I am hunting the papers up & shall write to Mr Hall the moment I possess them.

I am looking out for the plants you were going to send* & hope for a seedling (sucker or cutting) from the Crambe cordifolia, if impossible then *seed*, but I would *prefer* the others.

July Progress presumably *now* in your hands? Subscription is paid. The Natural History will be attended to. All pheasant papers are in your room, if we cannot get the pair of golden at a chance price, we must forego them. So far no reply from the Musselman; shall ask your dear mother to write again. Enclosed 6 Stps.

And now my dearest son I come to an important part, viz your Postcard of Saturday.* You wish me "not to cut off our noses" & make a "last bid for Mrs G". I am convinced you wrote in a hurry without giving the expressed matter reflection? It was the Ego which spoke & the brain had no voice! Honour must be untarnished! – A man is but a man when he can conscientiously self-respect himself, when his unobservable thoughts & actions are spotless. My dear Boy sink the Ego, burn the bridge & advocate the cutting off of noses whenever we are in doubt as to what is the honourable. Be abstract in judging "your" actions & thoughts, don't claim clemency from yourself or others, yet be clement to others. I want to see you a man with *absolute* control over himself & if I attach such great importance to that control it is because I consider it the Keystone to all bodily & mental happiness in which no person can have more interest than your wellwisher, your truest friend, your father. Cultivate therefore the inner man, radiate from within. The struggle in life demands protection of the Ego, no soiling.

Don't worry about the holidays. I have writen to Harry today, if that fails we shall endeavour to dispose of the holidays in the next possible profitable way.

Ever your loving father
Leu

177   [17.7.1894]*

My Dear Father,

I dont quite understand what was the matter with my postcard. I expressed the same thing when you came down here* & you did not say anything? Do explain more fully.

In what way would our honour be tarnished by trying again to get Mrs G's house. I can't see so do explain. ever your loving Son

Tankred

178   34 College Rd, Clifton

Sunday 22 July 94

My Dear Father

Why dont you write? Did you receive my post card?* Do write soon

Your loving Son
Tankred

179   Newfield

July 24th 94

My Blessed Boy,

I have only just noticed that *this* is your birthday.

Actually I have thought of it often but forgotten it was so very near.

Dear precious! I wish you & so we all do All happiness & goodness & gifts – that you may be a good upright noble useful man & that the world may some day be somewhat the better because you lived in it. and that *we* may always love one another more & more until death part us is the constant prayer of your

loving mother
Min.

We think you would like a pocket magnifying glass to carry about with you for a birthday present & propose giving one to you. I know your father & Tyra will write when I tell them

180   Newfield House, Forest Hill, Kent

24 July 94

My dear Son,

Foremost my best wishes for your birthday! A fathers prayers for blessings upon a beloved Son, they are yours! Try & be a truly true man, from top to toe! When the Sun smiles upon you, when success is yours, remain modest ever, & when disappointment frowns, be brave & strong, carry the burden without loss of love for nature, in whose book you will always find consolation & strength. I should like to bequeath to you my Glaubensbekenntnis [avowal of belief] to be handed on for generations to come, "Strong in ourselves, working from within".

Thank Mr Wollaston in my name for his kindliness, perhaps if he comes to London during the holidays & we are at home, he would spend a day with us, pray write him from us.

The musselman's answer, enclosed.

25.7.1894: 181 (TTB to LWFB)

I am afraid you made a miscalculation with your Scholarship; the Same carries you to July 95,* & if you do not pass then, but only in Novb 95, you will be 6 months without one, it be* then that you worked up for Woolwich & a Scholarship in July 95. – *I* would have secured one this July.* Mind the "style". If anything floors you it will be that "style" unless you take it *seriously* to heart. There is still time, but you should determine on it, from *this* minute & being so easy, you should *dictate* it to your mind & body & keep it with *a will* under control.

I am unaware that you mentioned Mrs Gard's house, during our presence at Clifton, had I heard it, I would have replied as before. Mrs G's behaviour was unworthy of our taking any further notice of her, certainly never when it demanded a forgetting from our side, because we would have in that instance been guided by selfish motives. I don't say do not forgive, but do not then be lead by ego –

I look forward with pleasure of seeing you soon.
Your affectionate
father Leu

[addition in TyTB's hand] dearest Tankred I am sorry not to have written for your Birthday but I only knew in the morning. I have got a canary. with heaps of love & kisses your loving Sis.

181   [25.7.1894]*

L.W.F.Behrens Esq*

as you say nothing of Cornwall I suppose the last letter* was of no avail? I cant read what Tyra wrote on your letter. The Scholarship would anyhow be no good for ½ a year, you would not get anything. What do you think of doing in the Holidays?
Tankred

182   Newfield House, Forest Hill, Kent

30 VII 94

My dear Boy,

The man's wife* refused to let us have the cottage; so Harry wrote. It is unfortunate & regrettable! As to what should be our next moves I cannot exactly define for the moment. You will be home to morrow, we will then go into it *at once* in all its length & breadth.

So until to morrow

Your loving father
Leu

183   22.8.94

[draft letter from LWFB to HSH] Dr Mr Hall, My boy found himself, last term, unable to follow you in Mathematics, as he thinks he ought in order to make sound progress & his idea is, he must not trouble you with questions.   Would you pray tell me, whether you consider the boy at the end of his tether* or if you believe that next term he will be able to follow? Hoping you have finer holiday weather than we have, I am very sny yrs LWFB

184   Clifton

Aug 23rd

Dear Mr Behrens

I am sure you need not fret about yr boy's Mathematics. He is young in comparison with others in his Set & if he sticks to his work, he will do very well, I have no doubt. He must not be afraid of asking questions – I don't mind it in the least so

174

long as the questions are relevant & to the point; sometimes questions are asked not in the proper spirit of enquiry, but in an argumentative dissatisfied manner. *This kind of thing* I feel bound to repress; it wastes time & serves no good purpose.

I am just home for a day or two – but am off again to-morrow. We have had very rough weather but not much rain.

Yrs sincerely

H.S.Hall

NEW TERM BEGINS

185   Newfield House, Forest Hill

Sunday Sept 23rd 94

Dearest Tankred

It is so very dull with out you, I do wish you were here. The Shrattenholz's are going to come to dinner to night & are going to play afterwards so Mother has asked The Parnells the Owsleys & Mr Schlund to come in after dinner. Sibyl came to tea yesterday, my room dose look so nice Smith has just put the pictures up. If you find any time to write please do.

What is your school like this term I hope it is nicer than usual. We all think Roy is very much like you now he has his hair short,* they are both getting on very well at school* I think. I am sending you a little pin cussion I hope you will like it

from your loving

Sis.

186   Newfield House, Forest Hill

Sunday 23rd – 94

Dear Tankred

We are all so sorry you are gone. Such a "lot of pears & apples" have fallen down lately, yesterday we picked up three bushels on the ground. Father is chiseling some very funny drawings wich he took from Seven churches* Ireland on the studio.* What is the weather like in Clifton it is dreadful here. I realy have no more to say & I also feel rather lazy so with best love from Roy & the rest

From your loving brother

Brian

187   34 College Rd, Clifton

Sept. 24. 94

My Dear Mother

I have got out of my form & also out of my French & German Sets & I may have got out of my Latin Set but that I dont know yet.* I have also not got a Study to myself. It is an awful swindle, Moor has given it to a fellow who has absolutely no right to it before me except that he has been longer in the house, I have been longer in the 5th form than he & I am also a form higher than he which ought to count more as he is on the modern side & I am on the military where it is much harder to get up. It is really impossible to do any *real hard* work when in a two study. You see the other fellow likes to have other people in to talk to & then one can't work. You see I don't allude to the actual preparation hours, but by *work hard* I mean do a little work for oneself out of school hours, & that one can easily do when in a one study, because there is never anyone to interrupt you unless of one's own free will. However here it is & it can't be altered this term so it is no good saying anything about it. But it is very unfair particularly as he has only to pass Smalls* at Oxford & I have to go to Woolwich.

Can I have leave to get a racquet to play racquets* with, I believe they cost about 15/-. If you don't feel inclined to pay for it, I mean you & Father, I shall pay for it, it is not necessary to send the money I can get & order here & put it down in the bill. I will write again soon, so good bye dear Mother

From your loving Son Tankred

188   Newfield

24 IX 94

My dear Son,

When difficulties are put in our way we neither despond nor grone! I say, we are *not* going to be done out of Woolwich. It is our privilege, to meet obstacles manfully, unhesitatingly & determinedly! What are you to do?

My advice is this. – You speak straight out to the "other fellow" of your study like this. Look here I have to work & mean to work. If you are going to have others in here, it will disturb my studies & we are *not* going to bring this matter before Mr Moor, but settle it *ourselves* like men. Let us arrange to have your friends here when it cannot harm my work. It has to be done, peacefully – if impossible then war.

Your loving father
Leu

189   34 College Rd, Clifton

Sept 30 – Aug* 1 94

My Dear Father.

thanks so much for your letter. I wish you would write to Mr Hall to make quite sure when I am going up for my Exam. Also ask him about the German & Chemistry if I could not do some Chemistry. And ask him if it is still so that if you go in on Chemistry you have to learn German there & if you go in on German you have to learn Chem there. I got out of my form & am now in the upper 5th Military. 5x. & I also got out of all my sets, so I am now am in the top set of all my work except French for which I am in the 2d. I do French & German with a German who comes from Elsass,* Otto Siepmann, I like his way of teaching better than that of any of the other modern language masters, it is more systematic.

8.10.1894: 190 (EFB to TTB)

How are Brian & Roy getting on.* "Learn hard & play hard" is going to be my motto this term. You dont seem to have understood abt the Study it is not from the fault of my companion, that was settled alright long ago; But however quiet & obliging he may be does not alter the fact that one can work *much* better in a one study. The fact is, I have been meanly cheated out of *my right* by the old hound,* I could give him a good hiding for it, it is simply his partiality for the other boy. What did he write about the anklets.

The only fault about my companion* leaves his books all about the study & if he wont pick them up nothing, no fighting would make him pick them up, he is about as obstinate as I am, & I dont like to pick them up for him, that is lowering myself. I have more to say but will write it in another letter as I have no time to write more now. So good bye dear Father from

your loving Son
Tankred

190   Newfield

Oct 8th 94

My Darling Boy,

This afternoon I sent you the rough proofs to look at & to hear what you think of them – The proof of Roy's photo in the high chair was the first they sent – but as the hair* was not visible & the expression bad, I asked for another & received the other – I have also asked to see rough proofs of the others. Let me have them all back at once. I hope you will be able to print the photo *well* you took of Roy in his hair just before it was cut.

Mr Edwards is giving Tyra her lesson & I am sitting with her hence this paper. – Emma intends returning home on Wednesday. Ever since you left dear, I have been immensely busy – arranging everything before the new maids came & I could not go about with Emma – in fact she helped very much & we all worked hard – but since Oct 1st when the new cook came we have been sight-seeing – playing hard, as you call it – & I have at last seen the Natural History Museum.* Really a beautiful place – one might spend months or years studying there. I hope we shall go there together.

We also went to the British Museum where there is a great improvement in all the arrangements so many interesting things are visible now which I suppose were formerly buried for want of room.

It is amazing the quantity of stolen goods* there collected together. The only balm to one's national conscience is to feel that they are any way preserved there for the scientists of all future ages.

Our dear small boys seem to be getting on nicely at their respective schools. Your father & I called on Mr Bryer to tell him we considered the lessons of the class to many & too advanced not only for Brian but for far older boys & also to tell him about the boy who bullied Brian & who took all his things & who actually told Brian if he (Brian) did not give him his chain he would tell Mr Bryer. Poor Brian believed he would get into trouble – The result of our visit was that the work of the whole class was reduced & the boy in question brought to order – Brians work now sits lightly upon him as Roy's does & both are very happy & look better in health, rounder & stronger & both more manly. They have each had a new acquaintance to tea. My next move is to see particularly about the games, as I think that part of their education most important, just as you do – I am very glad you have got out of all your sets (but French) & that "work hard & play hard" is your motto this term. Find a little time to write to me dear Boy for it is such a pleasure to me to have your letters – I do not write to you so often as I would because I too often feel too preoccupied & harrassed to write to you as I would like to do my dearest Boy – but I hope my household will go better now & that I shall contrive to get some time for myself & thoughts.

14.10.1894: 191 (TyTB to TTB)

When I hear Egouagya's lessons I do so wish I had had them myself, I would fain devote some years now to a training in classics & mathematics. I am ever so glad that you have a bent for the latter, it is a great satisfaction to me. The gong rings

love & hugs from your fond

mother Min

191   Oct 14th 1894

Dearest Tankred

I am very sorry not to have written for so long. aunt Emma has gone, we were all so sorry. Have'nt you had time to write to me yet? please do when you have time. Mother & father have just got Edith Owsley's wedding present it is 12 knives & falks for fish or dessert, they are very nice, I have made her a sideboard cloth with the inishalls in the middle

Mr Bird came to dinner yesterday, we all thought him very nice Roy is very fond of him. When do you come back?   I do wish you did not go to school. Do you know my canary has not begun to sing yet. We all send our best love to you & hope you are getting on all right   (I cant do it

your loving sis   properly)

Tyra

192   34 College Rd, Clifton

Sun. 14. Oct 94

My Dear Father,

Do write. I am sending you a small drawing (from nature). The drawing master* says it is rather good, But I must say I

180

cant see that it is, but as I know you like to see anything
that I have drawn, I send it you. I have a great deal of
work to do now, but I cant get down as well as I should
like, because I am in a two study, It cant be helped
though, I have arranged it as well as possible with the
other boy, & I am sure he is as equable as possible. thanks
for the paper, It was very interesting. Have you got the
distilling machine yet? Has Smith done my camera, & made
the dark room light tight yet. There is really no more just
now to say, but I will always write as often as I can, so
good bye dear father from your loving
Son Tankred.

Tell Smith to look in my Dark room. On the bottom big
shelf of all he will find a 7lb packet of Hypo.* tell him to
put it *at once* into the big jar that stands underneath & cork
it up.

193 Oct. 18th 94

My Darling Boy

In much haste I send on all I have of the toothpowder. I
will attend to your other request.

Tyra & Brian would so like to hear from you. I agree with
you about the photos & will send you one or two more
rough proofs. With love & hugs & blessings yr loving
Mother
Min.

194 18 Oct 94

Dear old Boy,

very glad to hear from you. *Shall write to you soon** – In the
meantime read enclosures.

181

Caro & Emma are waiting for letters from you are waiting
to send you Zwieback* etc etc

Your loving father

Leu

I am thinking what journey you & I might possibly take
together at Xmas & next summer

195   34 College Rd, Clifton

Sat. 20th Oct. 94

My Dear Mother

thanks for the tooth powder. You will be glad to hear we
won our second house match too, & also that your third
best nose got two good kicks so as to make it swell & it is
at present rather crooked as to the bridge but I expect as
soon as the swelling is down it will rectify itself. I got
rather knocked about getting 4 good kicks on the head, but
we won so it is alright. But now playing rackets I have
hurt my knee, either strained a muscle or put a sinew out
of place so that I will not be able probably to play for
about a week, but I will tell you for certain when I write
in a day or two as I have not as yet seen the doctor. Now
as to the Point of a hamper I think this term I will not
have money but a hamper, it will be the *2d* I have had
since I have been here so dont be surprised at a large
order.* Please send it as soon as you can. Father wrote in
his letter card of the 18th "Wait to send you 'Zwieback'
etc." I dont know what he means. Have the glasses from
Germany come & my knife? Do answer my letters.

Now the contents of the hamper. I want. about 20lbs of
jam not less. Strawberry, plum, currant, apple, perhaps some
pear jam & a pot of cherry "tutifruti".
a tin or two of sardines.
Send me that bottle of Tonicuin* I think it is in my
bedroom, in the cupboard.

21.10.1894: 196 (TyTB to TTB)

Also a Roast wing rib of beef, but let it be rather underdone than too much done you know how I like it, & also let it be a good big one like those we have at home, now dont let me be dissapointed in this, if you dissapoint me in the others which I dont expect you will. Then in addition send me some fruit whatever there is, I should appreciate this. You had better have it packed in a strong box from the top of the Garden somewhere I believe there are some; I have no more to write home now
So good bye dear mother from

your loving Son

Tankred.

Try & let me have the hamper by the middle of next week.

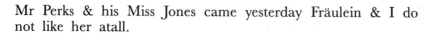

196*   Oct 21st 1894

Dearest Tankred

Mr Perks & his Miss Jones came yesterday Fräulein & I do not like her atall.

You know I am going to see Edith's wedding presents on wednesday I hear that she has 60.

I am so very sorry you have hurt your knee at foot ball* I hope you will soon be better & that your nose wont be spoiled. We all thought your drawing so very good.

I am sorry I have written such a short letter but I realy cant think of any thing to say.

Yesterday we had a vine tree on the table in honour of "The Perksman".
with heaps of love

from your loving sis

Tyra

197   Newfield House, Forest Hill

Oct. 24th 94

My Dear Boy

Mr Owsley is here – he seems to have no room at home with all Ediths presents & the preparations for the wedding on the 25th – Chet is quartered out.

You may imagine how sorry I am about my dear third best nose! I hope however for the best (noses do recover) (in time.) You told me that accidents at football occurred when boys were not playing up* generally?

I am glad you were first photographed. Do pray return me the other rough proofs I sent you & say what you think of them. Don't you think the laughing group most lifelike & good with the exception of Roy?

I would have sent you the parcel *this* week with pleasure *but* the roaster is being repaired & I know you would not care about a wing rib cooked in the oven. So I hope you will like it next week – on Tuesday or Wednesday. I will send fruit but not jam – it is too awkward to pack & you can buy it at Clifton 3lbs for 8½ (plum), 10½ (apricot) or so – & I will send you money for it instead. I hope you did not wish to give an entertainment this week particularly, or that if you did it will be as enjoyable & acceptable next week.

The new stoves have been in course of placing in the old library & in my bed room for the last three days & two nights so that there is no peace on this floor & in the kitchens I have been having the floors stained & varnished (in order to avoid scrubbing for the cook – our new cook seems to be very nice) by Smith in extra time. It really improves the look of the kitchens very much. We are considering the question of kitchen stoves now as ours burns so much coal – 10 or 12 scuttles at least twice as much as the old kitchener* but then with the old kitchener we have no hot water. Gill (the man at London Bridge) is coming to give us his advice I shall be so glad when all these things are done & we are enjoying the res-

Emilie Tunstall (Grandma)

Harry Bush, Brian, Roy, Leu: Newfield c1898

Leu: Newfield c1895

ults – In the gymnasium* I have gained the space where the stove was – for a boot cupboard or a chest of drawers if I can find one to fit.

The glasses have not yet come from Germany. Harry Bush came to dinner with Lilian & Mabel last Thursday, he was staying at Grandmas – he looks very well after his three years in India – rather stouter than he was. The firm he represented failed but he was almost immediately taken up by their opponents & he is here on business.

We expect Edith Bell with Dr & Mrs West to lunch on Friday if the weather is fine – Do write by return & let me know how the nose is & the knee & if you felt any the worse for the kicks in your head.
Love to you my dear old boy from us all especially from your loving mother

Min

198 [26.10.1894]*

My Dear Mother,

Thanks for your letter. Did you send me back with a whole packet or only 2 of these letter cards? Do send the jam. It can be packed quite safely by Smith. It is so much better than this shop jam. So do send it. Why dont you answer my questions? Ask Harry Bush from me if he ever received my second letter thanking him for the cookerie?* also ask him if he can get the little missing implements which belong at the side & which are missing in my specimen? I think all the groups bad & I think my left arm looks too stupid in all my Photos by myself. I wouldn't have any of them, rather let us go again. The single ones of Brian, Tyra, & Roy I think good though. will write again soon.

Tankred.

Please send stamps I use my last for the other letter*

199   Newfield House, Forest Hill

[28.10.1894]*

Dearest Tankred

I was so very pleased to have your letter. How your knee must have hurt you, I hope it will be alright soon.

When I talked of Miss Jones I thought you knew that Mr Perks was engaged. You know we had one of the young vine trees in a pot on the table in the dining room & picked the bunches off ourselves. Father thought you drew your leg very well. Edith Owsley was married last Thursday & I went to the wedding it was verry pretty. Sibyl, Miss Owsley* & one of Mr Boulton's sisters & a little friend of theirs were The bridesmaids. I believe that Edith had nearly a hundred presents, they were all so very nice too. When are you coming home. Father has given me such a nice picture for my room. Sibyl came over to tea yesterday, I asked Ethel & Violet but Mr Lambley won't let them go out on Saturdays is'nt it a shame.
Good buy
from your loving sis
Tyra.

200   [28.10.1894]* Sunday night

My Dear Boy

I will try to let you have your hamper on Wednesday. Please return the rough copy of photos to me *at once*. How is my 3rd best nose by this time? I think I only gave you one or two lettercards.

Your father does not know what he wrote to which you allude – It seems to me I always answer your questions as far as possible. I just enclose what stamps I have by me (four only) for the present. The clocks are all striking 12. Your father is

Tankred (photo of let198)

Tyra (photo of let1g8)

in bed so I will be off – No end of love to you my dear
old Boy from

Your loving Mother

Min.

One of Roys latest – apropos at one of Andersens tales
which he finds "dry" – "I suppose mother when I am older
I shall find all these tales wet!"

201   Newfield House, Forest Hill

Oct 31st

My Dear Boy,

I hope your hamper will have reached you safely to-day if
not last night & in good condition. As I went with your
father to spend the day at Edith Bells I could not actually
see it packed. The joint was roasted on Monday & ought
to be first-rate. I hope the fruit will not be crushed or the
jam spilt – & that you will enjoy it all – besides the joint
there were 2 boxes of sardines – 2 of buiscuits 3 pots of
jam containing about 11lbs & pears – I meant to have
had the joint boned & rolled but I daresay you prefer
carving it –

The new stove in my bed room is in & bronzed or rather
coppered & so effulgent that it warms one to look at it. A
stove like in your bedroom is to be put in the dining room
& one has been placed in the spare room – that makes
four new stoves – such a business.

At Ediths we played rather an amusing game "Telegrams"
take 12 letters of the alphabet haphazard – (say the first
letters of the 1st 12 words in some book) then decide
subject for telegram & each player composes a telegram
using 12 words beginning with the 12 Consonants in the
order given – The reading out is very funny. –

5.11.1894: 202 (TTB to EFB)

How are the nose & knee? photos received. Love & hugs from your fond mother

Min.

202 34 College Rd, Clifton

Mon. 5th Nov 94

My dear mother

I have not had any time till now to write to you nor have I much time now but I shall write again answering your letters tomorrow. The hamper arrived safely, thanks very much for it, the big pears though rather bruised were very good, & so were the others. The beef was just as I like it but was rather underdone which I find here is not a good thing as they don't even have the decency to keep ones meat in a larder, & so consequently it goes bad very soon, however I think we shall just finish the beef in time. Father wrote to me a letter card promising to write at length in a day or two dated oct.18. there was also something in it which I wrote & asked to be deciphered,* but that is how things are with us, I never get any of my questions answered at all. My nose is well again but rather knocked to one side & my leg is alright again now. no more news now so good bye dear mother

from your loving Son Tankred

203 Newfield

Nov 11th 94 Sunday

My Darling Boy,

The enclosed from Jumma – I have not yet written to him. I know he would like me to invite him at Xmas & I should like to give him pleasure. How do you feel about it? Let me know

188

but do not yourself send an invitation. It is rather difficult to know beforehand what one may be able to do. Dear! I dont know how you can say your questions are "never answered at all" as I go through your letters & answer one question after another when I write – what you *could* not decipher in your fathers letter he could not remember so I left it to him to reply (as he probably will). Mr Bird (Roys school master) & his mother were here this afternoon. Mr Bird seems to be very observant & sympathetic in his treatment of Roy – he finds he wants more keeping in order. he is too fond of mischief instead of doing his work.

Mr Geo. Allen has a little son.*

You did not say how you liked the jam. The holidays are really drawing near again. You will be pleased to hear that I have now a beautiful settee in my study instead of the green sofa. It fits in to the corner six feet either way broad & springy with six large square cushions against the wall. It is most luxurious & makes 4 or 6 seats & so gives us much more room & is a great improvement. In the gymnasium the space where the old grate was makes a capital boot cupboard & has a curtain before it which is a great gain (in its way) – the old mantelpiece in the spare room is covered in wood & is most harmonious with the new stove – which completes that room. I think you like to hear these little odds & ends. Brian seems to be doing well. Mr Edwards gives him extra latin which is a comfort to him & will also give him & Roy writing. I have been reading Andersens fairy tales* to both boys but Roy is such a little fidget he is scarcely still a moment. These readings always remind me of ours of old. Love & hugs from
yr. fond mother Min.

204* Nov 11. 94, Sunday

My Dear Mother.

Why do neither you nor *father* nor any of you write. You will be glad to hear we won our most important house match last week on Tuesday after a hard fight, we were all delighted. My nose though well wont go straight again, my leg is alright now. Do write & answer *all the* questions I have asked this term & I dont know whether I shan't want some new clothes this term, but that I will let you know later: Any way send me some more tooth powder by return *& a letter*. How are the boys? I am sorry I have not written to them *but there* is so little time, give them my love & greetings. So as there is no more at present to say goodbye dear mother from your loving Son

Tankred

205   34 College Rd, Clifton

Nov. 18. 1894. Sun

My Dear father

Why dont you write. generally when you say you will write you do so. I enclose your last lines,* what are the words underlined. I could not read them. We fought 4 of the strongest out of the 7 houses at football & won, beating the strongest* last. We thought then we had a clear field before us with the other three, however after a great victory often comes a severe defeat as with Hannibal's forces after Capua.* We have suffered a severe defeat from one* of these three houses; We fell to pieces before them. It seemed as though all the spirit of playing together & good combination had gone & the grit & hardness to beat even against a better team for which our house is well known, had gone. The want of combination by which we often beat stronger houses than us may be attributed to the fact of our confidence & the thought of "Oh, we shall win however slackly we take it", on the part of most of the team; the want of lasting power to the fact that the fellows thought they need not keep on training as they had before, & so had stodged* too much. But the loss of that courage & pluck & determination to win after they had scored the first point against us is unaccountable. Well the long & short was we suffered a severe defeat from a team much weaker than ourselves. All I think who care for the honour of the house feel very disgraced by this. However defeat is not always bad, many men have risen higher, greater, & better for getting a severe defeat & *taking it in the proper way*.* If one looks at ones faults committed at the defeat & determines to remedy them in the future, one can conquer yet, as Alfred the Gt & afterwards Fredrick the Gt. Such a defeat ought to be a life lesson to all connected with it; It ought not to carry its lesson only in the football field to make us play better individually by remedying our individual faults & also to learn never to behave as we have done in consequence of a great victory, but it ought to remain with each vividly throughout his life.* Whatever others may make out of it, I at least will make it a lesson never to relax one bit after a victory but rather always to improve no matter how puny the obstacles ahead may seem, it is thus that Rome fell. I shall also make it a lesson always to do my utmost during every moment of my life, as I look back on the game, I clearly see three mistakes I made these will forthwith be remedied on the football field, but these might not have been committed if I had done my utmost & if they had not been committed, the match might have been won. This is how every one of the team should feel about loosing the match, for if each had not played his part badly we should have won. My only consolation is that I shall create victory out of defeat & make this youthful defeat useful through my life. The actual defeat would not matter so much if as in the wars of Fredrick the Gt one could fight ones enemy again & thus retrieve what had previously been lost. Do ask mother to write soon & send me the tooth powder I asked for, give my love to Tyra & the boys who I hope play football too by this time. Last Wednesday we had a concert, I enclose the programme.* I liked no 1 & 5 best in Part I & I remembered the no. 4. from Henry VIII in Part II. I liked no. 9. best & part of no. 13 was very funny the music copying the sound of the cocks & hens very well. There is no more to say now so good bye dear father from

Your loving Son

Tankred.

Only 4 *weeks next* Tuesday to the holidays
Please *send some* stamps.
Did mother get my *letter card* last week?

20.11.1894: 206 (EFB to TTB)

206   Nov 20th 94

Darling Boy,

Your letter to your father yesterday quite inspirited me! It is curious to trace how the same causes produce the same results – in nations schools, families & individuals & I am so glad that *you* can see it & find it out for yourself. More anon from your loving Mother.

Min

You do not reply about *Jumma*.

207   nov 20th 1894

Dearest Tankred

How is your nose? I am so sorry that I have not written to you for the last three Sundays but the first Sunday mother & I were at Grannie's & the next I went to Ethel's from saturday till Tuesday & last Sunday Mother & I went to Church with the Lambleys & stayed to tea at their house. Is your knee all right yet? I have got such heaps to tell you when you come home I wish it was already the holidays. You know Brian comes up & has Latin with me & on the day I have handwriting with Mr Edwards, Brian & Roy both come & have it too.

What day do you come home?

You know mother has bought a new kind of sofa for her study it is very big & this shape –> & has six big cushions it is very comfortable & made of brocade.

I suppose you heard all about the hedge-hogs disappearing; I have no more to say.

from your loving sister
Tyra.

208   Newfield House, Forest Hill, Kent

25 XI 94

My dearest Boy,

I thank you for all your letters, of the 30 Sept/1 Aug 14 Oct & 18th Nov, they are a real solace to me. You complain of my not writing & you are right. My thoughts are always with you, my greatest wish is to see you a happy man & to write to you, I feel I ought to be myself, the man who loves nature, which always echoes joyfully in him. – If I have not written it is on account of that franchise vampyre,* which destroys the happiness of our home. Don't let me dwell upon it, suffice it to know that it is still there, undermining trust & faith & family – But let me reply to your different questions. Brian & Roy seem to be working into the school routine, they are both happy with their work. On the Anklets* 4/- were returned.

Your drawing from nature has pleased me immensely, it is good, continue to watch nature & render her truly. When you come home you can now *work* in the studio – the distilling machine has not come to pass. We will see to it together, as well as to the Camera. The Hypo has been attended to.

I am very sorry of your nasal accident. Considering that you played *Association?** it appears *to me* that you can only have met with it, through slipping in consequence of the play in *wet* weather? Otherwise it should have been impossible? What I want to know *by return* is was the nose *broken & where?* Was the *bone* broken?

Breakage of the Nose bridge *bone* is *very* dangerous if not *properly* healed & set, I have seen *frightful* consequence amongst my friends in consequence. (The consequences frequently appear *after years* only) So *do* write *explicitly. I, insist* upon its being *properly* set & if it has to be broken again. Your mother says you mentioned it being crooked? If the nose *was* a *bone* smash & is *properly* set it ought *not* to be crooked, but yet if it *were properly* set & crooked it could *easily* be got into its *right* shape by a wooden *nose* shape machine.

2.12.1894: 209 (TTB to EFB)

Do tell me *soonest* how the matter stands, as *I* shall come down to Clifton in case of need.

I am looking forward with pleasure to your holidays, I made up my mind *that you & I* will look after this Xmas & plan together – Your last letter of the 18th Nov has filled my heart with joy & hope. Continue in the right path – *no* mistaken ambition – the cause you are fighting for in life must have a *sound* basis – don't excuse hypocrisy ever (hypocrisy seems almost growing into a national religion in England). The lesson you should draw from your last experience summed up appears to me "Never underrate your enemy, nor be elated at a victory". Don't you think it is that? And another thing dear Boy as we are about it. – *Benefit* by the experience of your elders, there is Mr Hall one of *your* wellwishers, a man who takes a *real* interest *in you*. I am sure he feels you do not do justice to his advice. Pray think & consider. Do you imagine that his advice is simply to please himself? Fall in with his advice & try, cast the line of your own aside for a later period. You *can* do neat work if you like, you have *proved* it to me & you know *how* much it counts for in the exam. – Why will you throw your chances away? You *ought* to be *top* in style, *no* random work in Latin, nor weak or uncertain in french, or *silly* & *grotesque* in scriptures.* Your *German composition should* be good, your english composition *should* be excellent & *first class*. Set your heart to it & you *will* do it. I have *every* faith in *you* & feel sure you will show yourself worthy of it! Heartfelt greetings from your loving father

Leu

209 34 College Rd, Clifton

Dec. 2nd 94

My Dear Mother,

I should like Jumma to come very much but I dont know what other arrangements may be contemplated. You have not forgotten about the modelling have you? What have you done

194

about the Photo's? I am looking forward to seeing you on Tuesday fortnight. Although you may think you answer my questions you never do, & If you let me have my letters when I come home I will show you. Is the Studio in order yet? As I come home a week before Christmas this time I must arrange all the ordering of my clothes the day after I come home so as to have it off my mind at once. I want to do some work with Mr Edwards while I am at home, but we must settle about that when I come home. There is no more to Say so good bye dear mother from

your loving Son

Tankred

210   34 College Rd, Clifton

Dec 2d 94

My Dear Father

thanks for your letter & the tooth powder. The powder is horrid my teeth are getting quite yellow, it does not seem to clean them & also does not make a lather & is gritty to the teeth. I wish you had written earlier & I might have had some extra work this term in my most deficient subjects; however now it must be left till next term. I am looking forward to the holidays. Dec 18 – Jan 18 (about). I want you to get me some books; to *use these holidays* namely,

Salmon's Conics (*2d Hand*).
Loney's Elementary Dynamics. 2d Edition. &
Pt I. Elements of Statics & Dynamics. Statics.
Pt II   "   "   "   "   Dynamics
Cambridge Press.
& Greaves. Elementary Statics. Macmillan.

Let us these holidays really make up our minds what we are going to do at the beginning & not remain so uncertain as last holidays. I have many* waiting to be discussed with you when I come home. Have the things come from Germany yet?

Why did you not write to me for so long?

What makes you think we play Association? we play *Rugby* we always have. The nose wasn't broken only the bridge was bruised, It is beginning to get straight again now, I suppose a bruised bone takes some time to go down again. Do write soon

So now good bye from your

Loving Son Tankred

211   Newfield House, Forest Hill, Kent

5 Dec 94

My dear Boy,

Your mother turned the Hall into a meeting room* to day (meetings are apparently a "fashion" & will doubtless go the way of spelling bees).* Now I never did, nor will go with fashion & so I retired to my Tusculum* in the garden to use my time in replying to several letters, amongst which Yours of the 2nd. *Toothpowder*, the grit is ossa sepia (cuttle fish ground) very cleansing, producing *white* teeth *with us at forest Hill*. It is very unlikely that the Clifton atmosphere should have an effect upon the ossa sepia & thereby on your teeth in consequence? Or, that your fluor* of your teeth should be different from the family's?

Scrub, scrub, scrub, old fellow
And your teeth instead of yellow, –
Will be white as snow,
If you only do it so!

I think if you read my last letter *carefully*, it *indicates* to you sufficiently why I did not write for so long. I love to write to my son & usually refrain from doing so when I am out of tune. True, – discord only puts accord in so much bolder relief, – but I regard the *real* bas-relief* as the most perfect creation, *high* relief the world calls Rococo & Rococo is a rodomontade,* mostly creation gone mad!

MRS. BEHRENS

At Home,

WEDNESDAY, DECEMBER 5TH, 1894, 3.30 P.M.

Members of the ....
Ladies' Discussion Society and Friends are invited to
hear Mrs. GEO. BOOLE speak

ON THE

"Safeguarding of the Faculty of Originality in Children."

DISCUSSION TO FOLLOW.

The Rev. GEO. ALLEN in the Chair.

Newfield House,
36, Dartmouth Road, Forest Hill.

*An early reply is earnestly
requested.*

Invitation to Mrs Boole's lecture

Cover of Tyra's Hans Andersen

13.12.1894: 212 (LWFB to TTB)

Mr Edwards who is getting the books will work with you during the holidays, that is arranged.

What about Confirmation? Mr Glazebrook sent the usual paper.*

The things from Germany have arrived.

I was under the impression that you played Association, from what I heard from you & so was your mother.

The studio is nearly ready, I am anyhow already writing in it & hope to work in it by January. You may work *with me* there, if you like, but mind, work, & alone. Make up your mind what you wish to do, be it school work deficient subjects, art, or photographing. To go abroad is not feasible. I have several things I wish to see with you – Natural history Museum &c &c that I intend to work into our programme. Xmas Day as I mentioned before, you & I are going to take in hand.

Your loving father
Leu

212   Newfield House, Forest Hill, Kent

13 dec 94

My dear Boy,

We have sad trouble with Roy lately, who had a fit *for* naughtiness & disobedience which grieves me *very* much, as I dislike the application of the whip, believing in the appeal to honour – à propos of whipping – It was mentioned that a year ago *you* had passed the remark: "[My mother may beat me *but*]* My father *dare not* whip me & if he did, I shall make him suffer for it". I would like to have *your* version of *this*, for I can scarcely imagine that you allowed your temper to run away with you & make *such* an unlawful observation. Mind you, this is cited as a sequence* in Roy. If you nevertheless forgot

yourself, *Roy* regards* what you think & feel *today* about it.
You see how *necessary* it is that *you* should set a good
example & assist me in bringing a reasonable humane
bringing up about. There *must* be firmness *& obedience* to
elders in *particular* to father & mother. I give very little for
anyone who cannot be brought to reason by reason & who
has no honour I expect from you now some assistance in
this way & I wish to have *an answer* to my questions, which
I *don't* like to be passed over in silence on account of your
coming home now soon.
Next Tuesday I expect you & *before* this a reply
Your loving father
Leu

213 34 College Rd, Clifton, Bristol

Dec 16. 94

My Dear Father,

I dont recollect having said that at all & *certainly* not before
the children. That I may have said something like it I won't
deny. Since when any mention of such a thing has been
made, either with reference to me or any others of the
family it has made me angry & I know my temperament is
such that I should never feel towards you like I do, if such
should ever have taken place, it would I know without being
able to help it on my part leave a silent rancour in my
heart to think my *father* had beaten me; And since such a
state of things would make you suffer, I know, a remark
such as this may have escaped me except the first part
(added afterwards above the line in your letter). I tell you
quite plainly the truth, as I have never told you anything
but the truth; It may not be quite satisfactory to you, but I
know that would be the case, I have always felt so thankful
that such has never taken place, it would cast a shadow of
darkness on my home, which up to now never has been,
nor ever should be there. You know how it grieves me
when you are angry with me or indeed any others in the
family, true it sometimes shows itself in me in a burst
of anger & words which should have been supressed, but

nevertheless it is absolute unhappiness at the thought that things should be so. Home should be so sweet so happy all in union & harmony, the children show trust & obey implicitly their parents, it is for their own benefit to do so, – A rebuke from them should be enough & always taken to heart & acted on afterwards. I am sure I shall be better for having been brought up as I have without force & being treated as a sensible being & though it may have made me more unruly & more trouble to you for a time yet I am sure I shall turn out the better for it; I think I have arrived at a stage now when I can truly appreciate it, & make the true use of it. It grieves me *very* much that Roy should every* have experienced it, but as I dont know anything about it I can't say it might have* spared. The old saying "Spare the lash spoil the boy"* I don't believe in; When one has a father of that style, it makes one look on him rather as a master which is not the true filial feeling. So now good bye dear Father till tuesday from your ever

loving Son
Tankred.

214   Newfield House, Forest Hill, Kent

Dec. 16th 94

My Dear Boy,

Just a line to tell you what you know already, how glad we shall all be to see you on Tuesday! I have been very silent dear boy this term, but we must make up for it in the holidays which I hope will be happy ones for everyone. The boys & Tyra are reckoning upon them immensely. We are all most curious to know what sort of Xmas we shall have arranged entirely by your father & *you!* Very nice no doubt & quite a change Au revoir my dear old boy, with love & hugs always

Your loving Mother
Min.

199

215   Clifton College, Clifton, Bristol

Dec 27th 1894

Dear Mr Behrens

With regard to yr son's prospects, he could if you wish it go up for a try next June & he wd probably get a fairly good place; but I shd be inclined not to let him go up till November. He ought then to make a bid for a very high place, somewhere in the first six if he is capable of making sound progress all the coming year. He wd still have another try in case of accident, as he will not be 18 till July 1896.

He did very good work this term, but at present some of his Mathematical work is heavy & cumbrous. He wants a good deal of practice to gain readiness & skill to use the best & most *telling* Methods. As he has now covered (pretty well for a first reading) all the Woolwich course, we ought to be able to improve his work in the desired direction very materially in the next few months.

I promised to send him a Memorandum about holiday work. Will you please tell him that I shd like him to do the Woolwich papers V, VI for June 1890 & Nov 1890.
With all good wishes for the New Year
I am
Yrs sincerely
H.S.Hall

NEW TERM BEGINS

216   Newfield

Jan 21st 95

My Darling Boy,

I was sorry to see you go this morning though I feel I have much more time for the rest when you are not there. I hope

200

22.1.1895: 217 (TTB to EFB)

you reached Clifton – without a chill & still feeling well & that you will keep so all the term & be able to do your best work.

I send your list – *Send me* the size in paper of your sole for mocassins. I hope to write oftener this term & tell you what goes on – To-day Luke's wife Mrs Clary called. Such a nice woman. She could hardly speak to me at first. She told me that on the last morning Luke came Brian went into the workshop & said "do you know my papa is going to send you away" whereupon he took his tools & departed – she could scarcely believe there was no other cause & was most relieved to find that he had not been dismissed & that we were kindly disposed. She thought it most ignorant of her husband to behave in such a way & he has had no work since – she makes cricket leggings & has since she was a child has a fixed pay & keeps Luke & her old mother. She is *most* anxious that her visit to me should be kept a secret so I hope it has not been mentioned to Spall – *pray tell me* if you have said anything before him – because I would act accordingly.

Tyra's strain seems worse & I intend going to Lichtenberg again to-morrow morning, it does grieve me so. She is otherwise so well made & physically perfect.

I saw a woman to-day – (for a cook) so alarmingly plain – I am almost afraid to engage her, but she seems to be otherwise satisfactory & aimiable. The tea bell rings. I am afraid you omitted to say "goodbye" to Ethel & Violet did you? They left after lunch.

Love & hugs from yr fond mother
Min.

217   34 College Rd, Clifton, Bristol

22.I.95

Dearest Mother

this is a good beginning, a letter so soon – I arrived allright,

Mr Moor said he was surprised to see me so early so you
see what we did was alright.*

Have you said anything to Brian about Luke's affair? What
is going to be done, is anything? Has Bryant sent the fork
yet? I said nothing to Spall about it at all. I do Hope
Dear Tyra will get alright again surely she ought not to
Dance while it is still not healed up. I did say good bye to
the Lambley's. Dont forget this letter contains 3 questions.
So good bye Dear Mother from your ever loving Son
Tankred.

218   34 College Rd, Clifton

25.I.94*

My Dear Father

Please let me have the pictures as soon as possible. I did
not get into the VIth this term, no one was moved out of
our form. We are doing Schillers "Wilhelm Tell" this term
in German, which is very nice, it makes such a difference
doing a nice construeing book. Do Settle with Mr Hall
about my exam;* I don't want on any account to put off
my first try till November. It has always been your & Mr
Edward's idea that I should get in as early as possible.
Besides several of Mr Hall's former pupils whom he did
not wish to go in have in the end come out* very high
indeed, so why might not I too. Please don't put this off as
there would be some little alterations to be made pending
my Exam in June. Do get my silver watch done &
regulated by Tyler as soon as you can, it is so awkward
being without one here. Also write out my debt to you & I
will see if it lacks anything & then we can see how we
stand. Please send me some stamps. Also the envelope &
form which I have to send to Oxford* which I left in the
pot on the right hand side of the dining room mantlepiece.
So now good bye dear Father from
your loving Son
Tankred.

219 [26.1.1895]*

My dear Boy,

I hope to see Meadows about the pictures on Monday. To Mr Hall I wrote to night asking him to make arrangements for *June* Exam. The watch is already with Tyler *since yesterday*. Enclosed Mr Lynams Envelope, & Stamps. Your account with me stands so far:

brought forward from last a/c	£1	13	10
<u>Mean to pay</u> Batzer <u>but</u>	8	6	
Hope	0	19	11
Marshall*	1	3	
Randall*		9	6
Book		7	11
	£13	0	2

I hope you will succeed in June, doubtless as you mean to put your *whole* energy into your present work. *Personally*, I can*not* separate myself from my conviction that coming out with flying colours counts for more than a seniority. Mind there was a time, when you *yourself* declared to me, that unless you came out amongst the first three, you would *not* go!

Your loving father Leu

220   34 College Rd, Clifton

27.I.95

My Dearest Father

Thanks for the stamps & letter – I didnt remember anything was to be brought forward, however I expect you are right.

I thought this was it.	brought forward	1	13	10
	Hope		19	11
	Braces		2	6
	Marshall	1	3	

Randall		9	6
Book		7	11
Batzer	8	6	
Engelhart*		3	6
Stoneham		1	3
	13	7	5
amt due from you	8	10	
to be brought forward next time	4	17	5

Coming out with flying colours makes a good deal of difference no doubt. But as I said Mr Hall has had fellows who have gone in just as young as I & have got in bottom but have come out of Woolwich 1st or 2d or third. Now if I can get in in the first 20 I dont see, if I work hard why I should not get out high. If I get in below 20th I dont think I should go but the principle thing is to come out high say in the 1st 5 in the end, if I could be sure of doing that I should not mind. There is no more news now so good bye dear

Father from your loving Son
Tankred.

Please let mother see this.
£3 owed   16/- in hand
balance £2 4/-   to draw from my bank acct

221   Newfield

30 I 95

My dear Boy,

I have been in town with Louis today – seen after your pictures,* (etchings) which Meadows will frame & send *prepaid*, viz

Chelsea School
Words of Comfort
The Lady of the Swords
The Hall by Renoir
The Vanguard
Venice & Bath
I like to hear your appreciation. –

Louis Neuendorff, Maria, Hermann: c1896

Hotel & Badhaus zum Engel (see Biog Reg under Neuendorff)

I paid Mr Edwards 3/6 for you re Charlie's Aunt,* which I presume is right. I thought you had settled & luckily mentioned it; otherwise Mr Edwards would have gone without it.

Now I am off to the post & for a *round*, feeling cold in doors

Your loving father
Leu

222   Newfield

Jan. 31st 95

My Dear Boy,

I am glad you had nothing to regret on your late* return to school. Brian told us what he had said to Luke & is most unhappy at the consequences to Luke of his folly. He wrote a very nice letter to him on the strength of which Luke came down & told us how sorry he was that he had himself been so foolish. he said he had long since regretted it but had felt ashamed to come & say so; I only wish we could get him any employment* I suppose they don't want anyone at the College? Here people seem to be reducing the number of their workmen rather than increasing them. Bryant returned the fork. I took Tyra to Lichtenberg again he did not say anything particularly new – she is anaemic to which he attributes her tendency to lounge. I asked him if with the truss on she might do anything & he said "yes".

Mr Barlow gave us a pass for two to the stalls at Tooles theatre* so Lewis & Mr Edwards have gone together to see "Walker"* & "Paul Pry".* The frost is splendid 6 degrees. Our left path was watered & frozen over before the last snowfall & is splendid. On Saturday Sunday & on Monday we enjoyed it very much – both with our new & old sledges & two old metal tea trays. Tyra is very fond of coming down on one behind the sledge – It is so funny, often half way down she slips on one side & goes spinning down in front of the sledge & so far without hurt. We have frozen the snow heep which arrests us at the bottom for before, we continually swept through it. At first Lewis helped us nicely & seemed to like it but he does not care to any longer, but Chet is still faithful when he is free. Yesterday he took Tyra & Sybil to skate at the Palace* & they both got on very well – tomorrow perhaps Tyra & Sybil will try alone. Today was the dancing & I took her. It was bitingly cold waiting at the station afterwards. I asked what Miss Christmas would charge for making a pyjama suit. 7/6!! I must have some one here to help with them.

Lewis has given up the scent I disliked so much. Mr Eckers is engaged to be married – On Sunday Mr Sharman dined here & Mr Wendt & in the evening Ernest Schrattenholz came & we had some delightful music. I wish you could have been there dear! On Monday I had the pleasure of meeting Mrs Fawcett at dinner & hearing her lecture* afterwards at St John's Hall in the Devonshire Road where the Schrattenholz' concerts were held. This is a very scrappy letter dear Boy! but it is late & I am tired & I think you like just to hear the news. I forgot to say Brian gave Luke Grandma's half crown of his own accord. Do write to me soon & say if you feel quite well again & in good working order. With love & hugs. your fond mother
Min.

223   34 College Rd, Clifton

3.II.95

My Dearest mother.

I am sending the tracing of my foot [reproduced half size on p.208], you may as well order several pairs while you are about it. Did Smith make the new sledge & is it a good one how many does it hold? I do wish this weather had been in the holidays instead of now. Chet & I could have had such fun.

3.2.1895: 223 (TTB to EFB)

I hope Tyra is learning to skate nicely now; I don't think it very nice of Louis to desert the slide. I feel full of anxiety for June, it is impossible to get what I want explained* otherwise I should feel safe for I can work it up easily between now & then if only I understand it. The only, last refuge, I see is work about 6-8 hours a day all next holidays mostly with Mr E. I have no more news now so good bye dear Mother

from your loving Son
Tankred

I enclose a small drawing I made last term & finished this term of a rabbits skull.

Also 5/- would be acceptable to go on with in the way of Grub. acct enclosed of Money Spent, so that you can see how it is generally spent by me.

[enclosed account follows]

Ticket to L.B.*	3/½
Porter	2d.
Cab*	3/-
Ticket*	9/10½
Porter	6d.
paper & Bun	3d.
cab*	3/1½
	17/4½*
Kerosene	4d.
Stamps	6d.
Potted meat	2/-
Pen, Ink, & Ink Pot	1/4
	21/6½
House subscription	1/-
	22/6½
Ham	7/-
2 pots of jam	2/2
	31/10½*

So you see I had to borrow some

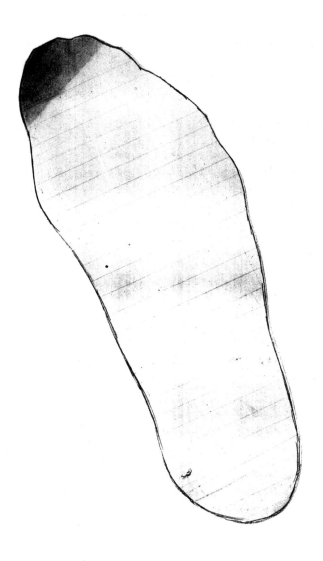

224   3.II.95

My Dear Father

The pictures have not yet arrived. I will tell you what I think of them when they arrive. thanks very much for them however beforehand. (as I know *you* like *most others* like thanks from any you *love* when you have rendered them a service) I thought I had reminded you of it. the total sum was I believe was between 3/6 & 4/- I cant exactly say what. When is the steam engine being erected? There is no more to say at present so good bye dear Father from
your loving Son Tankred.

225   Sunday 3 II 95

My dear Boy

We are all sitting in the Morning room & listening to Louis play which gives me a *great* deal of pleasure, being so fond of music & having none heard at home, so to say, for years. Besides Piano Louis plays the horn (Waldhorn)* which he learnt to *please his father* & of which he is very glad. It is at least pleasing to find one who, I daresay besides many others, regretted not having a father, whom he pleased & followed.* I wish you could hear Louis' horn, which comes very near the Cello in sound. I am thinking of taking Louis for a day or two to Bessy's Cove *if possible*, on the homeward journey. we might ?break the journey & see the College?

Engelhart claimed today 3/6 *from you*, is this right? Make it a rule *never* to leave *un*paid bills behind you.
Love from your father
Leu

My Dear Boy,

The skating weather lasts so splendidly that I feel inclined myself to try how I can get on upon the ice & looking over my skates I find they can be a little altered – but my dear Boy – what did you do with the key *and my straps!!* Tyra says "do give him my love!"

I took Brian & Roy to Dulwich Park* this morning & they get on very nicely. Tyra was there from 9.30 to 12.30 with Hauerl & Chet, & enjoys it very much. I am so glad they are all three in the way of skating well. Lewis is playing to us all the evening.

I wonder what you have been doing at Clifton. We do not hear often enough from you – dear – I must tell you that Tyras two teeth are just appearing in those two vacancies much to my satisfaction. Your father has been suffering the last few days from lumbago but to-night he is dancing about to the music as though he were quite himself again. Love to you my precious from your loving mother

Min

227   Newfield

5.2.95

My dear Son,

Thanks if they don't come from the inner man & his conviction, be damned, I dont want such & little care what others like or fancy on this point. What I do, I perform without calculation, or reckoning as to appreciation, less thanks. What *I* desire to make the acquaintance of, is the "inward" man. Unfortunately when Idealism & Realism meet, there will be Dualism,* wish that I could spare you that pang!

7.2.1895: 228 (LWFB to TTB)

We deem it right & justly so, to recognise a service of a fellow man. Is it illogical that those nearest to us, should enjoy *less* recognition? Are father, mother, brothers & sister greater strangers? Love without *Esteem* is a spurious article! –

Your drawing pleased me, there is hope – I paid Engelhart 3/6 from your a/c

Suppose you asked Mr *Wollaston* to explain what you want to know in Mathematics? From all you told me, he must be such a genial being, that if *you* put it in the right form to him, he might help you greatly – did you ever thank him for me? Shall I come down & speak to him?

Your father
Leu

228 Newfield

7.II.95

Dear Boy,

119 **Signalling.** Catechism of Army Signalling, by Majors Edge and Rhodes, post 8vo. *cloth*, 2/-
Aldershot, 1894

I bought the above for you & put it in your cupboard thinking you will have enough to read just now. Meadows says the pictures must be in your possession by Monday? I am going to have Rembrandts "Philosopher"* framed for you & keep it for the present in your room. To my mind a most valuable work, however doubtful whether you can appreciate it yet.

Recommending the enclosure to your observation I am

always your loving father
Leu

8.2.1895: 229 (TTB to LWFB)

229 34 College Rd, Clifton

Fri. 8, Feb. 95

My Dear Father

Thanks for the book* & picture. You misunderstood my last letter, I thanked you *there & then* because I knew you liked to be thanked; that had nothing to do with the thanks not coming from the bottom of my heart; As to Mr *Wollaston* helping me, that is impossible. I have to do geography now. So please send me Longmans, Macmillans & the Commercial atlases out of my book case & Longmans textbook of Geography a dark blue book. You dont mind, since I shall do Geography in the hours I used to do drawing, me doing Drawing as an extra do you? I have been tabogganing down some fine hills here lately instead of skating but now they are all spoil* by cinders having been put on them, so I shall have nothing to do If I do not skate on half holidays now so do please get me as soon as you can a pair of skates at the stores;* Let me have good ones as they last better in the long run. Ones like this I mean. enclose a rough drawing etc.* please, ask mother to write soon.
So now good bye dear Father
from your loving Son
Tankred

230 Newfield

11.II.95

My dear Boy,

I have forwarded your Geography books, adding a signalling book, which I thought, might interest you & which I bought for you. – I am sorry I was so far unable to go to the Stores re skates. Poor Roy is very ill fever 102-103 since friday. I am very much cut up & concerned about him; he reminds me of the time, when you at his age were so ill, I feel the same sorrows & pangs as then. Your lifes are so closely interwoven with me that I feel *intense* anguish when I see your healths imperilled, & the suffering you indure is only aggravated in me. – I tried Saturday but the Stores were shut – I have seen a german skate – "Columbus", which appears *to me* the thing *I* would choose, something like yours – but with *round* blades – & special iron bits *in* the boot soles extra fitted – they cost abt 18 or 20/-. Your good mother remarked, that whenever *you* wanted a thing, I had no hesitation in giving it to you & *then* the very best, whilst anything "they" wanted in clothes I grudged. Now I would suggest that you volunteered to pay it out of your money & I will make it up to you in other ways. – as to Mr Wollaston, I am *firmly* of the opinion that *you* should put the matter before *him* in a friendly way & ask him *his* advice. I am *sure* he *will* assist some way or another, but if *you prefer, I* will write to him?

Your loving father
Leu

231   Newfield

12 II 95

My dear Boy,

Roy has influenza with pneumonia complications; I had just called dr Wharry by wire. The poor little fellow's pulse* keeps at abt 103 since Saturday. Let us hope he will pass the crisis in a day or two allright. They are the same anxious moments I spent watching over your bed. I trust the dear little man will be spared to us –
God bless you

Your loving father
Leu

232   Feb 12th/95

Dearest Tankred

Have you had any of the skating? We have been having such a lovely time. After all Chet was able to take me skating when this weather came on, I have been several times with him & can go pretty well by my self, of cause I am not atall perfect but I can go well enough to quite enjoy my self. I do so very much wish you were here to enjoy it all. Some times Chet comes in at about 9.30 & we toboggan, it is so lovely. Louis has gone to Brighton to day.

I suppose you know that Mable is here, we have great fun skating to geather, poor Mable is so very frightened of falling you know. She sends you her best love & wishes you were her* to give her a prop. You know mother does look so very funny bundling about on the ice, she makes me split. I think you are a very naughty boy not to write to me, what do you mean by writing to Chet & Bad Heggs before me? Dr Warry came to day to see Roy & says he has been having Influenza & has Pneumonia mother will tell you all about it. We have such a very nice cook now, we all like her so, but she is as ugly as old boots poor soul.*

There was a dreadful fire just opposite us under the railway, it all flared up & looked so dreadful. Louis & father watched it & Brian & I went to see the ashes to day we also saw the fire men pass not the "West Kent"* of cause but some others. The "West Kent men" got there first but their hose burst. It was quite exciting. If only I had not been having my lessons father said he would have taken me too. The whole Owsley family* are very measly. We have hardly any water* we all feel so dirty. Mable feels like a pie already with a crust out side. Has'nt anything exciting happened at your place yet? I have had my chimney swept with the new thing Spall did it. Mable & I went to the Norwood Lake* to skate on Sunday afternoon it was rather nice. Chet came to breakfast in the morning & we then went to Dulwich Park to skate.
I hope to have a nice long letter from you before long
from your ever loving sis
Tyra.

233   34 College Rd, Clifton

13.II.95

My Dear Father,

I know parents are always rather over anxious than under for their children, & so I trust Dear Roy is not so bad really as would at first seem. Nothing could grieve me more than that he should be ill. Give him my love & tell him he is never out of my mind. As to the skates If I had wanted them given to me I should have said so, but I only asked you to get them for me. Do get them as soon as convenient & dont pay for a special patent to the detriment of the quality of steel in the blades. Thanks for the books. You dont say whether I may do drawing. It is really no good going to Mr Wollaston, in the 1st place he is no mathematical master & in the 2d I don't know him well enough, & in the 3d It would get to Mr Halls ears & he would take it as an insult to him. Why does mother not write. She knows besides I want to eat to live & she sends me nothing to live on. So now Good bye dear Father

from your loving Son

Tankred.

234   Newfield House, Forest Hill, Kent

13.II.95 11.30 p m

My dear Boy,

I know you like to know what is going on. – Roy – we expect the crisis to morrow. don't worry. whatever God ordains we have to take – I hope he will be spared. *Tyra* is down today with fever 103. Personally I attribute the whole thing to sledging & skating Enthusiasm. You *may* do these things like on the Continent, *provided* you use *their* experience, which people *here dont*, and hence the consequences!

Your loving father

Leu

PS Have yours of today – do drawing *by all means* dear Boy. Skates I will endeavour to get, let us have the best out,* never mind, *I* make it up *to you.**

Tell *me what* you want for living & I will do my best your mother is in the sick room & *cannot* attend –

My *treasures*, are *my* children if God takes them, I must submit, *he alone* knows my grief & anxiety – *don't you* be worried, suppose *I* came to Clifton?

235 34 College Rd, Clifton

14.2.95

My Dearest Father,

I do trust he will live thro' it I pray the Almighty may spare us all this pang & anguish. You say dont be worried, who could help being it who was his brother. I presume Tyra has not been told how bad he is. She does not seem to realise it in her letter of last night. Tell her I will write to her. I don't understand how people get ill over *skating & tabogganing*, I have always done it as yet without hurt. I should like 5/- or 10/-, I must have something to go on with when what I have is exhausted.
We are just off to bed so God be merciful to us in this extremity
ever your Loving Son
Tankred

236 Newfield

14 II 95

dearest Boy,

I hope Roy is saved, – Since 6 am, we have the fever *under*

100, abt 98½ normal; to 99½. Tyra is no worry but Mabel who was staying *here*, & unacountably *continued* staying *after* the illness *had* broken out, is now down too & in bed.

Shall I send you the *Mussel* book or keep it here?
Always your loving
father Leu

237   Newfield

Feb. 15th 95

My Dear Boy,

You have not heard from me directly for my hands have been quite full lately. Tyra has also had influenza but I am thankful to tell that since 6.a.m yesterday Roys temperature has been normal & Tyra's soon followed – in fact we took Tyra in time & she is now all right & just ready to enjoy her meals & recruit.* Mabel unfortunately has influenza now with a temperature of 103. She is in the large spare room & I am nursing her also – & writing now by the fire in her room. There are so many wants in a sick room. I have been going from one thing to another until now ever since 6.a.m. but I am so thankful to be able to make them all happy and comfortable & so relieved Tyra & Roy have got over the crisis & seem upon the road to recovery. I will just tell you what the programme is. Every 4 hours Roy has his medicine & a fresh linseed poultice – which latter is cooked on the gas stove in my room – we are *now* not so particular about 4 hours during the night – so I went to bed at 12.30 after administering a last poultice & medicine taking the temperature, respiration & pulse, noting also what food had been taken. Tyra has Roy's bed in the corner of my room where the crib used to be, & we all slept until 6.a.m. when I got up saw to the fire boiled some milk & barley water for both patients – made new poultice put it on gave medicine took temp. &c – washed hands & faces put Roy in Tyra's bed, aired his bed & made it (with yr fathers help) boiled more milk & barley water, ordered fish to be bought &

217

steamcd for Tyra's & Mabel's breakfast – made up Mabel's
fire, took her temperature gave her aconite* & what she
needed – had my own breakfast ordered dinner, &c – found
Dora not well – gave her castor oil in sloe gin – also to
Mabel gave out linen for poultices – Sundry other things.
Helped Lewis to accept an invite to a dance & to dinner
at Mrs Parnells & to arrange his clothes – our lunch –
childrens Mabels – wrote to Canon du Boulay to ask if
Your father & two young guests Lewis & his friend* could
go & stay there for two or three days before March 15th –
Sundry other invalid attentions & now here I am – you see
dear the kind of thing it is. I have wired to ask Wharry if
we may not discontinue the medecine & poultice now – We
are so sorry to have this stop put to our skating this
splendid frost – which continues amazingly. We were all
getting on so nicely in spite of the disrespectful way in wh.
Tyra writes of my performances. I hope to go on again
perhaps to-morrow. It is very nice in Dulwich Park – I wish
you were here – we have never seen you on skates. I enjoy
having Brian on the ice he gets on nicely too & so did
Roy on Sunday week* – the last time he was on – How I
wish we had taken his cold in time however I hope he will
quite recover & have no trace or weakness left.

I must answer yr questions later as they are not here –
your father is to set about the skates – I bought a pair for
4/6 with a screw at the back which *self adjusts* the heel &
sole clasps & are I think *first rate*. Those you describe cost
18/6 – they are lovely – Lewis' friend has them – but
plates must be inserted in the boots & Lewis himself does
not covet them. thinks something new is always coming out.

You spoke of food – I suppose you mean you want money
to pay for the ham &c? – however I will refer.*

I am glad you had good tobogganing. We all send our
dearest love & so does dear Mabel but most of all your
fond mother Min

238   Newfield

15 II 95

My dear Boy,

Roy's improvement is sustained so far & if no relapse occurs, we may probably consider him spared – Let us never forget the great Unknown, let us pronounce Him* whether we are in sorrow or in joy! Tyra seems better, Mabel has 103-104 fever. *Of course* people get ill whenever they try to defy Nature & behave senseless. Nature does not permit taking liberties, punishment follows. *"Untempered"* enthusiasm gets its set back. The boys & Tyra were tobogganing with your mother till midnight in very raw air to my mind insufficiently clad, which I regard next to gross negligence & crime. I found Brian in day time *wet* through & made him change, unluckily Tyra & Roy did not come to my notice. Your Mother forgets in pointing to *what* people do & endure *on the Continent, how* they do it & *under what* circumstances. Mabel, a fragile thing, cannot of all things take any risks – Now we have done ailing. What with being frozen out of water & servants short handed, & *doubly* worked, besides Mabel here, for which there was no reason the position is not exactly delightful. I thought Mabel had come to see the dentist* & was wondering if he was making her *several* sets of new teeth, when I was informed that she came here to skate – I was never asked whether such suited all parties – However never mind –

I think of running down to the Cove for 3 or 6 – six days with Lewis when Roy & Tyra are out of the wood. Brian keeps uncannily well & is getting stronger every day, going his own way, pleasant & no trouble to any one, working by himself & absolutely happy which is a blessing. – In him there appears to be the artist or scientist –

Enclosed P.O for 5/-. – Keep well & happy!

Do you think it to your benefit if I wrote to Mr Hall? regarding your work –

Your loving father
Leu

239   34 College Rd, Clifton

17.II.95 Sun

My Dear Father.

You say nothing abt skates do let me have them soon. I
should advise getting what I said but which only need
screwing on & do not need letting into the soles of the
boots. Thanks for the money. Do let me hear abt Roy as
he gets better. I am glad you are going down to the cove,
you can then see abt Harry's cottage & the arrangements
for the summer, mind don't forget. What about planting the
vines? I dont think one could write to Mr Hall except to
ask him if he thought I wanted any private help from him,
would he let me have it. Since the frost we have had no
end of boys down with Influenza* & some boys with
pneumonia, Lots of masters have been staying out too, &
so work is very much suspended. Instead of getting up at
6.30 now we get up at 7.45.

I like that very much & feel all the better for the extra
sleep. Give my love to all at home I will write to the
others later. So good bye dear Father from your
loving Son Tankred.

Please don't forget to send my watch when Tyler has
thoroughly put it in *good going order*, it is very awkward being
without it.

240   Newfield

18.II 95

My dear Boy,

The recuperative powers in a child are marvellous. Roy
appears to be picking up by the hour. He has been up for
a few hours & feels his legs again. dear Brian is the picture
of solidity & endurance – Tyra is up & has again her
lessons for the 1st time to day. Mabel is still in fever here.

You did not say whether you would like me to make a halt in Bristol, if I go to the Cove? Of course I shall think of the vines when down in Cornwall; no use planting now! From all I gathered from you, I always feared that Mr Hall had not the patience to explain to you things you wanted to know in *detail*? I thought it ought to be someone so patient like Mr Edwards. But if you fancy *Mr Hall*, tell me & I will consider the matter as to asking him.

re skates – your mother informs me that you wanted *now* a pair like hers ("celeronia")? To-day we have *at last* thaw & I am glad for it; for be it recorded that the laundress sent word today – (so bad are things here in consequence of want of provision against frost) – that she would be glad if we tried to do without clean linen for some time, for water she had none to wash in!! I daresay you have thaw at Clifton too & so I left the purchase of skates for you, I think we have done with skating this season! And I would rather you selected a *good* skate, than buy a make shift; which is only money thrown away. Either the Colombus skate or a good dutchman – there is now presumably time to choose for next season.

Tyler has your watch, but has not been down here – the one left with me I regulated nearly to 1 minute per week. –

I am so glad You kept well, take care of yourself – the cold has reached in some parts of Germany such a degree that they had to close the schools altogether. – We really had no great cold in England, we are only unprepared for it & what is worse with the turn of the weather, three days afterwards all will be forgotten, sufferings, much talked of improvements against reoccurence too & so we chock* along the old way as usual in old England!

Your loving father

Leu

241   Clifton College, Clifton, Bristol

Feb 19th 1895

Dear Mr Behrens

I don't think that private tuition is *necessary* in yr son's case, but I have no doubt that extra help of this kind wd make a difference of 200 or 300 marks to him in the Woolwich exam., & if you like me to do so I will reserve a place for him next term, so as to give him a little extra "polish" before the exam.

I don't know whether you have heard that I am one of the many victims to the prevailing epidemic of influenza. I haven't been out of the house for eleven days – My whole family & two servants have been down with this dreadful pest – 12 patients in all, & none of us yet fit to go out again. You will understand that I have been completely cut adrift from the School; I have a man doing my work, a first rate Mathematician, but what his experience of teaching may be I don't know.* I hope to be back again in a few days, but I shall not be disposed to take on any extra work this term as I am very much pulled down. While I am writing may I suggest (what I have already mentioned to yr son) that he might, if you care to entertain the idea, get considerable benefit in extra drawing lessons. There is a great deal of drawing in the *after** course at Woolwich & in our curriculum just before exam. the subject is apt to get crowded out as we have to pay so much attention to other things. I had made arrangements just before I was laid up for extra lessons* for one of my Woolwich candidates (Lewis mi)* & if you like me to do so I will, as soon as I get back, see if yr son cd go at the same times.

Yours sincerely

H.S.Hall

242   [20.2.1895]*

L.W.F.Behrens Esq*

Thanks for your letter. will write at length as soon as I can.

20.2.1895: 243 (LWFB to TTB)

You ask my advice about writing to Hall & outside envelope* you say "Am writing to H. by this post."? Can I have leave to get a *new* pair of breaches for the rifle corps, mine are now too small for me. please write the leave on a slip of paper by return so that I can show it to moor. Mother mistook abt the skates, I merely said I did not want to have to cut the boot sole & wanted only to have to screw a few screws into the sole which I could afterwards take out [unsigned but in TTB's hand]

243   Newfield

20 II 95

My dear Boy

I enclose you Mr Hall's letter received today, which you will read & *return soonest* possible for me to reply to. – I think it is essential that you should *now* work up *before* next holidays. Do you like (& *is it possible*) to have the private lessons by your *present* master in Mathematics? If so, I will ask Mr Hall to arrange such. You had better be put on to Mr Hall's list *next* term, as he suggests for "polish". What do you say about the Drawing lessons Mr Hall suggests?
Write by return to your

loving father
Leu

244   Newfield House

22.II.95

My dear Boy,

To *save* time, I decided, after having closed my last letter, to write to Mr Hall, therefore the *notice on envelope*. *New* breeches I regard a *mistake*, considering that June might see you leave Clifton. Have *yours lengthened* for *the time being*, they can be well let out, or put on,* probably at the waistband. If that won't do ask Mr Moor to sell yours & buy you a *clean 2nd* hand pair of a taller Boy, but I should think the first can be arranged.

Tyler brought your watch today, I want to time it for a few days & shall then send it on to you. – I am waiting for your reply re Mr Hall in order to answer him.

Your loving father
Leu

245   34 College Rd

24. Feb. 95

My Dear Father

the drawing Mr Hall suggests was what I had already written to you about.* By all means let me have extra work next term with Mr Hall. You must understand that the present Math master has nothing to do with the college. You might suggest the extra lessons with him to Mr Hall, he is very patient & does not mind explaining I like him very much. I may as well get a new pair of trousers it makes a difference only of 2/6. – to second hand ones & mine can't be altered, so do write me the leave, I will let you know soon when Aldershot* is, Louis might like to see it. Don't come & see me here unless you are alone or only with mother or Mr Edwards. So now good bye dear Father from your loving Son

Tankred.

Please show mother enclosed cutting, thanks for the map!

246 Newfield

24 II 95

Dearest Boy,

In vain waited I last night for the last post to bring me Mr
Hall's letter from you! –

Brook Smith's Book of Higher Mathematical questions – If
you are *not* using the same, *Mr Edwards* would like to look
at it. If you send it, say *when* you would like it *returned*.
Reply to *this soonest* & attend to it!

I believe I told you that Smith was down with influenza;
since yesterday Spall followed suit & is in bed, there seems
to be no progress possible since you left. We want Sun &
new life for Men like beasts seem half asleep.
Your loving father
Leu

247 Tuesday Feb 26. 95

L.W.F.Behrens Esq*

Posted a letter* Sunday night, dont know how it did not
reach you. I have not got the book Mr Edwards wants in
my possession. How is Roy & the other invalides.
Tankred

248 Newfield

Feb. 28th 95

My Darling Boy,

I send* you a pyjama suit I hope it will be to your liking, try
it on this very night – if not day – & let me know *by return*

if anything might be better. It is perhaps a little large but I have allowed for shrinking.

We have just been to see "the New Woman"* at the Palace. A play with a very good moral but by no means new. Your father & Lewis are going to dine to-night at Mr Pattenhausens a bachelors party for Mr Eckers (who is engaged), & I propose going with Tyra to Grandmas to have a hot bath as our pipes have not thawed yet. My patients are all better but I still keep dear Roy at home – the second gong! Love & hugs & best wishes & a nip for new*

from your loving Mother Min.

249   6 III 95

My dear Boy,

re trousers I send you the slip & hope you will sell yours. Why don't you write to Mr Edwards regarding the book in question is it in your *Box* & *where* is the key to it?

Roberts says he would be delighted to see us, questionable however if we can get away – When is Aldershot? It would be nice for Louis to see it. His stay is drawing now to an end. Roy is progressing favourably but unfit to go to School.

I write by this post to Mr Hall asking him to arrange private lessons for you with his representative & give you himself the polish before exam & let you have the drawing lessons.

Your loving father
Leu

250   7.III.95

My dear old Boy,

I presume you saw your report* ending 2nd March?

7.3.1895: 251 (TTB to LWFB)

There are three remarks:

"I wish he would realize that soon he will be called on to assume serious responsibilities as a VI form boy." Borwick

"I wish he were more *manly!*"? Moore*

"English essays
very variable seldom good"

All the other part is good & satisfactory.

Do *me* the favour & show Mr Moore & Borwick that you have & possess *the man* in you (I am afraid that both have perhaps no feeling for a youthful joke) so show them *the man* alone. As to English Essays it is clear to me that you *can* write *good* ones if you pin your will to it. Woolwich pays particular attention to essays & *values* them, so pray show your will there too & if you are in want of explanation write, Mr Edwards or myself are always ready to assist. Of course you know before sitting down to write, you should have made ready the analysis of your subject in your head & *logically well.*
Take courage, fare well & God bless you
                         Ever your loving
                                    father Leu

251   March 7th 1895*

My Dear Father

I am beginning really to think whether the army is the right place* for me. There I can never be my own master & in consequence I shall be liable to have people over me who may be much worse than me & yet treat me as a dog. Just so here I have sixths (prefects) above me whom I would not deign to look at, it is the school rule so they must be tolerated. Before they became sixths, I never annoyed them, in fact I left them alone & had nothing to do with them as below me; Now therefore to show their meanness of character they assert their newly begotten power* wherever they can to annoy one & speak to one as if one was a dog; I could remain quiet under them, as it is a school rule, if they *only* did their duty & at least behaved as their position behoves them. In that case I would only look at them as mere signs of the institution & no more. But as they behave I could not stand it & so the other night when he* came up & addressed me in his usual tone, I merely remark* that I thought he might at least treat us (the fifths) like equals & rather gentlemen, & not like dogs, & that I had never been spoken to as he spoke to me by any gentleman of my acquaintance.

This was in the lavatory* adjoining the bedroom whereupon he ordered me to go to my bed. I had done nothing & so he really had no right to say anything, so I told him I wished to drink some water & was not going, then two other fifths (friends of mine) came & backed me up so he was squashed for the time & had to shut up. (I had as I do every night been washing my teeth.)

So the next night the sixth as a body called me up & gave me a licking,* I suppose they thought they were going to reduce me to tears however I just calmly contemplated the despicable idiots (that is 3 out of the total 6) while they licked in & when they had finished put on my coat & laughed at them.

They then tried to get me censored amongst the fifths, but the fifths on the contrary sided with me so they had to subside. I and another boy have now drawn up & passed in the meeting of the fifths a code of laws for our constitution, as before we had only acted on traditional law which we found deficient. I will explain about Vth meetings etc when I come home. – So now the sixth have to knuckle under & treat us properly, having been thus well squashed. I have not told you yet that Mr Moor was ill at all as I thought he was getting better, but he died on Wednesday morning, influenza, pneumonia & other complications. You may imagine it is not a very pleasant situation. I suppose you will write a letter of condolence to Mrs Moor.* Dont forget what you say in it as I want to know how one writes such a letter as there is a great art in writing a

Brown's house: Mar/Apr 1895

Memorial bust of E N P Moor at Clifton

good one. I have not got a sou & I want money instead of a hamper this term so if you can I should like you to send me 2£; I don't know exactly how to manage you see the house are going to buy a wreath & I have not a "sou". I am using the Book* Mr Edwards wants at present. I am sorry I have neglected you so long but this letter has been being written for the past 10 days or so & I have not found time to finish it. One pays 2/6 to have new trousers & nothing if you get 2d hand ones, so they don't actually belong to one anyhow, so there is no selling them at all to be done.

So now good bye dear Father from your loving Son
                    Tankred.

Enclosed [reproduced beneath this letter] the Profile of one of our sixth. The eye is not right, but the eyebrow is.

Please send me a stick of indian ink I can't get any good ink here.

252   8/III 95

My dear Boy,

Man scarcely ever is really free & his own master unless he live by himself, & then* he is dependent! − Before we can govern, we have to practise discipline ourselves. The world is full of mean characters, & blackguards you find everywhere. In the Army & particularly in the Royal Engineers you are supposed to find studying & reflecting men, in fact gentlemen

8.3.1895: 252 (LWFB to TTB)

– one of the reasons why I advocated the RE for you. Before I can properly judge your case, I wish to know from you

1) Are these sixths (prefects) Boys from the *Army side* & going for Woolwich?

2) Do you mean to say that *three* attacked you?

3) In *what* did the licking consist?

Reply to these questions *exactly* & I will tell you *what I* would do. Laws as long as they exist, should be abided & it is *not* difficult to regard them without hardship, *always* provided you have *yourself in hand*. This is important & very necessary for you to learn. –

Whatever you have to endure in life & the brutality you have to suffer bear it well in mind, *not* for you to revisit on your fellow men as you rise, no – bear it in mind what you suffer & let it be *a preventive* – raise the world, never lower it.

Thanks for the sketch, if correct that head lacks *all* nobler quality, has nothing but the brute in it, & criminality.

Enclosed PO for 30/-. Copy of my letter to Mrs M – In writing letters, use head & heart & you won't go much wrong. I shall send you Indian Ink to morrow from the Studio – I think we missed a chance at Stevens* today, but I had no time to go
Reply to what I asked you
　　　　　　Your loving father Leu

Acknowledge receipt of PO *at once* please.

Just* notice that the remark abt "more manly" was from Mr Glazebrook & not Mr Moor. Mr Hall just writes* that it is impossible to find *extra* time in Mathematics for you *this* term, – so you have to work by yourself to the utmost.

8.3.1895: 253 (HSH to LWFB)

253   Kington Lodge, 9 The Avenue, Clifton

March 8th 1895

Dear Mr Behrens

I don't quite understand yr wishes about yr son. When I last wrote* I said that I did not consider extra tuition *necessary*, but that at the same time I felt that I cd do something to improve his Maths score next term.

I am now doing my full work again but I have not time *this term* for any more pupils, & I don't think I ever suggested private tuition this term. Of course I have no "representative"* now that I am in harness again, &, indeed, while I was laid up tho' there was a very able Mathematician doing my work he was quite inexperienced in Army work & had had very little practice at all as a schoolmaster.

I do not think it possible to find a Maths tutor for yr boy this side of the Easter holidays, as Mr Stevens is quite bowled over by the prevailing epidemic & I have taken on some of his work in addition to my own. Mr Hutchinson, the drawing master, has been laid up for more than 3 weeks & has only just got back to work – so that yr boy is just beginning with him as a half-term pupil.

Of course you have heard the sad news about Mr Moor's death – Tho' his long illness had left him in a state of extreme prostration & his death was not wholly unexpected it has cast a dreadful gloom over the place. He was so much liked by everyone, & had done so much for the School that he will be sorely missed for many a year.
I hope you are getting over yr discomforts now.
Yrs sincerely
H.S.Hall

254 Newfield

9 March 95

My dear Boy,

I expect my yesterday's letter in your hands. Indian Ink I posted this morning to you – Your mother is astonished not to have had an acknowledgement of the pyjamas from you. Have they not arrived? She sent them on the *2nd of March!*

Your weakness in english essays has ever since troubled me, considering that it is so easy in comparison to Mathematics. To score in Mathematics & *lose* points in essays seems somewhat out of reason. Pray reflect upon the fact that in the exam – essays *count* & you should not be licked* in that.

I am sure if you make once up your mind, you *can* do it. I have absolute confidence *in you* & would be pleased if you determined to give it your attention –
Ever your loving
father Leu

255 10.III.95

My dear Father.

Thanks very much for the P.O's duly to hand. I wish you would always send the amt* I ask for if you send any at all instead of always subtracting from it a small item. I dont want any more this term however, as what I have will suffice. It suggests to one the idea of asking for more than one wants in order to recieve what one really wants, besides you know I wont ever waste it. Of the pictures* in my study I like "Une halle" best, & the Vanguard. Then I like "The Queen of the swords" & "words of comfort". & then I think I like, "Sons of the brave" & "Venice" least, though I like them all very much. Thanks for the Indian ink. Do let me have my watch as soon as you have regulated it, it is so awkward being without one. I dont know what Borwick means by what he puts except the row I had with the sixth & How the Bogie knows anything about me I don't know, the only thing he can be thinking of is that I wear my trousers turned up which I know he objects to, as they are rather long* & it has been muddy this term. And what called forth the remark on my english essays so strongly, I scarcely know as we have only written one this term. The Sixths are prefects out of 40 in the School 2 only are on the M&E*. & neither of these are in our house. I said that as one* of these 3 miserable Sixths in our house (We have 6 altogether) always spoke to us as if we were dogs, I told him out straight that he didn't speak to us properly & we weren't accustomed to be addressed except as gentlemen, & for this & the rest of the little affair they gave me a licking each gave me two with the cane. However we have got the better of them now, so I am glad I sacrificed myself to gain our point.

Do Write to   Harrison & Sons (printers)
                   St Martin's Lane, London
for   "Regulations & syllabus for course of instruction"
        Royal Military Academy Woolwich

Were you can see the course of work to be gone thro' there. Mr Edwards might also like to look at it.
So now good bye dear Father from your loving Son
                        Tankred.

256   10.III.95

My Dear Mother.

Thanks very much for the pyjamas. They are very large but I will wait till they have been washed to see how much they shrink, before I tell you whether they will do as to size for new ones. Do write & tell me how Roy is. Do try & write oftener if you can, though you must have had a great deal to do lately when all have had the influenza.
So now good bye dear mother from your loving
                        Son Tankred.

I like the pyjamas very much the stuff, & the make is just as I like it.

I enclose two crests please put them with the other crests.*

257   [10.3.1895]*

[draft letter from LWFB to FB] Borwick dr Sir Will you kindly explain to me the powers & limits of power of the VI form boys. Is their serious responsibility supposed to exclude gentlemanly behaviour & permit cowardice? Can a praefect do no wrong & is therefore unpunishable? – If such is an existing error at Clifton I desire to expose it & have it rectified.

258   34 College Road, Clifton, Bristol

Mar 11

Dear Sir,*

In answer to your note, I may explain that VI form boys are responsible for the maintenance of discipline in the House & are entitled to expect unquestioning obedience to their directions, particularly from those whose position in the School & House should have taught them how vitally important to the success of the public-school system, here & elsewhere, is the loyal cooperation of every one high & low, with the endeavours of the VI form to maintain a high standard of conduct & manners. Of course the House- or Head-Master, or in the present sad circumstances the House-Tutor* exercise control over the VI form.

You will allow me to add that, had you known the circumstances of this case, I cannot but think you would have refrained from insinuations of cowardly & ungentlemanly conduct.

Yours faithfully
F.Borwick

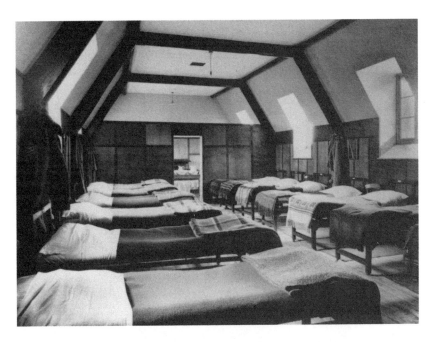

Brown's house, a dormitory and lavatory: early C20

Leu after the Franco-Prussian War

259   [12.3.1895]*

[draft letter from LWFB to FB in reply to letter 258]
Borwick Were my boy to behave as the VI form boys did,
I would most emphatically censure him & declare him a
miscreant. I would do more, I would insist upon his laying
immediately down the praefectship, as absolutely unfit for it.
As an old soldier* I lay the greatest value upon discipline.
But since the VI form alone, should not qualify a praefect
– the old adage of the sow's ear* still holds good in our
days, it would be a grave danger to entrust the power of
unquestioning obedience to an illmannered youth. But I
admit loyal cooperation with ruffians is difficult. I refrain
from expressing my usual view of the cane but I take note
of the matter & opportunity may arise where we have to
cross swords. –   A master may punish, a schoolfellow never
should have that authority. I suppose you know that all
byelaws have no standpoint before the law. No boy should
be allowed to inflict punishment – if you dont permit
fighting – the injury you do you seem to be unaware of.

260   Clifton College, Clifton, Bristol

March 14th

Dear Mr Behrens

I am sorry to be obliged to say that I have entirely failed
to decipher one sentence of yr last letter.* I have sought
the aid of 4 friends & have used a strong magnifying glass,
but I am still unable to make out the sentence which refers
to yr boy reading with ...."representative".

I think I told you in my last letter* that I had no
representative now that I was doing my own work, & at
this stage of the term (less than three weeks from the
exam) none of my colleagues wd take on a pupil even if
they had time. Yr son is regularly revising his work in
school with me & has no *new* work to read before the
Woolwich exam, so I think the question of revision need
not distress you in the least.

14.3.1895: 261 (LWFB to HSH)

Yes, Mr Moor's death has been a terrible blow to us all. He had been my personal friend since 1866 when we were together in the VIth, competing for the same prizes.

I am rather astonished to hear you say that you were not aware of the extent of the epidemic* outside London. It began here the first week in February & at one time there were more than 180 boys down with it, & at different times since the outbreak began, 17 masters besides myself have been down with the epidemic & incapacitated from work.

Mr Moor began a few days earlier than I did & when I was recovering he got an attack of pneumonia from which he had no strength to recover. It has been a most trying term for everyone. I hope yr invalids will soon be quite well again.

Yrs sincerely
H.S.Hall

261   14.III.95

[draft letter from LWFB to HSH in reply to letter 260] Newfield House, Forest Hill, Kent. Dear Mr Hall, Pray accept my apologies for my bad fist, which caused you such unnecessary trouble, the thought, unfortunately runs away with the pen. The word must have been pro tem or "been – representative".* I was under the impression, that your then representative was *yet* in Clifton & all I desired was, not to see you bothered by what you might consider unnecessary questions of a boy. However I submit willingly to your superior judgement in this matter & am quite satisfied with your arrangements as you think fit. The latest we have to expect now, is, I presume, the human foot & mouth disease. Always sincerely yrs – L.W.F.Behrens

18.3.1895: 262 (EFB to TTB)

262 Newfield House, Forest Hill

March 18th 95

My Darling Boy,

I send you the enclosed from Mr Allen in reply to it I recommended him not to sell* at all, as I think it a great mistake on his part but at the same time I may as well let you know about it.

Dear Boy! though I have not written I have been feeling deeply with you in all your experiences. I trust that all things will work together for good & right & justice some how or other, & I only trust that you strive with every fibre after the promotion & establishment of impartial & pure justice & endeavour to be unbiased by personal considerations – which is most difficult, & rarely accomplished. The meeting of 5ths you spoke of seems to me to be a very constitutional & proper thing, but I do not know if it might be regarded as insubordination.

I think you know that I have found a very gifted young musician to teach Tyra the piano & who lives near – so with him, Mr Sharman & Mr Ernest Schrattenholz I am able to have very nice music sometimes on Sunday evenings. We did yesterday – The Owsleys & Parnells joined us after dinner – Mother has a friend Mr Burnett who plays the cello, which I accompany & which is another source of musical pleasure & which I hope you will enjoy when you are here – If you could keep up your violin we could have such nice trios – there are very lovely ones which are by no means difficult. Louis left last Thursday.

We have had two or three such lovely days. Such a treat to see blue sky & summer light – we actually need no fires until the evening, & I have had the garden seats put out in their place. When do you come home.

Roy went to school to day for the first time he seems quite well again – but does not look very strong. Brian went to play

football with some small boys on Saturday for the first time – I am afraid he is not having all the advantages you had, in the way of discipline & sports which rather troubles me. I am thankful you have so far escaped influenza. With thousand loves & blessings your fond Mother
Min.

263   34 College Rd

Tues. March. 19th 95

My Dear Father.

Aldershot falls next monday, do come if you can. I saw a letter from you to Borwick our house tutor, I think. what was it about? Are you thinking of going to the cove these holidays? We come back 3 weeks today Tuesday April 9th* & have 3 weeks & 3 days holidays from then. I intend to devote all the holidays to good steady grind, to get over the ground to make sure of it as far as I can.
So now good bye dear Father from your loving Son
Tankred.

264   19.III.95

My dear Mother.

As I am rather pressed for time to get my work done my letter will be very short. About Mr Allen, if he is going to sell, I should like to *buy in part* if he is agreeable, & could wait 3 weeks till the holidays, he has I know some of the things I just happened to want. If he is pressed for time & wishes to sell all together, then if Father doesnt want it it must go.

I enclose the leaf of his letter. I think he is quite right, if he wants to give it up for the time such thinks* get worth less & less as better things are brought out. I am very glad you begin to play again so now good bye dear mother from your loving

Son Tankred

265   Newfield

20 March 95

My dear Boy.

Yours of the 10th & 19th inst. Suppose you asked me for £5 & I sent you *but* £*1*, you *have* to *take* it that were all I *would* send & in *this* spirit I *expect* you to *always* regard it. – Surely it does not follow that whatever we ask has to be fulfilled? As it happened I had just 30/- in my pocket, which I had turned into P.O. at once, so that you might not suffer delay.

Your new watch is perfect, but somehow or other I cannot regulate the old one, which will always lose. I shall try once more.

The papers from Harrison & sons we possess already.

I wrote to Mr Glazebrook & Borwick & am only waiting for their replies. Never will I allow any of mine to be trodden upon. *We* are one for all, & all for one! What I am driving at you will learn later. I am afraid I cannot come to Aldershot have too much work on hand. Your loving

father Leu

266 34 College Road, Clifton, Bristol

March 20. '95

Dear Sir.

Great pressure of work is partly responsible for my not answering your letter before: also I was anxious to allow an interval to elapse, before doing so, lest on a hasty perusal, I might be tempted into the use of hasty expressions which I am most anxious to avoid.

I can only say that to describe the action of the VI form in this matter as mean, cowardly, ill-mannered, ungentlemanly, & ruffianly, which are some of the epithets which you have permitted yourself to use, is as unfair as it is ridiculous, taking into consideration the fact that you are not acquainted with all the persons concerned, & have only heard "ex parte"* statements.

Your son was guilty of insubordination to the regularly constituted & recognised authorities, & punished accordingly.

Whether boys at School are properly entrusted with the power of punishment is a question that is open to argument: but I may point out that our system is the one which notoriously prevails at all public-schools, & that in sending your son here, you were, I presume, not unaware of that fact, & thereby assented to it.

Further, protests against the system are surely best addressed not to one, who has only to see that it is carried out properly, but to the Head Master who alone is responsible for the powers entrusted to the VI form; and who, I may add, was long ago well aware of the facts of this case.

Not that I wish to shirk my own share of the responsibility: I am quite ready to argue the general question, but I must beg that abusive epithets be not applied on insufficient information.

Yours truly
F. Borwick

21.3.1895: 267 (MGG to LWFB)

267   Clifton College, Bristol

March 21st

Dear Sir

I must apologise for being so slow to answer: but I have been unwell, and have an unusual press of business that must be got through.

What I meant by my remark* is that your boy does not take a proper attitude either towards work or towards authority. Instead of accepting instruction and rules of discipline, and making the best of them, as ordinary healthy boys do, he is querulous & critical. It not only makes him unhappy, but deprives him of a large part of the benefit of a public school education. A few days after making my remark I heard unofficially of some behaviour of his in the house* which painfully emphasizes this view of his character.

I had hoped that he would soon get into the sixth form and gain much from its spirit: but at present he is quite unfit to exercise authority.

Believe me

Yours sincerely
M.G.Glazebrook

268   24 March 95

[draft letter from LWFB to FB in reply to letter 266] Borwick Dr Sir, The interval you allowed to elapse, I notice, did not enable you to focus my letter. The epithets I permitted myself, were those I should have applied to the actions in question had they been perpetrated by a son of mine. desirous to follow the matter up, if needs be publicly, I now ask you to give me the "VI ex parte statement" though I regret thereby any augmentation of your work. May I take it that the evidence of a Vth boy has the same value as that of a VIth –

is the "unquestioning obedience" clause to be applied here also? As for the Clifton power & code with regard to corporal punishment by schoolfellows, may it suffice to tell you that I was unaware of it, for I *never* would assent to such miscarriage of justice, nor did I detect anything of the sort in the printed matter which came to my notice from the college. Awaiting your statement, for which I thank you by anticipation. faithfully yours

269   24/3/95

[draft letter from LWFB to MGG in reply to letter 267] Glazebrook dr Sir, I am sorry to hear that you are unwell & to add at such a time to your work. feeling obliged for your explanation & appreciating your criticisms, I must yet differ from you on certain points & you will observe the form masters notes* of the 2nd of March report do not coincide with your remark regarding work. Whilst strictly upholding discipline & obedience *to masters* I consider the power to inflict corporal punishment particularly so for minor offences by "schoolfellows", & their claim, as Mr Borwick terms it to *"unquestioning* obedience" as not only preposterous, but pernicious & I think the day has come when it should be considered publicly. The time when it was thought desirable to cast humanity into "one" mould is past, the dumb unquestioning heedless acceptance of everything must be very detrimental to the development of enquiring minds. – Undue power in the hands of boys, tho' they may have attained the dignity of the VIth form seems to me an anomaly. With regard to my son's *present* capacity for wielding authority I will not judge but only say that at Mr Lynam's he was from the very first considered most reliable, unqualifiedly trusted, with I remark a sense of justice & a gift for organisation. from what you say the inference to be drawn is that the Clifton system must be made responsible for the destruction of the above qualities & for his present unfitness, if that is so? Reluctantly you drive me into the camp of those who hold that day schools are best for the rising generation. The damage wrought by the injudicious exercise of power by "boys" does not conduce to the good fellowship which should play a large part in the benefit of a public school life not to speak of christianity. I am not sure whether I shall account its eradicating a work of yours. For the rest I am waiting for Mr Borwick's "VIth form ex parte statement" of the incident of which you say you hear unofficially – & if as I have reason to think the power at present wielded by the VIth has in this case been grievously abused, what I expect is, that the case should be *publicly* tried by you & the offenders at least suspended from their praefectship sincerely yours

270   34 College Road, Clifton, Bristol

Mar 26

Dear Sir.

Soon after receiving your letter, the Head Master saw me on the subject of the one you addressed to him: & told me that I need not prolong the correspondence any further, as he would communicate with you himself, after a close enquiry into the facts of the case.
Yours truly
F.Borwick

271   Clifton College, Bristol

March 26th 1895

Dear Sir

Your letter divides itself into two parts, which require separate answers.

26.3.1895: 271 (MGG to LWFB)

To the first part, which is a challenge of the whole principle of self government, which lies at the root of our public school system, I can only reply that I heartily believe in the system, and do not think it would be very profitable to enter upon a discussion of what certainly cannot be altered in our generation – The system is dear to the English people and suits their genius:* and they will not be touched by criticism which comes from a foreign point of view.

The second question is whether, given the system, there has been anything wrong about its administration. In order to answer that question I have myself examined the principal boys concerned. If the incident had been an isolated fact, I should have said that your son had been used harshly – But it is quite clear, in my judgment, that he has for a long time been a centre of mischief in the house, a leader of revolt against the legitimate authority of the Sixth, systematically insolent to the younger and weaker among them, while at the same time "truckling to the stronger". The occasion of his punishment was only the last straw, and by no means the largest. The Sixth regard him as the only dangerous boy in the house – that is, the only one who is always on the wrong side and has the power of leading others wrong. Such being the case I cannot think that he has been treated either with injustice or with harshness –

Indeed, after what I have heard from them and from Mr Borwick, I should not be at all sorry if he were* be removed at the end of the term – One is naturally unwilling to lose a clever boy just when he is likely to do the school credit by his success:* but the peace and order of a boarding house are much more important considerations. And for his own sake I think there might be some advantage in removing him from surroundings towards which he has taken a thoroughly wrong attitude. At the same time it would no doubt be better for all parties if he could really reform, and live loyally under our institutions –

Believe me, dear Sir,

Yours sincerely

M.G.Glazebrook

27.3.1895: 272 (LWFB to MGG)

272   27 March 95

[draft letter from LWFB to MGG in reply to letter 271]
Glazebrook Dr Sir Before replying at length to your letter
of yesterday, I should be obliged by your informing me,
whether the boys you examined were of the VIth form
only, or if those of the Vth who witnessed the incident as
well as my son were also questioned by you? – And of
what the offence *actually* consisted; which proved the last
straw?   I particularly wish to aver that my boy is absolutely
unaware* of my correspondence with either you or Mr
Borwick as I am most anxious to avoid unsettling him, or
encouraging him in any insubordinate attitude – this
particular controversy stands entirely between you & myself.
I am dear Sir Sincerely yours

273   Clifton College, Bristol

March 28th 1895

My dear Sir

The history of the last straw is as follows –

To the dormitory where your son sleeps there is attached a
small room in which the washhandstands &c are kept – No
talking is allowed in there or in the dormitories when they
are going to bed. Woollcombe, who is in charge of that
dormitory, heard your boy talking in the lavatory (as he has
often done before) and went in to quiet him – On his
denying it (falsely, I have good reason to believe),
Woollcombe told him to return to the dormitory. Instead of
doing so he remained there for some time, and then replied
to Woollcombe in what the Sixth thought a very insolent
way – So his offence was breach of order, disobedience,
insolence, and (probably) lying. Another of the Sixth is
quite certain that he heard him speaking at the time
referred to: but that charge was not pressed, as not being
capable of demonstration –

The boys whom I interviewed were himself, Woollcombe, and Meister, who is the head of the house. The last named is a boy of unusually high character, for whom I have the greatest respect. I did not send for your boy's two special friends in the Fifth, because one bears a very indifferent character, and the other is so weak and silly that no reliance can be placed upon him. (Please regard this last remark as strictly private. I do not like bringing in questions of other boys' characters.)

I daresay this account will sound rather like a storm in a teacup. But boys' lives are made up of small incidents, which relatively to them are of very great importance –

Believe me, dear Sir,

Yours sincerely

M.G.Glazebrook

274   Kington Lodge, 9 The Avenue, Clifton

March 28th 1895

Dear Mr Behrens

In a few days you will receive yr son's report,* & I am afraid you will be disappointed.

The fact is he has been falling off very much of late – both in quantity & quality his mathematical work for me has been considerably below the level of what it was at the end of last term, & I am sorry to say there have been during the last few days some symptoms of a return of that querulous attitude which I noticed & mentioned to you a year ago. I then remarked* that a certain want of docility & a tendency to argue about little details of work of which I do not approve & am obliged to correct, combined to make it extremely difficult for your boy's Maths work to progress satisfactorily. Last Easter you aided me by talking to the boy & impressing him with the necessity of cheerful acquiescence in my efforts on his behalf, & a marked improvement resulted. But if when I find it really necessary to correct certain errors & to find fault with details of arrangement & style, I am to be met by an attitude of grumbling self-defence, I really cannot answer for much solid progress between now & the June exam.

"You can take a horse to the water, but you can't make him drink", & without ready acquiescence in my ways & wishes I cannot make much of yr son's Mathematics.

It may be a question whether under the circumstances yr boy wd not do better next term with some other private tutor instead of myself. If he thinks so, do not scruple for a moment to choose some one else. My sole wish is to do the best for him.

Yrs sincerely,

H.S.Hall

275   [30.3.1895]*

[draft letter from LWFB to HSH in reply to letter 274] Dear Mr Hall The contents of yr letter sadly grieve me. The report of the 2nd having been favourable and your finding no fault in your last letter, I take it that the falling off of work as well as disobedience date but from that time namely the 14th inst this coincides with a very unhappy incident in the late Mr Moor's house in which my boy felt himself very unjustly dealt with – we have refrained from writing to him nor have we heard from him since just after the occurence. This has all no doubt been terribly upsetting to him as it would be to either of us in like circumstances & cannot fail to have affected his health & temper & capacity for work. He has always expressed the greatest respect & esteem *for you*, & I should regard it as the greatest personal favour on your part if you would speak to him seriously & *kindly* on the subject that he might really feel he had a friend to confide in in his form master it is very hard for a boy to steer without a friend and guide on the spot On the ....wrote* in the most cheerful way of the work he was going to do for you in the holidays namely 6 hours a day & you know he was willing & *anxious* to have done *extra* work *with you* during term had you been able to give it – ....looks forward to doing it *with you* next term – so he cannot be really *indifferent* now. I am convinced that the symptoms you speak of are but produced by this miserable affair (the details of which are so childish!) by this same post I am enjoining him the strictest obedience to masters I am sure and he is so too that he can do no better than with you I am truly sensible of.... very sincerely

276   Newfield House

30 Mar 1895

My dear Boy,

I am sure it cannot be your intention to cause us grief & sorrow, sleepless nights in the anxiety for your welfare & deprive us of our time, which we can spend better than in settling scrapes. disapproving of the power of inflicting corporal punishment in the hands of boys, I *strictly* & *unbendingly* insist upon the adherence to discipline & obedience *to Masters*. I refer you the enclosed copies* & *expect* you to speak to Mr Hall who *is a friend* to you, like a man Cease this querulous way, accept things as they are & *don't* believe you would be free if you had every thing your own way. We *all without* exception are the slaves of circumstances & there must be a law if social intercourse is to exist at all.

Consort with the good & noble. If you cannot find any, seek comfort in work & studies & keep to yourself, strictly regarding the law, by which you will earn the respect or enforce the same from others.

Just reason for a minute. If you engage some one to do a *particular* work according to *your* instructions, would you deem it satisfactory for that some one to keep on arguing with you? What would you think of the maestro of his craft, who permitted his apprentice to take up an attitude of grumbling querulousness, & self defence? No my good boy, that won't do, break with *that* style *once for all & ever*, for you will only create misery for yourself, & that must not be. Work thoroughly well & hard with *cheer* & keep up a *healthy* frame of mind.

How often have Mr Edwards & myself spoken about the "style"! It is *ruinous* in an exam to disregard it! Listen to *reason* you are now at an age when *reason must* prevail. Profit by the experience of your elders. Be a *protector* of the weak & *never* cringe to the strong. Let us act justly & fairly, for only then can you expect & demand justice.
Your true wellwisher & friend
Your father

277   Newfield

Mar 30th 95

My Dear Boy,

There was no time for me to write more to you by the 11.25.a.m post which has just gone & I hope the letters to you & to Mr Hall may go by it.

I am most *grieved* that you have made the place so thorny about you, but you will find through life that "as you make your bed so you must lie in it" & must have the moral courage to bear bravely whatever difficulties you find yourself in. Try to realize what the true cause of the difficulties is – acknowledge them frankly to yourself, & resolve to avoid them in the future – Parents may be indulgent to the faults of their children – in the way of punishment – however plainly they may see & deplore them, & endeavour by kindness & pointing them out only to remove them (as Mr Hall says you cannot *make* the horse *drink*) – *but* no one else will put up with any nonsense – & in fact errors & shortcomings bring inevitably their own punishment. I hope you will be able to appreciate the true meaning & *import* of Mr Hall's letter. It is very serious! His last report of your work & attitude (in the March

2nd report) was favourable & hopeful. I believe he feels kindly to you & is a really nice man. I wish you could throw yourself upon him & tell him *exactly* how the matter stands now & how it stood before & make a real friend of him & *ask his advice as to your course of action.* – & then work for him with *implicit obedience & all your might & main.* (It is absolutely useless when you are learning from anyone – to go in for your own private methods of work.) Do as we tell you, and make up your mind to be successful in your work. Be of good courage & take up a courageous cheerful attitude with regard to your whole surroundings.

Under the circumstances I am particularly glad that the school disperses five days earlier than was intended* & that we shall see you next Friday.

(I think now you will receive this & the other letters* together on Sunday morning.) Perhaps Mr Hall will send for you on Sunday afternoon. I hope he may, & that you will feel trustful & kind towards him & what he says – & not meet it with shyness & reserve "say you only wish what is just & to do the best". I have never doubted your truthfulness my dear boy – but I cannot help saying once more that Truth is ones best stronghold and defence! – Pray acknowledge to Mr Hall in what you know you have been mistaken or wrong. No one goes through life free of mistakes & errors, & if we take them in the true spirit they will prove stepping stones to better things.* I should like to hear from you – if Mr Hall sends for you. If you do not write – I shall think he has not said anything particular to you or invited your confidence, which will be a disappointment to me – He might of course only take the opportunity of saying a few words to you after a lesson or sometime in the week.

Whatever happens & however much I may regret what you do, you always have my sympathy, anxiety & love as you know. God bless you my dear Boy

Always your fond mother

Min

278   31.3.95

[draft letter from LWFB to MGG in reply to letter 271 and 273] My dear Sir, I presume you wish only the right, as I do & if either of us is in the wrong we admit it with good grace? I thank you for your letter of the 28th. Referring to your note of the 26th you will pardon me if the same struck *me* as unenglish. my demand is only for truth & fairness whether applied to a system or anything else & therefore specifically English. Place of birth I regard as a mere accident. I have not criticised but merely emphasized facts for consideration. for my own part I never underrate david.* if those who see drawbacks of a system remain silent it would never be altered or modified & I think you cannot wish the parents of your boys to be indifferent to your reports or not to know their full meaning. & I quite believe that the habits & methods of a professional lifetime are not to be discarded at a moment's notice. My belief is that very few of the english people have the *extent* of power entrusted to a VIth Boy – I certainly never heard nor dreamt of it. Of what the general english view would be, I have my own opinion. I think it is *not* an unreasonable or unfair demand to ask that such rule of power should be specified in the *school* circular so that parents & boys might see it clearly. I was glad (as the head is after all responsible for the underlings) you admit that had the incident been an isolated fact, you might have said the boy had been used harshly. Your opinion of the poor boy leaves very little good in him if any. Insolent to the weaker truckling to the stronger (unknown in family tradition) & "probably" lying a leader but always on the wrong side are as you may imagine for parents such scathing words which might make a father or mother despair, for were the above literally true, it would make me regard the boy as useless unfit material, who had but one chance open, the happy dispatch. Deeply grieved as I am that my boys headmaster should entertain such an opinion of him, I must let it pass in the hope that in your life time he will have an opportunity to force you to a different view. Permit me to report that at no time have I detected the slightest untruth in the boy. Well do I remember that whilst Mr Moor was still alive,* it was just then reason to believe he had stated "falsely & 'probably' lying"* & yet it turned out differently. The act committed by another boy was laid at his door; – he quietly denied having committed it but declined denouncing his schoolfellow (for me it would have been cowardly & mean) – Unfortunately the perpetrator lacked moral courage, he allowed my boy to suffer innocently – I deem it best not to express an opinion on your judicial procedure A remark at this stage I would consider not uncalled for The case was one of sound not sight; he was not speaking to himself. Others would have been in the lavatory, whom unfortunately you rejected as unworthy evidence (your private remarks will *go no further*) & those I presume were friends – It is true I have expressed the desire he should wash* his teeth face neck & hands before going to bed & in fact perform as many ablutions as the too limited opportunities permit (It seems this proves a hindrance to washing) I have probably to acknowledge myself the original cause of all the evil. I regret it but could scarcely foretell to what my love for hygiene might lead – I heartily concur with your remark "a storm in a teacup" It reminds *me* still more of the Nursery & *I* speaking personally never empowered a nurse to slap my children nor I think would you. As I mentioned at the beginning I wish but what is right & good & weighing the matter from *your* side I cannot but find that the VIth have acted like children who do not deserve to be entrusted with knives. As to "three 'flogging' one" the least said the best. With regard to implicit obedience to masters & loyalty there is no small fault* boy's side in my mind? I look back myself with pleasure to my own schooldays & with unfading admiration for our masters. That he might feel the same for his masters, has been my endeavour & the frustration of this I should regard worst in the whole case. There is no higher mission than that of a teacher; not all are born to it, it requires the genius for it You say small incidents are of great importance to boys. On the path to the University of Life, what deep ruts must any injustice leave Believe me dear Sir Yours sincerely

4.4.1895: 279 (MGG to LWFB)

279   Clifton College, Bristol

April 4th 1895

My dear Sir

I must ask you to excuse me for answering your letter rather briefly, for I have really no time just now, and do not like to delay longer. I am quite willing to concur in your wish that your boy should not leave; and I hope that he will do better in future.

I am not at all surprised that you think the evidence which I mentioned insufficient. But if you had been present when I took it, I think your opinion would be different. You know the difference between reading a newspaper report of a trial and sitting on the jury.

I think I ought to point out that it was stated in my last letter that, although the Sixth believed him guilty of lying, and say they have ample proofs of lying on a previous occasion, it was not lying for which they punished him, but systematic insubordination. A large part of your letter implies the view that the lie was the only thing; whereas in fact (just because, as you say, it was a case of sound, not of sight) it was not made a formal charge at all, nor punished.

The whole incident is most regrettable: but I think your boy brought it all upon himself. If he will be moderately civil to the Sixth next term it will all be forgotten.
Yours sincerely
M.G.Glazebrook

280   Kington Lodge, 9 The Avenue, Clifton

April 6th 1895

Dear Mr Behrens

I have been so busy since I got yr last letter that I have had

6.5.1895: 281 (TTB to LWFB)

no time to write.

I regret also that I did not have an opportunity of speaking to yr boy. I do not know that it was really necessary; if, as you say, he is in strict earnest about his work I hope I shall be able to take him in hand & do something for him.

You said something about working *6 hours* a day during the vacation: I sincerely hope you will discourage the idea of so much work as this, as I fear he wd come back "stale" & wd not stand the strain of high pressure right up to the exam. About 3 hours a day I think he may do safely & I have made suggestions for the proper employment of his time.

I hope he will come back in good health & vigour.
Yours sincerely
H.S.Hall

NEW TERM BEGINS

281   34 College Rd, Clifton

6. May. 95

My Dear Father.

May I have leave to get another racquet. I asked you before I left, but was in such a hurry that I forgot what you said. I got here alright, the exam begins on 25 or 26 June I forget which & lasts about 10 days. Are you going to Cornwall? I will write again soon. So good bye from your loving Son
Tankred.

Please answer per return

282   Newfield House, Forest Hill, Kent

7 may 95

My dear Boy,

If you cannot absolutely do without it, have a new racquet, if you can *avoid* the expense, do save & keep the old one.

Mother is writing to the Canon. you know *I* long to go to Cornwall.

Think of your style in work & writing
your father
Leu

283   34 College Rd

May 14th 1895

My Dear Father

thanks for your letter. I suppose the Canon wrote the usual. Please fill up the enclosed* & *note where to send it to*, & post it as soon as possible. Every hour of my time is occupied & it won't be from want of working if I dont get in. the exam begins June 25 & last* 9 days. So now good bye from your loving Son
Tankred

284   Newfield House, Forest Hill

May 15th

Dearest Tankred

I hope you are getting on alright at school. – Grandma & Lil

255

are here & what do you think? Lil is engaged to Mr Berdet (I do not know how to spell it.) I suppose you know him don't you? I think every body is very pleased. He is coming to dinner to night. I wonder what I shall have to call him. You must write & tell me what you think of it. Lil told me this morning. Please write to me soon dear. I suppose that you are working very hard now. How many weeks are there untill your exam?

Is it not a pitty all the gold fishes have died, first blackie then goldie & now silverie.

The garden is so lovely now. All the lilac is in full bloom
With best love from all
from your loving sis
Tyra.

285   34 College Rd

May 16. Thurs. 95

Dear Father

read enclosed.

[enclosed is printed Form 38 from Woolwich, dated 15.5.1895 (see Doc App LIV-LV), to which is appended a manuscript note: I am to add that your surname can only be described as "Behrens" unless you can produce legal authority for assuming the surname of "Tunstall-Behrens"]

& see if anything can be done. You see who it is one must see.

I have to do some work now So good bye from your
Loving Son
Tankred

please dont lose the paper.

286   Newfield

16 May 1895

My dear Boy,

Your enclosure was signed & duly forwarded by me. I think the address sent* will do, the omission of the hyphen* may have been a mere oversight only. –

Enclosed read Roberts & form of reply of mine. the Canon of course says *he* will be down there from 24 July to 15 Sept –

Tyra is still over the mats* for the drawers, although she is promised the cupboard.

Lil has engaged herself to be married to Mr Burdett.

When time read the enclosure*
Your loving father
Leu

287   17th May

[draft letter from LWFB in response to manuscript note appended to Form 38 in let285] Woolwich To General R.Gipps Sir My son T.Tunstall-Behrens has handed me your circular form 38 dated 15 May – I should like to point out for your consideration that my children are known by the name of Tunstall-Behrens, as you will perceive both in the Oxford* & Clifton certificates. The name will be his legally when he is of age & it avoids all confusion in his military career if as heretofore the name is passed on by *right of usage* which *I am advised is equally legal.* Awaiting your reply I am Sir Yrs obediently

288   Newfield House, Forest Hill, Kent

19th May 1895

Dear brother mine,

Father tells me he gave you a box for breeding larvae & killing bottle; but both are no more to be found. Have you left them at Oxford* or what have you done with them? I am fond of immediate attention to enquiries so an anser by return will oblige your brother. It may interest you to know that the smithy* is all most finished. I have undertaken to help with a lot of painting in the garden. Poor Roy is ill again, the chickenpox have hold of him & so I am not allowed to go to school for 3 weeks. Fräulein thought they were the smallpox.

Ever your
Brian

289   Newfield

May 20th 95

My Dear Boy.

On Friday your father wrote to General Gipps & is still awaiting his reply. Your dear father has such a bout of rheumatism that he can scarcely move & is in bed. but seems otherwise well. It is most trying for him as you may imagine. I know Tyra wrote to you about dear Lilian's engagement. I do not know if you have ever seen Mr Burdett, we all like him very much & as it is his kindness & goodness & pleasantness as well as his interesting qualities we prize I need not describe his appearance which is less youthful than one might choose for Lilian he belongs to one of the oldest if not the oldest firm of Solicitors in Grays Inn (Gamlen & Burdett). His name is Josiah & we call him "Jos"! Leu* was very nice to him & also to Lilian when they were here, & we had a charming evening quite an epoch making family evening, unfortunately Mabel being in Normandy* was not with us & we missed you dear –

Roy is geting nicely over his chickenpox though he has had them badly. the unfortunate part is having to keep Brian at home for four weeks – of course he may also have it still.* In the mean time he does some work with Mr Edwards, & is in all his glory painting in the garden – four doors to-day & some trellis. I hope to have good news to tell in a few days of the invalids & will write again soon. I hope you will keep well & calm for the exam precious & wish you success then & always! With our united fond love
Your loving Mother
Min.

290   Horse Guards, War Office

20 May 1895

The Military Secretary* presents his compliments to Mr L.W.F.Behrens & begs to inform him that in the absence of any legal document his son Mr Tankred Tunstall Behrens can only be known and described by the surname of "Behrens" that being the name shewn in the certificate of birth

291   Newfield

May 23rd 95

My Dear Boy,

I enclose a copy of the note from the Horseguards & yr fathers reply, which he sent after receiving the enclosed from Mr Burdett.*

23.5.1895: 291 (EFB to TTB)

The only other thing to do would be as I think I told you, would be for your father to adopt the name of Tunstall-Behrens himself which would cost £10: but it is not the expense which deters him, but the prospect of confusion & complications in his affairs which might be more troublesome & important than one can foresee. We can continue the T.Tunstall-Behrens as heretofore or if we decide that it is better to leave out the hyphen write it still the same way but without it – I send you Jos' letter (which please return) partly that you might see a letter of his & note what a nice letter it is – they are all like that.

I am writing in my bed room where your dear father has been laid up since Monday with *acute* rheumatism. it had been grumbling for some days since the cold weather but came on in the acute form at the breakfast table on Monday morning & we spent the whole morning waiting to see if he could not get upstairs & at last had to have him carried in a chair by Smith & Spall upstairs & lifted on to the bed – I sent for Dr Wharry – who ordered no smoking, no wine beer or spirits no tea or coffee (which only make the nerves acuter & more sensitive to pain). A farinaceous diet & the less food the better – until to-day at one o'clock he has taken nothing but arrowroot – & today a little fish & rice pudding. he is very gradually but decidedly improving. I thoroughly rub him all over morning & evening with (chloroform & belladonna). Roy is quite convalescent spent yesterday in the garden – but is weak still and is of course with Fräulein in quarantine. The forge is being erected under the spreading walnut tree* so as to include the fireplace – It rather spoils that part of the garden, blocking the fowl run, but is a nice place – or seems so to me.

Brian enjoys it all very much. I am sorry at present he is a dreadful dawdler over his lessons. It is such a pity – he gets up ever so early & then dawdles & wastes 2 or 3 hours over a few sums, but I hope to cure him – The water boots* have just come from Lewis Neuendorff & delight both boys. I wonder how the world is jogging with you this term? *Where* do you go for your exam on June 25th – I suppose all those who are going up, go with a master & put up together in the neighbourhood.*

4.6.1895: 292 (TTB to LWFB)

Yesterday Tyra & I went with Mr Ernest Schrattenholz to hear Burmeister the new great violinist a pupil of Joachim's & far surpassing him in technique he is 24 or 26 or younger – & is simply marvellous. I hope you will hear him later. Bye the Bye Have I told you of my new piano? Such a delight with a capital Delight! A Bechstein small grand* of the latest make & quite a choice specimen. Such a lovely instrument. You will enjoy it I know – & I feel bound to practice now! God bless you my dear Boy let me know how the Clifton world jogs – With no end of love from us all especially from your

fond mother
Min.

292 34 College Rd, Clifton

June. 4. 95

Dear Father

I am sorry I have not written before but all my time is taken up with work or the necessary exercise.

I hope you have quite thrown off your rheumatism. I knew it wd be no good unless you went yourself to the Cove. I certainly dont want to spend the holidays at Nunmuncton.* However you must decide abt going to the Gards I should not enjoy it if I knew you always disliked being in that house. I want some money please, we have 3/- house subscription which I have not paid, I also shd like some besides that to go on with as I have at present not a sou.

I shall be glad when the exam is over, it begins on the 25th & lasts 9 days. Please tell Brian that the things he wants* I believe dont exist any more. So now good bye from your loving

Son Tankred

Please let me have some stamps, this is my last.

293   Newfield

5 June 95

Dear Boy,

Enclosed cheque for £1 & 1/- in penny stps. I excuse you for not writing. Do your best & *mind*, – dont forget the "style". My rheumatism I am sorry to say is no better, on the contrary. It worries me so, because it prevents me from work, of which I have plenty & which I like & idle I shall never learn nor feel happy in – Et bien esperons! [well let us hope]

Your mother accepts the Gards house. Never mind my dislike, one has occasionally to make sacrifices. I quite admit I personally would never have anything to do with such persons & benefitted it me ever so much yet I go to see you & your brothers & sister enjoy themselves with their mother. Mrs Gard does not exist for me, as far as I am concerned. God bless you my son

Ever your loving
father Leu

[addition by EFB] My dear Boy – the *fact* is, that you & your father are the two for whom we go to Bessy's Cove – no one else. I do not mean to imply that we are not happy to go there – but we could all be very happy in many other places – God bless you Dear.

Your loving mother
Min.

Your father *progresses steadily* but not so fast as we could wish.

294   34 College Rd, Clifton

June 6. 95

My Dear Father.

thanks very much for the money & stamps.

I wish under the circumstances the house had not been accepted Since all points to me & says "We sacrifice ourselves to you". I shan't be able to enjoy myself at all under these circumstances. I wish it had been arranged otherwise. It is just time to go to bed, so good bye

from your loving Son

Tankred.

295 June 10. 6.30.P.M

Dear Father.

I think it better if you dont come down here. I agree with you & we will decide not to go to camp.* Has Mr Wollastons plant* come to flower the one here is just flowering? I suppose we shant be able to have Roberts for the 1st 2 weeks or so. So I am writing to him as to how it stands, I suppose we better when we know make an arrangement with the Allens for the interval. I am also writing to Roberts to get the tackle in order. If matters stand for going on Aug. 1st I shall have to follow anyhow for we dont go back till July 31 & Shd have to do some shopping 1st. However we can talk that over when I come to town abt July the 6th* it will be. I hope your Rheumatism has left you. I am straining every nerve, but don't seem to feel very hopeful.

Yours.

Tankred.

296 13 June 95

My dear Boy,

Received report* – the remark "his singularly ugly handwriting which is often very difficult to read will tell against him, I fear" & "fair except as regards style" (English Composition) confirms the old dilemma "Style" Style & Style again! Just give

263

it *a thought*, when you are working in exam. I have drawn
your attention frequently to it. I don't want to worry you,
only remember that "style counts more than you wot of".
Go on fearlessly!

with Love your father
Leu

297 Sunday morning. June 16th 95

My Darling Boy

Ever so many things are calling out for me to do them but
I have been wishing every day to write to you & so I come
to tell all the little odds & ends. It is a most heavenly
Sunday morning & Tyra & I are writing at the table near
the studio shaded by an awning. I wish you were here to
enjoy it too –

Tyra is writing* to Emma & wants me to spell every word
– she makes out she cannot spell "meine liebe Tante" [my
dear aunt] – however the day is lovely Sunday morning is
so peaceful & unlike other days – & now Col. Wood has
left the last house* in Derby Villas, no one can see us *here*.
A little Persian kitten, a new acquisition of Tyra's is frisking
about. Mabel brought it back from her visit to the
Marquise of Banneville in Normandy & so we call it
"Monsieur le Marquis de Banneville" nothing less! He takes
great liberties & it is wonderful how tolerant "Mummy" is
of the newcomer. Jove & Chloe however nearly settled him
yesterday, taking him for a rat. he had of course no chance
against them but lay on his back & kicked & scratched
with all fours – when Spall came to the rescue with one of
his gentle kicks. Our two small boys went down to Margate
(by boat) with Fräulein last Wednesday for a week – Roy
really wanted the change, after his chickenpox & I thought
Brian would be all the better. Grandma & Mabel have been
staying at Margate & found the lodgings for them. I went
to see them (Granny & Lil & Mabs – at Kensington)
yesterday & really Mabel looked blooming! round & rosy.
Lilian will not be married until January,* I believe.

Emma Neuendorff: Newfield 1893

Mummy

Time flies and we with Time.
Stonehenge, Nov, 9th, 1912.

Min in a biplane

16.6.1895: 297 (EFB to TTB)

I am rather sorry not to come to the Guthrie commemoration this year. Mr Glazebrook's note in your report was "I hope he may be (or will be* successful.)" to which I say a very hearty *Amen!* my precious! Do not be over anxious about it however. How glad we shall be to see you when the exam is over & hear all about it – on July 5th I believe you said? You know I should think it was rather a pity for you to miss that camps week at Aldershot, for the sake of the experience & the sociability & esprit de corps – but of course we shall be glad to have you as soon as possible at Bessy's Cove.

I think of taking Lil & Mab's bicycle there with me, keeping it at the packet* or the blacksmiths or at nurse's,* & taking exercise upon it – while you & father are on the sea. I think it would do me more good than anything & I believe Tyra would like it too, we could go together* on it Tyra & I – & *you* & I, if you had a liver attack thro' lack of exercise as sometimes happens! Do not think I mind going there. I like to go where everyone else enjoys going & I mean (D.V*) to enjoy & profit by it myself! & I expect everyone else to do the same. The lunch gong is actually sounding! It always rings too soon on Sundays! & the nice peaceful part of the day is so soon over!

All this time I have taken Tyra to her dancing & such things & what with going out with your father, every morning is more than taken up. I am taking some music lessons & can practice but very little. I suppose I told you of the lovely new Bechstein piano & how much I enjoy it, it is a real pleasure. –

Battersea Park* has become quite a fashionable rendezvous this season for all the lady bicyclists* & I expect to go to see them with Digby Green to-morrow morning. Mrs Wharry is wishing to bycycle now that Magara* is closed & was going too but is prevented.
God bless you my precious here is a visitor
your loving Mother
Min.

298   34 College Rd

Jun 17. 95

Dear Father.

I hope your rheumatism has left you. I am thinking of all the odd things to be done before going to Cornwall. Do send me the £2 as we have to pay the man* in advance. Also please write at the end of the letter "You may bring home a Martini* if you can get leave to have it." & just sign your name, so that I can show that without the rest of the letter. It is necessary to get leave from home before you borrow a rifle for the holidays.
so now good bye from
your loving Son
Tankred.

Please thank mother for the Hamper arrived

Has Roberts written yet?

299   Newfield House

June 28th 95

My Darling Boy

We are thinking of you going through your exams in the heat & hoping that you are getting on bravely all the same – I have understood that you are coming home on July 5th & Tyra has refused an invitation to the Peglers for that weekend – to be with you then. She has just left for the midterm holiday at Brighton* to which all the old girls are invited from Friday to Monday – It is a great pleasure to her to go.

The boys enjoyed their ten days at Margate & have come back tanned & bonny. I am going to have Lil & Mabs Tandem over, for Tyra & me to ride for the sake of the exercise, & take it

Mabel and Lilian on their tandem: Aug 1890

Lilian and Josiah Burdett

to Cornwall with me & I think of trying to improve my swimming before we go down – by practicing in these swimming baths* only I dislike going in a "loving tub" so much. I hope you have exercise & fresh air in between the exams – but I dare say some one sees to that in your case but I heard at New Cross* of an examination room with half the roof of glass & absolutely nothing open on one of the hottest afternoons, spectacles slipped from noses & pencils from fingers it was awful. –

God Bless you my Precious we all pray for your success & shall rejoice to see you. Undying love from

Your fond mother
Min.

I am just going to make a blind for the glass roof* of the studio. –

300   34 College Rd, Clifton

Sun. 30. June 95

Dear Father

I hope your rheumatism has left you at last. Please thank mother for her last letter; I am glad the exam is nearly over; I believe I have at last overworked myself, I cant get rid of a headache I seem to have continually now. Have you any objection to my coming home on Friday next & having about a weeks stay at home as I have the viva* on Monday the 8th. If you dont mind, would you write to Mr Glazebrook & say that I feel overworked & that you think it is *very* desirable. You had better write, it would not be much good my asking him on my own hook.* I think this will be allowed if you write, as it has been allowed before I believe, & if you tell him that I have been working *very* hard both during last *holidays* & this term. I have written to Roberts about the necessary arrangements, but we will discuss this when I come home, also all other things we might want I will try & think of. I have only 4 more different exams left to do now I am thankful to say, It is awfully hard work & I shall be glad when it is all over. I must do some work now, so good bye dear Father From your loving son

Tankred.

301   Newfield House, Forest Hill, Kent

1 July 95

My dear Boy,

I agree & shall be glad to have you near me from friday next to the following Monday week, in which sense I write by same mail to Mr Glazebrook.

I am sorry to say my rheumatism is not gone yet, I am now trying Hensel

Your loving father
Leu

302   Newfield

July 16th

My Dear Boy,

If your nose bleeds again lie on your back. the blood then runs away through the right channels as you suggested, I have just read about it. Hänsel says it has no bad significance – just a little natural relief & the blood finding its way out where it comes out easiest – we were sorry to lose you* dear – I do hope in Cornwall we shall have leisure to enjoy one another – Here there is always so much business on hand.

When you leave Clifton for the holidays, mind you do the proper thing in saying adieu to the masters, & giving thanks where thanks are due! You know I love true courtesy! How shall we know the result of your exam? by the newspapers? or will you be personally informed?
Love to you Blesséd from yr loving Mother
Min.

18.7.1895: 303 (TTB to LWFB)

303   18.7.1895*

L.W.F.Behrens Esq*

Thanks for cheque received this morning. What arrangements have you made, & what day are we going away?

Tankred

304   34 College Rd, Clifton

July 20. 95

Dear Father

Please keep a piece or two of that parchment Smith has & put it in the box on my landing. Has some wire come for me? Let Smith get 1lb of copper wire of medium thickness & also put it in the box. Please send me 6 stamps as this is my last & I may want to write a few more letters. Has Roberts answered my letters yet? Do get rid of your rheumatism. Mr Perks Has kindly sent me the chart.

So now good bye from your

loving Son Tankred.

305   34 College Rd, Clifton

Sunday. July. 28. 95. 3.30 P.M

My Dear Father.

thanks for your letter. I am so glad your rheumatism is better. I am looking forward to coming home on Tuesday particularly as I dont feel quite up to the mark. Please dont forget to think of proper sketching apparatus. Also please ask mother to have some Iron & Salt to take with us. If you have no objection to my having the usual journey money 25/- please let me know by *Monday evening*. As they are not going to allow us more than the bare fare, & I dont like that, I like to be provided in case of accidents, if possible. I* you object to my having the above, dont trouble to write.

So now good bye from

your loving Son

Tankred

306   Sale Cottage, North Road, Hertford

August 2nd 1895

My dear Tankred,

Every day since the exam I have looked for what I knew I should find sooner or later, & this morning's Standard* tells me of your success. I feel so truly glad, & hasten to assure you what a very real pleasure it is to me to congratulate you (*once more*) most sincerely, & also on the high place* you have taken. I have cut out the list & shall preserve it amongst my treasures. I hope you are now enjoying a well earned rest. As I do not know your Cornwall address I must direct to Newfield House. Will you please tell your Mother I was so sorry not to have found the time to call after her pleasant garden party, which I enjoyed so much. With my love to you all

Always Affectionately yours

Florence Etheridge.

307*   Newfield House, Forest Hill

Aug 3. 1895

Dear Master Tankred

I trust you will pardon me, But I feel I must Congratulate you for being so successful with your Examination. I felt quite excited when Mr Edwards told me yesterday & I sincerely hope

Florence Etheridge

Silverdale, Sydenham.

Mrs & Miss Etheridge's school

James Spall

Corner of Westwood Park (on the left) and Honor Oak Road, Forest Hill: c1900

as you go through Life you will always be Successful with all your Undertakings.

Please tell your Father Everything is progressing Satisfactorily at Newfield & Believe me to

Remain yours
Obediently
J.Spall

308   Isle of Cumbrae,* NB

[6.8.1895]*

T.T.Behrens Esq*

Heartiest Congrats – I call it splendid –
C.C.Lynam

ADDITIONAL LETTERS

19A   [23.10.1892]*

Dear Mother

Dont send the gas elongator, if you could spare that incandescent burner* which used to be behind the Piano in the Library & if it is in order send that but not the *gas elongator*. If I cant have the incandescent burner I will see about getting a reading lamp. Send my provisions in one of those old sample boxes which are in the studio have my name painted on it so

that it will serve me as a play box for odds & ends
in haste your loving Son
                                        Tankred

36A London

13 XII 92

My dear Tankred,

Your box with coins arrived safely containing your birthday-
wishes. Pray forgive me that I have not thanked you before;
although retarded, my thanks are not the less sincere &
heartfelt, as I always appreciate any attention paid to me.
Had I not been busy in squaring my affairs in town, I
would have written you long letters, for I have lots to
discuss. In a week's time you will be starting for home, so I
leave now everything until we meet & remain as always
with a good grip
                           Your loving pater
                                        Leu

49A 36 Sussex Sq, Brighton

[18.2.1893]*

Darling Tankred

Please do write to me soon. I realy cant write you a long
letter to day because I have nothing to say.

Some of the teachers have got up a hand writing club & I
am going to belong to it & so is Ethel.

we also have a hoop club & if we go to the equarium with
out letting the hoop drop we get a prize & I have got two
it is not very difficult.

I hope Father will come down & see me. no more to say
from your loving Sister
Tyra.

58A   Newfield House, Forest Hill, Kent

d. 14. März 93.

Lieber Tankred!

Roy und ich haben jeder einen Axt bekommen. Vater hat
mehrere Bäume gefällt und wir haben die Rinde abgehackt.
Jetzt hacken wir die Äste klein. Für zwölf Bündel bezahlt
Vater einen Penny.
Dein
dich liebender Bruder
Brian.

[14th March 93// Dear Tankred,// Roy and I have each
got an axe. Father has felled a lot of trees and we have
stripped off the bark. Now we are cutting the branches
small. For twelve bundles father pays a penny.// Your//
loving brother// Brian]

65A   Newfield House, Forest Hill, Kent

[7.5.1893]*

My Precious Boy

No word from you has reached me since you left. I trust
that no news is good news – but I am pining for news of
some sort from you & shall hope to hear on *Monday*. I shall
try to write myself to you – to-morrow – I just enclose
dear Tyra's letter & Roberts! with my dearest love
always your fond Mother
Min

How do you find the *military side*? What is the difference in
practice.

109A 34 College Rd, Clifton, Bristol

[1.12.1893]*

My dear Father

do write & tell me why you do not write, I can't understand it, it is now nearly 4 weeks since I last had a letter, & I think I have written every week. I will write a longer letter sometime during the week there is no news now. I was exceedingly sorry to see in the paper that Dr Webb of Aspatria died the other day from pneumonia, I suppose you know this by now however. So Good bye dear Father ever your loving Son

Tankred

116A 36 Dartmouth Road, Forest Hill*

[25.1.1894]*

Darling Tankred

I am making you a very small little paper book but cannot finish it because I do not know when you are coming home. I think the Lambleys are coming on Saturday till sunday afternoon.

This is my plan for the present

time	Monday	Tuesday	Wednesday	Thursday	Friday
9 to 10	French	German	French	German	French
10 " 11	Practis*	Practis	Practis	Practis	Practis
11 " 11.15	Lunch	Lunch	Lunch	Lunch	Lunch
11.15 to 1.30					
prep for	Mr Ed	Mr Ed	Mr Ed	Mr Ed	Mr Ed
			Afternoon		
5.30 to 7.30					
Lesson*	Mr Ed	Mr Ed	Mr Ed	Mr Ed	Mr Ed

25.1.1894: 116B (RTB to TTB)

I am so sorry but I cannot write in Gold Ink because it takes such a long time. I said to Roy, "now what are you going to say to Tankred", so he said "Oh, That I would love him to send me a big piece of lickeris." (I dont know how to spell it.)

Thank you very much for your letters. The parcle had just gone a little while before the letter came.
There is no more to say
from your loving sis
Tyra.

116B Newfield House, Forest Hill

[25.1.1894]*

Dearest Tankred,

We have a little stove & Tyra cooked some sweet stuf in it today. Do write to me soon do send me a long pipe of Licorice. Pater gave us a plate of brass for an ornament, & he also gave Tyra a picture that he painted.
from your loving brother
Roy.

118A [5.2.1894]*

Dearest Tankred

Thank you very much for your letter, There is not much news except That the big hall floor has got to be taken up* of the fungus. Mother & I certainly do not take much exercise infact mother does not take any. Ethel & Violet came home with me last Saturday & stayed till Sunday evening we had such fun.

28.3.1894: 138A (LWFB to ENPM)

Practis on my time table. Music Practising. My room is getting on lovley & I have cot* a brown wodden curtain rod but mother has not found curtains yet. Smith is a very nice man but very quiet. I have asked Mr Edwards about the paper cutting. I have no more to say. Good buy Dearest Tankred

from your loving sis
Tyra.

138A [28.3.1894]*

[draft letter from LWFB to ENPM replied to in letter 142] Dr mr moor Viewing the labour of a teacher a high calling (as I do), you can easily understand that any discord between him & a son of mine is sore to me. – the duty of parents, inculcating truth honour & justice, necessarily fosters keenness in either. I could not permit your remarks in my son's reports to pass by without remonstrating with him* & I am very sorry to find that a most bitter feeling possesses him that you have dealt unfairly with him – doubting for a moment his truthfulness, for which I vouch. He has put the matter plainly before me & although manliness naturally forbids to defend himself at the sacrifice of exposing others, I regret that his word should be doubted because he refuses rightly to act meanly. I hold that the strongest attachment should exist between boys & their teachers for life,* for they are the coming men & disciples & the morale of the world should be raised. Will you favour me by removing a barrier which I do not like to exist between you & my boy. Yrs sincerely

My dear Tantrud,

Your box with coins arrived safely containing your birthday-wishes. Pray forgive me that I have not thanked you before, although retarded, my thanks are not the less sincere & heartfelt, as I always appreciate any attention paid to me. Had I not been busy in squaring (squaring) my affairs in town I would have written you long letters, for I have lots to discuss. In a week's time you will be starting for home, so I leave ~~now~~ now everything until we meet & remain as always with a good grip

Your loving pater

Lay

London 13 XII 92

Original of let36A

36 Sussex 82

<u>Brighton</u>

Darling Tankred

Please do write to me soon. I realy cant write you a long letter to day because I have nothing to say.

Some of the teachers have got up a hand writing club and I am going to belong to it so is Ethel.

I also have a hoop club. If we go to the aquarium without letting the hoop drop we get a badge. I have got two it is not very difficult.

I hope Father will come down to see me.

no more to say

from your loving Sister

Ira.

NEWFIELD HOUSE,
FOREST HILL, KENT.

Original of let58A, in a German script (size reduced)

My Precious Boy

No word from you has
reached me since you
left. I trust that no news
is good news - but I am
pining for news of some
sort of from you & shall
hope to hear on Monday
I shall try to write myself
again - tomorrow -
I enclose dear Syra's
letter & Lo___ with
my dearest love -
always your fond
Mu___
Mu___
(How do you find the military side?
that is the ___
is ___)

NEWFIELD HOUSE,
FOREST ___, KENT

Original of let65A

34 College Rd
Clifton
Bristol

My dear Father
          do write & tell me why
you do not write, I can't understand
it, it is now nearly 4 weeks since
I last had a letter, & I think I have
written every week. I will write a
longer letter sometime during the week
there is no news now. I was exceedingly
sorry to see in the paper that Dr Webb
of Aspatria died the other day from
pneumonia, I suppose you know
this by now however. So Good bye dear
Father ever your loving Son
                          Tankred

Maulfield House
Forest Hill

Dearest Tankred.

~~Tyra~~ We have a little stove & Tyra cooked some sweet stuff in it to day. Do write to me soon do send me a long pipe of Licorice. Pater gave us a plate of brass for an ornament, & he also gave Tyra a picture that he painted.

from your loving brother
Ray.

COMMENTARY: DATES & MONEY

WHAT DAY OF THE WEEK?

1st of the month fell on the following days:

	J	F	M	A	M	J	J	A	S	O	N	D
1892									Th	Sa	Tu	Th
1893	Su	W	W	Sa	M	Th	Sa	Tu	F	Su	W	F
1894	M	Th	Th	Su	Tu	F	Su	W	Sa	M	Th	Sa
1895	Tu	F	F	M	W	Sa	M	Th				

1	8	15	22	29
2	9	16	23	30
3	10	17	24	31
4	11	18	25	
5	12	19	26	
6	13	20	27	
7	14	21	28	

DATES OF TERMS

TERM 1	16.9.1892-20.12.1892	begins at let1(TTB 14)
TERM 2	20.1.1893-11.4.1893	begins at let39(TTB 14)
TERM 3	5.5.1893-1.8.1893	begins at let65A(TTB 14)
TERM 4	22.9.1893-22.12.1893	begins at let95(TTB 15)
TERM 5	23.1.1894-10.4.1894	begins at let116(TTB 15)
TERM 6	4.5.1894-31.7.1894	begins at let146(TTB 15)
TERM 7	21.9.1894-18.12.1894	begins at let185(TTB 16)
TERM 8	18.1.1895-5.4.1895	begins at let216(TTB 16)
TERM 9	3.5.1895-30.7.1895	begins at let281(TTB 16)

MONEY CONVERSION

Approximate modern values are as follows:

$$£1 = £100 \qquad 1/- = £5 \qquad 1d. = 40p$$

COMMENTARY: CLIFTON

Clifton College, Clifton, Bristol

The school was opened in September 1862 in the burgeoning Bristol suburb of Clifton, on the pattern of Thomas Arnold's reform of the public school system at Rugby, and after the example of the new public schools founded at Cheltenham and Marlborough in the 1840s. In proposing the foundation in 1860, Dr John Addington Symonds (1807-71), an eminent physician, "an influential resident of Clifton", and the father of the identically named John Addington Symonds (see Biog Reg under ENPM), affirmed that public education (as distinguished from private education at home) "conformed to the general genius and character of the British people: the competition, the emulation, the struggles, the very collisions which occurred in public education suited the struggling, whilst hardy, conquering English mind...Education, competition, examination were the order of the day" (Winterbottom, *Clifton*, p.12 and see let271 and Doc App XVI-XVIII).

The first headmaster (1862-79), John Percival, established Clifton as a flourishing school, and he took seriously the founding intention that the school was to be for Clifton children and encouraged day boys from Bristol (sometimes snobbishly looked down upon as sons of the new rich from semi-detached villas, see Winterbottom, *Clifton*, p.23 and Potter, pp.42-3) as well as boarders from further afield. From the beginning there was both a Classical and a Modern side and also an unusual emphasis upon science (and the creation of the Military and Engineering side in 1875 derived from this; see Potter, p.39, the endnote on **old Cliftonian officers** in let79 on Clifton's military tradition, and the endnote on **mathematical colleagues** in let145), even though the classical emphasis of the traditional public school curriculum predominated, with its ambition to send boys to Oxford and Cambridge rather than Woolwich and Sandhurst. Other notable features of the school almost from the beginning were its provision for Jewish boys (see Biog Reg under Polack) and the degree of insistence on compulsory games, as one element of a strenuousness directed in part, so we might suppose, against sexual activity and in part intended to encourage a distinctive spirit (see Biog Reg under Grace, endnote on **chapel** in let1, and let205). By the time of Glazebrook's headmastership the school was settled in its ways, but had lost some of the élan of the early years.

280

COMMENTARY: NEWFIELD

Newfield House, 36 Dartmouth Road, Forest Hill, Kent
(now London SE)

This house (arrowed at the bottom centre of the map of
Forest Hill on pp.282-3) began life as two semi-detached
villas (1 and 2 Newfield Villas) built in 1848 west of the
railway line to London (poorer houses were gradually built
close to or east of the line, on lower ground in the typical
Victorian way) in an area much favoured by German
immigrants in the second half of the nineteenth century.
The two villas were occupied in 1862 by William Hall and
James Lintop and were still separate in 1875, but by 1877
LWFB had leased either one or (at least by 1888) both –
then known as 36 (Newfield House, on the corner facing
Derby Villas) and 38 (Lansdowne Villa) Dartmouth Road –
and afterwards called them jointly Newfield House. When
LWFB bought the combined property (in area about an
acre and a quarter) in 1889, he had already made
connecting doors between the two original villas (see the
advertisement of the sale at Doc App XLIV-XLV), and
thereafter he devoted himself to the making of furniture
and fittings and to modifying both house and garden to his
taste and needs, principally (during the years covered by the
letters) by building a new studio in the steeply rising garden
well away from the main building (see let119 & 130 and
Dorothy Harlow's letter at Doc App LVIII; one is reminded
that when William Morris set up house everything "had to
be re-invented" – *Later Victorian Britain*, p.134). The house
was sold in 1912 (see Biog Reg under Spall); it lost most of
its garden in 1936/37, but the house (divided into flats)
survived until the mid1960s, when it was demolished to
make room for a block of flats.

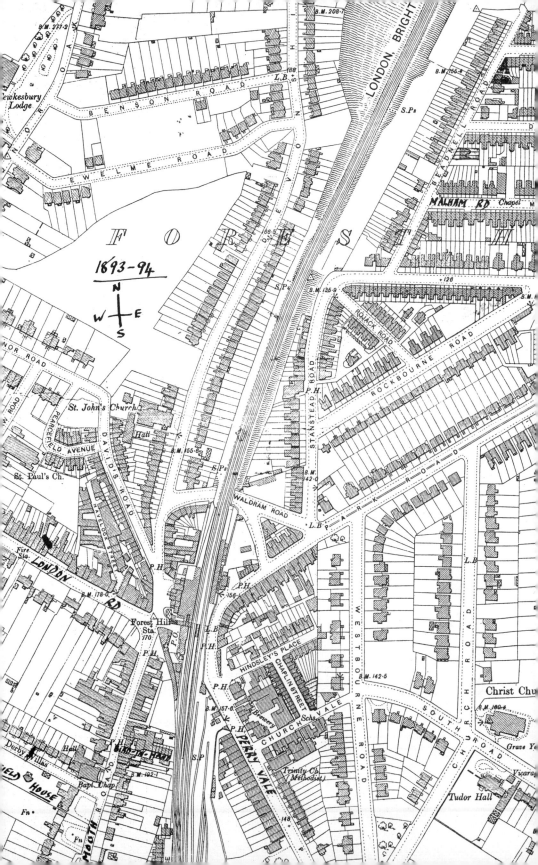

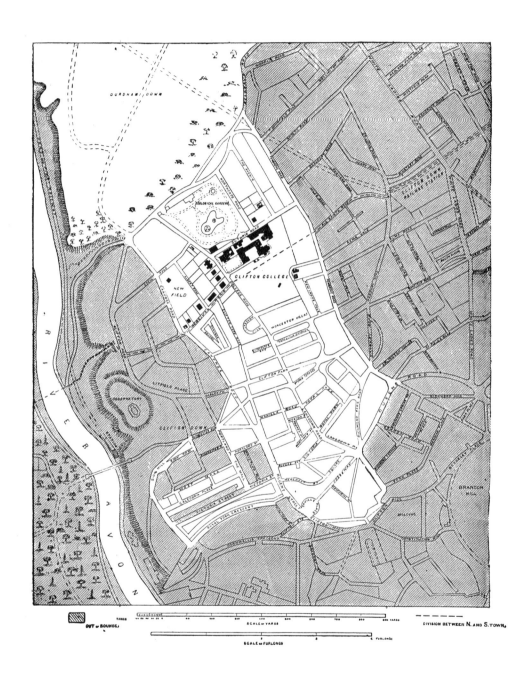

COMMENTARY: FAMILY TREE (in cols left to right)

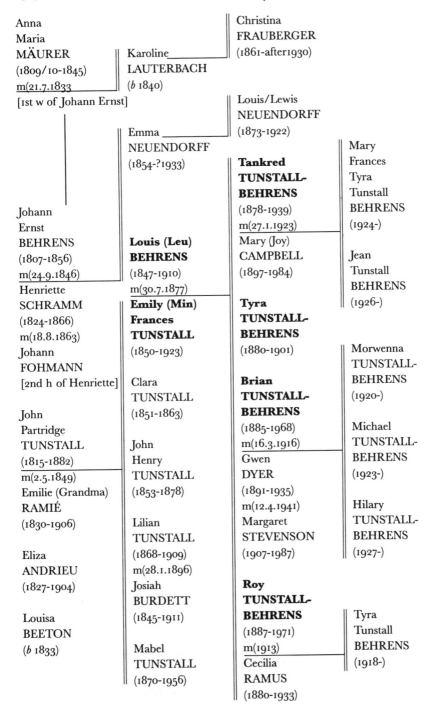

Anna
Maria
MÄURER
(1809/10-1845)
m(21.7.1833
[1st w of Johann Ernst]

Karoline
LAUTERBACH
(b 1840)

Christina
FRAUBERGER
(1861-after1930)

Emma
NEUENDORFF
(1854-?1933)

Louis/Lewis
NEUENDORFF
(1873-1922)

Mary
Frances
Tyra
Tunstall
BEHRENS
(1924-)

Johann
Ernst
BEHRENS
(1807-1856)
m(24.9.1846)
Henriette
SCHRAMM
(1824-1866)
m(18.8.1863)
Johann
FOHMANN
[2nd h of Henriette]

Louis (Leu)
BEHRENS
(1847-1910)
m(30.7.1877)
Emily (Min)
Frances
TUNSTALL
(1850-1923)

Tankred
TUNSTALL-
BEHRENS
(1878-1939)
m(27.1.1923)
Mary (Joy)
CAMPBELL
(1897-1984)

Tyra
TUNSTALL-
BEHRENS
(1880-1901)

Jean
Tunstall
BEHRENS
(1926-)

Morwenna
TUNSTALL-
BEHRENS
(1920-)

John
Partridge
TUNSTALL
(1815-1882)
m(2.5.1849)
Emilie (Grandma)
RAMIÉ
(1830-1906)

Clara
TUNSTALL
(1851-1863)

John
Henry
TUNSTALL
(1853-1878)

Brian
TUNSTALL-
BEHRENS
(1885-1968)
m(16.3.1916)
Gwen
DYER
(1891-1935)
m(12.4.1941)
Margaret
STEVENSON
(1907-1987)

Michael
TUNSTALL-
BEHRENS
(1923-)

Hilary
TUNSTALL-
BEHRENS
(1927-)

Eliza
ANDRIEU
(1827-1904)

Lilian
TUNSTALL
(1868-1909)
m(28.1.1896)
Josiah
BURDETT
(1845-1911)

Roy
TUNSTALL-
BEHRENS
(1887-1971)
m(1913)
Cecilia
RAMUS
(1880-1933)

Louisa
BEETON
(b 1833)

Mabel
TUNSTALL
(1870-1956)

Tyra
Tunstall
BEHRENS
(1918-)

COMMENTARY: BIOGRAPHY

BIOGRAPHICAL REGISTER

This register lists the names of people and animals occurring in the letter text and endnotes, excluding names mentioned simply as those of shops and shopkeepers or suppliers (where any detail will be found or indicated in the letter or endnote at first mention). If a name as it appears in a letter cannot be found in that form in the main alphabetical sequence (or with some minor names, absorbed into the main entry for the family name), it will be found cross-referenced to that sequence in the list of <u>informal uses</u> which here follows the list of <u>abbreviated initials</u> used in page headings and elsewhere. Entries dependent upon an immediately preceding entry begin with italic capitals.

Abbreviated and informal uses

BTB	Brian Tunstall-Behrens
CCL	Mr Lynam
EFB	Mrs Emily Behrens
ENPM	Mr Moor
FB	Mr Borwick
FE	Miss Florence Etheridge
HR	Harry Richards
HSH	Mr Hall
LWFB	Mr Louis Behrens
MGG	Mr Glazebrook
RRG	Gen Gipps
RTB	Roy Tunstall-Behrens
TTB	Tankred Tunstall-Behrens
TyTB	Tyra Tunstall-Behrens

Aunt Eliza	Madame Eliza Andrieu
Boss	Hugh Eyre C Beaver
Brian	Brian Tunstall-Behrens
Caro	Caro Lauterbach
Chet	Chet Owsley
Dora/Dore	Dora Peters
Edith	Edith Owsley
Egouad(g)ya	Mr Edwards

COMMENTARY: BIOGRAPHY

Emma	Emma Neuendorff
Ethel	Ethel Lambley
Fräulein	Fräulein Wehrmeister
(Grand)mother/Grandma/Grannie	
	Emilie Tunstall
Harry	Harry Richards
Jos	Mr Josiah Burdett
Jumma	James Lynam
Leu	Mr Louis Behrens
Lilian/Lil	Lilian Tunstall
Louis/Lewis	Louis Neuendorff
Luke	Luke Clary
Lumpi	Roy
Mabel/Mabs	Mabel Tunstall
Marjorie	Marjorie Monkhouse
Min	Mrs Emily Behrens
Miss B	Miss Bagguley
Mr E(d)	Mr Edwards
Mrs G	Mrs Gard
Mrs M	Mrs Moor
Patty	Sophia Pattenhausen
Roy	Roy Tunstall-Behrens
Sybil	Sybil Owsley
Taglioni-lumpi	
	Roy
Tankred	Tankred Tunstall-Behrens
the archdeacon	
	Canon du Boulay
the aunties	Lilian and Mabel
the bogie	Mr Glazebrook
the boys/the children	
	Brian and Roy
the canon	Canon du Boulay
the head (master)	
	Mr Glazebrook
the Perksman	Mr George Perks
Tina	Tina Frauberger
two aunts	Emma and Caro
Tyra	Tyra Tunstall-Behrens
Violet	Violet Lambley
Xenia	Janet Beaver

ADAMS, Revd Henry Cadwallader (1816/17-after1896) prolific author of children's books

AFFLECK-GRAVES, Dermot (1879-1912) schoolboy at Clifton 1892-96; Royal Military Academy, Woolwich (3rd in competitive entrance examination Dec 1896) and Royal Engineers; left the army and joined the Public Works Department 1911

AGNES household servant at Newfield, originally housemaid and later parlourmaid

ALBERT, Prince (1819-1861) consort of Queen Victoria

ALFRED the Great (849-901) king of the West Saxons

ALLAN (mistakenly Allen), William (b 1832/33) had three sons, Joseph, Thomas and Charles, all four fishermen in Bessy's Cove, near Penzance, Cornwall (mentioned only in let295 & 298)

ALLEN, Mr (Revd) George William (?1859-?1913) educ London College of Divinity; lived in 1892 near Newfield at 9 Brownhill Road, Catford Bridge and in 1893 at 33 Bloomsbury Square, London WC; curate of St Nicholas Cole Abbey in the City of London 1887-93, where he baptised all the children of LWFB and EFB 13.9.1892 (noted in the Baptismal Register that TTB's name, as the others, corrected to Tunstall-Behrens "at parents' written request"; see Biog Reg under George Perks); skilled amateur photographer; organised and gave lectures at the Christo-Theosophical Society which he had founded in February 1890; some of these lectures published in 1892 as *"Things to Come" being essays towards a fuller appreciation of the Christian idea* (see Bibliog; the Preface is reprinted as Doc App L-LI); also published a book of poems c1892; m a "very young wife" (let110) Ellen Emma 1893, a son, Lionel Raymond, b 7.11.1894; curate of Nun Monkton (dioc of Ripon) 1893-97, his address then being Nun Monkton Rectory, York (see Biog Reg under Hancock and Shuttleworth and endnote on **St Nicholas Cole Abbey** in let66)

ANDERSEN, Hans Christian (1805-1875) Danish storyteller

COMMENTARY: BIOGRAPHY (Andrieu)

ANDRIEU, Madame Eliza Ann (née Ramié) (1827-1904) widow of Mathieu-Maurice Andrieu (1813/14-1887); lived at 6 rue de la Trinité in Paris (see Family Tree)

ASHBY, Leonard Beauclerk (1875-1954) schoolboy at Clifton 1890-93; head of TTB's house 1892; Trinity College, Cambridge; became a clergyman (dioc of St Alban's); wrote popular theology

BADAMS, Miss ?governess in the Lambley household

BADLEY (mistakenly Baddeley), Mr John Haden (1865-1967) founded Bedales in Haywards Heath, Sussex in 1893, a school (then as now) inspired by a liberal and humane philosophy very different from that of the rising generation of public schools in the nineteenth century (see p.280)

BAGGULEY (mistakenly Bagallay/Baggalay), Miss M E (1862/63-1938) matron/sister/mistress at the Dragon School (known as "the Bag") 1889-1929

BALFOUR, Arthur James (1848-1930) statesman and philosopher; Conservative prime minister 1902-05 (see DNB)

BALLER, Mrs lived at The Grange, Clapham Common, London SW

BARFF, Edward James (1864-1936) educ Clifton and Trinity Hall, Cambridge; master at Clifton 1887-1927

BARLOW, Mr Henry his daughter a pupil of Mr Edwards; family lived near Newfield at Birkendale, Taylor's Lane, Upper Sydenham

BARNETT, Mrs Louisa Ramié (née Beeton) (*b* 1857) estranged cousin of EFB; EFB's father, John Partridge Tunstall, became a partner in 1868 in a colonial merchanting enterprise (with offices in the City of London and Victoria, British Columbia) with Henry Coppinger Beeton (*b* 1827) who was his brother-in-law (husband of Louisa, who was sister of Emilie Tunstall and Eliza Andrieu) and Louisa Barnett's father; John Henry Tunstall (see Biog Reg under EFB) went to work in the British Columbia offices of this firm in 1872 (see Nolan, p.18) and only left for New Mexico and his death when the partnership broke up and John Partridge Tunstall withdrew from the firm in 1876; there was then a rift between the sisters Emilie Tunstall and Louisa Beeton (see Nolan, p.123 and Doc App LXVII); no doubt LWFB met EFB because his City interests and her father's were very similar; Louisa Barnett lived at 7 Great George Street, Park Street, Bristol; there were three sons and a daughter (Magnus, Samuel, Mary and Stephen), born between 1880 and 1892, to her marriage with Francis Barnett, the eldest child, Magnus, dying in 1892 (see Family Tree)

BARRIE, James Matthew (1860-1937) playwright and novelist (see DNB and Biog Reg under John Toole)

BEAVER, Mrs Cerise (née Eyre) (1856-1922) mother; after husband's death went first to live with her mother (see Biog Reg under Eleanor Maria Eyre) at Eyrecourt Castle near Banagher, Co Galway, Ireland, and afterwards near Newfield at a house called Colbrae, and then at Highlands, Amersham, Bucks

BEAVER, Mr Hugh Edward Campbell (1843-29.8.1892; see let23, but *Burke's Irish Family Records* gives the date of death as 27.8.1892) father; *d* at Johannesburg in S Africa

BEAVER, Hugh Eyre Campbell ("Boss", no doubt a nickname acquired by the little eldest son in S Africa) (1890-1967) son; industrialist and engineer (see DNB)

BEAVER, Guy Duncan Campbell (1891-1947) son; Indian army

BEAVER, John Dennistoun Campbell (2.1.1893-1918) son; killed in the First World War

BEAVER, Janet Ada Campbell ("Xenia") (19.2.1886-after 1952) Mrs Beaver's niece by marriage

BECHSTEIN, Karl (1826-1900) German piano maker

COMMENTARY: BIOGRAPHY (Behrens)

BEHRENS, Mr Louis Wilhelm Ferdinand ("Leu") (1.12.1847-8.7.1910) *b* (the first child of his father's second marriage; see Biog Reg under Lauterbach) Wiesbaden, "in the kingdom of Prussia" (as the naturalisation papers put it; Wiesbaden was the capital of the Duchy of Nassau, independent until annexed by Prussia in 1866); baptised a Protestant, as both his parents were 26.12.1847 (in the birth register he is Ludwig, the German form of Louis, no doubt because both his deceased paternal grandfather, who had been a locksmith in Braunschweig, and his maternal grandfather were Ludwig); fought in Franco-Prussian War 1870-May 1871 (the only one of his soldier companions to survive this terrible ordeal); resident in England from August 1871, living first at 2 Chillington Villas, Penge Road, Norwood Junction, London, SE (a mile or two from Newfield, see p.281; this is now 22 Penge Road, South Norwood; the substantial semi-detached house was occupied from the 1860s to the 1890s by the Rishworth family, with whom LWFB was evidently a lodger); contacts with England from before 1871, since he had been known to some of his British-born referees at naturalisation for twelve years; ceased to be a Prussian subject 13.5.1872; successful London coffee merchant (Behrens and Landsberg of London and Santos in Brazil, his office at 71 Eastcheap, London EC; finally left by 1893); became naturalised British subject 23.7.1878, the day before TTB's birth, when living at Newfield, to which he had moved at marriage; skilled amateur artist; bought land in Bessy's Cove, S Cornwall, beginning perhaps in 1894/95 (see let239 & 240), and more substantially before TyTB's death; he died there suddenly after an operation for appendicitis (see Family Tree, Biog Reg under Barnett and Doc App LVIII-LXVI)

BEHRENS, Mrs Emily Frances ("Min"; née Tunstall) (9.4.1850-23.8.1923) *b* at 14 Liscombes Cottages, Dalston, London E; evidently went away to school at some point (see let26); family lived before her marriage at 7 Belsize Terrace, Hampstead, London NW where the Tunstall family moved in 1869 and where they remained for some years before the move to 187 Adelaide Road, Hampstead; greatly loved by her brother, John Henry Tunstall (see his letter at Doc App XLII-XLIII); John Henry Tunstall murdered in New Mexico in the Lincoln County War 18.2.1878 (see Nolan, p.273), just a few months before birth of TTB, whose hyphenated surname was in memory of EFB's brother; after LWFB's death she moved restlessly from place to place and was living at 72 Normandy Avenue, Barnet, on the northern edge of London, when she suffered the "severe accident" which finally led to her death (see Family Tree, Biog Reg under Barnett and Emilie Tunstall and Doc App LXVII)

BELL, Mr Theodore & Mrs Edith lived at Downside, Epsom, Surrey (see Biog Reg under Mrs Hall)

BELLA cousin of ?EFB; engaged to Mr Jones 1894

BIRD, Mr (Revd) Arthur Frederick Ryder (1860-?1928) son; educ St Edmund Hall, Oxford; ran Forest Hill School near Newfield at 13 Honor Oak Road, Forest Hill (where he lived with his widowed mother, Mrs Fanny Bird *b* 1824/25) 1886-1903; *m* Edith Owsley 25.10.1894

BLACKIE (*d* 1895) a Newfield goldfish

BLACKWELL, Mr lived at Mitre Court, Plough Lane, Purley, Surrey

BLAKE, William (1757-1827) poet and painter (see DNB)

BLEULER (mistakenly Bloiler) party in a law suit against LWFB

BLEWITT, Maj-Gen Charles (1824-1907) husband of Mrs Beaver's first cousin by marriage (Isabella Blanche Beaver 1844-1939)

BOOLE, Mrs Mary Everest (1832-1916) writer on mathematics and education (see Bibliog under *A Boolean Anthology* and Doc App LII-LIII); lived at 16 Ladbroke Road, Notting Hill Gate, London W

BORWICK, Mr Frank (1866-1945) educ Clifton and Trinity College, Oxford; master at Clifton 1892-1926; house tutor in TTB's house 1893

COMMENTARY: BIOGRAPHY (Boulton)

BOULTON, Mr one of his sisters a bridesmaid at Edith Owsley's wedding 25.10.1894

BOYS, Professor Charles Vernon (1855-1944) physicist (see DNB)

BROOKSMITH (mistakenly Brook Smith), Eldred John edited *Woolwich Mathematical Papers* 1888-1910

BROWN, Revd Thomas Edward (1830-1897) Manx poet; educ King William's College, Isle of Man and Christ Church, Oxford; master at Clifton 1863-92; housemaster of TTB's house before ENPM 1864 (it was known as Brown's house still when TTB arrived and then became Moor's house, and then in 1922 again Brown's house when it was decided that all houses should be known by the names they had had at the end of Percival's headmastership; merged with another house and renamed Moberly's in 1994) (see DNB)

BRUNEL, Isambard Kingdom (1806-59) engineer (see DNB)

BRYANT ?gardener at Newfield; ?to replace Luke Clary in 1895 (see endnote on **employment** in let222)

BRYER, Mr Thomas ran Elliott (i.e. Eliot) Bank School near Newfield at 7 and 8 Eliot Bank, Forest Hill

BURDETT (mistakenly Berdet), Mr Josiah (1845-1911) solicitor with Gamlen and Burdett in Gray's Inn, London WC; childless widower at marriage with Lilian Tunstall in 1896 (see Family Tree)

BURGER ?friend of LWFB

BURMESTER (mistakenly Burmeister), Willy (1869-1933) German violinist, pupil of Joachim

BURNE-JONES, Sir Edward Coley (1833-1898) painter; baronet 1894 (see DNB)

BURNETT, Mr friend of Emilie Tunstall who played the cello

BUSH, Harry second cousin of EFB, businessman home from three years working in India 1894

BUSH Mr T Shropshire friend of Mr Allen

CAMBRIDGE, Violet & Lucy daughters of a family that lived near Newfield

CHARLES XII (1682-1718) king of Sweden

CHATTERTON, Thomas (1752-1770) poet (see DNB)

CHITTY, Alexis ?husband; childhood friend of EFB's; lived at 20 Elsworthy Road, Chalk Farm, London NW; Amy Chitty ?wife; Fraser Chitty ?son

CHLOE a Newfield dog

CHRISTMAS, Miss Mary (*b* 1868/69) dressmaker; lived with her parents near Newfield at 3 Derby Villas, Forest Hill

CHURCH, Maurice Richard (1872-1901) schoolboy at the Dragon School 1884-86; farmer and then prospector in British Columbia 1894-98; master at the school 1898-1900; killed in the Boer War (mentioned only in let139)

CHURCH, Professor Alfred John (1829-1912) scholar and prolific populariser of the classics; educ Lincoln College, Oxford; professor of Latin at University College, London 1881-89 (A E Housman's chair 1892-1911)

CICERO, Marcus Tullius (106-43BC) Roman writer and philosopher

CLARY, Luke young (?because called by his first name) gardener (?because working with Spall; see let67) at Newfield; lived with his wife and her old mother

COBBE, Miss Frances Power (1822-1904) philanthropist and religious writer; joint-secretary of National Anti-Vivisection Society 1875-84 (see DNB)

COLUMBUS, Christopher (1451-1506) discoverer of the New World

COX, Nina   lived near Newfield, friend of Rex Earle

CRANE, Walter (1845-1915)   artist (see DNB)

DAVID   (*d* 962BC) second king of Israel

DE BANNEVILLE, Léontine Francisca Thérèse de Biederman Furony, Marquise (1847-1911) Austrian by birth, *b* in Vienna, where she met her diplomat husband, Gaston-Robert Morin, Marquis de Banneville (1818-1881); lived at Banneville la Campagne, near Troarn, close to Caen in Normandy, France

DE BANNEVILLE, Monsieur le Marquis (*b* 1895) a Persian kitten at Newfield

DEWAR, Professor James (1842-1923) chemist and physicist; invented the forerunner of the thermos flask for the storage of low-temperature gases (i.e. the "frozen air" of let116) c1892 (see DNB)

DICKENS, Charles John Huffam (1812-1870) novelist (see DNB)

DU BOULAY, Canon (Ven) Henry Houssemayne (1839/40-1925) educ Exeter College, Oxford; (BA 1863; MA 1892); rector of Lawhitton (dioc of Truro) and archdeacon of Bodmin 1892-1923; a sporting and fishing cleric, he had a holiday house called the Haven on the S Cornish coast in Bessy's Cove

EARLE, Beatrice   young friend of Xenia Beaver, lived near Newfield

EARLE, Rex   teacher in Dover, previously at Eliot Bank School (see Biog Reg under Bryer); friend of Chet Owsley and of Nita Cox

COMMENTARY: BIOGRAPHY (Eckers)

ECKERS, Mr perhaps mistakenly for Mr A Eggers, who lived near Newfield at Holme Lodge, Forest Hill

EDWARDS, Mr Oliver (*b* 1853/54) headmaster of St Bartholomew's Church of England National School (an elementary school founded in 1832) near Newfield at the corner of Kirkdale and Sydenham Park, Upper Sydenham (see endnote on **Board schools** in let116); he was still at the school in 1920/21 (see endnote on **The wreck of the golden fleece** in let136)

EDYE (mistakenly Edge), Major Lourenço (see Biog Reg under Rhodes)

ELIZABETH I (1533-1603) queen of England

ESCOMBE, Francis Jerram (1877-1938) schoolboy at Clifton 1892-95; Trinity Hall, Cambridge; became a stockbroker, and was well known as a Cambridge rowing coach

ETHERIDGE, Miss Florence E ran (with her mother) an elementary school near Newfield at The Briars, 13 Silverdale, Lower Sydenham

EUCLID (c300BC) Alexandrian mathematician; teaching of geometry was usually based on his *Elements*

EYRE, Mr William Henry Gregory (1860-1925) brother of Mrs Cerise Beaver; youngest and only surviving son, inherited Eyrecourt Castle on death of father in 1890

EYRE, Eleanor Maria (*d* 1922) mother of Mrs Cerise Beaver; wife of John Eyre; eldest daughter of Hubert Butler Moore of Shannongrove House, Pallaskenry, Co Limerick, Ireland

FAIRBANKS, Walter (1852-1924) educ Clifton and Clare College, Cambridge; master at Clifton 1875-96; housemaster of Watson's house 1893

FAWCETT, Mrs Henry (i.e. Dame Millicent Fawcett) (1847-1929) leader of the women's suffrage movement (see DNB)

COMMENTARY: BIOGRAPHY (Festing)

FESTING, Richard Arthur Grindall (1875-1957) schoolboy at Clifton 1889-94; head of TTB's house 1894; Queen's College, Oxford; Ceylon civil service

FITZGERALD, Edward (1809-1883) poet and translator (see DNB)

FRAUBERGER, Philiphina Tina (i.e. Christina; née Lauterbach) (1861-after1930) *m* Georg Iungius 1883 (one daughter, Irene Eugenia); *sec m* Heinrich Frauberger 10.2.1892; lived at Gneisenaustraße 13 in Düsseldorf; wrote in June 1892 an article urging the renewed popularity of a kind of lacework called tatting (Schiffchenspitze); in 1894 as Vorsteherin der Kunststickereischule [principal of the fine embroidery school] in Düsseldorf published a *Handbuch der Spitzenkunde* [handbook of lacework]; was still in the same position and living in the same street (now at no 36) in 1921 when she published vol 2 of a *Handbuch der Schiffchenspitze* (vol 1 publ in 1914) (see Family Tree, Bibliog under Frauberger, Biog Reg under Emma Neuendorff and Doc App XLVI-XLIX)

FRAUBERGER, Heinrich (1845-?1919) husband; scholarly writer; for many years was Direktor des Kunstgewerbe-museums [director of the arts and crafts museum] in Düsseldorf

FREDERICK II the Great (1712-1786) king of Prussia

GARD, Mrs Elizabeth (*b* 1829/30) lodging house keeper in Bessy's Cove, S Cornwall, with her two daughters, Anna and Janie

GATTIE, A W dramatist

GENTH (mistakenly Gent), Wilhelm commission merchant; lived near Newfield at 19 Tyson Road, Forest Hill; party in a law suit against LWFB

GILBERT Roberts' partner in or near Bessy's Cove, S Cornwall

GIPPS, Gen Sir Reginald Ramsay (1831-1908) military secretary at the War Office 1892-96

GLADSTONE, Mr William Ewart (1809-1898) statesman and author; *m* Catherine (1812-1900); prime minister, for the fourth and last time 1892-94 (see DNB)

GLAZEBROOK, Mr (Revd) Michael George (1853-1926) educ Balliol College, Oxford; (third) headmaster of Clifton 1891-1905 (see DNB)

GOETHE, Johann Wolfgang (1749-1832) German poet and dramatist

GOLDIE (*d* 1895) a Newfield goldfish

GRACE, William Gilbert (1874-1905) son of Dr W G Grace (1848-1915; a Clifton doctor, the legendary cricketer, and captain of Gloucestershire, who played often in the Close – "the field behind the College", see let19 – at Clifton, which was used by Gloucester County Cricket Club – see also Newbolt's poem *Vitai Lampada*, 1892); schoolboy at Clifton 1887-93; Pembroke College, Cambridge; became a schoolmaster

GRANT, Sir James Hope (1808-1875) general (see DNB)

GREAVES, John (1854-1913) educ Christ's College, Cambridge; fellow of Christ's 1879; *A Treatise on Elementary Statics* 1886

GREEN, Digby lived at 50 Eaton Terrace, London SW

GRUNDY, Sydney (1849-1914) barrister 1869-76; then full-time dramatist; hostile towards Ibsenism

GUTHRIE, Canon John (1793/94-1865) educ Trinity College, Cambridge; chairman of the first Council of Clifton; his wife, Caroline, built the chapel at Clifton as a memorial to him (opened 15.6.1867); the yearly Commemoration was originally of this gift, the first one being held on 22.5.1868

COMMENTARY: BIOGRAPHY (Hall)

HALL, Capt of the 6th Warwickshire Fusiliers; lived at Aldershot (his wife was the niece of Mr Bell)

HALL, Mr Henry Sinclair (1848-1934) educ Clifton and Christ's College, Cambridge (BA Mathematics 1873; MA 1886); schoolfriend of ENPM in the VIth form 1866; (first old boy to become) master at Clifton 1873-99; head of Military side 1875; *m* with a large family; retd early after success of his mathematical textbooks to devote himself to fly fishing (see Biog Reg under Stevens, and Potter, pp.38-9)

HÄMERT, Mr   lived near Newfield

HANCOCK, Revd Thomas (?1840-?1903) lecturer of St Nicholas Cole Abbey 1884-?1903 (see Biog Reg under George Allen)

HANNIBAL (247-182BC) leader of the Carthaginians against Rome in the Second Punic War

HARRIS, Thomas Lake (1823-1906)   mystic (see DNB)

HAUERL   friend of Louis Neuendorff

HEGGS, Bad   lived near Newfield

HENRY VIII (1491-1547)   king of England

HENSEL (or else Hänsel) author of a medical dictionary of some sort, perhaps John George Hansel, who published his *Compendium medicinale* in London in 1730

HICHENS (mistakenly Hitchens/Hitchins), Mr James Harvey (1858/59-1938) educ Epsom and Queen's College, Oxford; master at Cheltenham 1890-95

HILLARD, Revd Albert Ernest (1865/66-1935) educ Christ Church, Oxford; master at Clifton 1890-99; wrote classical textbooks (the writing of schoolbooks was something of a habit with Clifton masters; see Biog Reg also under HSH, ENPM, Siepmann and Stevens)

COMMENTARY: BIOGRAPHY (Holt)

HOLT, Betty (i.e. E D) schoolgirl at Roedean 1891-92; lived at 54 Ullet Road, Sefton Park, Liverpool

HORACE (i.e. Quintus Horatius Flaccus) (65-8BC) Roman poet

HUGHES, Mr lived near Newfield

HUNTINGTON, Revd Henry Edward (1860-5.3.1893) educ Malvern and Keble College, Oxford; master at Wellington 1885-89; housemaster at Malvern 1889-93 (W J G Purnell's housemaster)

HUTCHINSON, Mr George William Caldwell (1849-1930) educ Clifton; drawing master at Clifton 1886-1907

IBSEN, Henrik (1828-1906) Norwegian dramatist

IRVINE, John Henry (1877-by1954) schoolboy at Clifton 1890-95; Corpus Christi College, Oxford; became a barrister (no practice)

IRVING, Sir Henry (1838-1905) actor; knighted 1895 (see DNB)

JAEGER (or else Jäger), Gustav (1832-1916) professor of zoology and physiology at the University of Stuttgart; in a work called *Gesundheitspflege* (c1880; translated immediately into English by Lewis R S Tomalin as *Health Culture*) he suggested that it would be much healthier for human beings to be dressed entirely in clothing made of animal fibres, especially wool; a leading article in *The Times* for 4.10.1884 was devoted to the idea of this new health cult (see endnote on **jaeger** in let15)

JOACHIM, Joseph (1831-1907) German violinist and composer; the favourite violinist of English audiences all his life

JONES, Miss engaged to Mr George Perks 1894

JONES, Mr civil engineer; engaged to Bella 1894

JONES, Wilfred Henry (1874-1944) schoolboy at Clifton 1888-Dec 1892; Emmanuel College, Cambridge; became a schoolmaster

JUNO (afterwards Jove) (*b* Feb 1894) a Newfield Irish terrier

KEALL, Harry William Fitzgerald (1878-after1947) schoolboy at Clifton 1890-95; Magdalen College, Oxford

KENNEDY, Benjamin Hall (1804-1889) the "greatest classical master of the century"; *The Public School Latin Grammar* 1871 (see DNB)

KROEKER, Mr & Mrs lived near Newfield at Cedar Lodge, 19 Honor Oak Road, Forest Hill

LAMBLEY, Ethel M S daughter; schoolgirl at Roedean 1891-93 (her parents then living in Brazil, where LWFB had trading interests), left two terms before TyTB; her name for Tyra was "Tibs" and Tyra's for her was "Lims")

LAMBLEY, Violet E K daughter; schoolgirl at Roedean 1892-93, left two terms before TyTB

LAMBLEY, Mr & Mrs parents; afterwards family lived at Croydon, Surrey

LAUTERBACH, Caro (i.e. Karoline, but spelt usually with a C) Elisabethe Friederike (née Behrens) (*b* 1840) child of first marriage of her Protestant father (her mother was a Catholic), who was a master saddler or harness maker, and worth the modestly substantial sum of about 15000 guilders at the time of his second marriage; *m* Emil Lauterbach (*d* 1877) 1860 (see Family Tree)

LAWRENCE, Miss Penelope (1856-1932) the eldest of the three sisters who founded (what by 1899 became known as) Roedean School (in TyTB's time the school, then known as Wimbledon House School, was at 36 Sussex Square in Brighton); educ Newnham College, Cambridge; headmistress of Roedean 1885-1924

LAYDEKKER, R writer on natural history

LEWIS (minor), Henry Lester (1879-1953) schoolboy at Clifton 1892-95; Royal Military Academy, Woolwich (1st in competitive entrance examination, Dec 1895) and Royal Engineers (mentioned only in let241, all other references to Lewis are to Louis Neuendorff)

LICHTENBERG, Georg Philipp Justus Ludwig surgeon; of 47 Finsbury Square, London EC

LIVY (i.e. Titus Livius Patavinus) (59BC-16AD) Roman historian

LONEY, Sidney Luxton (1860-1939) educ Maidstone Grammar School, Tonbridge and Sidney Sussex College, Cambridge; afterwards professor of mathematics at Royal Holloway College, University of London; *A Treatise on Elementary Dynamics* 1889; *The Elements of Statics and Dynamics* 1891

LONGFELLOW, Henry Wadsworth (1807-1882) American poet and novelist

LYNAM, Mr Charles Cotterill (1858-1938) educ King William's College, Isle of Man and Hertford College, Oxford (BA Mathematics 1882); began teaching at (what by 1921 was known as) the Dragon School, Oxford 1882 (before 1921 the school was known as the Oxford Preparatory School or sometimes Lynam's); *m* Catherine Alice 1885, son and daughter; (in TTB's first term became) headmaster (known as "the skipper") of the Dragon School 1886-1920 (was known for his advanced views); highly skilled and passionate sailor; TTB and he lifelong friends (fulfilling in this instance LWFB's wish, see let 138A & 278); buried at sea (as TTB was shortly afterwards) (see DNB)

LYNAM, James Whitehead ("Jumma") (1878-1938) youngest brother of CCL; schoolboy at the Dragon School 1887-92; farm pupil at Howstrake Farm, Onchan, Isle of Man 1892-97; master at the school 1905-10; afterwards a farmer in Canada and Australia

COMMENTARY: BIOGRAPHY (Lynam)

LYNAM, Dr Robert Garner (1859-1922) brother of CCL; educ King William's College, Isle of Man and King's College, London; doctor in Oxford and school doctor at the Dragon School 1890-1922

MACFADYEN, Eric (1879-1966) rubber-industry pioneer; schoolboy at the Dragon School 1890-93 and Clifton 1893-97; Wadham College, Oxford (see DNB)

MACPHERSON, W D L school secretary and bursar at Clifton 1864-1912

MADDEN, Mr missionary with the Universities' Mission to Central Africa

MAJOR family holidayed in Sennen, Cornwall

MANN, Thomas (1856-1941) trade-unionist and communist; it was "the dock strike of 1889 which brought John Burns and Tom Mann to the front as the "new" labour leaders" (Holbrook Jackson, p.28); he was also concerned about women's suffrage and for instance addressed a meeting on "the programme of the Women's Franchise League" near Newfield in Upper Norwood that EFB attended on 17.5.1893 (see endnote on **association** in let47 and DNB)

MANNS, August (1825-1907) German by birth; conductor at the Crystal Palace 1855-1901; the principal source of classical music at popular prices for many years (as important as the Proms in the twentieth century) were his Oct-Apr Saturday afternoon concerts at the Crystal Palace; naturalised 1894; lived in Norwood, London SE (see DNB)

MANTON, Joseph (mistakenly John) (?1766-1835) gun maker (see DNB)

MARTINI, Frederick (1832-1897) Swiss (by adoption) rifle maker

MAY, Princess (i.e. Princess Victoria Mary of Teck, afterwards Queen Mary) (1867-1953) *m* Duke of York (afterwards George V) 6.7.1893

MCCOLBY   cook at Newfield

MEISTER, Gerald Carl Quintus (afterwards Gerald Charles) (1876-1954) schoolboy at Clifton 1890-95; head of TTB's house 1895; King's College, Cambridge; became a schoolmaster; retired to live at the Dragon School

MELLOR, Maud schoolgirl at Roedean 1892 (arrived at the school before TyTB); lived at Royhouse, Heaton, Bolton

MILTON, John (1608-1674)   poet (see DNB)

MONKHOUSE, Marjorie M an older schoolgirl at Roedean 1890-94 whom TyTB dearly loved; she died young like TyTB

MOOR (mistakenly Moore), Mr Edward Norman Peter (1851-6.3.1895) TTB's housemaster; educ Clifton and Balliol College, Oxford (BA Lit Hum 1874; MA 1876); schoolfriend of HSH in the VIth form 1866 (the obituary seems in error in saying he came to Clifton only in 1867; see let260 and Doc App XXXVIII); while still in the VIth form met the author, John Addington Symonds (1840-1893; see DNB and p.280) in Dec 1869, and for about two years they were lovers, but "although Norman responded to his advances, he was in turn attracted to younger boys" (Grosskurth, p.129; see also Potter, pp.100-8); (third old boy to become) master at Clifton 1874-95; *m* Emily Sibella, who had a brother (see endnote on **Mrs Moor** in let251) 1878, two daughters; (in TTB's first term, cf CCL, became) housemaster 1892-95 (and was followed, in TTB's last term, by W W Asquith, brother of the future prime minister; see Doc App XIV); published in 1892 a translation of Cicero, *de Oratore* (Book I) (see Bibliog under Cicero, Biog Reg under Brown and Doc App XXXVII-XXXIX)

MORICH, Mr R J German by birth; educ University of Berlin; master at Clifton 1892-1900, previously at Manchester Grammar School 1875-92; his wife also taught at Clifton

MORRIS, Miss   TyTB's "special teacher" (let20) at Roedean

COMMENTARY: BIOGRAPHY (Morris)

MORRIS, William (1834-1896) poet, artist, manufacturer and socialist (see DNB and Biog Reg under Stepniak)

MUMMY a Newfield cat

NEUENDORFF, Auguste Emma (née Behrens) (1854-?1933) *m* 1872; she and her husband (Hermann Joseph Neuendorff – 1846-1901) and then her son kept a large hotel (with 130 rooms) in the centre of Wiesbaden where the hot springs are, the Hotel & Badhaus zum Engel at Kranzplatz 6, until it passed from their control into French hands after the First World War; she lived for two years with Tina Frauberger in Düsseldorf after the death of her son, and then in Wiesbaden, for the last ten years utterly dependent on regular quarterly sums of money from BTB, with the assistance of TTB (EFB, for whom Emma felt the affection of a sister, had begun this assistance just before she died in 1923, and Tina had also asked EFB for help with money in 1922) (see Family Tree)

NEUENDORFF, Louis/Lewis (1873-1922) son; *m* Maria Lugenbühl (1877-after1933) 1896 (three sons, Hermann *b* 1900, Karl *b* 1902, and another) (see Family Tree)

NEWBOLT, Henry (1862-1938) poet; educ Clifton and Corpus Christi College, Oxford (see DNB and Biog Reg under Wollaston)

NIGHTON, Mr & Mrs rented Cliff Cottage in Bessy's Cove, S Cornwall from Harry Richards

OWEN family friends of Mr (?George) Perks in Bristol

OWSLEY, Mr John W (*b* 1840/41) father; barrister; family lived near Newfield at 9 Derby Villas, Forest Hill

OWSLEY, Bertha E (*b* 1841/42) mother

OWSLEY, Miss Cicely G (*b* 1868/69) daughter; *m* 1909

OWSLEY, Catherine Edith (*b* 1870/71) daughter; *m* Mr Bird 25.10.1894

OWSLEY, George Chet (i.e. Chetwode) (*b* 1873/74) son; schoolboy at Eliot Bank School (see Biog Reg under Bryer); as a doctor certified the death of Emilie Tunstall 24.2.1906

OWSLEY, Sibyl B (*b* 1882/83)   daughter

PARNELL, Dr Gerald Crécy (*b* 1849/50) doctor; lived with his wife, Mary E L (*b* 1849/50), and son near Newfield at 86 London Road, Forest Hill

PATTENHAUSEN, Mr Charles O (*b* 1836/37) son; commission merchant; family lived near Newfield, first at Rose Cottage, Perry Vale, Forest Hill and later at Priory Villa, Sydenham Road, Lower Sydenham

PATTENHAUSEN, Sophia ("Patty") (*b* 1840/41) son's wife

PATTENHAUSEN, Mr father (not living with son and son's wife at time of 1891 census; mentioned only in let111)

PATTINSON (*d* ?1894) workshop employee at Newfield (see endnote on **averse to** in let115)

PAXTON, Sir Joseph (1803-1865) architect and landscape gardener; designer of the Crystal Palace (see endnote on **Palace** in let30 and DNB)

PEGLER, Mr & Mrs Holmes family lived near Newfield at Strathmore Lodge, 25 Sydenham Park, Upper Sydenham; their son Ernest later wrote poems to TyTB

PELLISSIER, Eugène French by birth; master at Clifton 1874-96

PERKS, Mr Robert William (1849-1934) elder brother; lived at 11 Kensington Palace Gardens, London W and the family house, Claverley, in Chislehurst, Kent (see let69); *m* Edith Mewburn 1878; MP for the Louth Division of Lincolnshire 1892-1910; (see Bibliog under Denis Crane and DNB) (mentioned in let69 & 106; probably all other references to Perks are to George Perks)

COMMENTARY: BIOGRAPHY (Perks)

PERKS, Mr George D younger brother; succeeded his brother, Robert, in the legal firm Robert had helped to build up in Leadenhall Street, London EC when Robert retired from active practice in 1892; advised LWFB about the possible official change of his surname to Tunstall-Behrens 3.11.1892 (see also let291); engaged to Miss Jones 1894 (probably all references to Perks with the exception of those in let69 & 106 are to him)

PETERS, Dora (mistakenly Dore) German parlourmaid and seamstress at Newfield

PLACE, Charles Otley (1875-1955) schoolboy at Clifton 1890-93; Royal Military Academy, Woolwich and Royal Engineers

PLANT, Lt-Col (& Hon Col) Edmund C (*d* 1902) educ Bristol Mining School; (engineering) drawing master at Clifton 1867-1902; CO of Cadet Corps until 1893

POLACK, Revd Joseph (1856-1932) a rabbi; educ Jews College and University of London; master at Clifton and housemaster (not the first; the house was in being by 1878) of Polack's house for Jewish boys 1890-1923

POOLE, John (?1786-1872) dramatist and miscellaneous author (see DNB and Biog Reg under John Toole)

PRINSEP, Val (i.e. Valentine) Cameron (1838-1904) painter (see DNB)

PURNELL William John Geldard (1876-1949) schoolboy at the Dragon School 1886-90, at Malvern 1891-93 and then (a day boy at) Wellington 1893-94 (where his father was a housemaster); became a stockbroker, and Fellow of the Royal Philatelic Society (see Biog Reg under Huntington)

PUTZGER, F W German geographer

REMBRANDT (i.e. Rembrandt Harmensz) (1606-1669) Dutch painter

COMMENTARY: BIOGRAPHY (Renoir)

RENOIR, Auguste (1841-1919) French impressionist painter

REX (d Mar 1894) a Newfield dog

RHODES, Major Elmhirst joint author (with Major Lourenço Edye) of a *Catechism on the Manual of Instruction in Army Signalling*, 1889

RICHARDS, (sea)Capt Harry (i.e. Henry) J (b 1817/18) owned Cliff Cottage in Bessy's Cove, S Cornwall

ROBERTS cook at Newfield (mentioned only in let44)

ROBERTS, (Mr) William (1846/47-1922) fisherman in Bessy's Cove, S Cornwall; did for the Behrens family the kind of thing described in let156

ROOK, Eustace H dentist; lived near Newfield at 68 London Road, Forest Hill

SALMON, George (1819-1904) mathematician and divine; *A Treatise on Conic Sections* 1847 (see DNB)

SARAH parlourmaid at Newfield; left 16.6.1893

SCHARLIEB, Dr/Mrs Mary Ann Dacomb (1845-1930) gynaecological surgeon (see DNB)

SCHILLER, Johann Christoph Friedrich von (1759-1805) German poet and dramatist

SCHLUND, Mr Theodor lived near Newfield at Frankfort House, Manor Road, Forest Hill; *m* with at least one daughter

SCHRATTENHOLZ (mistakenly Shrattenholz), Mr & Mrs Ernest lived at 22 St George's Square, Regents Park, London NW

SCHUBERT, Franz Peter (1797-1828) Austrian composer

SHAKESPEARE, William (1564-1616) dramatist

SHARMAN, Mr Percy V violinist, pupil of Joachim; lived at 223 Gipsy Road, West Norwood, London SE; his father, J Schutz Sharman, a surgeon, was the householder

SHUTTLEWORTH, Revd Henry Cary (?1851-after1896) rector of St Nicholas Cole Abbey 1883-after96 (see Biog Reg under George Allen)

SIEPMANN, Otto (1861-1947) a German from Alsace; pioneering teacher of modern languages; educ University of Strasbourg; master at Clifton 1890-1921 (see DNB)

SILVERIE (d 1895) a Newfield goldfish

SMITH workshop employee at Newfield, to replace Pattinson in 1894

SMITH, Charles (1844-1916) educ Sidney Sussex College, Cambridge; master of Sidney Sussex College 1890-1916; *An Elementary Treatise on Conic Sections* 1882

SMITH, Edmund Henry Cocks (1854-1935) educ Wellington and Trinity College, Cambridge; master at Clifton 1877-1922

SOMERVILLE, Annesley Ashburton (?or Ashworth) (1858-1942) educ Queen's College, Cork and Trinity College, Cambridge; master at Eton 1885-1922; *A First French Writer* 1889

SOPHIE cook at Newfield (?or household servant acting as such)

SPALL, James (b 1857/58) gardener at Newfield; lived nearby at 45 Malham Road, Forest Hill; the only servant to be left a bequest (£100) in LWFB's will; left employment with the Behrens family after the move from Newfield, May 1912

SPENCE (mistakenly Spense), Mr Charles Hickson (1858-1912) educ Jesus College, Cambridge; master at Clifton 1884-1912; head of Modern side 1892

COMMENTARY: BIOGRAPHY (Stapley)

STAPLEY, Mrs friend of EFB, probably the wife of Henry Stapley who lived near Newfield at 1 Bird-in-Hand Cottages, Forest Hill

STEPNIAK (i.e. Sergius Mikhailovitch Kravchinsky) (1852-23.12.1895) a leader of the Russian Revolutionary party; settled in London 1885; killed by a train on a level crossing near his home at 31 Blandford Road, Bedford Park, London W; William Morris' last open-air appearance was to speak at his funeral, outside Waterloo station on 28.12.1895

STEVENS, Mr Frederick Haller (1852/53-1934) educ King's School, Warwick and Queen's College, Oxford; master at Clifton 1876-1904; collaborated with HSH on some of his textbooks

STURT, George (1863-1927) wheelwright and writer (see Bibliog under Sturt and DNB)

TAGLIONI, Marie (1809-1884) the "most prominent danseuse of the century" (see DNB)

TAIT, Charles William Adam (1845/46-1913) educ Rugby and Queen's College, Oxford; master at Clifton 1873-1904

TECK, Duchess of (1833-1897) mother of Princess May

TENNYSON, Alfred, Lord (1809-6.10.1892) poet (laureate 1850-92) (see DNB)

THOMAS, Walter Brandon (1856-1914) actor, dramatist and song writer

TOOLE, John Lawrence (1830-1906) actor and theatrical manager; played title role in John Poole's *Paul Pry* for first time 1852; leased the Folly Theatre 1879-95 (called Toole's 1882); played Jasper Phipps in J M Barrie's *Walker, London* 1892 (see DNB)

TOWNSHEND, Charles, 2nd Viscount (1674-1738) of Rainham, Norfolk (see DNB)

COMMENTARY: BIOGRAPHY (Trollope)

TROLLOPE, Anthony (1815-1882) novelist (see DNB)

TUCKER (Mr) fisherman like Roberts, no doubt living in or near Bessy's Cove, S Cornwall

TUNSTALL, Emilie (née Ramié) (1830-1906) lived at 187 Adelaide Road, South Hampstead, London NW and afterwards in Kensington, London W; *m* in St Pierre, Jersey; *d* at Newfield, death certified by Chet Owsley (see Family Tree and Biog Reg under Chet Owsley)

TUNSTALL, Lilian (1868-1909) there were three sons and a daughter of her marriage with Josiah Burdett (Scott, John/Jack, Eleanor/Ella and Graeme) born between 1897 and 1903; Graeme died young and the others were orphaned in childhood (see Family Tree)

TUNSTALL, Mabel (1870-1956) unmarried (see Family Tree, and Doc App LXVII-LXVIII)

TUNSTALL-BEHRENS, Brian (12.8.1885-25.5.1968) educ (after Miss Etheridge and then in Sept 1894 Mr Bryer's school) Channel View (Prep) School, Clevedon, Somerset (with RTB) 1897-98, Dulwich (as a day boy) 1898-1904 and Pembroke College, Oxford (matric 1905; BA Chemistry 1911); inherited the land in Cornwall (see Family Tree and Biog Reg under LWFB and George Allen)

TUNSTALL-BEHRENS, Roy (6.9.1887-29.4.1971) educ (after Miss Etheridge and then in Sept 1894 Mr Bird's school) Channel View (Prep) School (with BTB) 1897-98, the Dragon School 1899, Repton (briefly), Marlborough 1902 until he left abruptly at Christmas 1904 (see let134) and St John's College, Oxford (matric 1907; no degree); left for Canada late in 1907, began to buy land in Lindsay, California 1910, after some financial arrangement with his brothers as a result of LWFB's death and set up there permanently as a fruit grower (see Family Tree and Biog Reg under George Allen)

TUNSTALL-BEHRENS, Tankred (24.7.1878-16.4.1939) the name Tankred (a variant form of Dankred) not so rare in Germany then as now, because of the nineteenth-century vogue for legendary heroic figures; 8¾lbs at birth; educ the Dragon School (where he was known as "Tinker" and was CCL's first boarder; and is listed as T T Behrens, not Tunstall-Behrens) 1886-92; (with a mathematical scholarship worth £25, after an unsuccessful attempt at Rugby; and see let138) Clifton 1892-95; Royal Military Academy, Woolwich (7th in competitive entrance examination, June/July 1895); passed out 3rd, commissioned into the Royal Engineers 1897; in the army he was not permitted to use the hyphenated surname (see Biog Reg under EFB, George Allen and George Perks, and Index under Surname) which he had with difficulty asserted at Clifton, and his children did not have the hyphen; served on the Anglo-German Boundary Commission in Uganda 1903-06; served on the Boundary Commission in Bolivia 1910-13; wounded in France Oct 1915 (returned to the front 1916); served on the Austro-Italian Boundary International Commission 1920-23; retired from the army with the rank of Lieut-Colonel 1926; returned to the Army as Garrison Engineer at Shorncliffe and Lydd 1934; buried at sea like CCL (see Family Tree and Biog Reg under CCL)

TUNSTALL-BEHRENS, Tyra (19.9.1880-16.1.1901: 2.30p.m.; see Biog Reg under Victoria) the name Tyra from a feminine form of the Scandinavian god Tyr, son of Odin and younger brother of Thor, with also a chiming glance at the German *teuere* [dear, beloved] (Lilian Tunstall called her "Tibby"; see also Biog Reg under Ethel Lambley); educ Roedean 1892-93, left at the end of the Michaelmas term (see endnote on **sports** in let95 and Biog Reg under Lawrence), St Leonard's in St Andrew's, Scotland 1896-98, where Dorothy Harlow was a schoolfriend, and Westminster Art School in London 1899; Tyra probably died of the still poorly understood Guillain-Barrié disorder (see Family Tree, Biog Reg under George Allen and Doc App LVII-LX)

VAN SOMMEREN, William Weymouth (*b* 1876) schoolboy at Clifton 1890-94; Burma military police and Indian army

VASSALL, Gilbert Claude (1876-1941) educ Charterhouse and Oriel College, Oxford; master at the Dragon School (eventually co-headmaster) 1900-41; frequent companion of CCL's (as "the mate") on cruises

COMMENTARY: BIOGRAPHY (Vaughan)

VAUGHAN, William Wyamar (1865-1938) educ Rugby and New College, Oxford; master at Clifton 1890-1904; house tutor in TTB's house until end 1893; headmaster of Rugby 1921-31 (see DNB)

VECQUERAY, John William Joseph (?1830-1901) educ Notre Dame de la Paix, Namur, Belgium 1841-48; master at Rugby 1859-1901, previously at a prep school in Bruges, 1851-59; *A German Accidence for the use of Rugby School* 1856 (later revised for general school use)

VERGIL (i.e. Publius Vergilius Maro) (70-19BC) Roman poet

VICTORIA (1819-22.1.1901) queen of England

WALKER, Mrs friend of EFB

WARD workshop employee at Newfield

WATSON, Revd Henry Charles (1843-1925) educ University College, London and Trinity College, Cambridge; master at Clifton 1870-1900; first housemaster of Watson's house 1878-93

WEBB, Dr Henry John (1853-28.11.1893) principal of Aspatria Agricultural College in Cumberland

WEHRMEISTER, Fräulein Marie governess to Brian and Roy for five or six years; did some nursing training while in England (see let69)

WENDT, Mr O lived near Newfield at Friedheim, Sydenham Park, Upper Sydenham

WEST, Benjamin (1738-1820) painter (see DNB)

WEST, Dr & Mrs lived near Newfield

WHARRY, Dr & Mrs R lived at 7 Cambridge Gate, Regent's Park, London NW

COMMENTARY: BIOGRAPHY (Wharry)

WHARRY, Olive (*b* ?1889) daughter; schoolgirl at Roedean 1902-04; she died young like TyTB

WILLANS, Mrs R H (*d* 1897) mother; lived at Haywards Heath, Sussex and then near Regent's Park, London NW

WILLANS, R H K son; of the Connaught Rangers

WILLANS, T James son; of the Connaught Rangers, seconded to the Indian staff corps

WILLANS, R StJ evidently the youngest son; tried again for Sandhurst June 1894; later of the Northumberland Fusiliers

WILSON, Revd James Maurice (1836-1931) educ Sedbergh and St John's College, Cambridge; (second) headmaster of Clifton 1879-91 (see DNB)

WOLLASTON, Mr George Hyde (?1845-1926) educ Clare College, Cambridge; master at Clifton 1873-99; ran the botanical garden and museum at Clifton; first housemaster of North Town (one of the two day boys' houses; and was there Henry Newbolt's much loved and respected housemaster; see Potter, p.35) 1875

WOOD, Col family lived near Newfield at 13 Derby Villas, Forest Hill (see endnote on **house** in let297)

WOOLLCOMBE, Basil Richard (1878-1943) schoolboy at Clifton 1892-96; VIth former in charge of TTB's dormitory 1895; became a solicitor

WORCESTER, Marquis of (1847-1924) afterwards 9th Duke of Beaufort

WRIGHT, Mr & Mrs Walter lived near Newfield

ENDNOTES

Letter 1
Sunday see Dates of Terms and a method of calculating days of the week on p.279
fresh...new a usual misquotation of the last line of Milton's *Lycidas*
chapel see Biog Reg under Guthrie; the chapel was extended in 1910 to its present size; Newbolt's poem *Clifton Chapel*, written in 1898, expresses perhaps what is in EFB's mind here:

> This is the Chapel: here, my son,
>   Your father thought the thoughts of youth,
> And heard the words that one by one
>   The touch of Life has turned to truth.
> Here in a day that is not far
>   You too may speak with noble ghosts
> Of manhood and the vows of war
>   You made before the Lord of Hosts...

we i.e. RTB, BTB and Fräulein (see let13)
Brighton i.e. to school at Roedean (see Biog Reg under TyTB and Lambley); it was TyTB's first term at Roedean just as TTB's first term at Clifton; EFB actually herself took TyTB on 27.9.1892 (see let13); TyTB wrote home on 17.7.1893: "I shall be so glad to be home agan scholl is so nasty I do hate it so."
"ship called Tyra" see let196; this was perhaps a little boat made for BTB and RTB by TTB in imitation of a boat-shaped shuttle (Schiffchen, see illustration drawn from Tina Frauberger's *Handbuch der Schiffchenspitze* on p.lvi) sent with a lacework set to TyTB (?for her birthday) by Tina Frauberger (see Biog Reg); the German phrase for "Tyra's shuttle" would be *das Tyraschiffchen*, which could be re-translated as "the ship called Tyra"; after Tyra's death, LWFB and his sons had a "boat called Tyra" (see the photograph facing p.lviii of this 13ft St Ives built 'punt', which still survives fragmentarily).

Letter 2
ADDRESS i.e. the Dragon School
keepsake see let13
be friends it was so (see Biog Reg under CCL)

COMMENTARY: ENDNOTES (let3)

Letter 3
Moors House see Biog Reg under Moor and Brown
5£ see Money Conversion on p.279
altogether TTB has the sums of money the wrong way round, no doubt because of the 5/5 chime; the expense for fives is enormous, perhaps a covert way of helping to pay for the fives courts, which were built in the 1890s
Corps the Corps (whose CO was at this time Col E C Plant) was not compulsory, as it later became (from First World War until 1970); it had been founded in 1875 as the Engineer Cadet Corps and remained an engineer corps until 1929; at its foundation it was stated that it "should rank as one of the games of the school...and that it should as far as possible have the same organization as the other games" (see endnote on *play up* in let100) – "A great many fellows pass direct in to the Royal Military Academy at Woolwich...For, see, we have an Engineer Cadet Corps, and that gives us a better chance of learning the practical work than most fellows have" (*Chat about Clifton*, p.102)

Letter 4
DATE clearly precedes let5
Military side boys arriving at Clifton chose at once the Classical side (for university) or the Modern side (for business); if intended for Sandhurst or Woolwich they would join the Military side (normally after age 16) from the Modern side; TTB began on the Modern side (see let7) and joined the Military side in the summer of 1893 (see let66), i.e. just before his fifteenth birthday (see endnote on **power** in let251, p.280 & Doc App XVI-XVIII)

Letter 5
DATE TTB mentions "Fathers letter of yesterday" in let7; I take it that this means TTB *received* this letter on 24.9.1892, so that it would have been written the day before
cheque for £1 see let3; LWFB was presumably a little puzzled by TTB's account of the necessary payment for fives
mother tongue as of course it was LWFB's
master for German i.e. O Siepmann
Woolwich this is the first mention of TTB's preference; possibly mentioned by HSH in the letter to LWFB noted earlier in this letter

pater   public school (Latin) slang for "father"

Letter 6
DATE   clearly immediately follows let5
list of payments   see Doc App XIX

Letter 7
resurrection pie   i.e. filled with leftovers
Middle 5th   forms were not necessarily age related, and boys did not move up automatically each year; the VIth form was chiefly for boys going to Oxford and Cambridge (see let255)
Smutty words   but see let138
Irishman   i.e. almost certainly D Affleck-Graves, who seems with TTB to have been the only new entrant from outside Clifton (as distinct from the junior school) to Brown's house in Sept 1892; the Bristol/Ireland connection was strong because of trade
so small   see let19; the system was to sleep in dormitories and live in the studies in day time, with the dormitories then out of bounds
the downs   the large area of common land immediately to the north of the school, beyond the Zoo
my name   see Biog Reg under EFB, TTB, George Allen and George Perks; the school register has TTB under both Behrens and Tunstall-Behrens in the index, though in the entry for him the elements are not hyphenated (see let291); in the school list of 1892 he is simply Behrens (but see endnote on **5.y.** in let70)
write   for "writing"
form   TTB was in the Middle Vth (initially 14 boys, no one else from his house; form master C H Spence, who was also form master of the Upper Vth, with 13 boys); Mr Spence taught Scripture, Latin, History, Geography and English Literature; for Mathematics, TTB was in set 3 with 18 boys – this is the "form" he refers to here – taught by HSH; for French Conversation and Composition, he was in a set with 11 boys, taught by E Pellissier; for French in general, in set 5 taught by C W A Tait; for German, in set 3 taught by J Polack (from which, oddly, he is marked as absent); for Geometrical and Plan Drawing, he is in a set taught by E C Plant; he does not seem to have been in a Science set
Lines & Twine   i.e. fishing tackle

COMMENTARY: ENDNOTES (let8)

back home   see let1

hot baths   at the Dragon School, by contrast, considerable care was taken about such arrangements; in his Dec 1895 copy of the *Draconian*, TTB would have been able to read about the new plunge bath which "can be heated to about 80 degrees Fahrenheit"

28 boys   the Middle and Upper Vth together actually came to 27 boys

he   for "here"

a good many   on the Jewish house, see Biog Reg under Polack and p.280

London Bridge   the train fare from Forest Hill to London Bridge is much more in let223 (see endnote on **L.B.**)

extra 1d.   i.e. presumably for any additional letter to LWFB (but the 1d. is spent on let8 in the event).

Clifton   the village area, a quarter of a mile south of the school; by 1892 all the present suburban buildings had been built, though when the school was founded it was out in the fields, with only the Zoological Gardens (founded 1835; see endnote on **Zoological Gardens** in let103) for company

the bill   see let3

about it   i.e. German (see let5)

head boy   i.e. L B Ashby

Scholarship   TTB was one of seven scholars in his year at Clifton

begging   for "beginning"

Letter 8

adress any letters   TTB is presumably concerned about the exact form of his name on the envelope, that he should have an initial and not a Christian name (see let33) and a hyphenated surname

Letter 9

most of my time   after retiring from his work in the City (see let14)

acct   i.e. account

home ministry   i.e. arrangements about servants (see let13)

Sandhurst   see let6

Gebraucht...gewinnen   LWFB slightly misquotes from *Faust* (Part I, lines 1908-9), perhaps not immediately remembering the amusing circumstance that this is actually the devil, in the

disguise of Faust, giving no doubt good sound advice to a student
force perhaps an anglicising of "forte"

Letter 10
DATE clearly immediately follows let9

Letter 11
christened Tunstall-Behrens see Biog Reg under George Allen
School Secretary i.e. W D L Macpherson, who had been secretary from the beginning of the school; see endnote on **my name** in let7

Letter 12
Brockley i.e. Brockley Combe, a narrow tree-clad steep dry limestone valley about five miles south of Clifton (see let15)
Drags a drag was a heavy four-horsed cart

Letter 13
Newfield see p.281 and the address at the head of let116A
letter...father i.e. let2
laurel i.e. bay
Brighton i.e. Roedean
Worthing see let1
Bergen i.e. mountains; BTB and RTB of course speak German with Fräulein, whose written English at least, however, was good (see also let134)

Letter 14
DATE 8th for 9th
you plainly both parents visited TTB at Clifton (see let11)
Pall Mall perhaps a copy of *The Pall Mall Gazette* (a London daily evening newspaper), though the concern seems more than might be justified by so relatively slight a production; *The Pall Mall Magazine* cannot be meant because it only began publication in May 1893
room i.e. EFB's study at Newfield
where to see let12; TTB doesn't know where Brockley Combe is
his visit see let17

319

to Malvern actually on this occasion the Malvern contingent came to Clifton for these Cadet Force exercises, as we see from the mention of the Clifton suspension bridge in let15

Letter 15
attack for "attach"

jaeger kind of woollen cloth from which vegetable fibres are excluded as unwholesome, originally manufactured in the late nineteenth century by Dr Jaeger's Sanitary Woollen System Co Ltd; the so-called Woollen Movement "in which the unlovely garments advocated by Dr Gustave (sic) Jaeger played a conspicuous part" was an offshoot of the whole movement towards "Rational Dress" which accompanied the move towards the social emancipation of women in the late nineteenth century. "The first Jaeger retail shop was opened in 1883 at Fore Street in the City." (Adburgham, p.159, and see also Biog Reg under Jaeger and endnote on **patent** in let23)

Tanin i.e. tannic acid

2 Hrs. i.e. at about 2½ mph

Brockley coon see let12; TTB clearly *heard* the name rather than read it on a notice

Suspension bridge i.e. Brunel's famous suspension bridge at Clifton, opened 1864

Letter 16
DATE clearly immediately follows let15

geography school examinations tested knowledge of the geography of the Holy Land and of Greece and Rome; not quite what LWFB might have thought useful

Letter 19
MR. H i.e. Moor's house; this is the standard abbreviation as used in the *Cliftonian*, the Clifton College magazine (see Biog Reg under Brown)

DATE clearly immediately follows let18

boys clubs this public school mission in the St Paul's area of Bristol was started by a committee of masters, Old Cliftonians and boys in 1875; in 1882 a mission hall was opened; in 1886 St Agnes became the first church to be built for a public school mission; a boys' and a girls' club were built in the 1890s, and there were summer camps and sports fixtures for the boys of the mission (W H Jones was one of the officers for the 1892 summer camp for 112 boys; see also Potter, pp.48-9 and endnote on **Board schools** in let116)

Aldershot a regular army camp in Hampshire which was an alternative venue for field days

shop in our road David Emery (ham and beef warehouse), 13 Dartmouth Road, Forest Hill, near Newfield

galley pots i.e. gallipots, small earthen glazed pots, esp as formerly used by apothecaries for ointments and medicines

menier Menier's is a fine dark chocolate

maté tea i.e. tea from Paraguay

Letter 20
last letter i.e. let19, but see endnote on **last letter** in let21

Bedales see Biog Reg under Badley

Letter 21
last letter this must presumably be let19, but the mention of the incandescent burner later in the paragraph "as in last letter" seems to refer to let19A, which was perhaps sent at the same time

house match clearly there was a system of matches lasting for several days, rather like test match cricket; the system was changed in 1893 (see let108); in the house competition mentioned in let21 TTB's house actually came 6th out of 8 – "there is far more excitement over the football House matches than over the cricket. We play the Rugby Union game, and a match lasts for three days, one hour each day unless one side scores two goals, when the game is finished. If neither side manages to score two goals in the three days, the match is decided by points" (*Chat about Clifton*, p.102)

workshops these were for making and repairing things for Newfield (see p.281)

Letter 23
third i.e. J D C Beaver

mother i.e. Eleanor Eyre

Eyrecourt Castle one of only two important mid-seventeenth-century country houses in Ireland to survive into the twentieth century (abandoned after 1920), near the Shannon estuary in Co Galway (see Bence-Jones and Biog Reg under Beaver and Eyre)

writing i.e. handwriting; the report must have said (unjustifiably, see original of let109A following p.276) nasty things about TTB's handwriting, as later reports do (see Doc App X & XIV for comment on TTB's handwriting; this particular report is missing from the incomplete collection of reports in Doc App I-XV)

Hoare of Messrs Hoare & Sons (Merchant Tailors), Central House, 252 & 255 High Holborn, London WC

patent i.e. patent no.18189, dated 14.11.1889, for "Improvements in women's and children's dress"; EFB's patent was part of the whole movement towards "Rational Dress" and reminds one of Lady Harberton's divided skirts "known as 'dual garmenture'" (Adburgham, p.159, and see endnote on **jaeger** in let15 and note on **10% royalty** in let90)

Letter 26

insult because the housemaster was responsible for the catering in his house

present cook see let13

Meadows shop H & F Meadows (Picture Frame Makers ...Printsellers, Dealers in Works of Art); the shop was well situated, at 59 Gracechurch Street, London EC

N.B. North Britain, i.e. Scotland (see let308)

a for "are"

expresses it slightly adapted quotation from *In Memoriam* i, where this is the "truth" which Tennyson actually magnificently rejects as he begins his poem (see let277); Tennyson had died only a month before this letter (see endnote on **the loveliest & the best** in let72)

Letter 27

DATE noted by EFB as received on 13.11.1892

lecture the lecture was on "Quartz Fibres": Professor Boys "proved to the complete bewilderment of the sceptical that it is possible for the light of a candle in a village several miles away to exercise an appreciable influence upon us!" (*Cliftonian*, Dec 1892, p.424)

Letter 28

open it it must have been a combination lock

Letter 29
DATE   noted by EFB as received on 21.11.1892
as   for "a"
cap   i.e. W H Jones

Letter 30
King Lear   see let38
Palace   i.e. Crystal Palace, designed by Sir Joseph Paxton to be the home of the Great Exhibition in Hyde Park in 1851; it covered 19 acres, was 108ft high, had a steel frame of 3300 columns and 2300 girders, and was glazed with nearly 300,000 panes of glass; it was moved to a site near Sydenham in 1854, destroyed by fire in 1936; the Saturday concerts at the Crystal Palace, closely associated with Schubert and under their conductor, August Manns, with many Germans in the orchestra, were a focus of expatriate German social life in the area (see Biog Reg under Manns)

Letter 31
Christmas   he didn't (see let109)
packet   i.e. a birthday present (see let33)
letter to day   perhaps let30 was delayed

Letter 32
odd folks   probably a children's annual or magazine

Letter 33
DATE   TTB clearly writes back urgently after receipt of let32
Tankred on my letters   TTB doesn't want his Christian name but only an initial on the envelope, the public school form then and long afterwards being use of surnames and embarrassed concealment of Christian names

Letter 35
DATE   as postmark

Letter 36
boot's   i.e. servants employed to clean boots and shoes and no doubt to do other jobs in the house

Letter 38
Lyceum   theatre in London's West End

Doctor   i.e. Dr Garner Lynam

Letter 39
***Genth* case**   clearly a civil action by LWFB to do with his business affairs, probably involving the German commission merchant of that name who lived near Newfield (see Biog Reg) and was of course in the same kind of business (see let54 where TTB spells the name as it would be pronounced in German)

Letter 40
DATE   92 for 93
burning   perhaps the burning in of her name or initials (cf. TTB's umbrella in let100)
glasses   i.e. looking glasses (see let48)
Hulbe   Georg Hulbe, owner of the Kunstgewerbehaus [arts and crafts emporium] at Lindenstraße 43-47, St Georg, Hamburg, with other branches in Hamburg and also in Berlin, Copenhagen and Wiesbaden

Letter 41
I   for "I'm"

Letter 42
G.   i.e. Genth
double tax   an unstamped letter was charged at double the rate to the recipient
her houses   Emilie Tunstall owned large premises close to the Corn Exchange in Romford which were converted into two adjoining shops and leased to Messrs Pink (Ironmongers) from 25.3.1894 at an annual rent of £140, and to W Pearson (Jeweller) ?from the same date at an annual rent of £90

Letter 43
reader   see let44 and Biog Reg under Somerville

Letter 44
father wrote   missing
runs   i.e. cross-country runs
comforter   i.e. woollen scarf
***Hope* of Cheapside**   (?shirtmaker) of Cheapside, London EC
Prayers...go   slight misquotation from *Hamlet* III.3

Letter 45
DATE as postmark
the brazen serpent painting by Benjamin West of the event in Numbers XXI.9
hippacea "hippace" was "caseus equinus", i.e. cheese made of mare's milk, and had medical uses; perhaps "hippacea" was an ointment made of the same substance

Letter 46
Bloiler case TTB evidently misspells the German name Bleuler; this is clearly a civil action rather like the Genth case (see endnote on **Genth** case in let39)
book i.e. Somerville (see let43)
Have omits "you"
they i.e. presumably problems based on the theorems; perhaps the following "they" refers to practice problems TTB had done before

Letter 47
Nil desperandum i.e. nothing to be despaired of; quotation from Horace, *Odes* I.vii
middle fifth see endnote on **form** in let7
association Tom Mann was founder and member of many labour unions and organisations; in 1885 he affiliated himself with the socialist movement, and the association referred to here seems plainly a socialist one
stores i.e. probably the Supply Stores (grocers and provision dealers), 15 & 17 Dartmouth Road, Forest Hill, near Newfield; possibly an early form of the shop that sold everything, if it is the same place that sold skates in let229 & 230

Letter 48
Houghton George Houghton & Son (photographic apparatus manufacturers), 89 High Holborn, London WC (see let52)

Letter 49
bygones conceivably this may have had something to do with the family difficulty noted in Biog Reg under Barnett

Letter 50
tool basket see let32; TTB had had only "juvenile tools"

COMMENTARY: ENDNOTES (let51)

Letter 51
envelope missing

Letter 52
Progress *a monthly illustrated record of technical and scientific advance*, vol 1, no 1 (July 1892)
class see endnote on **form** in let7

Letter 53
in...world the "not of the world" theme is common in e.g. I John, but this precise "in but not of" formulation is not Scriptural (Shakespeare uses a somewhat similar formulation at *Cymbeline* III.4.138-40)
practical help see endnote on **St Nicholas Cole Abbey** in let66

Letter 54
DATE TTB will almost certainly have written on the Sunday, after receiving let53 on Sat 25th
Tyler this is either Edward Tyler (watchmaker), 42 Exmouth Street, Clerkenwell, London EC; or Richard Tyler (watchmaker), 45 Cleveland Street, London W; probably the former
Jew's i.e. J Polack

Letter 55
1st first thing, immediately
other fellow i.e. J H Irvine

Letter 57
report see Doc App I
second edition see let44

Letter 58
DATE must be a Sunday after the date of let57
St Mary Redcliffe's church described by Queen Elizabeth I as "the fairest, the goodliest, and the most famous parish church in England" and made doubly famous by Chatterton
carvings the 1200 roof bosses in the church are very varied, with for example representations of a maze, a jack-in-the-green (several of these), a mermaid, besides armorial designs
god for "good"

COMMENTARY: ENDNOTES (let60)

Letter 60
Siegle   August Siegle (English and Foreign Bookseller), 30 Lime Street, London EC
report   see Doc App I

Letter 62
DATE   clearly follows let60, and written most likely on the Sunday following the two Penpole races
before   see let58
penpole   the name of these long-distance races came from a spot overlooking Avonmouth called Penpole Point (seven miles from Clifton); the land between Clifton and the point remained farmland until the 1920s; the Long Penpole (run on this occasion on 25.3.1893) was from Clifton towards Penpole and back, and the Short Penpole (run on this occasion on 23.3.1893) was part of this course – "on half-holidays there are longer runs. These are the school runs called "Big Penpole" and "Little Penpole." The latter is for boys under sixteen only. The object in these runs is "to come in," that is to say, to finish within ten minutes of the hares. To do this is none too easy for, in the first place the course for "Big Penpole" is about ten miles over a very hilly country; secondly, the country is a good deal intersected with dykes, which are too wide to jump over, consequently you have to jump *into* them and clamber out the best way you can on the other side..."Little Penpole" is a shorter course, but every bit as sticky" (*Chat about Clifton*, pp.102-3)
one boy   i.e. F J Escombe;
1st boy   i.e. H W F Keall, who completed the race in 54min 52sec
4th & 6th boys   i.e. W W van Sommeren and C O Place; the winner completed the race in 63min 33sec

Letter 63
children   for "children's"
vide   for example

Letter 64
letter   see let54
paddington   the London railway terminus for trains from Bristol

special train this was an early train specially arranged to carry a large proportion of the boarders from the school to London

Letter 65
Bessy's Cove for family reasons, the more usual name, wherever it occurs in the letters (i.e. in let65, 156, 167-71, 225, 293 & 297), has been replaced by this name drawn from the 1891 census of the spot
horse i.e. gym horse; TyTB *was* in the drilling eight, together with Maud Mellor
hepeling i.e. helping
Lambleys i.e. Ethel and Violet Lambley

Letter 66
St Nicholas Cole Abbey see Chadwick, vol 2 on the social gospel in the late 1880s and 1890s: "The Christian Socialist H.C.Shuttleworth and his curate Thomas Hancock preached a social gospel in St Nicholas, Cole Abbey, in London, and thereby filled a hitherto empty church." (p.281)
school life they had left Roedean
C.T. i.e. Christo-Theosophical Society (see Biog Reg under George Allen)

Letter 67
DATE letter completed on May 22nd and 23rd
rat trap perhaps family slang for a wire-fronted bookcase with locking doors (?to keep picture books safe from the little boys)
Derby horse race run yearly at Epsom, Surrey, established 1780

Letter 69
only goes Ethel Lambley, another special friend, had left Roedean the previous term
German Hospital in Dalston, London E, founded 1845

Letter 70
routine see Doc App XX
5.y. this was one of two forms on the Military side (11 boys, one other boy in TTB's house, form master F H Stevens); TTB's name is now written as Tunstall-Behrens
do for "don't"

scol. i.e. scholarship

holidays i.e. as distinct from half holidays; these were for Commemoration (see Biog Reg under Guthrie)

law suits i.e. Genth and Bleuler

Cricket (School) Eleven the team was captained by W G Grace, son of the legendary cricketer – "He is a good bowler, and has played for the county. He is also a very clever scholar" (*Chat about Clifton*, p.102)

Having omits "given"

Letter 71

Draconian the Dragon School magazine

Exam i.e. for a scholarship

Marlborough 1893 was Marlborough's jubilee, and as part of their celebrations they invited Clifton Rifle Corps to a field day, along with Bradfield, Wellington, Winchester, Malvern and Rugby; the event took place in Savernake Forest

Oxford i.e. the Dragon School (see Biog Reg under CCL)

played i.e. at cricket; W G Grace practically won the match single-handed; the XI actually won 5 matches in the season, drew 2 and lost 2

weather the school was an official Meteorological Office weather centre until 1916

Letter 72

gardener i.e. J Spall

the loveliest & the best perhaps an echo of stanza xxi of Fitzgerald's *Rubáiyát of Omar Khayyám*:

> Lo! some we loved, the loveliest and the best
> That Time and Fate of all their Vintage prest,
> Have drunk their Cup a Round or two before,
> And one by one crept silently to Rest.

(see Newsome, p.258 on the way in which Fitzgerald's poem – though in fact it was published in 1859 – was perhaps the most popular of the 1890s, as Tennyson's *In Memoriam* perhaps of the mid-century; see also Doc App LXIV & LXVI)

Letter 74

seen you LWFB and Mr Edwards went to Commemoration (see let76)

Letter 75
electric light the first practical electric light bulb was produced in 1879, and the first electricity generated for public and domestic use was by the Central Power Station in Godalming, Surrey, in 1881
thing for "think"
certain hours the mains water supply was evidently not constant; the "pipes indoors" were clearly connected to a storage tank system

Letter 77
scholarship this was a Council scholarship for boys under age 15, tenable for 2 years; at £50 per year (double TTB's year's entrance scholarship of £25) it paid just over half the annual fees (for boarders) of £90; E Macfadyen also got one (see Doc App XXXI, under III.C)

Letter 78
marked papers i.e. presumably the exam papers TTB had made notes on (see let75)
station presumably Forest Hill station near Newfield
Band of Union presumably the "Social reform Union" of let47
holidays EFB clearly didn't read let76 to which she added a postscript

Letter 79
DATE dated from the mention of the royal wedding
old Cliftonian officers see Doc App XXIII-XXX for the list of officers printed in the *Cliftonian*; 43 Cliftonians were killed in the Boer War, 578 in the First World War, in which the Commander-in-Chief, Douglas Haig, was also a Cliftonian
Royal Wedding see Biog Reg under Princess May

Letter 80
yours i.e. your family
Staff i.e. the military Staff Corps of senior officers
Russian & Persian i.e. have a special skill in difficult languages; TTB later for a while had a Russian tutor
you for "he"

COMMENTARY: ENDNOTES (let81)

Letter 81
DATE presumably LWFB received this letter on the 10th (see let82)

Letter 82
letter from Tyra i.e. let81
small man i.e. RTB, who was the youngest and naughtiest of the children

Letter 83
DATE presumably LWFB received this letter on the 13th (see let84)

Letter 84
Enclosure evidently information from Mrs Beaver; see EFB's postscript
town i.e. central London

Letter 85
DATE noted by LWFB as "received 17 July 93"

Letter 86
home rule was the political issue of the hour; Gladstone's second Home Rule Bill was rejected by an overwhelming majority in the House of Lords in Sept 1893

Letter 87
wild women's presumably because about women's rights
Chigago for "Chicago"; the women were no doubt returning from the World's Columbian Exposition, held in Chicago (then the second largest city in the USA) in 1892-93 to commemorate the 400th anniversary of the discovery of America by Columbus
Brother i.e. W H G Eyre

Letter 88
DATE presumably this letter was enclosed with let90 for TTB's birthday on the 24th
doubled your scholarship see endnote on **scholarship** in let77

COMMENTARY: ENDNOTES (let89)

Letter 89
DATE presumably this letter was enclosed with let90 for TTB's birthday on the 24th
workmen i.e. in the workshop at Newfield

Letter 90
10% royalty see endnote on **patent** in let23; the dresses evidently sold expensively at 5gns (i.e. £5.5.0) each
Libertys "Liberty's of [originally 218A] Regent Street was born [in the late nineteenth century] out of Arthur Lasenby Liberty's involvement with the aesthetic movement, in which oriental silks, furnishings, pottery and artwork played an influential part" (Adburgham, p.156, and on the "Japanese craze", p.157)

Letter 92
in 93 i.e. if TTB were to try the last exam under the old system

Letter 93
when i.e. about when you expect to arrive
London Bridge the London railway terminus for trains from Forest Hill
latest 2 p m LWFB has second thoughts about "before 3.30"

Letter 94
DATE noted by LWFB as "received 31/7/93"

Letter 95
Tina & her husband married a relatively short time, and clearly EFB had not yet met Heinrich
for them in the event only BTB went
you suggested was TTB expresing doubts about the army? (see let251)
sports there was much emphasis on sport at Roedean; but TyTB plainly wanted to leave at the end of the previous term (see endnote on **Brighton** in let1), and it seems pressed her wishes urgently after going back for the new school year in Sept 1893 (but see also let112); in let115 LWFB is clearly content also that she should leave Roedean; Sydenham High School, founded by the Girls' Public Day School Trust in 1887, was near Newfield at Longton Hall, Westwood Hill, Sydenham

COMMENTARY: ENDNOTES (let96)

Lobbs John Lobb (bootmaker), 296 Regent Street, London W

winter garden the landlord of the Mogul tavern in Drury Lane, London WC, turned the building next door into a music hall which was eventually known as the Winter Garden theatre, but this name also plainly stood for the whole establishment, since EFB and LWFB ate there

Arts & Crafts exhibition the aim of the Arts and Crafts movement was, as a protest against the ugliness produced by industrial manufacture, to make objects once again beautiful; this 1893 exhibition, the fourth, was criticised, however, by one reviewer as "the work of a few for the few"; the first three exhibitions were in 1888, 1889 and 1890, and thereafter the London exhibitions (in the New Gallery in Regent Street, London WC) were triennial

Letter 96
every day see endnote on **saturday** in let98
companions TTB is clearly now sharing with more than one other boy
cant for "can"
tailor i.e. probably Batzer (see endnote on **Batzer** in let163)
sets TTB is now taught Maths by HSH; Latin by E H C Smith; French by W W Vaughan; and German by E J Barff

Letter 97
before EFB has not yer received let96, written the day before

Letter 98
nib i.e. the "Stylographic pen" of let104
nuiense for "nuisance"
saturday Miss Etheridge actually came to Newfield to teach the boys (see let100) but RTB has a shorter school week because he is the younger
barbielous schmerzen a half-German phrase for "bilious pain" (see let137)

Letter 99
DATE together with let98 in the MS

Letter 100

note   replaced by the model letter in let102

play up   Newbolt's famous poem *Vitai Lampada*, written in 1892 but not published until 1897, uses this schoolboy cry (see Biog Reg under Grace and endnote on **Corps** in let3)

Letter 101

letters   i.e. presumably the letter to TTB and the note to ENPM

his note   i.e. the note intended for him

possibly   omits "see"

Letter 102

division   see Biog Reg under Barnett

Letter 103

Zoological Gardens   these were on the other side of the road from TTB's house, so that in bed at night the boys must have been able to hear lions and elephants (see endnote on **Clifton** in let7)

Letter 104

DATE   Oct.32. for 1 Nov

Enrights Castleconnell   John Enright & Son (rod maker), Castleconnell, Co Limerick, Ireland

smashed   they were of course clay pipes

sent   for "send"

Father's Studio   see p.281

Letter 105

st   i.e. stomach (see let110)

Letter 106

W.G.G.   his initials were actually W J G

housemaster   i.e. H E Huntington

Employers Liability Bill   this would be the annual debate on the yearly renewal of the Employers' Liability Act (first passed in 1880), which extended the grounds on which an employee could be awarded damages for injuries sustained at work

little place   "'But the place they give us is so unpleasant,' said Mrs Bonteen. 'There are worse places even than the Ladies' Gallery,' said Lady Laura. 'And it is as well to make oneself

COMMENTARY: ENDNOTES (let107)

used to inconveniences of all kinds.'" (Anthony Trollope, *Phineas Finn* (1869), chap 36)
post marks   he is evidently collecting postmarks from cards and envelopes (see endnote on **204** in let204)

Letter 107
DATE   probably written on the Sunday following let106
M&E   i.e. Military and Engineering side, a usual abbreviation

Letter 108
of   for "on"
three days   see let21
send   for "sending"

Letter 110
Perry Vale   a road near Newfield
influenza   there was a serious world epidemic at the end of 1889 and beginning of 1890, which reached London in Nov 1889; and then milder outbreaks in England in each of the years 1891-94, with a more serious one in 1895 (see let241 & 260)
bowels   see let105
14/6   but see postscript to let111
while...work   slightly modified quotation from John IX.4

Letter 111
mother   see let107
paper   see endnote on **paper** in let211
about   omits "it"

Letter 112
implicitly   unquestioningly
Marazion   railway station near Penzance, Cornwall

Letter 114
DATE   clearly immediately follows let113

Letter 115
wire   i.e. send a telegram
necrosis   mortification of bone tissue
Girton   Girton College was founded in 1869 and re-established in Cambridge in 1873 as part of the movement towards proper

education for women
St Andrews   i.e. St Leonard's (see Biog Reg under TyTB)
home   see endnote on **sports** in let95
Brighton   i.e. Roedean
averse to   Pattinson sounds like the kind of workman so admired by George Sturt in *The Wheelwright's Shop*, who allowed the natural shape of a job needing to be excellently done to determine the time it took, and who was satisfied with the skilled use of the tools he knew; LWFB represents the new age

Letter 116
Infants...cry   slightly adapted quotation from *In Memoriam* liv
more light   at 9 in the morning on the last day of his life, 22.3.1832, Goethe felt lively and asked for more light in the room which had been darkened to ease him; he died 3½ hours later; the words are plainly attractive metaphorically, even though they were in origin a practical request
means of progression   this seems more like a reference to such things as railways than to social progress
Board schools   in 1811 the Church of England founded a National Society for educating the poor in the principles of the established church (see Biog Reg under Edwards), as a counter to the first major voluntary attempt at educating the poor with the founding of the undenominational British and Foreign School Society in 1808; in Apr 1844 the formation of the Ragged School Union was the beginning of another voluntary attempt at education for the poor in London; its schools merged with the so-called board schools set up under local school boards to form a national system of elementary education by the Elementary Education Act of 1870 (as did the Ragged School set up by masters and boys of Clifton in 1868; see Potter, p.48); two Acts of Parliament, in 1876 and 1880, made school attendance compulsory (raising the attendance figure from about two million in 1876 to about four million in 1881); in 1891 elementary education was made free of charge
telephone   the first words were spoken by telephone on 10.3.1876; by 1887 there were about 26000 subscribers in England; by 1891 there was a telephone link between London and Paris (see also endnote on **electric light** in let75)
frozen air   see Biog Reg under Dewar

Letter 117
oilers i.e. oilskins

Letter 118
Podopholin for "podophyllin", a purgative medicine
matter it looks as though the earlier you arrived the better your chances of the study you wanted

Letter 119
DATE letter completed on Thursday Feb 8th
Lansdowne lawn see p.281
overseer i.e. the District Surveyor
The Transgressor by A W Gattie (1894)
Bademeister i.e. oversee her bath
no exercise see let118A

Letter 120
can for "can't"

Letter 121
invitation see let69
law suit with Bleuler (see let135)
purse Hulbe also specialised in leatherwork
Zeiser's see let140
coal mines the lecture was to the Scientific Society, in the Chemistry Laboratory, with 100 members and visitors present
Cairotherion for "Cheirotherion"
caws for "corms", bulb-like stems
napthaline for "naphthaline", a distillation of coal-tar
Blanch's John Blanch & Sons, the leading nineteenth-century gunsmith; the firm was established in 1809 and in the mid1890s had its premises at 39 Fish Street Hill, London EC
Eastman's see endnote on **Kodak** in let135

Letter 122
DATE supplied from let125
Juno the little dog was actually male (see let136) and later its name was changed to Jove
lessons see let116A
steam bakerie i.e. in which the oven was heated by steam carried in pipes

Charlie Lucken *Charlie Lucken at School and College* by H C Adams (1886)

Letter 123
DATE supplied from let125
Tranked for "Tankred"

Letter 124
DATE supplied from let125

Letter 125
separate letters which they also answered separately in let122-125
youngest boy i.e. R StJ Willans
regiment see Biog Reg under Willans

Letter 126
DATE postmarked in London on the 17th; this is the postcard of the 16th referred to in let135
SKETCH OF BUILDINGS this does not seem to be a view of any Clifton buildings

Letter 129
DATE TyTB's examination was on the 23rd (see let130) and is in this letter to be "tomorrow"
General i.e. Maj-Gen C Blewitt
Two thousand years ago subtitled *The adventures of a Roman boy*, by Professor A J Church (1885); this was TTB's book (see let136)
there omits "are"
Mr Edwards see endnote on **Colbrae** in let130

Letter 130
is omits "it"
Colbrae this must be the name of her house and must be near Newfield because TyTB went to tea (see let129) and was back in time for Mr Edwards' lesson (presumably after his school day was over) at 5.30 (see let116A)
Concert i.e. Albert, the Prince Consort

Letter 133
DATE clearly follows let132, which EFB wrote on Sat 3rd

COMMENTARY: ENDNOTES (let134)

central Africa the lecture was actually on Wed 28th and was given by Mr Madden, a member of the Universities' Mission to Central Africa, founded in 1859; clearly TTB didn't take to missionary lectures

Letter 134
dreadful **evil** i.e. sex between boys; common and commonly opposed in public schools, either by a kind of hysteria or an inhibited and (it was hoped) inhibiting silence
unspotted...world James I.27
master builder Ibsen's *The Master Builder* was first produced in England in 1892, and the following year it was one of six plays by Ibsen produced for English audiences, with whom this shocking new playwright was very popular
gardener i.e. J Spall
theory see let262

Letter 135
bad faring i.e. a worrying prospect (as regards the exam)
1895 the year of TTB's Woolwich exam
Kodak George Eastman (1854-1932), founder of Eastman Kodak, produced the famous Kodak hand-held camera in 1888; it was relatively simple to operate, used rolls of film, and so made amateur photography really feasible
just now i.e. with the building of the studio
nolens volens willy-nilly
report see Doc App VI
I have had...be led from ENPM's comment
The wilson in commemoration of J M Wilson; see let180 and Doc App XXXII

Letter 136
Clifton mistakenly for Aldershot (see let137)
The wreck of the golden fleece the story of Jason and the Argonauts seems unlikely to be intended by this title; perhaps TyTB intends a reference to Dickens' *The Wreck of the Golden Mary* (1856) in *Christmas Stories*; or perhaps there was in fact a book of exactly the title set down here; the boys mentioned must presumably be the boys of Mr Edwards' school (cf. Mr Lynam's boys in let116) because in the 1891 census he has a wife living with him but no children, and he would hardly be old enough to have sons already living away from home

339

Letter 137
Aldershot on Mar 14th the Clifton Engineer Cadet Corps paraded at 6.45 in the morning, arrived by train at 10.30 and commenced battle at 12.00; they left at 4.30 and arrived back at Clifton at 7.30
nipped i.e. by cold
some days ago this can't be let136

Letter 138
DATE TTB didn't *send* the letter till the 27th (see let140)
before i.e. earlier
my master i.e. W W Vaughan
get a mark i.e. presumably, get any marks for correct answers
the master i,.e. R J Morich
Zizer for "Zeiser"
it omits "is"
dictated i.e. the lines were of text to be written out, and TTB was helping by dictating them; the text was probably Vergil
privileges i.e. so that he wasn't more severely punished
head of the house i.e. R A G Festing
accused omits "me"
fifth power i.e. disciplinary status in the house of the Vth form
the for "that"
barge see let141
report omits "to"
think for "thing"
bunted see let141
wanted omits "to"
"pi" sanctimonious (slang abbreviation of "pious")

Letter 139
We i.e. a party from the Dragon School
Dorchester large village with an abbey church eight miles from Oxford

Letter 140
werther...College dear Herr Zeiser, Forgive me for only now thanking you for your kindness. Father has meanwhile given me a knife, and because I must be careful of my budget I have decided against a purchase, but I thank you most sincerely all

COMMENTARY: ENDNOTES (let142)

the same. With best wishes to Frau Zeiser and you, Yours
TTB Clifton College
seeked i.e. sought my company

Letter 142
Latin tutor i.e. E H C Smith

Letter 143
DATE clearly follows let142

Letter 144
report see Doc App VII

Letter 145
form master i.e. F H Stevens
mathematical colleagues on the exceptionally high standard
of mathematical work at Clifton, see Potter, pp. 62 & 113; and
for examples of examination questions in mathematics, see Doc
App XXI-XXII

Letter 147
circular letter see Doc App XXXIII-XXXIV
question i.e. in the circular letter

Letter 148
apparent steel i.e. the barrel of forged iron polished to
look like steel

Letter 149
DATE probably immediately follows let147

Letter 150
DATE as postmark
L.W.F.Behrens Esq addressee of postcard
man i.e. Macarthey (see let151 & 172)

Letter 151
regular see endnote on **Rugal** in let152
parole i.e. watchword

Letter 152
Rugal in let151 LWFB wrote "regular" (see endnote), and in

response to TTB's underlining glosses it "Rugal" (i.e. "regular Rugal")
cant for "can"

Letter 155
unsuitable omits "a"
there see let156
ironclads ships cased with iron plates

Letter 156
gib for "jib"
Norfolk system Charles, 2nd Viscount Townshend (known as "turnip Townshend", a landowner in Norfolk, initiated in the eighteenth century the *Norfolk* or *four-course rotation system*, which replaced the year of "bare fallow" with the cultivation of turnips and other root crops, and so also made possible the winter feeding of cattle

Letter 160
the Royal this was a hotel on College Green in the heart of Bristol, now reconstructed as the Swallow; there was a statue of Queen Victoria opposite its entrance, unveiled 1888
dear there were clearly difficulties between LWFB and EFB at this time about women's rights (see let161 & 164)
tale quale as it stands

Letter 161
Council Room a fine room at the end of the Library, where the College Council met, and a convenient centre for gatherings of up to about 50, though more room could be had by spilling out into the museum end of the Library

Letter 162
report see Doc App VIII

Letter 163
Batzer of R Batzer and Hughes (Ladies' and Gentlemen's Tailors), 10 Gracechurch Street, London EC

Letter 164
franchise question see Biog Reg under Mann
questionable though they did in fact go (see let165)

Letter 165
from for "for"
screuge variant spelling of "scrouge", a well established London colloquialism, meaning here "squeeze"

Letter 166
Scholarship see endnote on **scholarship** in let77

Letter 167
DATE the letter was actually written on the 8th (see let172)

Letter 169
glass studio i.e. probably the same as the vine (or orchard) house; LWFB's studio was also roofed with glass (see let299)
we called i.e. when they went to Commemoration

Letter 172
plant written in another hand (?Wollaston's) is "Crambe cordifolia (Caucasus)", which is a hardy perennial of the cabbage family, having clouds of small fragrant white flowers in branching sprays, grows to a height of 6ft
9th TTB says "no" meaning he did *post* it, as LWFB says (see let170) on the 9th, but he has forgotten that he dated it the 10th
Stoneham Frank & Edmund Stoneham (booksellers), 79 & 129 Cheapside, London EC
man at Croydon i.e. Macarthey, living on the Surrey edge of London (see let150 & 151)

Letter 173
enclosed i.e. let171
Sennen in Cornwall, the westernmost village in England

Letter 174
DATE as postmark
L.W.F.Behrens Esq addressee of postcard

Letter 175
L.W.F.Behrens Esq addressee of postcard

Letter 176
send LWFB clearly has not yet received let175

Saturday i.e. let174

Letter 177
DATE as postmark
here i.e. for Commemoration

Letter 178
post card i.e. let177

Letter 180
to July 95 see endnote on **scholarship** in let77
be perhaps for "would be better"
this July see let135

Letter 181
DATE as postmark
L.W.F.Behrens Esq addressee of postcard
letter see let176

Letter 182
man's wife i.e. Mrs Nighton (see let171)

Letter 183
tether i.e. at the limit of his capacities

Letter 185
hair short RTB evidently had his long hair cut after his 7th birthday, no doubt on going to a proper school for the first time
school see Biog Reg under RTB and BTB

Letter 186
churches omits "in"
on the studio i.e. decorating the studio with wood engravings of celtic emblems

Letter 187
know yet TTB was now in HSH's form, 5x (initially 11 boys); for Mathematics he was also in HSH's set; for French in set 2 and for German set 1, both with O Siepmann (see let189); for Latin he was in set 1 with A E Hillard; he was taught freehand drawing by G W C Hutchinson

COMMENTARY: ENDNOTES (let189)

Smalls i.e. Responsions, the first (i.e. entrance) of three examinations for the Oxford BA

racquets Clifton participated in a racquets competition from 1886, and was one of a small number of schools to have a racquets court (built in 1872)

Letter 189

DATE Aug for Oct

Elsass TTB uses the German form of the name Alsace, no doubt following Otto Siepmann's usage; this was a region always disputed between Germany and France, annexed by Prussia after the Franco-Prussian War

getting on i.e. at their respective schools

old hound i.e. ENPM

companion omits "he"

Letter 190

hair i.e. newly cut (see let185)

Natural History Museum in Kensington, London W, opened in 1881

stolen goods i.e. treasures acquired by imperial or military seizure

Letter 192

drawing master i.e. G W C Hutchinson

Hypo i.e. Hyposulphite (for fixing photographs)

Letter 194

soon TTB wrote a note against this "now. Nov. 18.", plainly when he sent the letter back to LWFB for decipherment of Zwieback on Nov 18th (see let202 & 205)

Zwieback this can only mean "rusks"; ?conceivably a private joke word used for "chatter, gossip"

Letter 195

order see let19

Tonicuin i.e. tonic wine of some sort

Letter 196

196 the printed letterhead figure is clearly of the "ship called Tyra" (see endnote on this in let1)

foot ball actually at racquets (see let195)

Letter 197
playing up see endnote on *play up* in let100
kitchener cooking range
gymnasium this is perhaps more likely to be what we would call the schoolroom (using the German sense) than a place for gymnastics

Letter 198
DATE as postmark
cookerie evidently some kind of camping stove
other letter evidently a letter sent to TyTB at the same time as this, for which she thanks TTB in let199

Letter 199
DATE last Thursday was the Owsley wedding, the 25th (see let197), yesterday was Saturday the 27th
Miss Owsley i.e. the elder sister, Cicely

Letter 200
DATE the hamper was sent on Wednesday the 31st (see let201), and here on Sunday is promised "on Wednesday"

Letter 202
deciphered see let195 and endnote on *soon* in let194

Letter 203
little son i.e. Lionel Raymond
Andersens fairy tales no doubt from the copy TyTB was given as a Christmas present by Lilian in 1885 (see let200)

Letter 204
204 written across this letter in EFB's hand is "keep the crests & stamps for you & post marks for Brian" (see let106 & 256)

Letter 205
last lines i.e. let194, see endnote on *soon*
strongest i.e. School house
Capua a city just north of Naples in Italy, in ancient times of vital strategic importance to Rome; occupied by Hannibal in 216BC after the great defeat of the Romans at Cannæ; he and his army wintered there too and were said to have slumbered

amidst its delights

one   Brown's house lost in the final round to Fairbank's house (i.e. Watson's house; on naming of houses, see Biog Reg under Brown)

stodged   i.e. lain about eating too much instead of training

proper way   see let26

his life   see Newbolt's popular poem *Vitai Lampada* (and endnote on ***play up*** in let100)

programme   see Doc App XXXV

Letter 208

franchise vampyre   i.e. the insistent, draining issue of votes for women

Anklets   see let189 and Doc App XIX on Gaiters

Association   i.e. Soccer (see let210)

scriptures   see Doc App X

Letter 210

many   omits "things"

Letter 211

meeting room   the meeting (with George Allen in the chair) was to hear Mrs Boole speak on the "Safeguarding of the Faculty of Originality in Children"

spelling bees   spelling competitions

Tusculum   i.e the studio; Cicero had a favourite villa in this town twelve miles from Rome

fluor   calcium fluoride

bas-relief   a form of mural decoration which, by contrast with the dramatic projection of rococo, projects very little from its background; the Renaissance terminology distinguished between *basso-rilievo, mezzo-rilievo* and *alto-rilievo* (high relief); LWFB does not relish the starkness of contrast between his present discontents and his domestic ideal

rodomontade   boastful bragging

paper   see Doc App XXXVI, evidently sent before its printed date of 10.12.1894

Letter 212

[My...*but*]   inserted above the line (see let213)

sequence   i.e. RTB taking on the opinions and attitudes of his eldest brother

regards i.e. would also be influenced by your present attitude

Letter 213
every for "ever"
have omits "been"
Spare...boy slightly modified quotation from Proverbs XIII.24

Letter 217
alright see endnote on **late** in let222 and Dates of Terms on p.279

Letter 218
DATE 94 for 95
exam i.e. the entrance exam for Woolwich
came out i.e. passed out of Woolwich (see Biog Reg under TTB)
Oxford i.e. to the Dragon School; see let219

Letter 219
DATE clearly comes between let218 & 220
Marshall most probably to be identified with Frederick Charles Marshall & Co (tailors), 34 King Street, Cheapside, London EC
Randall Henry Edward Randall (boot and shoe maker), 134 Cheapside, London EC
Book presumably this is not a proper name

Letter 220
Engelhart Ernest Engelhart (hairdresser and perfumer), 103 Devonshire Road, Forest Hill, near Newfield

Letter 221
pictures see let225
Charlie's Aunt for *"Charley's Aunt"* by Walter Brandon Thomas (1892)

Letter 222
late term began on 18.1.1895 (see p.279) and TTB went back on the 21st (see let216)

employment perhaps there was difficulty because Luke Clary had already been replaced by Bryant, so that there was no longer a job for him at Newfield

Tooles theatre see Biog Reg under Toole

Walker *Walker, London* by J M Barrie (1892) (see Biog Reg under Toole)

Paul Pry by John Poole (1825) (see Biog Reg under Toole)

Palace i.e. Crystal Palace

lecture the lecture was on "The Duties of Women as Citizens", and the motion was carried "That this meeting approves the extension of the Parliamentary franchise to women householders"

Letter 223

explained see let183

L.B. i.e. train to London Bridge from Forest Hill (perhaps a mistaken price, see endnote on **London Bridge** in let7)

Cab from London Bridge to Paddington railway station

Ticket i.e. train from Paddington to Bristol

cab from Bristol to Clifton

17/4½ incorrect total (would be more nearly correct if the Forest Hill/London Bridge fare were as in let7)

31/10½ incorrect total

Letter 225

Waldhorn French horn

followed the sentence makes sense if "regretted not" is taken as an inversion, i.e. = did not regret

Letter 226

DATE dated from let225

Dulwich Park near Newfield

Letter 227

Dualism omits "I"

Letter 228

Rembrandts "Philosopher" Rembrandt was commissioned in 1652 to paint a "philosopher" and the following year completed *Aristotle Contemplating the Bust of Homer*, this may be the painting referred to

Letter 229

book TTB thinks the signalling book is in his cupboard at Newfield (see let228), though in fact LWFB sent it shortly afterwards (see let230); it is curious that LWFB speaks in let230 of the signalling book as though TTB had not already referred to it

spoil for "spoilt"

stores see endnote on **stores** in let47

drawing etc missing

Letter 231

pulse i.e. presumably temperature (see let234)

Letter 232

her for "here"

poor soul see let216

West Kent the West Kent Volunteer Fire Brigade Station was at 25 London Road, Forest Hill, near Newfield; it had been established in 1871, and these new premises had been opened in Oct 1892

Owsley family except presumably Edith, who was now married

water because the pipes were frozen

Norwood Lake near Newfield

Letter 234

out available

to you see let230

Letter 237

recruit recover health

aconite as a medicine to relieve fever

his friend i.e. probably Hauerl; the friend was evidently one of the skating party, as Hauerl was

Sunday week see let226

refer i.e. to let233; EFB has plainly not yet seen let235, in which money is specified

Letter 238

pronounce Him an odd phrase (less odd would be "proclaim"), perhaps meaning "declare his goodness"

dentist i.e. E H Rook

COMMENTARY: ENDNOTES (let239)

Letter 239
Influenza see endnote on **influenza** in let110

Letter 240
chock for "jog"

Letter 241
don't know see let245
after i.e. subsequent
extra lessons i.e. with G W C Hutchinson (see let253)
Lewis mi i.e. H L Lewis ("mi" = minor, indicating an elder brother at the school)

Letter 242
DATE as postmark
L.W.F.Behrens Esq addressee of postcard
envelope missing

Letter 244
put on added to

Letter 245
about see let229
Aldershot i.e. the field day

Letter 247
L.W.F.Behrens Esq addressee of postcard
letter i.e. let245

Letter 248
send actually sent on 2nd Mar (see let254)
the New Woman by Sydney Grundy (1894); a recent play, but EFB means the *sentiments* were "by no means" sympathetic to the "new" way of things; there were plays at the Crystal Palace theatre on Tuesday and Thursday afternoons in 1895 and EFB is writing before dinner on a Thursday after returning from the performance; Grundy's feeble satire had just finished its successful London run at the Comedy theatre, and so was available for suburban performance (see Beckson, pp.143-4)
nip for new as we would say, "pinch punch the first of the month"

COMMENTARY: ENDNOTES (let250)

Letter 250
report see Doc App XII
Moore this is actually MGG's comment, as LWFB later notes (see let252); ENPM had died the previous morning (see let251)

Letter 251
DATE the letter was being written for about ten days, as TTB says at the end, and was dated on completion
place see endnote on **you suggested** in let95
power clever boys on the Classical side were rapidly promoted into the VIth form though they might be younger than Vth form boys on the Military side (see let255 and p.280)
he i.e. B R Woollcombe (see let273); the house photograph of Brown's house facing p.228 dates from March/April 1895 (term ended on 5.4.1895), when FB (centre rear, bearded) was in temporary charge, after the death of ENPM (see Biog Reg under ENPM); the six VIth formers are wearing boaters, the captain of the house, G C Q Meister, stands rear left against the wall, and TTB stands, in a cap, rear right against the door; B R Woollcombe (who was about the same age as TTB) is probably one of the younger looking VIths; the photograph was perhaps made as a keepsake for Mrs Moor as she left
remark for "remarked"
lavatory washing place
licking beating
Mrs Moor who had lost her husband, her home and her income (her brother came to help run the house immediately after ENPM died)
Book see let246 & 247

Letter 252
then i.e. even then
Stevens perhaps for "Stephens" and a reference to the ink manufacturer Henry Charles Stephens (1841-1918), whose offices in the mid1890s were at 17 Aldersgate Street, London EC, with the factory at Gillespie Road, London N; perhaps there had been some kind of sale
Just i.e. I just
just writes let253 arrived by the evening post of the day it was written, giving time for a postscript here before let252 was posted late on the 8th (see let254)

Letter 253
last wrote see let241
representative HSH clearly quotes LWFB's term (see let249 and endnote on **last letter** in let260)

Letter 254
licked LWFB evidently has TTB's beating in mind

Letter 255
amt i.e. amount (see let251)
pictures see let221
rather long ENPM had earlier commented on an "untidiness which is apparent even in his personal attire" (Doc App III)
M&E see endnote on **M&E** in let107
one i.e. B R Woollcombe

Letter 256
other crests see endnote on **204** in let204

Letter 257
DATE clearly immediately precedes let258

Letter 258
Sir clearly directed to LWFB, answering let257
House-Tutor i.e. FB himself, since ENPM had died

Letter 259
DATE clearly follows let258; FB replied on the 20th (see let266) after an admitted delay
old soldier see Biog Reg under LWFB
sow's ear "you can't make a silk purse out of a sow's ear"

Letter 260
yr last letter LWFB evidently replied to let253, which he notes receipt of in let252
my last letter see let253 and endnote there on **representative**
epidemic see endnote on **influenza** in let110

Letter 261
representative i.e. LWFB now quotes the phrase with a dash for the previously illegible part, so it originally read "been pro tem representative"

COMMENTARY: ENDNOTES (let262)

Letter 262
sell i.e. probably photographic equipment; TTB speaks of it in let264 as equipment that is likely to be superseded

Letter 263
9th see Doc App XL, which alters the date to the 5th

Letter 264
thinks for "things"

Letter 266
ex parte in the interests of one side

Letter 267
remark see let250 and endnote there on **Moore**
house see let251

Letter 269
form masters notes see Doc App XII; HSH's general comment was "Improved generally, seems to be more in earnest about his work", and under Mathematics: "Making excellent progress"

Letter 271
genius see p.280
were omits "to"
clever...success LWFB underlines these words and comments in a marginal note: "how does that combine with your remark attitude towards work letter 21st" (see let267)

Letter 272
unaware see let263

Letter 274
report see Doc App XIII
remarked see let145

Letter 275
DATE sent by the same post as let276
wrote see let263 (the suspension marks here and three lines later indicate gaps in the MS)

Letter 276
copies i.e. presumably enclosed copies of let274 & 275

Letter 277
intended see endnote on **9th** in let263
other letters i.e. perhaps let276 (with its enclosures) and a brief note from her (missing) which EFB seems to refer to at the beginning of this letter
stepping...things see endnote on **expresses it** in let26

Letter 278
david i.e. ?the underdog (the lone voice), against the Goliath of a system
alive see let138A & 142
'probably' lying LWFB quotes let273
wash see let95 & 96
fault omits "on the"

Letter 283
enclosed evidently a form from Woolwich (but not Form 38 of let285; see let286)
last for "lasts"

Letter 286
sent i.e. from which it was sent
hyphen LWFB has not yet had Form 38 (see let285)
over the mats i.e. ?extremely eager for (perhaps the image is of a jumper reaching so far that he comes to ground beyond the landing mats)
enclosure i.e. LWFB's "form of reply" to Roberts

Letter 287
Oxford i.e. the Dragon School

Letter 288
Oxford i.e. the Dragon School
smithy i.e. clearly the forge of let291

Letter 289
Leu this is the only occasion in the correspondence on which EFB refers to LWFB in this way

COMMENTARY: ENDNOTES (let290)

Normandy   staying with the Marquise de Banneville (see let297)

still   i.e. may yet show evidence that he has contracted it

Letter 290
Military Secretary   i.e. Gen Sir R R Gipps

Letter 291
Mr Burdett   who was no doubt advising on the legal position about the hyphenated surname (see Biog Reg under George Perks)

under...tree   the first lines of Longfellow's *The Village Blacksmith* are in EFB's mind:

    Under a spreading chestnut-tree
    The village smithy stands...

water boots   waders

neighbourhood   TTB actually sat the Woolwich papers at Clifton, and afterwards went to Woolwich for the viva (see let300)

Bechstein small grand   this still survives, in excellent order, and a very fine instrument; it is a 6ft 3in baby grand in a walnut veneer finish, made in 1894 (no. 35638)

Letter 292
Nunmuncton   for "Nun Monckton", where George Allen was curate

wants   see let288

Letter 295
camp   see let297 and Doc App XLI

plant   see endnote on **plant** in let172

6th   actually the 5th (see let301)

Letter 296
report   see Doc App XIV

Letter 297
writing   in German

house   see map of Forest Hill; this was the house (no 13) furthest from the junction with Dartmouth Road

January   see Family Tree

will be   the words were: "I hope he will be successful" (Doc App XIV)

COMMENTARY: ENDNOTES (let298)

packet   the pub was called *The Falmouth Packet*

nurse's   probably no connection with the "old nurse" of let124

together   it was a tandem

D.V   Deo volente [God willing]

Battersea Park   just south of the Thames

bicyclists   the invention of the "safety" bicycle (much resembling the modern design) in 1876, its popular manufacture by 1885, and the pneumatic tyre of 1888 led to an explosion in the popularity of cycling, first for men, and then as a mode of freedom for the "new woman" (see Holbrook Jackson, p.35 and Newsome, p.254); EFB became an enthusiastic cyclist and kept a *Cycling Register* of expeditions made from 1896-1903 (later, at Stonehenge on 9.11.1912, she experimented with flying, as a passenger in a biplane)

Magara   no club or company of this name appears in the Post Office directories for London in the 1890s; however, the excavations at the ancient city of Megara Hyblaea, near Syracuse in Sicily, began in 1891, and perhaps we may speculate that Mrs Wharry was in some way involved at the London end

Letter 298
the man   i.e. presumably W Allan (see let295)

Martini   see Biog Reg under Martini

Letter 299
Brighton   i.e. Roedean

swimming baths   the swimming baths in Dartmouth Road, near Newfield, were opened in 1884

New Cross   a district a mile or two north of Forest Hill; the "examination room" was probably at the Goldsmiths' Institute (afterwards Goldsmiths' College), opened in 1891

glass roof   see endnote on **glass studio** in let169

Letter 300
viva   see endnote on **neighbourhood** in let291

hook   authority

Letter 302
lose you   TTB was at Newfield after the exam until the 15th (see let301)

357

Letter 303
DATE as postmark
L.W.F.Behrens Esq addressee of postcard

Letter 305
I for "If"

Letter 306
Standard *The Evening Standard*, a leading London daily newspaper, evidently arriving in Hertford the following morning
place see Biog Reg under TTB and Doc App LVI

Letter 307
307 letter written to TTB in Cornwall

Letter 308
ADDRESS Great Cumbrae Island, between the island of Bute and Largs on the mainland; CCL was evidently on a cruise
DATE the postcard was redirected from Newfield to Cornwall, and the forwarding postmark was 7.8.1895
T.T.Behrens Esq addressee of postcard

Letter 19A
DATE probably sent with or immediately following let19 (see endnote on **last letter** in let21)
burner the incandescent gas mantle was invented in 1884

Letter 49A
DATE Ethel Lambley left Roedean at the end of the first term (i.e. Apr) 1893, so this gives a limiting date; EFB particularly mentions TyTB's handwriting in let52, and had clearly had a letter from her in Brighton in let50, which we may presume was in answer to one from EFB announcing the healing of the family quarrel written at the same time as let49; we may suppose that TyTB wrote to EFB, and with that letter enclosed this one for TTB, immediately she received the equivalent of let49

Letter 65A
DATE the Monday referred to is probably 8.5.1893, since let66 also has a reference to the new experience of the Military

side; this letter was then probably written on the Sunday before the 8th

Letter 109A
DATE Dr Webb died on 28.11.1893, so this is perhaps to be dated a day or so earlier

Letter 116A
ADDRESS this is the only occasion in the correspondence on which Newfield is given its ordinary postal address, no doubt because TyTB was writing over a printed Roedean heading and could use the "36" of that Brighton address (see Biog Reg under Lawrence)
DATE in let118A the Lambleys came last Saturday and stayed till Sunday (i.e. 3-4.2.1894); in this letter that visit is looked forward to, and in let117 TTB sends TyTB a note of term dates, clearly in response to her remark in this letter and to EFB's remark in let116 which no doubt enclosed let116A
Practis i.e. music practice (see let118A)
Lesson see endnote on **Colbrae** in let130

Letter 116B
DATE the liquorice dates this with let116A

Letter 118A
DATE in let119 EFB refers to TyTB's comment about exercise, so presumably this letter was written at some point in the several days it took for let119 to be written
up omits "because"
cot for "got"

Letter 138A
DATE presumably this was written immediately after LWFB received let138, which was not actually sent until the 27th
with him see let135
for life see let278 and Biog Reg under CCL

COMMENTARY: INDEX

INDEX TO LETTER TEXT

References in this index are to **letter numbers**; people and animals in the main alphabetical sequence of the Biographical Register, however referred to in the letter text, appear as they are recorded there; the index includes matter mentioned in the endnotes as immediately relevant to the letter text; a name in capitals indicates an entry in the Biographical Register.

Aberdeen 156
Aconite 237
ADAMS, Revd Henry Cadwallader (see under *Charlie Lucken*)
AFFLECK-GRAVES, Dermot 7
Africa 60,62,63,133,155,163
AGNES 13,67
ALBERT, Prince 130,131
Aldershot 19,69,121,135,136,137,138,140,245,249,263,265,295,
    297
ALFRED the Great 205
ALLAN, William 295,298
ALLEN, Lionel Raymond 203
ALLEN, Mr (Revd) George William 20,21,26,37,42,44,46,47,
    48,50,53,54,57,58,65,66,110,203,262,264,292
ALLEN, Mrs Ellen Emma 110
Alsace 189
Analytical Conics 118,120,135,138,140
ANDERSEN, Hans Christian 200,203
ANDRIEU, Madame Eliza Ann 95,100,101,102,103,104,105,
    106
Antivivisectionists 34
Aquarium 49A
Aristotle Contemplating the Bust of Homer 228
Arithmetic 70,71,72,120,135,140,291
Army (see also under Soldiers & Officers) 251,252
Arrowroot 291
Art 211
Artist 238
Arts and Crafts 95
ASHBY, Leonard Beauclerk 7
Aspatria (agricultural college in Cumberland) 109A
Atlas (see under Maps)

DOCUMENTARY APPENDIX

CLIFTON COLLEGE.

FEBRUARY, 1893.

MODERN SIDE.

Name _Behrens, T. T._

Place in School List below which he ought not to fall _11ᶜ_   Term in the Form _2ⁿᵈ_

WEEK.	1st.	2nd.	3rd.	4th.	5th.
Place in 56					
Form of 19 Boys		19ᵗ		6ᵗ	
Latin	rather better I think : but he has no foundation of grammar.				
Divinity { O. T. ...	f.				
N. T. ...	f				
History	good.	improved in care and style fresh.			
Geography	v. fair.				
English	better : fails badly at times : theme poor.				
Drawing Set	r.f.				
Mathematics 3 Set 2 *Term in the Set*	much improved, except in style.				
French 5 Set ⅔ *Term in the Set*	not doing so well as he should.				
German 3 Set 1 *Term in the Set*	v. fair.				
Chemistry 4 Set	doing very fairly.				
Physics Set					
Private Tuition in					

DILIGENCE, REGULARITY, PUNCTUALITY, GENERAL CONDUCT, ETC.

A general improvement I think : I am sorry his french report however is bad , and it is a very low set.

I hope he is getting on better this term. I think he fails from want of patience and temper. and is apt to blame others rather than himself when he does not succeed

C. H. Spence. _Form Master._

W. W. Vaughan _House Tutor._

ELMoor. _House Master._

Head Master.

The next Ordinary Report will be sent at the end of Term.
A Weekly Report is sent home with each Day Boy every Monday Morning.
Term ends on TUESDAY, April 11.

CLIFTON COLLEGE.

APRIL, 1893.

MODERN SIDE.

Name _Behrens. T. T._

Place in School List below which he ought not to fall ___ 11ᵗʰ   Term in the Form ___ 2ⁱ

WEEK.		6th.	7th.	8th.	9th.	10th.	DILIGENCE, REGULARITY, PUNCTUALITY, GENERAL CONDUCT, ETC.
Place in	5·b.		11ᵗʰ		14ᵗʰ		15ᵗʰ	He has done much better this
Form of	19. Boys							term : I should advise his
Latin		better, but still dreadfully inaccurate.						going on the Military side
Divinity {O. T. ...		good						as soon as possible.
N. T. ...		fair						
History		fair: answers often very well						I think the sooner he gets
Geography ...		written work still very rough.						started on his military
English								career the better. he is a
Drawing Set		v.f.						very steady trustworthy boy
Music								and is sure to do well.
Mathematics Set 3ᵈ / Term in the Set 2ᵈ		decidedly better: but his style is still very poor.						
French Set 5ᵗʰ / Term in the Set 1ˢᵗ		better						
German Set 3ᵈ / Term in the Set 1ˢᵗ		v.f.						
Chemistry Set								
Physics Set								
Private Tuition in								

_____ C. H. Spence. _Form Master._
_____ W. W. Vaughan _House Tutor._
_____ Vschuvor. _House Master._
_____ (signature) _Head Master._

Boarders return on FRIDAY, May 5th, 1893.
The College re-opens with Service in Chapel, at which all must be present, on SATURDAY, May 6, at 9 a.m.
The School Lists will be forwarded about April 20th.

[P. T. O.

CLIFTON COLLEGE.

JUNE, 1893.

MILITARY SIDE.

me _Behrens T. T._

ace in School List below which he ought not to fall ___8^{th}___   Term in the Form ___1^{st}___

WEEK.	1st.	2nd.	3rd.	4th.	5th.	DILIGENCE, REGULARITY, PUNCTUALITY, GENERAL CONDUCT, ETC.
ace in _59._	—	$\frac{T}{12}$	$\frac{a}{12}$	$\frac{a}{12}$	$\frac{a}{12}$	In spite of his low places -
rm of _12_ Boys						Due chiefly to his change
thematics _2nd_ Set / Term in the Set _1._		Doing well - but he should take more pains to keep the style of his work neat and orderly.				from the Modern to the Military Side - I think he is on the whole doing
tin _3rd_ Set _II._ Term in the Set _I._		Prose better: translation still poor but better.				well. He works willingly and with interest; but he should try to be neater.
ench _4th_ Set _I._ Term in the Set _I._		Moderate: could do better.				
inity { O. T. ...		Satisfactory				I hope he is getting on better
{ N. T. ...						this term. He should try to
awing		Very fair.				cure this defect of untidiness
rman _3rd_ Set _I._ Term in the Set _I._		Very fair.				which is apparent even in personal attire.
emistry Set		—				~~~~
story		—				
ography		Is getting on.				
vate Tuition in						

F. Stevens — Form Master.
W. W. Vaughan — House Tutor.
EM Moor — House Master.
_M_ — Head Master.

The next Ordinary Report will be sent at the end of Term.
A Weekly Report is sent home with each Day Boy every Monday Morning.
Term ends on TUESDAY, August 1.

CLIFTON COLLEGE.

JULY, 1893.

MILITARY SIDE.

Name _Tunstall - Behrens T._

Place in School List below which he ought not to fall __8 _t___   Term in the Form __1 st___

WEEK.	6th.	7th.	8th.	0th.	10th.	DILIGENCE, REGULARITY, PUNCTUALITY, GENERAL CONDUCT, ETC.
Place in Form of _2_ Boys	_5,3_	_12 st_	_12 T_	_12 tt_	_12 th_	_12 th_	He seems to me to have worked steadily and with
Mathematics _2_ Set Term in the Set _1_		works very well and shews intelligence ; …… …… …… …… …… in style.				intelligence. I hope that his place in the Form will be higher next term
Latin _3_ Set Term in the Set _1_		Very well.				
French _4_ Set Term in the Set _1_		Moderate. could do better.				He is rather inclined to be childish he should cure this now. WWV.
Divinity { O. T. …		Quite satisfactory				
{ N. T. …						
Drawing … …		Very fair.				12 th in her order. Mr Steven tells me he did a very … examination. ……
Music… … …		-				
German _5_ Set Term in the Set _…_		Fair but inaccurate.				
Chemistry Set		—				
History … …		—				
Geography … …		Good				
Private Tuition in						

_____ Form Master.

W. W. Vaughan House Tutor.

EuMoor. House Master.

_____ Head Master.

Boarders return on FRIDAY, September 22, 1893.
The College re-opens with Service in Chapel, at which all must be present, on SATURDAY, September 23, at 9 a.m.
The School Lists will be forwarded about August 10th.

[P. T. O.

V

CLIFTON COLLEGE. (Military Side.)

Report for the Five Weeks ending *December 9th* 189*3*

Name *Tunstall-Behrens T.*   Form *5 4*   Average Age of the Form *16-5-*

Place in Form at the beginning of Term, below which he ought not to fall _ *5*   Term in the Form *2·³*

WEEK OF THE TERM.	6th.	7th.	8th.	9th.	10th.	REMARKS.
Place in Form of ... *M*...Boys	*5*	*5*	*7*	*9*	*26*	*Quite satisfactory: he has worked well through- -out the Term.*
Mathematics *1* Set *Term in the Set*		*Very industrious: will do well in time.*				
Latin ... *Term in the Set*		*now and then good: improving in Composition*				
French *3* Set *Term in the Set*		*Very weak, but I hope he has been trying to do his best.*				Form Master *F.H.S Estlin.* He will I hope, make up his mind to exert all his influence on the right side.
Scripture		*Satisfactory.*				
German or Greek *3* Set *Term in the Set*		*Very fair.*				House Tutor *W.W.Vaughan* Satisfactory – but I do feel with Mr Vaughan that it is a critical time with him & that he must take his line decidedly.
Chemistry		–				*7th in new order.*
Drawing		*doing well*				
Special Work or Private Tuition in						House Master *M.M.Moor.*

Head Master [signature]

[P. T. O.

A Weekly Report is sent home with each Day Boy every Monday Morning.

VI

CLIFTON COLLEGE. (Military Side.)

Report for the Five Weeks ending February 24ᵗ 1894

Name _Tunstall Behrens T._   Form _5·y_   Average Age of the Form _16-3_

Place in Form at the beginning of Term, below which he ought not to fall _2·⁰_   Term in the Form _3·⁰_

WEEK OF THE TERM.	1st.	2nd.	3rd.	4th.	5th.	REMARKS.
Place in Form of ..12....Boys	5ᵗ	4ᵗ	4ᵗ	4ᵗ		Quite satisfactory: he is coming on well. — but he should pay more attention to the _style_ of his work.
Mathematics 1ˢᵗ Set 2ⁿᵈ Term in the Set	Very steady and diligent: but his work is at present rather crude and unfinished. He is however working with older boys than himself.					
Latin ... 2ⁿᵈ Set 1·⁰ Term in the Set	Improving: his unseen translation is good: prose fair.					
French 3·⁰ Set 2·⁰ Term in the Set	Much improved; he is working well.					Form Master _F. H. O'Brien_
Scripture	Satisfactory					
German or Greek 2·⁰ Set 1ˢᵗ Term in the Set	Fair: not painstaking enough.					House Tutor _H. Borwick._ I have had to speak very seriously to him about the line he is taking in the house. He lets himself be led, I think, instead of trying to lead.
Chemistry	-					
Drawing	Very fair					
Special Work or Private Tuition in						House Master _M. Moor._

Head Master _[signature]_

A Weekly Report is sent home with each Day Boy every Monday Morning.   [P. T. O.

CLIFTON COLLEGE. (Military Side.)

Report for the Five Weeks ending _March 31st_ 189 _4_

Name _Tunstall-Behrens, T_   Form _5·3_   Average Age of the Form _16·4_

Place in Form at the beginning of Term, below which he ought not to fall _2·3_   Term in the Form _3·3_

WEEK OF THE TERM.	6th.	7th.	8th.	9th.	10th.	REMARKS.
Place in Form of ...14...Boys	4th	1st	2nd	6th	4th	His work for the last week or two has been somewhat less satisfactory. He certainly has ability; but he estimates it himself too highly, and thus is inclined to place himself in a wrong attitude towards anything like correction or reproof.
Mathematics 1st Set 3rd Term in the Set	He has some ability, but he will not make great progress until he is more docile. He is too fond of defending his own work.					
Latin ... 2nd 2nd Term in the Set	Not working so well of late, I think. His prose composition is fair.					Form Master _F.H.S.P._
French 3rd Set 2nd Term in the Set	Fair: he can do well, but his work varies too much.					
Scripture	Satisfactory					House Tutor _T. Borwick_
German 1st Set Greek Chemistry 1. Term in the Set	Fair: his grammar is poor.					He is a difficult boy to deal with & is very unwilling to be corrected. His excuses are always plentiful & sometimes trivial. But I am convinced that he is at bottom a good fellow & will come all right.
History and English	His English writing shews some ability, but it is often done in a slovenly way.					
Drawing	Very fair.					
Special Work or Private Tuition in						House Master _E.M.Oakeley_

This is very far from satisfactory —   Head Master _M.G.G._

A Weekly Report is sent home with each Day Boy every Monday Morning.   [P. T. O.

VIII

CLIFTON COLLEGE. (Military Side.)

Report for the Five Weeks ending June 9th 1894

Name *Tunstall-Behrens T*   Form *5⁴*   Average Age of the Form *16-4*

Place in Form at the beginning of Term, below which he ought not to fall *2·*   Term in the Form *3·*

WEEK OF THE TERM.	1st.	2nd.	3rd.	4th.	5th.	REMARKS.
Place in Form of ...12... Boys	-	2	4	3	3	He is doing very much better, and is making good progress. The weak side of his work is its inaccuracy and want of style.

Mathematics / Set   1·· Term in the Set — *A marked improvement this Term: but he has still much to learn in the matter of style.*

Latin ... 2ⁿᵈ Set ·   1·· Term in the Set — *Working better - but wanting in style.*

French 3· Set   3·· Term in the Set — *He is getting on, but he must pay more attention to spelling.*

Form Master *F. H. Slaters*

Scripture ... ... *Satisfactory*

good in the House.

German 2·· Set ~~or Greek~~ ~~or Chemistry~~   2·· Term in the Set — *Fair - but very inaccurate.*

House Tutor *F. Borwick* .

History and English — *His English writing is intelligent, but wanting in accuracy.*

Drawing ... ... *Very fair.*

More satisfactory. He seems to have settled down. He must remember that he will soon be in the VIth form, & ought now to be setting an example of quiet & orderly behaviour.

House Master *EM Moor.*

Special Work or Private Tuition in

Head Master *M. G. G.*

A Weekly Report is sent home with each Day Boy every Monday Morning.

[P. T. O.

CLIFTON COLLEGE. (Military Side.)

Report for the Five Weeks ending July 15th 1894

Name Tunstall-Behrens, T.   Form 5 y   Average Age of the Form 16·6

Place in Form at the beginning of Term, below which he ought not to fall 2   Term in the Form 3

WEEK OF THE TERM.	6th.	7th.	8th.	9th.	10th.	REMARKS.
Place in Form of /1 ...... Boys	2	2	2	2	2	He has worked more steadily this term on the whole.
Mathematics 1 Set (2 Term in the Set)	Works diligently, but has a poor style.					
Latin 2 (3 Term in the Set)	Quite satisfactory - he has worked steadily.					
French 3 Set (3 Term in the Set)	His work is fair, but not as good as it should be if he is to make much of the subject: he has done better lately.					Form Master F. H. Sleine
Scripture	Moderate. I have had occasion to speak of some inattention.					He seems to me a steady boy in the House.
German 2 Set / Greek / Chemistry (Term in the Set)	Has improved: he is becoming more accurate.					House Tutor F. Borwick.
History and English	His English Essays are fair but not always very accurate.					I have had no fault to find with him this term
Drawing	Very fair.					2 in new order
Special Work or Private Tuition in						House Master

Head Master

A Weekly Report is sent home with each Day Boy every Monday Morning.

[P. T. O.]

X

CLIFTON COLLEGE. (Military Side.)

Report for the Five Weeks ending Oct 27th 1894

Name _Tunstall Behrens T_   Form _5x_   Average Age of the Form _16-9_

Place in Form at the beginning of Term, below which he ought not to fall _6_   Term in the Form _1_

WEEK OF THE TERM.	1st.	2nd.	3rd.	4th.	5th.	REMARKS.
Place in Form of ..12...Boys	—	7	7	6	=6	

Mathematics / Set 4 Term in the Set	making progress; but he does not improve much in style at present. He must give attention to this; it is most important	making fair progress on the whole, but he wd. do better if he made greater efforts to fall in with the advice of his teachers. He seems at times to be more anxious to take a line of his own.
Latin... ...1... / Term in the Set	a random worker; might do much better work.	
French / 2 Set / Term in the Set	weak & uncertain.	Form Master H.C. Hall
Scripture	not very good; his answers are sometimes silly, or even grotesque.	
German or Greek or Chemistry / Set / Term in the Set	fair; composition poor.	House Tutor F. Borwick.
History and English Composition	weak, & disfigured by an untidy style & handwriting.	He seems to me to have much improved. I hope we are beginning to understand one another better.
Drawing	V. fair	
Special Work or Private Tuition in		
——————		House Master EMMoor.

Head Master [signature]

A Weekly Report is sent home with each Day Boy every Monday Morning.

[P. T. O.]

CLIFTON COLLEGE. (Military Side.)

Report for the Five Weeks ending _Dec 1st_ 1894

Name _Tunstall-Behrens_   Form _5x_   Average Age of the Form _16-8_

Place in Form at the beginning of Term, below which he ought not to fall _6_   Term in the Form _1_

WEEK OF THE TERM.	6th.	7th.	8th.	9th.	10th.	REMARKS.
Place in Form of 12.....Boys	4	4	6	2	6	I have been very well satisfied lately.

Mathematics / Set — Term in the Set 4 — Is steadily making progress; at present his work is rather crude in style & his methods cumbrous, but time will cure these faults.

Latin ... / ... Term in the Set / — The last half of the term has shewn considerable improvement.

French 2 Set — Term in the Set / — fair, promising.

Form Master _A W Hall_

This is satisfactory

Scripture ... ... — Generally very fair.

German / Set — ~~Greek~~ ~~Chemistry~~ / Term in the Set — fair.

House Tutor _F Bourich._

This is most encouraging.

~~History and~~ English Composition — Very uncertain. Sometimes he writes sensibly & shews intelligence.

Drawing ... ... — Doing well.

2nd is now over. Capital.

Special Work or Private Tuition in

House Master _E M Moor._

Head Master

A Weekly Report is sent home with each Day Boy every Monday Morning.   [P. T. O.

CLIFTON COLLEGE. (Military Side.)

Report for the Five Weeks ending *March 2nd 1895*

Name *Tunstall-Behrens* Form *5x* Average Age of the Form *16-9*

Place in Form at the beginning of Term, below which he ought not to fall *2* Term in the Form *2*

WEEK OF THE TERM.	1st.	2nd.	3rd.	4th.	5th.	REMARKS.
Place in Form of *14* ....Boys	—	3	2	—	2	

		REMARKS
Mathematics *1* Set *5* Term in the Set	*Making Excellent progress.*	*Improved generally. Seems to be more in Earnest about his work*
Latin ... *1* Term in the Set *2*	*Keeps a better level than last term*	
French *2* Set Term in the Set *2*	*doing better than at the beginning of term*	Form Master *A. E. Hall*
Scripture	*r.f. to good.*	*I wish he would realise that soon he will be called on to assume serious responsibilities as a VI form boy.*
German *1* Set or Greek or Chemistry *2* Term in the Set	*fair*	House Tutor *F Borwick*
History and English Essays	*very variable; seldom good.*	
Drawing	*Working well.*	
Special Work or Private Tuition in		
		House Master

I wish he were more manly —

Head Master *[signature]*

A Weekly Report is sent home with each Day Boy every Monday Morning.

[P. T. O.]

CLIFTON COLLEGE. (Military Side.)

Report for the Five Weeks ending _March 30th_ 189 _5_

Name _Tunstall-Behrens T_ Form _5 x_ Average Age of the Form _16-9_

Place in Form at the beginning of Term, below which he ought not to fall _2_ Term in the Form _2_

WEEK OF THE TERM.	6th.	7th.	8th.	9th.	10th.	REMARKS.
Place in Form of 14 ...... Boys	2	= 3	3	5	2	At times displays a want of docility wh. makes my work difficult & retards his progress.
Mathematics 1 Set Term in the Set 5	Has not improved lately, but has rather fallen off.					
Latin ... 1 Term in the Set 2	Work going on very satisfactorily.					
French 2 Set Term in the Set 2	Has been coming on better of late.					Form Master _H W Hall_
Scripture ...	fair					I trust most sincerely, that we shall have a pleasanter term after Easter. He will be given every encouragement the result will [rest] in his own hands
German 1 Set Greek Chemistry 2 Term in the Set	fair; his composition is weak.					House Tutor _H Borwick_
History and English Compos.?	rather poor.					
Drawing	Improves.					House Master
Special Work or Private Tuition in						

Head Master [signature] [P. T. O.

A Weekly Report is sent home with each Day Boy every Monday Morning.

CLIFTON COLLEGE. (Military Side.)

Report for the Five Weeks ending _June 8th_ 1895

Name _Tunstall-Behrens T._ Form _5x_ Average Age of the Form _17-2_

Place in Form at the beginning of Term, below which he ought not to fall _1_ Term in the Form _3_

WEEK OF THE TERM.	1st.	2nd.	3rd.	4th.	5th.	REMARKS.
Place in Form of _16_ ...... Boys	—	2	1	2	1	

		REMARKS
Mathematics 1st Set / Term in the Set 6	Working well, but he is not making much improvement.	He has not gained much ground of late, & he is no riper for competition for the highest places in the Woolwich list. But he may do very creditably. His singularly ugly handwriting, & is often very difficult to read will tell against him, I fear.
Latin ... 1 Term in the Set 3	Takes pains but is poor, especially in Unseens.	
		Form Master _H.S.Hall_
French 2 Set Term in the Set 3	Disappointing; his standard is not high.	
Scripture ...	Fair.	
German 1 Set or Greek or Chemistry 3 Term in the Set	fair.	House Tutor _F.Borwick._
History and English Composition	Fair except as regards style	
Drawing ...	good.	
Special Work or Private Tuition in Mathematics	Has worked very steadily, but I must confess to some disappointment as to results.	House Master _W.W.Asquith._

I hope he will be successful   Head Master _[signature]_

A Weekly Report is sent home with each Day Boy every Monday Morning.   [P. T. O.]

CLIFTON COLLEGE. (Military Side.)

Report for the Five Weeks ending _July 13th_ 1895

Name _Tunstall-Behrens_ Form _5x_ Average Age of the Form _17 – 2_

Place in Form at the beginning of Term, below which he ought not to fall _1_ Term in the Form _3_

WEEK OF THE TERM.	6th.	7th.	8th.	9th.	10th.	REMARKS.
Place in Form of 16 ... Boys	1	1	not placed			A good term's work 2d. I hope maybe rewarded with success
Mathematics 1 Set Term in the Set 5	Has worked steadily all through the term.					
Latin ... 1 Term in the Set 3	fair; takes pains					
French 2 Set Term in the Set 3	fair on the whole; comp.s weak					Form Master _S. D. Hall_ I heartily wish him success.
Scripture	Satisfactory.					
German 1 Set ~~Greek~~ ~~Chemistry~~ 3 Term in the Set	fair					House Tutor _H. Berwick._
History and English Composition	fair, but rather erratic					I am glad to see the form report of his work; and wish I could speak with equal praise
Drawing	good					of the line he has taken in the house – tho' here I am
Special Work or Private Tuition in Mathematics	Has worked with interest & intelligence.					inclined to believe there has been an improvement on last term. House Master _W. W. Asquith_

I hope he has passed high –

Head Master _[signature]_

[P. T. O.]

A Weekly Report is sent home with each Day Boy every Monday Morning.

THE EDUCATIONAL COURSE OF CLIFTON COLLEGE.

The School consists of the following parts:—

    (1) The Upper School, for boys between 13 and 19, which is divided into three departments—the Classical Side, the Modern Side, and the Military Side.

    (2) The Junior School, for boys between 10 and 14, which prepares for the three departments of the College.

    (3) The Preparatory School, for boys between 7 and 11, which prepares for the Junior School.

The numbers of each part of the School are limited—the Upper School to 460, the Junior School to 140, the Preparatory School to 45.

PREPARATORY SCHOOL.—In the Preparatory School boys receive a thorough grounding in English subjects, French, Latin, and Arithmetic. Their play is systematic, and is superintended by the Masters. Their schoolrooms are in a separate building at some distance from the College.

JUNIOR SCHOOL.—The Junior School have separate buildings within the College precincts, and a separate part of the playground. Their hours are so arranged that they cannot have communication with the older boys. They all learn English subjects, French, Latin, and Mathematics. In the Third Forms Greek is taught to those who are being prepared for the Classical Side of the College, while boys intended for the Modern and Military Sides learn extra French and Mathematics. The games are carefully organized, as well for town boys as for boarders, and are superintended by Masters.

UPPER SCHOOL.—On entering the Upper School a boy has to choose between the Classical and the Modern Side. (Boys intended for the Military Side remain on the Modern Side until they reach the Upper Fourth Form.) A boy who is intended for the University or the Indian Civil Service should join the Classical Side, unless he is to specialize in Mathematics or Science. Those who are intended for Business generally join the Modern Side. Where the profession is not yet decided it is generally better to join the Classical Side.

Every boy is placed in a " Form." On the Classical Side the Form Work consists of Scripture, Latin, Greek, History, Geography, and English Literature, and occupies about 20 hours in School each week, besides preparation. On the Modern Side the Form work comprises the same subjects, with the exception of Greek, and occupies about 10 hours in School. The rest of the work, on both Sides alike, is done in " Sets," *i.e.*, groups of boys chosen from different " Forms " according to their capacity in each special subject. The Mathematical Sets throughout the School, and the German and Science Sets in the Upper Half, are common to the two sides of the School.

It is now necessary to say a few words about the separate work of the two sides.

CLASSICAL SIDE.—In the Third and Fourth Forms all boys learn French and Science in Sets. In the Fifth Forms French is a voluntary subject, and each boy has to choose between German and Science. The Form work becomes somewhat elastic, so that boys are able, to some extent, to cultivate special tastes, especially a taste for History.

MODERN SIDE.—In the Third Forms all boys learn French, Drawing, and Natural Science in Sets. In the Fourth Forms Drawing ceases to be compulsory, and German is begun, while French and Science are carried further. From the Upper Fourth a large number of boys pass into the Military Side. Those who are not intended for the Army pass up into the Modern Fifth Forms, where considerable facilities are given for special work. In those Forms all boys do English, Scripture, History, French, and Drawing; and they may choose any two of the three subjects—Latin, German, and Science. Those who are strong in Mathematics, Science, or Modern Languages are able to devote a large amount of time to any one of the three. Those who are going to the Universities now join a special Greek class, in which they learn the small amount of that language which is required in order to pass at Cambridge.

THE MILITARY SIDE is open only to boys who reach the Upper Fourth Form before they are 16, and are able to reach a certain standard in Mathematics. The work of this side is carefully regulated to enable boys to pass direct from the School into Woolwich, Sandhurst, or Cooper's Hill (Indian Woods and Forests). As a rule only boys preparing for those three examinations are admitted to the Military Side; but occasionally boys are allowed to enter it who are intended for the profession of Civil Engineering.

SIXTH FORM.—Boys are promoted from both Classical and Modern Upper Fifths into the Sixth Form. The whole Form attend the Head Master's lessons in Scripture and English; but for other subjects they are divided into two main branches. In one of these are placed all boys whose special subject is Classics, but they continue to give four hours a week to Mathematics, and four to either German or Science, until their last year. The other division comprises all those, whether promoted from the Classical or the Modern Fifth, who are to devote themselves mainly to History, Science, Mathematics, or Modern Languages. These do a moderate amount of Greek and Latin as a Form, doing their special work in Sets. Such boys on the Military Side as are qualified by their attainments rank as part of the Sixth Form, and share the Scripture lessons, though the rest of their work is done in the Military Sets.

October, 1892.   M. G. GLAZEBROOK.

Clifton College Engineer Corps.

Memorandum for information of Parents as to Cost to Boys on joining.

The Subscription of 21/- per Term covers the cost of all outfit and equipment except Gaiters (5/9) and Gloves (9d.) These free outfits will have been issued before, but will be in good serviceable condition; no charge will be made for alterations in fit. In all cases where new Tunics and Trousers are supplied, there will be an extra charge of 5/- for Tunic and 2/6 for Trousers. The parents' authority must be given in writing for all new uniform. No extra expense is incurred, either for additional outfit on promotion, or for the cost of Ammunition at the Rifle Range.

There are two Public School Field Days annually: one in March at Aldershot, the other in October in the West of England. The cost of travelling, &c., for boys selected to attend is, for the former about 12/-, and for the latter from 5/- to 7/6.

(*Signed*)   EDM^D. C. PLANT, *Col.,*
Commanding 2nd G.V.R.E. and Clifton College Cadets.

APPROVED.

(*Signed*)   *Head Master.*

CLIFTON, 24/9/90.

XX

MORNING.	SUNDAY.	MONDAY.	TUESDAY.	WEDNESDAY.	THURSDAY.	FRIDAY.	SATURDAY.
8.45—10	Old Testament (prep)	N. T.	french	Trigonometry	German	prepare 1 hr extra during the week for this Geography	Latin
10—11	O. Testament.	German	Trigonometry	German	Trigonometry	Euclid	french
11.15—12.15	Chapel	Latin	Latin	Algebra	french	Latin	Algebra
12.15—1.15					Latin		Mensuration
AFTERNOON.							
			Geometrical Drawing	french (prep)		1 hr extra prep for this Geomet: Drawing	
3—4		Theme	Euclid (prep)	french		french	
4—5	Chapel	french	Euclid	Latin (prep)			
5—6		Algebra	German	Latin		Algebra	
EVENING WORK.	N. Testament (prep)	1½ hr Latin 1½ hr french	1 hr. German 1 hr Algebra ¾ hr french	1 hr German 1 hr Latin ½ hr french	1½ french 1 hr Euclid	1½ hr Latin 1 hr french	1 hr German Theme.

3.1091

CLIFTON COLLEGE.

CHRISTMAS. 1892.

HIGHER ALGEBRA.

V. 1 β., 2 ; I. Mil. do 7 questions from Part II.
V. 3 ... ... do 7 questions, not more than 3 from Part I.
V. 4 ; II. Mil. ... do any 7 questions.

PART I.

MARKS.

1. A ratio of greater inequality is decreased by adding the same number to each of its terms.

   Find the number which subtracted from 14, 34, 36, 111 will make them proportional.

   If $b : a :: 7 : 8$ and $x : y :: 2 : 3$ and $a : y :: 11 : 21$, find the ratio of $2b + 7x : 2y - 3a$. 7

2. Deduce the algebraical definition of proportion from the geometrical definition.

   If $a : b :: c : d :: e : f$,

   shew that $(a^2 + c^2 + e^2)^{\frac{1}{2}} : (b^2 + d^2 + f^2)^{\frac{1}{2}} :: a : b$
   and that $a^3 d^2 f = b^3 c^2 e$. 8

3. When is one quantity said to vary as another quantity ?

   If $A \propto BC$ and A is 6 when B is 5 and C is 7, what is C when A is 9 and B is 5 ?

   If $(x+1)^2 \propto y^3$ and if $y = 2$ when $x = 2$, find the relation between x and y. 7

4. Sum to n terms the arithmetical progression

   $$a + (a+d) + (a+2d) + \ldots\ldots$$

   Write down the 17th term of the series 3, -1, -5, -9.

   Find the nth term of the arithmetical progression whose first term is $a + b$ and common difference $a - b$.

   Find the first three terms of the arithmetical progression whose 10th term is -100 and whose 48th term is 128. 10

5. Sum to n terms the geometrical progression $a + ar + ar^2 + \ldots\ldots$

   In what case can a geometrical progression be summed to infinity ?

   Sum (1) $32 + 48 + 72 + \ldots\ldots$ to 6 terms ;

   (2) $9·6 + 7·2 + 5·4 + \ldots\ldots$ to infinity.

   Find the sum of five numbers in geometrical progression, the second term being 5 and the fifth term being 625. 10

CLIFTON COLLEGE.

CHRISTMAS, 1892.

HIGHER TRIGONOMETRY.

[No one may attempt more than NINE *questions.]*

Set V. 3 may do any EIGHT.

Set V. 2 may take FIVE *from Part I.*

II. Mil. may take FOUR *from Part I.*

Set V., 1 β, and I. Mil. may take ONE *from Part I.*

PART I.

MARKS.

1. Establish the formula for the expansion of $\cos(A+B)$. Hence or *otherwise* prove that $\sin(90°+A)=\cos A$, and $\cos(180°+A)=-\cos A$.　　10

2. Find the value of $\tan(A-B)$.

   Express $\tan^2\theta$ in terms of $\cos 2\theta$.

   Prove the identities

   (1) $\cos(A+B)\cos(A-B)=\cos^2 A\cos^2 B-\sin^2 A\sin^2 B$;

   (2) $\sin A=\dfrac{\sin 2A\cos A}{1+\cos 2A}$.　　12

3. Establish the formula for $\cos\theta-\cos\phi$ in terms of the product of $\sin\dfrac{\theta+\phi}{2}$ and $\sin\dfrac{\theta-\phi}{2}$.

   Prove (1) $\dfrac{\cos A-\cos 3A}{\sin 3A-\sin A}=\tan 2A$;

   (2) $\cos(420°+A)+\cos(60°-A)=\cos A$;

   Hence deduce the value of $\cos 105°+\cos 15°$.　　10

4. Prove that $\dfrac{\sin A}{a}=\dfrac{\sin B}{b}=\dfrac{\sin C}{c}$.

   In any triangle

   (1) $(a+b)\cos C+(b+c)\cos A+(c+a)\cos B=a+b+c$;

   (2) $\tan\dfrac{A+B}{2}=\cot\dfrac{C}{2}$.　　12

OLD CLIFTONIAN ARMY LIST.

The Editors of *The Cliftonian* have much pleasure in printing the following List of Old Cliftonians Serving in the Army, which has been drawn up with great labour by E. H. M. Leggett, R.E., hoping that it may be of interest to Cliftonians, and asking them to let the Editors know of any omission or error they may notice.

CAVALRY.

REGIMENT.	RANK.	NAME.	HOUSE.	REMARKS.
2nd Life Gds...	Lieut. ...	Brinton, J. C. ...	Oakeley ...	
1st Drag. Gds.	Capt. ...	Younghusband, F. E.	School ...	prob. Ind. Stff. Cps.
,, ,, ,,	Lieut. ...	Marter, W. M. ...	Oakeley ...	
4th ,, ,,	Capt. ...	Brinkley, C. M. E....	Poole ...	attached O.S.Corps
5th ,, ,,	Major ...	Hemming, F. W. ...	School ...	Brevet Lieut.-Col.
3rd Hussars ...	Major ...	Scott, J. S. R. ...	Brown ...	
,, ,,	Major ...	Alexander, R. G. ...	School ...	
,, ,, ...	Capt. ...	Pirie, D. V. ...	School ...	
7th ,, ...	Capt. ...	Haig, D. ...	School ...	
8th ,, ...	Lieut. ...	Sandwith, L. ...	School ...	
9th Lancers ...	Capt. ...	Little, M. O. ...	Jn. School	A.D.C. to Lord-
,, ,, ...	Lieut. ...	Campbell, D. G. M.	Wiseman	Lieut. Ireland
11th Hussars...	Capt. ...	Salt, T. A. ...	Moor ...	Adjutant
13th ,, ...	Capt. ...	Wiggin, E. A. ...	School ...	
19th ,, ...	2nd-Lieut.	St. Quentin, E. S. ...	Watson ...	
21st ,, ...	Lieut. ...	Taylor, A. H. M. ...	Grenfell...	

ROYAL ARTILLERY.

RANK.	NAME.	HOUSE.	REMARKS.
Major ...	Hay, E. O. ...	Town ...	R.H.A., Aldershot
,, ...	Baker, J. V. V. ...	Town ...	Rawul Pindi
,, ...	Lowther, W. G. ...	Town ...	Devonport
,, ...	Bowles, F. A. ...	Brown ...	Mt. Batt., Rawul Pindi
,, ...	Brunker, J. M. S. ...	Town ...	Field Batt., Meerut
,, ...	Smith, E. A. ...	School ...	Madras
,, ...	Harrison, R. A. G. ...	Brown ...	Gibraltar
,, ...	Piers, H. O. ...	Brown ...	Campbellpore
Captain ...	Hay, A. E. ...	Town ...	Field Batt., Athlone
,, ...	Block, M. W. P. ...	Dakyns ...	Ceylon
,, ...	Savile, W. C. ...	Town ...	Asst. Insp. Stores, Devonport
,, ...	McLeod, R. M. G. ...	Harris ...	Field Batt., Bellary
,, ...	Armitage, E. H. ...	Harris ...	R.H.A., Trimulgherry
,, ...	Thornton, S. V. ...	School ...	Adj. Mil. Art., Scarborough
,, ...	Darley, G. R. ...	School ...	Field Batt., Ipswich
,, ...	Lambert, W. ...	N. Town ..	Asst. Insp. Stores, Woolwich
,, ...	Baker, G. D. ...	Brown ...	Singapore

XXIV

ROYAL ARTILLERY *(continued).*

RANK.	NAME.	HOUSE.	REMARKS.
Captain	De Jersey, C.	School	Field Batt., Ahmedabad
,,	Tisdall, A. L.	Oakeley	Adj. Mil. Art., Londonderry
,,	Watkins, L. G.	Wiseman	Indian Ord. Dept.
,,	Moore-Lane, W.	Dunn	Adj. Vol. Art., Dover
,,	Ducrôt, L. H.	Brown	Gosport
,,	Harrison, H. C. V.	N. Town	Adj. Vol. Art., Blackburn
,,	Young, A. D.	Oakeley	Field Batt., Hyderabad
,,	Cooper, E. S.	Oakeley	Insp. P. F., Portsmouth
,,	Cookson, W. W.	Wiseman	Indian Ord. Dept.
,,	Macbean, W. A., p.s.c.	Oakeley	Field Batt., Newcastle
,,	Graham, L.	Bart.	Field Batt., Aldershot
,,	Fasson, D. J. M.	Bart.	Halifax, N.S.
,,	Fowler, F. C.	Brown	Jamaica
Lieut.	White, G. F.	Brown	Field Batt., Bareilly
,,	Raby, M. H. B.	Watson	Field Batt., Campbellpore
,,	Gooch, J. S.	N. Town	Campbellpore
,,	Prescott-Decie, C.	Bart.	R.H.A., Aldershot
,,	Heath, F. W.	Brown	R.H.A., Woolwich
,,	Pringle, G. O. S.	N. Town	Egypt
,,	Boulnois, W. A.	Bart.	R.H.A., Woolwich
,,	Phillips, T. R.	Watson	Indian Ord. Dept.
,,	Seagrim, D. G.	S. Town	Native Artillery
,,	Pack-Beresford, A. W.	School	R.H.A., Rawul Pindi
,,	Woodcock, H. S.	Grenfell	Southern Division
,,	Taylor, H. W.	Oakeley	R.H.A., Umballa
,,	Williams, M. S.	Wiseman	R.H.A., Woolwich
,,	Parsons, E. H. T.	N. Town	Field Batt., Weedon
,,	Owen, F. C.	S. Town	Field Batt., Bangalore
,,	Buckle, A. S.	School	Supt. of Expts., Shoeburyness
,,	Brett, H. G.	Watson	Mt. Batt., Rawul Pindi
,,	Bellairs, N. E. B.	Watson	Gosport
,,	Thomson, A. F. R.	Grenfell	R.H.A., Aldershot
,,	Oldham, F. T.	N. Town	Field Batt., Ahmednugger
,,	Craster, E. H. B.	School	Mt. Batt., Umballa
,,	De Brett, H S.	Watson	Field Batt., Ahmednugger
,,	Horne, J.	Bart.	Field Batt., Aldershot
,,	Harington, E. C.	Bart.	Rangoon
,,	Bowring, A. H.	Bart.	Field Batt., Aldershot
,,	Hinton, G. B.	S, Town	Malta
,,	Probyn, D. G.	Bart.	Field Batt., Mooltan
,,	Townsend, S. C. C.	Grenfell	Cape of Good Hope
,,	Pinhey, W. M.	Bart.	Half-pay
2nd-Lieut.	Osborne, L. L. H.	N. Town	Isle of Wight
,,	Boyce, A. H.	Watson	Rangoon
,,	Cottingham, H. L.	Watson	Malta
,,	Baillie, G.	Phelps	Gibraltar
,,	Macdougall, J. T.	Watson	Malta
,,	Evans, W.	N. Town	Trimulgherry
,,	Lloyd, H. G.	Grenfell	Field Batt., Campbellpore
,,	Tilney, N. E.	Grenfell	Field Batt., Newcastle
,,	Currie, I. B. F.	Wiseman	Malta
,,	Oldfield, L. C. L.	S. Town	Attock
,,	Hood, Hon. N. A.	School	Gibraltar

ROYAL ENGINEERS.

RANK.	NAME.	HOUSE.	REMARKS.
Major	Maycock, S. M.	Town	Halifax, N. S.
Captain	Turton, W. H.	Town	Assistant Instructor, Chatham
,,	Jackson, H. M.	Dakyns	Survey of India
,,	Horniblow, F. H.	Town	Cork
,,	Baker, W. W.	Brown	War Office
,,	Browne, C. A. R.	Brown	Assam Railway
,,	Vidal, W. S.	Brown	Instructor in Submarine Mining
,,	Hemming, E. H.	Dunn	Aden
,,	Boyd, M. A.	Town	Instructor in Submarine Mining
,,	Jones, L.	Dakyns	Edinburgh
,,	Leahy, C. A.	School	Ordnance Survey
,,	Pringle, J. W.	Town	Intell. Division War Office
,,	Kent, H. V.	Oakeley	Pembroke
,,	Painter, A. C.	Oakeley	Portland
,,	Broke, H.	School	Ordnance Survey
,,	Birdwood, H. C. I.	Watson	A.E., Simla
,,	Young, J. R.	School	Assistant Instructor, Chatham
Lieut.	Liddell, W. A.	School	A.E., Rangoon
,,	Evans, W. W.	N. Town	S. and M., Bangalore
,,	Stokes-Roberts, E. R.B.	School	E.E., Madras
,,	Enthoven, C. H.	Oakeley	Halifax, N. S. (ordered home)
,,	Lloyd, F. L.	Oakeley	S. M. Co., Hong Kong
,,	Lee, R. P.	S. Town	Telegraph Batt., Aldershot
,,	Clauson, J. E.	Bart.	Staff College
,,	Prentice, H.	Wiseman	India
,,	Pilcher, A. J.	Wiseman	Indian Survey
,,	Wilson, C. S.	School	Aldershot
,,	O'Shee, R. A. P.	S. Town	Falmouth
,,	Austin, H. K.	N. Town	Mombasa, E. Africa
,,	Lathbury, H. O.	Oakeley	A.E., Attock
,,	Watherston, A. E. G.	Bart.	Fd.Co., Aldershot
,,	Home, J. G. L.	Watson	Submarine Mining Co., Bombay
,,	Rivett-Carnack, S. G.	Bart.	E.E., Meerut
,,	Pike, C. B. F.	S. Town	Malta
,,	Carmichael, J. F. H.	Bart.	A.E., P.W.D., Burmah
,,	Smyth, W. C.	Oakeley	A.E., East Coast Railway, India
,,	Hibbert, W. G.	Brown	N.W. Railway, India
,,	Dumaresq, A. H.	Watson	Cork, Submarine Mining Co.
,,	Denis de Vitré, P. T.	N. Town	Bridging Batt., Aldershot
,,	Lees, W. E.	Brown	Bombay
,,	West, R. H.	Watson	S. and M., Kirkee
2nd.-Lieut.	Leggett, E. H. M.	Grenfell	L. and N.W. Railway
,,	Stokes, W. A.	School	Secunderabad
,,	Polwhele, R.	School	Midland Railway
,,	Barstow, J. B.	N. Town	S.M.E., Chatham
,,	Vickers, C. E.	School	,, ,,
,,	Elliott, C. G. E.	Bart.	,, ,,

XXVI

INFANTRY.

REGIMENT.	RANK.	NAME.	HOUSE.	REMARKS.
1st Royal Scots ...	Major ...	Money, R. F. K. ...	Brown ...	
,, ...	Lieut. ...	Versturme, H. P. ...	Dunn ...	
2nd R.W. Surrey .	Lieut. ...	Cowper, H. M. ...	S. Town...	
3rd Buffs ...	Captain ...	Vertue, N. H. ...	Wiseman .	Adj. 2nd Battn.
,, ...	Lieut. ...	Cobbe, C. C. ...	Grenfell...	
,, ...	2nd-Lieut.	Perkins, Æ. C. ...	Grenfell...	
4th Rl. Lancaster .	Captain ...	Somerville, T. C. F....	Harris ...	A.D.C.toLt.Gen.
,, ...	Captain ...	Haynes, A. ...	S. Town...	Cape of G. H.
,, ...	2nd-Lieut.	Borrett, C. A. ...	Brown ...	
5th Northum. Fus.	Captain ...	Willmott, W. A. ...	Oakeley...	Adj.North.Vols., Hexham
6th Rl. Warwick...	Major ...	Helyar, H. W. ...	Harris ...	Adj.Vls.,Bir'ham
,, ...	Captain ...	East, C. C. ...	Watson ...	A.D.C.toG.O.C., Madras
7th Rl. Fusiliers...	Captain ...	Forbes, W. L. ...	Watson ...	Adj.Vls.,Aberd'n
,, ...	Captain ...	Nicholson, H. H. ...	School ...	Adj. Vols., Peter-
,, ...	Captain	Menzies, S. ...	School ...	head
,, ...	Lieut. ...	Fowler-Butler, R. ...	School ...	Adj. 1st Batt.
,, ...	Lieut. ...	HelyHutchinson,R.G.	School ...	
,, ...	Lieut. ...	Thurburn, W. L. ...	Grenfell...	
8th Liverpool ...	Captain ...	Campbell, G. ...	School ...	
,, ...	Lieut. ...	Van der Gucht, R. L.	S. Town...	
,, ...	2nd-Lieut.	Austin, F. J. ·...	N. Town..	
9th Norfolk ...	Captain ...	Borton, C. E. ...	Hartnell...	
10th Lincoln ...	Captain ..	Rawlinson, W. C. W.	School ...	
11th Devon ...	Captain ...	Briggs, F. C. ...	Harris ...	Adj.Vols.,Exeter
,, ...	Captain ...	Ellicombe, G. J. ...	Dunn ...	Ad.Vl.,New.Abt.
,, ...	Captain ...	Goodwyn, N. J. ...	Dunn ...	Adj. 2nd Batt.
,, ...	Lieut. ...	Law, J. P. ...	Bart. ...	
,, ...	2nd-Lieut.	Marshall, C. H. ...	School ...	
12th Suffolk ...	Lieut. ..	Unwin, R. B. ...	United ...	
13th Somerset L.I.	Captain ...	Payne, R. L., D.S.O.	Town ...	
,, ...	2nd-Lieut.	Rawling, C. G. ...	School ...	
14th W. Yorks. ...	Captain ...	O'Donell, H. ...	Town ...	Adj. 1st Batt.
,, ...	Lieut. ...	Lang, G. G. ..	Oakeley...	
15th E. Yorks. ...	2nd-Lieut,	Tawney, C. J. ...	Bart. ...	
16th Bedford ...	2nd-Lieut.	Appleby, G. F. ...	Brown ..	
,, ...	2nd-Lient.	Stallard, R. M. ...	Watson ...	
17th Leicester ...	Captain ...	Burnett, J. G. L. ...	Harris ...	Adj.Vols.,Leices.
,, ...	Lieut. ...	Tredgold, J. A. T. ...	Grenfell...	Att. A. S. C.,
,, ...	Lieut. ...	Smith, H. S. ...	Brown ...	[Curragh
18th Royal Irish...	Lieut. ...	Armstrong, W. M. H.	Wiseman..	
19th Yorkshire ...	Captain ...	Elton, A. B. ...	Town ...	
,, ...	Lieut. ...	Maitland, H. R. S. ...	Oakeley...	
20th Lanc. Fus. ...	Lieut. ...	Newnham, P. F. ...	N. Town..	
21st Rl. Scots Fus.	Captain ...	Lean, K. E. ...	School ..	St.Stff.Off.Beng'l
,, ...	Captain ...	Thurburn, A. H. ...	Brown ...	Adj. 1st Batt.
22nd Cheshire ...	Captain ...	Tod, A. G. W. ...	S. Town...	Att.O.S.C.Malta
,, ...	Captain ...	Clifford, W. R. ...	Wiseman .	

INFANTRY *(continued)*.

REGIMENT.	RANK.	NAME.	HOUSE.	REMARKS.
22nd Cheshire ...	Lieut. ...	Stone, A. B.	Watson ...	
„ ...	Lieut. ...	Adair, A. C.	Wiseman .	
„ ...	2nd-Lieut.	Mayo, H. E.	School ...	
23rd Welsh Fus....	Captain ...	Cooper, A. F.	Dakyns ...	
24th S.W. Bord....	Lieut. ...	Canning, A.	S. Town...	
„ ...	2nd-Lieut.	Williams, W. A. G....	Tait ...	
25th K.O.S. Bord.	Captain ...	Hemphill, F.	Hartnell...	
„ ...	Lieut. ...	Going, A. C.	Oakeley...	
„ ...	Lieut. ...	Robertson, E. Q. ...	School ...	
26th and 90th	Major ...	Rawlins, H. de C. ...	School ...	
Cameronians	Lieut. ...	Blackburn, L. D. ...	School ...	
„ ...	Lieut. ...	Vandeleur, C. B. ...	Brown ...	
„ ...	Lieut. ...	Murray, F.	Brown ...	
„ ...	Lieut. ...	Davis, G. J. ...	S. Town...	Prob.In.StaffCp.
27th and 108th	Captain ...	Armitage, J. L. ...	Harris ...	p.s.c.
Enniskilling Fus.	2nd-Lieut.	Chapman, R. B. ...	Laxton ...	
„ ...	2nd-Lieut.	Sime, C. G.	Bart. ...	
28th and 61st	Major ...	Archdale, M. E. ...	School ...	
Gloucester	Captain ...	Baxter, C. F.	School ...	
„ ...	Captain ...	Willcock, S.	Harris ...	Adj. 2nd Batt.
„ ...	Captain ...	Fyffe, B. O.	S. Town...	
„ ...	Lieut. ...	Carmichael, G. C. I.	Bart. ...	
„	2nd-Lieut.	Hunter, C. W.	N. Town..	
29th and 36th	Lieut. ...	Norbury, C.	School ...	
Worcester	Lieut. ...	Bennett, C. H.	Brown ...	
„ ...	Lieut. ...	Cayley, D. E.	Grenfell...	
„ ...	Lieut. ...	Birdwood, H. B. ...	Grenfell..	
„ ...	2nd-Lieut.	Fagan, A. P. D. ...	N. Town ..	
30th and 59th	Captain ...	Haynes, C.	School ...	Act.Pay.1st Batt.
East Lancashire	Captain ...	Pile, L. L.	Dakyns ...	Att. A.S.C., St
„ ...	2nd-Lieut.	Browne, C. E.	S. Town...	Lucia
31st and 70th	Lieut. ...	Tew, H. S.	School ...	
East Surrey	Lieut. ...	Hart, A. H. S.	Brown ...	
32nd&46th D.C.L.I	Lieut. ...	Grant, A. G. W.	Watson ...	
33rd and 76th	Major ...	Jenkins, V.	Cay ...	Brevet Lt.-Col.
West Riding	Captain ..	Anderson, W. J. ...	S. Town...	
„ ...	Lieut. ...	Higginson, A. J. M....	School ...	
34th & 55th Bord.	Lieut. ...	Stack, L. O. F.	Oakeley ...	
„ ...	Lieut. ...	Bosanquet, J. T. I....	Brown ...	
„ ...	2nd-Lieut.	Pigott, A. F. H. ...	S. Town .	
35th and 107th	Lieut. ...	Burbury, J. H.	United ...	
Sussex	2nd-Lieut.	Daunt, R. B.	S. Town .	
37th and 67th	Major ...	Macdonald, R. P. ...	School ...	D.S.O.
Hampshire	Captain ...	Munro, L.	Town ...	p.s.c., Brig. Maj.
„ ...	Captain ...	Mactier, H. C. ..	Brown ...	[Gibraltar
„ ...	Lieut. ...	Bewsher, W. D. ...	Wiseman .	
38th and 80th	Captain ...	Barlow, H.	Watson ...	
S. Staffordshire	Lieut. ...	Cozens, R.	School ...	
„ ...	2nd-Lieut.	Campbell, D. W. A....	S. Town...	
39th & 54th Dorset.	Lieut. ...	Dalgliesh, E. E. C....	Grenfell...	
40th and 82nd	Major ...	Kellie, R. H.	Town ...	
S. Lancashire	Captain ...	Moggridge, J. A. ..	Dakyns ...	
„ ...	Captain ...	Shekleton, H. P. ...	N. Town ..	

XXVIII

INFANTRY *(continued)*.

REGIMENT.	RANK	NAME.	HOUSE.	REMARKS.
40th and 82nd	Captain ..	Smythies, R. H. R....	N. Town ..	
S. Lancashire	Lieut. ...	Lewis, C. E.	School ...	
,, ...	2nd-Lieut.	Oakeley, E. F. ...	Grenfell ...	
,, ...	2nd-Lieut.	Clarke-Jervoise, E. J.	Grenfell ...	
41st & 69th Welsh	Captain ...	Goodwyn, J. H. ..	Dakyns ...	Adj. Vols., Tai-
42nd and 73rd	Captain ...	Galbraith, G. H. L...	Oakeley ..	[bach, S. Wales
Black Watch	Lieut. ...	Turner, H. S. ...	Wiseman .	
43rd and 52nd	Captain ..	Luard, R. C. ...	Bart. ...	
Oxford L.I.	Lieut. ...	Childers, E. M. ...	Hartnell ..	
,,	Lieut. ...	Cuyler, Sir C. ...	School ...	
44th & 56th Essex	Captain ...	Machell, P. W. ...	Watson ...	Att. Egpt. Army
45th & 95th Derby	Captain ...	Brittan, R. ...	Town ..	
49th & 66th Berks.	Captain ...	Southey, J. H. W. ...	Brown ...	
51st and 105th	Captain ...	Heath, H. N. C. ...	Brown ...	Brevet-Major
York. L.I.	Captain ...	Elles, A. W. ...	Watson ...	A.D.C. to G.O.C.
,, ...	Lieut. ...	Jones, F. W. ...	Watson ...	[Bengal
53 & 85 Shrops. L.I.	2nd-Lieut.	Luard, E. B. ...	S. Town ..	
60th K.R. Rifles ...	Lieut. ...	Watson, J. K. ...	School ...	
62nd & 99th Wilts.	Lieut. ...	Beadon, A. E. ...	School ...	
63rd and 96th	Captain ...	Melville, C. C. ...	Dakyns ...	
Manchester	2nd-Lieut.	South, H. M. W. ...	Brown ..	
64th and 98th	Major ...	Wood, C. E. W. ...	Harris ..	
North Stafford.	Captain ...	Lindner, A. J. ..	Dunn ...	
,, ...	Captain ...	Geldard, F. ...	Brown ...	Adj. S.Staff.Mil.,
,, ...	Captain ...	George, A. ...	Dakyns ...	[Lichfield
,, ...	2nd-Lieut.	Bliss, C. ...	Brown ...	
65th and 54th	2nd-Lieut.	Cotes, G. R. H. ...	Watson ...	
York and Lanc.	2nd-Lieut.	Norrington, F. C. S..	N. Town ..	
,, ...	2nd-Lieut.	Colston, H. K. ...	Brown ...	
,, ...	2nd-Lieut.	Sykes, W. E. ...	Watson ...	
68th and 106th	Major ...	Wiehe, F. G. A. ...	School ...	
Durham L.I.	Captain ...	Bush, B. E. ...	S. Town...	
,,	Lieut. ...	Luard, C. C. ...	Bart. ...	Act. Paymaster
71st and 74th	Captain ...	Synge, R. F. M.F.M.	Brown ...	
Highland L.I.	Lieut. ...	Cowan, J. W. A. ...	Watson ...	
,, ...	Lieut. ...	Begbie, G. E. ...	Grenfell ...	
72nd and 78th Sea-	Major ...	Mackenzie, K. R. ...	Brown ...	
forth Highland'rs	Captain ...	Spottiswood, A. A. ...	Dakyns ...	
,, ...	Lieut. ...	Galloway, H. B. ...	Grenfell ...	
,, ...	Lieut. ...	Vandeleur, R. S. ...	Brown ...	
75 & 92 Gord. Hgrs.	Lieut. ...	Macnab, G. R. ...	School ...	
83rd and 86th	Captain ...	Cliffe, H. M. ...	Oakeley ...	
R.I. Rifles	Lieut. ...	Christie, E. J. ...	Wiseman .	Adj. 1st Battn.
87 and 89 R.I. Fus.	Lieut. ...	Pike, M. J. W. ...	S. Town...	
88th and 94th Con-	Major ...	Maclean, A. W. D....	School ...	Adj. Mayo Mil.,
naught Rangers	Captain ...	Hume, J. J. F. ...	Town ...	[Castlebar
,, ..	Lieut. ...	Murray, S. J. ...	Brown ...	
91 & 93 A.& S.Hgrs.	Lieut. ...	McNeill, M. ...	Wiseman .	
100th and 109th	Major ...	Kaye, A. E. C. ...	Harris ...	
Leinster	2nd-Lieut.	Searle, A. V. ...	Hartnell ..	
101st and 104th ..	Major ...	Penny, F. H. ...	Town ...	
Munster Fus.	Captain ...	Hall, C. A. K. ...	School ...	
,,	Captain ...	Congdon, A. E. S. ...	Town ...	

INFANTRY *(continued)*.

REGIMENT.	RANK.	NAME.	HOUSE.	REMARKS.
101st and 104th	Lieut. ...	Tizard, H. E. ...	Phelps ...	
Munster Fus.	Lieut. ...	Bourne, W. F. ...	Watson ...	
102nd and 103rd	Major ...	Miles, G. A. ...	Town ...	
Rl Dublin Fus.	Lieut. ...	Higginson, C. H. B...	School ...	
„	... 2nd-Lieut.	Harcourt, J. S. M. ...	S. Town...	
West India ...	Lieut. ...	Master, A. G. ...	Oakeley ...	
„ ...	Lieut. ...	Tredgold, W. L. ...	Oakeley ...	Att. O.S.C.

DEPARTMENTAL CORPS.

CORPS.	RANK.	NAME.	HOUSE.	REMARKS.
Army Service	Captain ...	Hamnett, G. E. ...	Dakyns ...	From R.A.
„	Captain ...	Pile, L. L. ...	Dakyns ..	From E. Lanc. Rgt.
„	Lieut. ...	Tredgold, J. A. T. ...	Grenfell ...	From Leicstr. Regt.
Ordnce. Store	Captain ...	Brinkley, C. M. E....	Poole ...	From 4th Drg. Gds.
„	Captain ...	Tod, A. G. W. ...	S. Town...	From Cheshire Regt.
„	Lieut. ...	Tredgold, W. L. ...	Oakeley ...	From W. Ind. Regt.
Medical Staff	Surg.-Maj..	Peck, F. S. ...	Town ...	Indian Medl. Dept.
„	Surg.-Capt.	Jones, F. W. C. ...	Dakyns ...	Bombay
„	Surg.-Capt.	Squire, W. P. ...	Oakeley ...	Shoeburyness
„	Surg.-Capt.	Manifold, C. C. ...	Brown ...	Indian Medl. Dept.

ROYAL MARINES.

ARTILLERY.			LIGHT INFANTRY.		
RANK.	NAME.	HOUSE.	RANK.	NAME.	HOUSE.
Captain .	Brittan, E. P. ...	Town	Major...	Horniblow, A. E. ...	Town
Captain .	Gaitskell, W. J. ...	School	Captain	Brittan, C. G. ...	Town
Lieut. ...	Poole, G. R. ...	N.Town	Lieut....	Bayliff, R. L. ...	N.Town
Lieut. ...	Brooke, C. L. ...	Oakeley	Lieut....	Garrett, J. R. ...	S. Town
			Lieut....	Hawkins, T. H. ...	N.Town

XXX

INDIAN STAFF CORPS.

RANK.	NAME.	HOUSE.	RANK.	NAME.	HOUSE.
Lt.-Col..	Gouldsbury, D. E. ...	School	Lieut....	Marlow, B. W. ...	Dakyns
Major ...	Kellie, E. C. ...	Town	,,	Younghusband, L. N.	School
,,	Maisey, F. C. ...	Brown	,,	Moore, F. L. ...	Brown
,,	Bird, W. J. B. ...	Town	,,	Chitty, W. W. ...	Oakeley
,,	Field, W. C. F. ...	School	,,	Pilleau, A. L. ...	S. Town
Captain.	Stuart, C. J. L. ...	Town	,,	Harrison, T. A. ...	Watson
,,	Marshall, W. S. ...	Town	,,	Stuart, D. F. ...	Oakeley
,,	Pollock, F. G. ...	Jn. Sch.	,,	Woodcock, W. C. M.	Wisemn.
,,	Brownlow, C. B. ...	School	,,	Batten, F. G. ...	N.Town
,,	Cunliffe, E. W. ...	Town	,,	Birdwood, W. R. ...	Oakeley
,,	Younghusband, G.W.	Town	,,	Parker, H. R. E. ...	School
,,	Sandwith, J. R. ...	Jn. Sch.	,,	Parker, N. T. ...	Wisemn.
,,	Pakenham, W. W. V.	Brown	,,	Campbell, G. P. ...	Grenfell
,,	Priestley, F. J. B. ...	Town	,,	Strachey, B. ...	Bart.
,,	Boswell, W. L. ...	Dunn	,,	Palin, P. C. ...	N.Town
,,	Thomson, W. D. ...	Brown	,,	Senior, H. W. R. ...	N.Town
,,	Christie, J. H. ...	Watson	,,	Brandreth, E. ...	School
,,	Younghusband, G. J.	School	,,	Peacocke, H. B. ...	Oakeley
,,	James, H. ...	Town	,,	Chitty, E. R. I. ...	Oakeley
,,	Pirie, C. P. W. ...	Town	,,	Priestley, C. E. W....	N.Town
,,	Lock, G. H. ...	Dunn	,,	Vaughan, R. E. ...	Watson
,,	Rideout, F. C. W. ...	Dakyns	,,	Grove, H. M. ...	N.Town
,,	Owen, E. O. ...	Town	,,	Newnham, W. F. ...	S. Town
,,	Cave, H. C. E. ...	School	,,	Crosthwaite, J. G. ...	Wisemn.
,,	Priestley, H. W. ...	N.Town	,,	Whitehead, J. H. ...	Brown
,,	Grey, E. ...	Brown	,,	Elsmie, A. M. S. ...	Grenfell
,,	Thwaytes, E. C. ...	School	,,	Hill, F. B. ...	N.Town
,,	Trevor, H. ...	School	,,	Stevens, J. L. C. ...	Bart.
,,	Edwards, F. M. ...	Oakeley	,,	Browne, H. M. ...	S. Town
Lieut....	Pinhey, A. F. ...	Dakyns	,,	Morris, D. O. ...	School
,,	Pritchard, C. H. ...	Watson	,,	Bethune, H. ...	Bart.
,,	Whyte, C. W. F. ...	S. Town			
,,	Beames, D. ...	Brown		*Probationers.*	
,,	Priestley, G. W. ...	N.Town			
,,	Palin, G. W. ...	N.Town	Captain	Younghusband, F. E.,	School
,,	Bradshaw, F. E. ...	S. Town		C.I.E. ...	
,,	Pollard, J. H. ...	School	Lieut...	West, W. G. M. ...	Oakeley
,,	Watson, E. H. ...	Dakyns	Lieut....	Peck, A. W. ...	S. Town
,,	Carnegy, C. G. ...	Wisemn.	Lieut....	Vivian, A. G. ...	S. Town
,,	Young, F. P. ...	Oakeley	Lieut....	Davis, G. J. ...	S. Town

CLIFTON COLLEGE.

SCHOLARSHIPS FOR 1893.

At least Eleven Scholarships, varying in value from £25 to £50, and admitting of augmentation to £90, will be open for competition in June, 1893 :—

I.—JUNIOR SCHOOL SCHOLARSHIPS—One or more of £25, open to boys under 14 who have entered the Junior School under the age of 11½. Tenable for two years, or until election to a Council Scholarship.

II.—ENTRANCE SCHOLARSHIPS—Open only to boys under 14 on March 31st, 1893, who have not previously entered. Tenable during the holders' stay at the College.

(*a*) * One or more of £50.

(*β*) * One or more of £25.

Free Nominations and Entrance Exhibitions securing admission to the College in September, may be awarded to boys who do well in the Examination but fail to obtain Scholarships.

III.—COUNCIL SCHOLARSHIPS—Open to Members of the College, as well as to those who have not yet entered.

A. Tenable for two years at the College, open to Boys under 17 on March 31st, 1893.

(*a*) The GUTHRIE Scholarship of £50.

(*β*) One or more of £25.

B. Tenable for two years at the College, or till election to another Scholarship, and open to boys under 16 on March 31st, 1893.

(*a*) One or more of £50.

(*β*) One or more of £25.

C. Tenable for two years at the College, or till election to another Scholarship, and open to boys under 15 on March 31st, 1893.

* Two or more of (*a*) £50 or (*β*) £25.

IV.—The CAY Scholarship of £20 a-year, for Mathematics, tenable for one year ; but the holder is re-eligible.

V.—A MODERN LANGUAGE Scholarship (English, French, and German), value £20, tenable for one year only.

* For these Scholarships a certain allowance of marks on account of age is made in favour of young boys.

CLIFTON COLLEGE.

SCHOLARSHIPS FOR 1894.

At least Eleven Scholarships, varying in value from £25 to £50, and admitting of augmentation to £90, will be open for competition in July, 1894 :—

I.—JUNIOR SCHOOL SCHOLARSHIPS—*One or more of £25, open to boys under 14, on March 31st, 1894, who entered the Junior School under the age of 11½. Tenable for two years, or until election to a Council Scholarship.

II.—ENTRANCE SCHOLARSHIPS—Open only to boys under 14 on March 31st, 1894, who have not previously entered. Tenable during the holders' stay at the College.

(a) * One or more of £50.
(β) * One or more of £25.

Nomination Scholarships, of the value of £5 a year and securing admission to a large house in the College in September, are awarded to not more than six boys who do well in the Examination but fail to obtain Scholarships.

III.—COUNCIL SCHOLARSHIPS—Open to Members of the College, as well as to those who have not yet entered.

A. Tenable for two years at the College : open to Boys under 17 on March 31st, 1894.

(a) The WILSON Scholarship of £50.
(β) One or more of £25.

B. Tenable for two years at the College, or till election to another Scholarship : open to boys under 16 on March 31st, 1894.

(a) One or more of £50.
(β) One or more of £25.

C. Tenable for two years at the College, or till election to another Scholarship : open to boys under 15 on March 31st, 1894.

* Two or more of (a) £50 or (β) £25.

IV.—The CAY Scholarship of £20 a-year, for Mathematics, tenable for one year ; but the holder is re-eligible.

V.—A MODERN LANGUAGE Scholarship (English, French, and German), value £20, tenable for one year only.

* For these Scholarships a certain allowance of marks on account of age is made in favour of young boys.

CLIFTON COLLEGE,
April 28, 1894.

DEAR *Mr. Behrens*

A new regulation has just come into force at
the Royal Military Academy, Woolwich, which may
affect your Son's prospects to some extent.

Hitherto, in the course of studies at Woolwich,
Chemistry has been a compulsory subject, while German
has been voluntary. But whereas the Science course has
been so straightforward and easy that Candidates, without
previous knowledge of the subject, have had no difficulty
in reaching the required standard, the Examinations in
German have been of a more searching character. Moreover, no Candidate has been allowed to score anything
in this voluntary subject unless his marks reached half
the maximum allotted to it.

These facts have influenced us in helping our
Woolwich Candidates to choose the most suitable group
of subjects for the Entrance Examination. As Mathematics, Latin, and French are subjects taken up by every
Candidate, the fourth subject has been either German or
Chemistry, which have been alternatives in our curriculum; lately we have recommended German in preference
to Chemistry, unless a Candidate has a decided aptitude
for Science, or has shown some incapacity for linguistic
study.

The new regulation which has just come to my
knowledge leaves the choice of subjects for Entrance

untouched, but, in the course of studies at the Royal Military Academy, no one in future will be allowed to take up a voluntary Modern Language, while the Science course is to be extended, and is to carry more weight in the Examinations.

It would appear, therefore, that Candidates who go up for the Competitive Examination with German instead of Chemistry may be somewhat handicapped at Woolwich, and it becomes necessary to inquire whether it is not worth while in some cases to substitute Chemistry for German before it is too late. It will not be wise to make a change of this kind if it merely substitutes a weak subject for a strong one, and so imperils the chance of success in the Competitive Examination; but in cases where not much progress has as yet been made in German and there is reasonable time left for the study of Chemistry, the question of taking up Chemistry instead of German is worthy of consideration, and I commend it to your notice. At the same time I should add that we cannot recommend any one to begin Chemistry as a Woolwich subject unless he has *at least five School terms before him*.

If you have any strong desire for the change in your Son's case please communicate with me as soon as possible.

Yours faithfully,

H. S. HALL.

Programme.

Part I.

1.	OVERTURE...	...	"Sosarmes"	...	...	*Handel.* *(1685—1759)*
2.	TRIO	...	...	"Prelude"	...	...	*Mendelssohn.* *(1809—1847)*

      Violin—Mr. F. GARDNER.
      Harp—Miss FLORENCE LANE.
      Organ—Mr. F. ROOTHAM.

3.	PIZZICATO SERENADE	...	...	...	*K. Müller-Berghau.*
4.	THREE DANCES ("Henry VIII.")	...	...	*E. German.*

    (By permission from Messrs. Novello & Co.)

      I.—Morris Dance.
      II.—Shepherds' Dance.
      III.—Torch Dance.

5.	LARGO IN G (for Strings, Harp, and Organ)	...	*Handel.* *(1685—1759)*
6.	VIOLONCELLO SOLO..Notturno (Op. 88)	...	...	*I. Lachner.*

      Mr. J. POMEROY.

7.	ROMANCE (from SERENADE)	...	...	...	*Mozart.* *(1756—1791)*
8.	CONCERTO in F ma (Op. 5)	...	...	...	*Corelli.* *(1653—1713)*

    Adagio—Allegro—Sarabanda—Gavotta.

Part II.

9.	OVERTURE...	...	"Lohengrin"	...	...	*Wagner.* *(1813—1883)*
10.	TRIO	...	...	"Hymn to St. Cecilia"	...	*Gounod.* *(1818—1893)*

      Violin—Mr. T. CARRINGTON.
      Harp—Miss FLORENCE LANE.
      Organ—Mr. F. ROOTHAM.

11.	MEXICAN SERENADE	"Mandolina"	...	...	*Otto Langey.*
12.	THREE MELODIES	...	...	...	*Schumann.* *(1810—1856)*

      I.—Abend Lied.
      II.—Nordisches Lied.
      III.—Träumerei.

13.	SCÈNES HUMORISTIQUES (Op. 61)	...	...	*H. Léonard.*

      I.—The Rooster and Hens.
      II.—The Cat and Mice.
      III.—The Donkey and Driver.

14.	HUNGARIAN MARCH..	"Faust"	...	...	*Berlioz.* *(1803—1869)*

XXXVI

December 10th, 1894.

DEAR SIR,

The Bishop of the Diocese intends to hold a Confirmation in our Chapel towards the end of next March. If you wish your son to be confirmed, I shall be obliged by your communicating with his *Housemaster* to that effect before January 18th.

I am, dear Sir,

Yours faithfully,

M. G. GLAZEBROOK.

IN PIAM MEMORIAM.

NORMAN MOOR,

OB. PRID. NON. MART. MDCCCXCV.

ÆT. 44.

There must have been many among those who gathered round the grave of Norman Moor, who felt that it closed over one whose life had been of unspeakable value, whose death was an irreparable loss to the School. There has been no one, with the exception of him whose sudden death we all were mourning not much more than a year ago, who was so widely known to Cliftonians of almost every generation, and so widely loved. Like him, Norman Moor seemed to many of us the depositary, the embodiment of the best traditions of the place. Both alike had caught the spirit of him who moulded them in their early years as boy or master here, and whom they both alike loved and venerated with truest piety. We, his colleagues, went instinctively to the one or the other, when we felt our need of help in forming a right judgment on some question, in which their intimate knowledge of the history of the School, their genial sympathy, their fearless integrity, their clear-sighted discernment of the right, made their counsel of inestimable value. From the time when Norman Moor won his Balliol Scholarship, now more than five-and-twenty years ago, Clifton had always been proud of him. The promise of those early days has been repeatedly and abundantly realized since then; never perhaps more fully than in the little book which he gave to the world not very long since, and which proved, to others besides ourselves, at once the ripeness of his scholarship and the skill of his pen. In the Close no less than in the Class-room his influence has brightened and stimulated our common life; and we shall not readily forget the charm of that affectionate manner which, alike in work and in play, warmed and won the hearts of so many whose lives as boys or as masters have been spent at Clifton.

He has been taken from us, not perhaps " ere his prime," but in the fulness of his powers, and, as it must seem to us, long ere we could spare him. He has left us a legacy of loyalty to high ideals and to our best traditions, and the tradition which he has himself created should have power to inspire and animate us who remain. May the knowledge of the deep affection which was felt for him by all who know and care for Clifton help to alleviate in some degree the bitter grief of those who were nearest and dearest to him.

Norman Moor was born at Kingsbridge in Devon on January 10th, 1851. His grandfather was a master at Rugby School under Dr. Wooll and Dr. Arnold; and his father, from whom he inherited his gift of scholarship and personal charm of manner, was master of Kingsbridge School. After his early education at Ashbourne School, he went in 1865 to Leamington College, where the Rev. E. St. J. Parry recognised and developed his great ability. In May, 1867, on Mr. Parry leaving Leamington, he came to Clifton College. He was placed in the lower bench of the Sixth Form, and came out head of it at Midsummer. In September, 1868, he succeeded J. A. Neale as head of the School, gained a Balliol scholarship in November, 1869, and left at the end of that Term. During this short but eventful time he saw many changes in the young School, and exercised a great influence for good. He was present at the opening of the Chapel, saw the building of the houses that are now Mr. Moberly's and Mr. Tait's, and by his personal influence made easier the difficult change from School House to Cock House match at cricket and football. He was in the Eleven one year, and made sixty-nine against G. F. Grace's bowling in the Lansdowne match, an achievement which he always remembered with satisfaction. He got his cap; and was a good long-distance runner, coming in first several times in the old days of the runs before the Long Penpole was thought of, and when every run was a race from start to finish. He was an excellent and devoted head of the Town, taking the greatest pains in the organization of their games. At Oxford he gained a first-class in Moderations and a

second-class in the Final Classical School. In the
Summer Term of 1874 he came back as Sixth Form
master under Dr. Percival. In the autumn of that year,
when the Towns were separated, he was appointed
tutor of the North Town; but finding this too heavy to
combine with the Sixth Form work, he resigned it in
1875. He took pupils for a short time in Mr. Dakyns'
house, and relinquished this for the same reason; but
as all members of Dakyns' and Bartholomew's house
will well remember, he never lost his interest in the
welfare of that house, and was always a welcome guest
at their House Suppers. In December, 1878, he
married Miss Emily Powell, and took the small house
that is now Mr. Smith's; but resigned it in 1880, that he
might give all his energies to the classical teaching of
the Sixth. In September, 1892, he succeeded the Rev.
T. E. Brown as House Master, and though his career
there was short, all who came under his gentle influence
will cherish his memory.

The following is an extract from THE TIMES:

" The premature death, from illness following influenza, of Mr. E. N. P. Moor, one of the chief Classical
masters at Clifton College, will be lamented by a very
large number of friends. As a boy at Clifton he became
head of the School, played in the cricket eleven, and
was the first of Dr. Percival's pupils to obtain a
scholarship at Balliol, being elected in 1869 together
with Mr. Asquith, the present Home Secretary. At
Oxford he was known as an accomplished scholar, and
enjoyed the friendship of such men as Professor T. H.
Green, Mr. R. L. Nettleship, and Professor Andrew
Bradley. On taking his degree in 1874 he was brought
back to Clifton by Dr. Percival as Sixth Form master,
and in that position acquired and retained an influence
both among Masters and boys which has been of singular service to the School. His graceful scholarship
and delicate taste, his laborious patience in teaching,
were, in the opinion of his ablest pupils, unrivalled; a
rare charm of manner, combined with the strength of a
wholly sweet and noble character, made him dear to
generation after generation of Clifton boys; and thus
at any gathering of Cliftonians his has been for many
years the most familiar and the most welcome presence."

XL

CLIFTON COLLEGE, BRISTOL,

MARCH 25TH, 1895.

DEAR SIR,

The outbreak of influenza, from which the School suffered in February, was practically over before the end of that month, and we have had no other illness, except a few colds. But the Medical Officers of the School tell me that the severe weather and the depressing circumstances of this term have somewhat affected the average vitality of boys and masters, and they are anxious for some addition to the holidays, in order that we may begin next term in full vigour. It has therefore been thought advisable to relieve the boys of the strain of examination, and to send them home on FRIDAY, April 5th, instead of the following TUESDAY.

I am sorry that I could not give you longer notice, but it is only in the last two days that the need of the change has become clear to us.

I remain, DEAR SIR,

Yours very faithfully,

M. G. GLAZEBROOK.

ENGINEER CADET CORPS.

CLIFTON COLLEGE, BRISTOL,
June 6th, 1895.

DEAR SIR,

There will be a Public Schools Volunteer Camp at Aldershot this year, from Tuesday, July 30th, till Tuesday, August 6th, and as a strong desire to attend it has been expressed by several members of the Corps, it has been decided that a detachment will be sent if the attendance of a sufficient number can be guaranteed.

I therefore write to ask whether you wish your son to join this camp, and beg at the same time to give you the following particulars.

Such camps have been held for the last six years—in 1889 and 1890 with the Home Counties Volunteer Brigade at Churn in Berkshire, and since then at Aldershot, where they have been very successful in all respects, largely owing to the great interest taken in them by the military authorities. In 1894 detachments were sent from Bradfield, Cheltenham, Haileybury, Harrow, Marlborough, Rugby, Sherborne, Wellington, Winchester, and other schools. For various reasons our Corps has never attended this camp, but the unanimous testimony of representatives of other schools as to the benefits attending such a week's instruction, together with the strong wish that has been expressed by several members of the School, have induced us to take steps to send a detachment this year.

Expense.—It has been decided that the amount charged for the week in Camp, including railway fare to Aldershot, shall not exceed £1 10s. 0d. per head.

Discipline.—The members of Corps taking part are subject to the ordinary school rules as regards smoking, entering public-houses, &c., and the town of Aldershot and North and South Camps are "out of bounds." In other respects the Volunteers—Officers, N.C.O.'s, and Sappers—are subject to Military Law.

Recreation.—There is a Recreation Committee, which arranges for games and amusements when the Volunteers are off duty.

Site.—The camp is situated in the private grounds of Government House, by the kindness of H.R.H. the Duke of Connaught, commanding the Aldershot Division.

Organisation.—If as many as 50 rank and file attend, the Corps will be formed as one company, otherwise it will form part of a company along with a detachment from some other school. The battalion will be under the command of a Regular Officer.

As at present arranged, the detachment will proceed to Aldershot on Tuesday, July 30th. No one will be expected to leave before Tuesday, August 6th, except for special reasons. The Volunteers will be dismissed at Aldershot on the latter date, and arrangements about luggage will be made to suit individual cases.

I shall be greatly obliged if you will let me know *on or before June 15th*, whether your son will attend the Camp or not.

I am,
Faithfully yours,
D. RINTOUL, *Capt. 2nd G.V.R.E.*,
Hon. Capt. C.C.E.C.

P.S.—I desire, as Head Master, to express my hearty approval of Captain Rintoul's proposal. I believe that boys will gain great advantage by joining the Public Schools' Camp.

M. G. GLAZEBROOK.

XLII

Lincoln, Lincoln Co, New Mexico

June 4th 1877

L.W.F.Behrens Esq

My Dear Sir,

I last night received the tidings from the hands of my Father Mother & Sister, that my sister Minnie had engaged to become your wife;

It would be quite impossible for me to express to anyone, what my feelings were at the receipt of such news, of which I had had no previous intimation whatsoever; I suppose that Minnie has told you of the strong attachment that exists between us, (*so much* stronger, I am happy to say, than is generally the case between brother & sister) & the effect that such intelligence would be likly to have upon me. For I hold Minnie's happiness *dearer* than life itself, & the *slightest* risk of it, is in my eyes more serious than a crime. Not knowing you, I can but be guided in my opinion of you by the description given in the letters I received concerning you; and as the subject touches me so deeply, so my feelings towards you will be deep whether of love or hate.

To be worthy of the possession of so rich a prize as I consider Minnie will be, to the man who has the fortune to have her as his wife, he ought to be the *best*, of *The Best of Men*; her purity & simplicity of mind are such, that they make her character almost *divine*. I have never known her to make an ungenerous or uncharitable remark concerning anyone in my life, neither have I ever known her to express a thought, that indicated anything but purity of mind or motive, from our *earliest* childhood up.

My love for her has been such all my life, that I have never felt that I cared for anyone *at all* in comparison with her, & I have been selfish enough always to hope that she would never marry, & that my parents, sisters & myself would have her undivided affection. All my hopes of success in life have begun continued & ended in the thought of acquiring means to enable me to live *with* her, & *for* her. – If I were blind to her worth I might expect less of a brother-in-law than I do of you, but you are undertaking to make the joy or the sorrow of the idol of three hearts, for no one on earth was ever more adored by Father, Mother & Brother than my *Dear Dear* Sister is; we are as completely wrapt up in her, as ever a lover was in the object of his love; & if possible more so, for we *know* her worth. This may savor to you of rapsody, but it is but the expression of feelings, produced by a *knowledge* of the *exceptional* worth of my *beloved* Sister. You cannot have failed to notice after becoming as intimate in our family as you must have done, that the several members that you have met, have the strongest love & admiration for each other, I would caution you against believing too implicitly what you may hear about myself, as I have lived away from home, *very* nearly all my life, & (as you know) *entirely* during the last 5 years, consequently, it is impossible for me even to have a *strong* family likeness to the rest, & the life I am compelled to lead on the frontier of civilization, you can well imagine, has not the most refining influence possible. It is entirely superfluous for me to tell you, that you have my Father's & Mother's entire confidence, for you could wring their heart's blood from them, more easily, than their consent that you should become their son-in-law unless you possessed it.

Having the consent of my Father, Mother & sister to enter our family, it is only graceful (to say the least of it) on my part, to give you mine, & add my voice to the welcome they give you, for I am quite sure that if you are worthy to become Minnie's husband, you are far more than worthy to become my brother, so that unless some unforseen occurrence should sunder us, we will think of each other as brothers, & for the present, with every confidence *in*, & wish, for your future happiness & success

I remain
Your affectionate Brother
John H. Tunstall

P.S. I cannot tell you how much I regret that the extremely critical position of my affairs renders it impossible for me to leave here, for ever so short a time, for at least 8, & perhaps 18 months.

LOT 2.

TWO SEMI-DETACHED

FAMILY RESIDENCES,

Desirably situate, adjoining Lot 1, and known as

"NEWFIELD HOUSE," AND "LANSDOWNE VILLA,"

Nos. 36 & 38, DARTMOUTH ROAD,

FOREST HILL.

Each having an Excellent Garden, well planted with Fruit Trees and Shrubs, and comprising in all an Area of about
AN ACRE AND A QUARTER.

"NEWFIELD HOUSE" contains

On the Second floor,

TWO BED ROOMS, BOX ROOM, NURSERY, and a Room lighted by a Skylight.

First floor.

TWO BED ROOMS, each fitted with a marble chimneypiece, and a DRAWING ROOM, BATH ROOM, with fitted Bath, hot and cold supply of water (the Bath and Lavatory are the property of the Tenant, and removable by him); and a W.C.

Ground floor.

ENTRANCE HALL, DINING ROOM,

STUDY or PANTRY, with cupboard; Wine Cellar, KITCHEN, SCULLERY, WASH-HOUSE, Larder, Coal House, W.C., and way out to Garden. Side Entrance from DERBY VILLAS. Yard with

SMALL COACH-HOUSE AND STABLE,

There is a Carriage drive in front, and a capital GARDEN at the rear of the House, with Lawn, Vinery, Forcing House, Potting Shed, and Summer House.

Which are now utilised for other purposes.

"LANSDOWNE VILLA" contains

On the Second Floor.

THREE ROOMS, each with fireplace, and a Cistern Room.

First Floor.

FOUR ROOMS, three with marble chimneypieces; BATH ROOM, with fitted Bath, hot and cold water laid on; Lavatory, and a W.C.

Ground Floor.

ENTRANCE HALL, DRAWING ROOM, AND DINING ROOM,

Each fitted with a marble chimneypiece;

CONSERVATORY, KITCHEN, with dresser and cupboards; SCULLERY, sink and water laid on; TWO LARDERS, Fruit Room, Coal Cellar.

The House is approached by a Carriage drive, and there is an excellent GARDEN at the rear, with Lawn, Greenhouse, Potting Shed, Fowl House, and Vinery.

The two Houses are held under one Lease, dated the 16th November, 1849, for a Term of 88 years from the 25th December, 1848 (leaving 47½ years unexpired from the 24th June, 1889), at the low Ground Rent of £23 per Annum. Communicating doorways have been made between the two Houses, and they are both let to L. W. F. Behrens, Esq., on Agreement for 6 years from the 25th December, 1888 determinable by the Tenant at the end of the third year by giving 6 months' previous notice, at a Rent of

£200 PER ANNUM.

The Tenant covenants to pay all Rates and Taxes, except Tithe or Tithe Rent-charge, and Landlord's Property Tax.

The Palm House, Orchid House, glazed Lean-to on wall, and a few other Fixtures are the property of the Tenant, but such of the Fixtures as belong to the Vendors will be included in the Sale.

A considerable sum of money has been recently expended upon the Drainage and Sanitary Arrangements of the two Houses.

XLVI

Sonderabdruck zweier Auffätze von Frau C. Frauberger aus dem General-Anzeiger, Düffeldorf.

I.

Aus der Kunftftickerei-Anftalt.

Die Frivolitäten-Arbeit.

(Occhi, Makuk.)

Düffeldorf, den 9. Juni 1892.

Keine Arbeitsart hat fich einer fo rafch wechfelnden Beliebtheit und Unbeliebtheit zu erfreuen und zu beklagen gehabt, wie die Frivolitäten-Arbeit.

Die echt franzöfifche Bezeichnung fteht weder mit der Herkunft, dem Ausfehen, der Anwendungsart der Arbeit, noch mit dem Werkzeug, mit dem fie ausgeführt wird, im Zufammenhang. Hier und da begegnet man der italienifchen Benennung „occhi" (Augen), deren Berechtigung fich auf die augenförmigen Mufterungsarten ftützt. Wir Deutfchen geben uns leider erft feit den letzten zwei Jahrzehnten die Mühe, deutfche Worte für Fremdworte, zumal franzöfifche zu finden und zu erfinden. Doch haben fich verdeutfchte Fremdwörter im Laufe der Zeiten derart eingebürgert, daß man, will man keinen Aufruhr im kleinen heraufbefchwören, Bezeichnungen, die als feft-ftehend betrachtet worden find, nicht ohne weiteres umändern kann.

Der Name der Arbeit, die in Syrien, im befonderen in den Klöftern des Libanon, ihre Heimat hat und eine Hausindustrie bildet, ift dort „Makuk". Die Arbeit felbft dient als Befatz an Vor-hängen, Kopf- und Schleiertüchern, wie fie von den orientalifchen Frauen getragen werden, hat aber in den orientalifchen Nadelfpitze, „Kochakia" genannt, die in Smyrna Hausindustrie ift und größere Mannigfaltigkeit der Mufter zuläßt, eine überlegene Gegnerin ge-funden. Nur der Eintönigkeit der Mufter der Frivolitäten-Arbeit ift ihr zeitweiliges, der Vergeffenheit Anheimfallen zu fuchen, wie dies auch während der letzten 15—20 Jahren in einzelnen Gegenden bei uns der Fall war.

Das aufwachfende weibliche Gefchlecht fchaut mit Verwunderung auf das Werkzeug, das zu der Arbeit gehört. In frifcher Jugend-blüte ftehende Mädchen erinnern fich dunkel einer älteren Anver-wandten, die fie vor Jahren mit dem Gerät hat hantieren gefehen; auf der Höhe des Lebens ftehenden Frauen fällt der Befitz eines kleinen Käftchens ein, das feit der Jugendzeit in der unterften Lade des Legekaftens unbeachtet ruht. „Ach ja! das ift ja die niedliche Arbeit, von der wir behaupteten, daß fie weiße Hände mache! Gewiß, ich erinnere mich noch, wie wir auf der Schulbank während der Schulftunden heimlich daran arbeiteten, denn es war ja damals eine wahre Frivolitäten-Manie! Und die reizende anmutige Arbeit foll wieder gelehrt werden?! Da muß ich mir denn doch das

6

Käſtchen hervorſuchen! Es iſt ja wahr, die heutige Mode mit der
vielen Paſſementerie iſt ſo ganz und gar dazu angetan, eine Arbeit
wie Ochi zu verwenden!" — Und ſo weiter geht es! Die Stickerei-
und Kurzwarengeſchäfte werden, wenn ſich das geſuchte Werkzeug
zu Hauſe nicht mehr findet, darum befragt. Als Spielerei wird
mit der Arbeit begonnen, ſie wird Mode, wird auf allerlei Weiſen
verwendet und' wird wieder — vergeſſen.

Aber können und kennen ſollte man ſie. In der Tat iſt die
Frivolitäten-Arbeit die niedlichſte aller weiblichen Handarbeiten und
gibt, wie das engliſche Spiel Lawn Tennis in amazonenhafter Weiſe
für den Körper, für die Hände in echt weiblicher Beſchäftigungsart
Gelegenheit, anmutige Handbewegungen zu zeigen.

Das Werkzeug, das „Schiffchen", iſt einer verdickten und ver-
kürzten Netznadel (Filetnadel) ähnlich. Es beſteht aus zwei leicht
gebogenen, in der Mitte ungefähr 1½ bis 2 Zentimeter breiten und
6 bis 7 Zentimeter langen, auf beiden Seiten zugeſpitzten Bein-
platten, die, einander gegenüberſtehend, auf ein kleines Holz- oder
Beinpflöckchen befeſtigt werden und zwar ſo, daß ſich die Spitzen
der Platten leicht berühren. In das Pflöckchen iſt ein Loch zum
Durchziehen und zur Befeſtigung des Arbeitsfadens gebohrt, der,
zwiſchen den Platten hindurchgehend, über das Pflöckchen gewickelt
wird. Beim Ankauf eines Schiffchens achte man darauf, daß die
Spitzen der Platten gut federn, damit ſich der aufzuwickelnde Faden
hindurchführen läßt und während des Arbeitens dennoch genügend
feſtgehalten wird.

Im vorigen Jahrhundert waren die Schiffchen zuweilen reich
verziert, und da man mit weſentlich ſtärkerem Faden, wie gedrehte
Seidenſchnüre arbeitete, auch umfangreicher. Vor 20 Jahren ge-
brauchte man bereits die kleinen Schiffchen und verwendete zumeiſt
Leinen- oder Baumwollfaden, ſelten die Seide. Die damals beliebten
Zwiſchenſätze und Spitzen dienten zum Ausputz der Wäſche, zu
Kragen und Manſchetten; die Sterne, die zu Deckchen und Decken
aneinandergefügt wurden, zum Bedecken von Sofa- und Seſſellehnen.

Die Zeiten ändern ſich und raſcher noch die Moden! Die Frivolitäten-Arbeit machte der Häkelarbeit Platz, die als dauerhafter
gilt und größeren Muſterreichtum geſtattet. In alle Handarbeits-
gebiete drängt ſie ſich ein, entlehnt überall Muſter und, mir fällt
eine Strophe aus einem, in Frankfurter Mundart geſchriebenen
Gedichte Stoltzes ein:

Sie hat geſtrickt, auch! Sapperlot!
Egal! des will ich meene!
Un hat geheekelt wie e Gott
Die Deckercher, die ſcheene;
For's Diſchi, Kanabee un Bett
Nebſt der Schawell, warum dann net?
Wie ääch der Vatter breeckelt_
's ward alles immerheekelt.

Die Frivolitäten-Arbeit iſt, ſo unfaßbar ſie manchem auf den
erſten Blick erſcheint, nicht ſchwierig, wenn man darauf achtet, die
meiſtens ungeſchickte linke Hand richtig und im richtigen Augenblick

7

zu bewegen und die rechte Hand in Ruhe zu halten. Wenn der Faden auf das Schiffchen gewickelt ist, nimmt man das Fadenende zwischen Daumen und Zeigefinger der linken Hand. Die rechte Hand hält das Schiffchen, von welchem der Faden etwa 20 bis 25 Zentimeter Länge abgewickelt ist, und führt es über die gespreizten Finger der linken Hand bis zum Fadenende zwischen Daumen und Zeigefinger, den Faden spannend, während die linke Hand den Faden zu dem Fadenanfang faßt. Der Teil des Fadens, der von dem Schiffchen ausläuft, wird über den kleinen Finger der rechten Hand gespannt und das Schiffchen selbst mit Daumen und Zeigefinger gehalten. Nun führt man das Werkzeug zwischen Mittel= und Zeigefinger der linken Hand, unterhalb der Schlinge, die über die Finger gelegt war, hindurch und oberhalb derselben zurück, zieht den Schiffchenfaden fest an und beläßt ihn, ohne weitere Bewegung der rechten Hand, die zur größeren Ruhe eine Stütze etwa auf der Tisch= platte findet, in der ruhigen Stellung. In der geringsten unzeitigen Bewegung liegt zumeist die Klippe, an welcher Anfängerinnen scheitern.

Die linke Hand hat sich während des Anziehens der rechten geschlossen, ohne jedoch die zwischen Daumen und Zeigefinger fest= gehaltene Schlinge loszulassen. Nun spreizt sie die drei anderen Finger mit einer leichten Handdrehung aus und schürzt dadurch die Schlinge, die sich durch das Einschieben des Schiffchens gebildet hatte, an Daumen und Zeigefinger heran. Die nach unten gekehrt gewesene Schlinge wendet sich dadurch nach oben und wird von dem Teil des Fadens gebildet, der um die linke Hand gelegt war, also nicht von dem, von dem Schiffchen auslaufenden Faden. Läßt sich die Fadenschlinge noch durch den geformten Knoten hin= und her= ziehen, so ist der Knoten richtig gebildet und geschürzt gewesen.

In der, ohne Abbildung der Händestellung schwer zu erklärenden und nicht zu erlernenden Bewegung liegt die ganze Schwierigkeit der Frivolitäten=Arbeit.

Bei dem zweiten Knoten wird das Schiffchen von rückwärts durch die Schlinge der linken Hand geschoben. Das feste Anziehen des Schiffchens, die Ruhe der rechten Hand, das Schürzen des Knotens durch die linke Hand geschieht in der gleichen Weise wie beim Bilden des ersten Knotens. Die zwei verschiedenen Knoten heißen zusammen Doppelknoten. Ist eine Anzahl derselben aneinander= gereiht, so zieht man sie zusammen, indem man die um die linke Hand gelegte Schlinge freigibt und das Schiffchen anzieht. Dadurch bildet sich ein "Auge", das durch Schleifen (Picots) reicher gestaltet wird. Durch Neben=, An= und Übereinanderreihen von Augen, durch Arbeiten mit zwei Schiffchen und zwei Farben, läßt sich die Frivolitäten=Arbeit trotz der nicht zu leugnenden Eintönigkeit reiz= voll gestalten. Und kann man der Häkelarbeit nicht ganz entsagen, so bietet sich ihr Gelegenheit, Arm in Arm mit den Frivolitäten, den Rest des Jahrhunderts in die Schranken zu fordern.

In dem neuen Material zweifädiger, gedrehter, waschechter Seide (Soie double Nr. 40) in den schönsten Farben, die neuerdings in den Handel gelangt ist, bietet sich ein Faden, der außerordentlich verwendbar zur Herstellung von seidenen Frivolitäten ist. Auch dickere gedrehte Schnüre sind, sobald das Schiffchen entsprechend größer ist, zu verarbeiten. Zum Abschluß der Kleidersäume, als Besatz von Kragen und Ärmeln, als Zwischensatz und Spitze einer seidengestickten Decke, zu einer Anzahl von Gegenständen, wie: Arbeitsbeutel, Eisdeckchen, zu jedem textilen Gegenstand, der einen schmalen, zierlichen Abschluß gebraucht und verträgt, ist den Damen in der Frivolitäten-Arbeit Gelegenheit gegeben, sich auf mühelose Weise zu beschäftigen. Das in einem kleinen Etui verschlossene Schiffchen, einige Strängchen Seide, eine Häkelnadel zum Verbinden der Schleifen, sind leicht in der Tasche zu bergen und mitzunehmen. Und die verzeihliche Koketterie, seine Gelegenheit zu benützen, weiße Hände in anmutige Bewegung und Arbeit zu versetzen, die dazu noch das Plaudern gestattet, wären das nicht triftige Gründe, die Frivolitäten-Arbeit aufzunehmen, zu erlernen und zu üben?

Tina Frauberger.

L

PREFACE.

A VERY few words of introduction are needed here. The essays contained in this volume were all read at meetings of the Christo-Theosophical Society during its first year of existence; and perhaps a brief description of that society may not be out of place. It was started in February, 1890, in a very unostentatious way, and has steadily prospered. Its object was to show that there is a great deal more in the Gospel of Christ, when profoundly understood, than might be supposed by those who know it only as it is presented in too many pulpit utterances and conventional treatises. In this its—to us—crude form Christianity seems undoubtedly to have a work to do among the great mass of unexercised intellects to whom our presentation would be, at first, unintelligible; and it is no part of our purpose to oppose or denounce any presentation that seems true and helpful to any of our brethren. But there are many others who must either find some higher presentation or cease to call themselves Christians; and to these the Christo-Theosophical Society addresses itself. Its method is as follows: It starts with a certain presentation which has been arrived at simply by thinking out what is really involved in the belief in God as 'Our Father.' This basis is an absolute universalism, and a negation of the essentiality of evil, which, if essential, must be the antithesis to God, so that to predicate its essentiality would demonstrably be to deny His.   It is suggested as a starting-point ; a ground of hope that there may be much more of still fuller good and clearer knowledge beyond, and the society's work is by united effort to strive for a continually growing apprehension of those sublime truths which are the 'things to come' of the title of this volume.

In an Appendix will be found a somewhat fuller account of the position of the society, to which the reader desiring further information is referred.

In the general conviction that the Gospel of Christ is a profound philosophy, far wider and deeper than is by the mass of professing Christians supposed, the contributors to the present volume are in warm agreement.   Beyond this, as to the particular apprehension and enunciation of the details of that profounder view, the society does not seek, or expect to find, perfect unanimity.   Each writer is responsible for his own contribution alone, and the society is only committed to any of them so far as this—that it asserts that the views put forward herein are all worthy of earnest attention.

G. W. A.

LII

Introduction

The collected works of Mary Boole amount to more than fifteen hundred pages. Among them is found a regular and passionate insistence on the real—but widely ignored—significance of her husband's work, and a vision of mathematical education that is powerfully relevant, but still unrealised, today.

This selection sets out to provide a brief introduction to her writings in order to stimulate a wider awareness of her thought. The numbers in brackets at the end of each extract are page number references to the collected works in the now out-of-print 1931 edition.

Mary Everest, later the wife of the mathematician George Boole, was born in 1832. Her father, a rector, was a friend of Babbage and Herschel who as students had initiated various reforms in mathematics at Cambridge. Her mother was the sister of a classics professor at a college in Cork, where Boole was to hold the chair of mathematics. When Mary was five her father became seriously ill and the family moved to France, so that he could be treated by Hahnemann, the founder of homeopathic medicine. Mary grew up bilingual. An early interest in mathematics was aroused by a teacher who gave her private lessons in arithmetic; many years later she wrote a charming account of this inspiration. Her father's health improved and the family returned to England when Mary was eleven.

Mary first met George Boole on a visit to her uncle in Cork. After the hard struggle of the early years, Boole was just beginning his great work. His masterpiece, *An investigation of the laws of thought*, was published in 1854 and was dedicated to Mary's uncle. Her father died the following year, and they married soon after. It was a successful marriage; though Boole was seventeen years her senior they were close companions, and Mary was able to share her husband's interests—she became a devoted disciple.

They had five daughters. The youngest was only six months old when Boole died of an attack of pneumonia in 1864. Mary was then 32 years old.

In the following year she took a post at Queen's College, London. Opened in 1847, this was the first college of higher education for women. Though unable to award degrees, it gave something more valuable, at least to some of the pupils; one of Mary's was to write later, "I thought we were being amused not taught. But after I left I found you had given us a power. We can think for ourselves, and find out what we want to know."

After a few years Mary left the college to become for a brief time the secretary of James Hinton, a writer on ethics and evolution as well as a skilful ear-surgeon, who had been a friend of her father. She was interested in the aspect of his work that most of his friends found unimportant, namely 'the art of thinking itself, which he, as well as George Boole, believed to be the true key to the physical and moral regeneration of mankind'.

In the twenty years after her husband's death Mary Boole supported and raised a family and read, corresponded and discussed over a wide range of themes and with a large circle of friends (some of whom are mentioned briefly in an appendix—see p. 75). Committed to spreading her husband's ideas about mathematics she also developed her own thoughts on education. She studied the works of Thomas Wedgwood, the son of the famous potter, and a friend of Darwin. She developed the ideas of the French logician and mystic, Gratry, and related them to those of her husband. At the same time she became more and more involved in spiritualism and theosophy with a curious amalgam of ideas from Hebrew ritual, Indian mysticism and Western science. At the age of 50 she embarked on a series of books and articles, publishing regularly up to the time of her death in 1916 at the age of 84.

Much of her writing has not been to twentieth century tastes though many contemporary young people have been rediscovering her themes. She was interested in the occult, homeopathy, vegetarianism, anti-vivisection—and love. But the practical common sense of her lesson notes, *Lectures on the logic of arithmetic* (1903, when she was 71), and the pioneering insights of *The preparation of the child for science* (1904) had their impact on progressive schools in England and the U.S.A. in the first decade of the 20th century. She invented curve-stitching and for many years cards marked for this purpose were known as Boole cards (see p. 35). Her first book, published in 1883 but written in the sixties, was a pioneer work on mental hygiene. In *the mathematical psychology of Gratry and Boole* (1897) and one of her last books, *The forging of passion into power* (1910), she showed an understanding of the unconscious far ahead of her time.

Most educationists today appear to have other things to write about than dowsing rods and so on. Certainly other things than love. Few achieve the clarity, the vision and the highly relevant insights of Mary Boole.

Form 38.

Woolwich.

In any further communication upon this subject, it is requested that the words "Woolwich" may be written at the head of the letter, which should be addressed to the Military Secretary, Horse Guards, War Office, S.W.

HORSE GUARDS, WAR OFFICE, S.W.

15 May 1895.

Sir,

With reference to the application you have made, to be allowed to attend the examination for admission to the Royal Military Academy at Woolwich, I am directed by His Royal Highness the Commander-in-Chief to inform you that the necessary instructions, showing the hours and places for your examination in the subjects specified in the Regulations, will be issued to you in due course by the Civil Service Commissioners, by whom the examination will be conducted.

I am further instructed by His Royal Highness to request you to notice specially, that in the event of any unfair practice being discovered during the examination, not only will the examination of the offending candidate be cancelled, but he will forfeit all claim to be considered eligible for a commission in Her Majesty's Service.

In the event of your being declared a successful candidate at the literary examination, you will be required to attend for medical examination in London, and your admission to the Royal Military Academy will then depend upon the report of the Medical Board as to your fitness for military service.

If you have not already done so, it is essential that you furnish me with an address at which your parent or guardian may be communicated with during the next three months, and any unavoidable change of address should be at once made known to me.

All the requisite articles of uniform will be provided for the successful candidates at the Academy, on their arrival there.

I am to add that your surname can only be described as "Behrens" unless you can produce legal authority for assuming the surname of "Tunstall-Behrens".

I am,

SIR,

Your obedient Servant,

R. GIPPS,

Lieut-General,

Military Secretary.

J. J. Behrens Esq

H W V 750 6—94 4 18 7

Wool.
MKS. Q.

CIVIL SERVICE COMMISSION.

SIR,   2 AUG. 9⁵

    I am directed by the Civil Service Commissioners to inform you that at the recent competitive Examination of Candidates for admission to the Royal Military Academy, Woolwich, your place in order of merit was ————7———— and that you are ———— — ————one of the successful Candidates.

    You passed the Obligatory portion of the Examination.

    The following Statement shows the marks obtained by you :—

	Subject.	Maximum.	Marks.
Class I.	Mathematics	3,500	3163
	Latin	2,000	1387
	French ⎫ alternative	2,000	
	German ⎭	2,000	1149
	English Composition (including Spelling and Hand-writing)	1,000	612
	Geometrical Drawing ...	1,000	819
	Total. Class I.	9,500	7130
Class II.	Higher Mathematics ...	2,000	1227
	German ⎫ alternative	2,000	
	French ⎭	2,000	911
	Greek	2,000	
	English History	2,000	
	Chemistry	2,000	
	Physics	2,000	
	Physiography and Geology ...	2,000	
Class III.	Geography	500	428
	Freehand Drawing	500	327
	Total Marks.		10,023

    If you should hereafter be nominated as a Queen's Cadet, Honorary

Y. Y. Behrens Esq.

Number in Examination ——

W B & L (412w)—53543—500-12-94

My Darling Precious Tankred,

Such news as I have to write breaks my heart to tell our dear girl is so ill, She has had influenza since the 27th of December but I hoped it would be over like your fathers & mine but on the 8th of Jan – her temperature after returning to normal was up again so I sent for Wharry – he reported favourably in the morning but after he was gone the symptom of numbness & pins & needles in the finger tips & toes increased & rose & rose until her frame is paralysed up to the sternum – she feels nothing. Dr Gee the specialist says it is "ascending paralysis" – & gave us little hope – but while there is life there is hope. Dr Hart is capital – keen earnest leaving not a stone unturned & it maybe that the Lord will restore her to us – but the last two nights I have thought every moment would be the last of her dear life. Today however Wharry & Hart think & hope the crisis is passed – the disease has not increased & may have turned. Well one clings to every grain of hope. she is fed through the nose every 6 hours with milk water brandy & medecine – having great difficulty in breathing often gasping for breath – Your kind letters were a joy to us & your beautiful New Years calenders are lovely one hangs in dear Tyra's room, her Sanctum sanctorum – & mine in my room with its sweet daily thought from one I love so dearly – Do you think shirts too unromantic a present! I quite enjoy the thought that when you don your shirt you think of your mother. I wish it were a snowy Armour to shield you from every form of evil an invisible armour which no one guessed of. Well darling it is shirts I give as well as Pudding – so unromantic!

God bless you Darling & help you to bear the anguish which you share with us. Gods will be done.
Love from your fond mother

Tyra sends you her dear love & has said several times have you written to Tankred. I cant write much as I cannot bear to be away from her

LVIII

11 Bardwell Road, Oxford

6th June, 1964

Dear Hilary

How curious you should be still so interested in "Tyra" for it is now I think about 60 years since she died. I had seen a lot of her after she left school, visiting at her house & she at mine, & her death was my first greatest shock. For 3 days before I had been to see her hearing she had a bad cold & we talked for long in her bedroom her cold had nearly gone & she was going to get up after I left to have a dress fitting. And the next I heard was a letter from your grandmother 3 days later saying paralysis had set in first at her feet; & within a day had reached her heart.

I think Tyra was a few months older than I was & was not in my form but I was in 6th3 & she in 6th2. I think I was more practical & she was intellectual, she did *not* want to tinker with tools or mathematics (as I did) & had none of the tastes in that direction like "Tankred & Brian". Neither your grandfather or those two, would cease to alter a house. In fact your Grandfather whom we all thought, a difficult man never ceased to alter that dreadful house at Forest Hill or its furniture, & he kept on the premises a skilled reparer of antique furniture always reparing something. I think Tyra was like her mother & they were both kind & fairly domesticated, she was very dark & rather stocky & an absolutely different type to her brothers.

The time when I saw a lot of her was either the summer before or after we left school.

We went together for 3 weeks to a domestic economy school held in an old farm house. And we enjoyed ourselves in a very snobbish & light hearted manner. We had come from quite a different background to that of any of the other girls, who were more obedient less spirited & of a working class. We both received lectures on disrupting the routine.

In those days families like ours all kept at the least 3 servants, & did not bother to learn domestic economy, as we were doing.

I do so well remember the woman of about 40 who kept the establishment & who had a tame parson whom she adored.

They had composed the morning prayers for her school of some 18 girls. We stood in 2 rows facing one another, and there was daily a long prayer. Which ended "For the devil walketh about like a roaring lyon seeking whom he may devour", & we all roared out Thanks be to God; Tyra & I facing one another & trying not to laugh. Also Tyra had an unusually good alto voice, & I was singing suprano at concerts, so we held silence, with little piping by girls round us & struck out loud at a prearranged verse, & startled the community.

We once also pulled all the dormitory curtains by attatching strings to their ends & during the night managed to terrify the neumerous scotch girls they believe in ghosts. We used to meet our train at Euston, I think it was, & travel up together some 30 girls or so on a night train to St Andrews where we were at St Leonards school. That school, Cheltenham, & the one at Brighton, were the only girls schools of our day run like boys public schools, and houseing some 400.

Tyra & I were new girls the same term & for the first year slept in the same dormitry; which was very nicely arranged like little rooms with curtains at the passages. I left when I was not quite 17 to go with my parents to India & Tyra stayed longer at school.

Tyra & I were both good at hockey & Lacross. I think we were both in the house team during our first year. I remember we were more unsentimental than most school girls, for we never "schwermed" over mistresses, or were sorry when term was over.

I think "Tyra" was very devoted to her mother, & rather resented your grandfather's excentricities & his throwing money on eternally altering the Cornish house.

The above paragraph need not be repeted to Bryan.

I think I have now told you all I can remember. I fear I am not writing as clearly as I used.

Anyhow I have *not* been well since I saw you & therefore it

LX

has taken some time & courage to write all this.

I don't think anyone will remember me in 60 years & think
it touching you should want to know about Tyra.
                    Yours sincerely
                    Dorothy Harlow

[note by Hilary Tunstall-Behrens appended to the text] This
letter was written to me after a short meeting in Oxford,
where Mrs Harlow lived, when father and I were visiting
Pembroke for a centenary celebration and in the evening
went across to talk to Mrs. Harlow who was the daughter
of a great friend of the family called Forrest.

MR. L. W. F. BEHRENS.

A correspondent writes :—

"Cornwall has lost one of its foremost agriculturists in Mr. Louis Wilhelm Ferdinand Behrens, who died last week at Forest-hill, Kent. Although he had not been settled in the county for a great many years, he had become a leader in all those methods of intensive and garden culture whereby the district round Penzance has been able to compete with far more Southern latitudes in the London and other markets. In his sheltered fields Mr. Behrens last year ripened maize, an achievement almost unparalleled in England. Along the cliff edge he introduced masses of beautifully flowering creepers, which, in seasons of autumn drought, could be sacrificed most beneficially for the sheep. It was characteristic of the man to see what ornamental growths could be turned to use in emergency. This season he was growing, with the aid of those artificials particularly recommended by Austrian experience, a considerable area of sugar beet, and amid all his energies he was ever accessible to neighbouring farmers, to whom he was ready to reveal all his methods and delighted to impart the knowledge which he had often acquired but newly, and that at considerable outlay.

"Mr. Behrens, who was aged 62, served all through the Franco-Prussian War and preserved a vivid memory of such battles as Wörth and Mars-le-Tour. In private life he was a particularly brilliant talker, a collector of English modern pictures, and himself an amateur artist of not a little achievement. In politics Mr. Behrens was a strong Conservative and Tariff Reformer."

THE LATE MR. BEHRENS.

A very animated, attractive, and engaging personality has been withdrawn from us in the terribly sudden and premature decease of Mr. Louis Frederic Behrens. Agriculturist and man of science, Mr. Behrens was indeed in his sixty-second year, but his commanding presence and fine physique appeared to forbid the very idea of change. Probably no landowner of recent years has done more for Cornwall than Mr. Behrens. Beginning almost invariably with feuds, meeting with ingrained prejudice against every new idea, Mr. Behrens won his way among the small farmers and labourers of South-West Cornwall until at the time of his passing he was already looked up to as the man who was experimenting, trying, searching for the benefit of all. Intensive culture in a dozen forms which the genial air of Marazion and St. Hilary invited—soy beans which will only flourish where there is no frost, La Bresse fowls which sell so well for the table when bred in Brittany—and, therefore, why not in Cornwall? —these were but some of Mr. Behrens's attempts to which his neighbours might ever have access, welcome to note failure as well as success, frankly told outlay as well as receipts. Last year the fine weather of later September enabled him to secure ripe maize cobs, a triumph rare indeed upon English soil. His German knowledge and interests made him an enthusiastic champion of sugar beet cultivation in this country, and his world-wide travelling had left him with a sentiment of nothing but wonder for the people who did not safeguard their obvious interests by a scientific tariff. The last communication which we had with this gifted pioneer of a truly scientific agriculture related to the nuisance of weeds spreading from ill-farmed or derelict land. The excellent Act which is at present in force in Canada appeared to him to be worthy of enactment in the United Kingdom. Weeding on his own property cost him annually considerably over a hundred pounds, and of this, since he went in for high farming and kept a good staff, he was almost certainly justified in believing that by far the greater proportion was entailed upon the well-farmed land by the neglected and weed-ridden properties of the neighbourhood. The matter is of very special interest to all good farmers, and few better memorials to Mr. Behrens's memory could be found than in parliamentary attention to this practical demand of a life-long worker in the cause of clean and good farming.

The news of the death of Mr. Behrens will be regretted by his friends in West Cornwall.

Those who knew him best held him in great respect. He was a man of distinguished appearance and strong individuality. A natural kindliness of heart was sometimes hidden by a brusque manner; and a determination to stand by legal rights was often accompanied by many a benevolent action. It was unfortunate that a few local residents disputed his right to certain pathways. He resented their manner, and won his case when the matter was threshed out in the High Court in London. Mr. Behrens then made some concessions to the public. He was interested in experiments in sugar beet growing; had a chemical laboratory on his premises, tried to acclimatise various shrubs, and was interested in social problems, and in the Cornish Fishery. He attended the recent Royal Cornwall Show.

Mr. Behrens worked his farm on scientific lines, and in the carrying out of his ideas became a large employer of labour. His death, at the age of sixty-two, came as a great surprise to the people living in the neighbourhood, who for the most part were unaware of his illness. It was only on Monday last that medical aid was summoned, and then no immediate danger was anticipated, but on Thursday it was decided to call in additional medical advice, and three doctors were in attendance that night, but on Friday morning the end came. In accordance with the expressed wish of Mr. Behrens, his body will be cremated in London.

"ONE AND ALL" NOTES.

There was a Door to which I found no Key:
There was a Veil past which I could not see:
Some little Talk awhile of Me and Thee
There seem'd—and then no more of Thee and Me.

This is the thirty-second quatrain of the Rubaiyat of Omar Khayyam, the Persian poet, whose poetical philosophy was cast into imperishable verse by Edward Fitzgerald.

It is in a little booklet, and has against it a pencil mark to call my attention to the enigma of life and death. The pencil mark was made by a hand which is now nerveless and never will trace another line. And across the title page are the words:

"With a friend's greetings.
Sept. 1905.
L. W. F. B."

The friend, the donor of the little book, was Mr. L. W. F. Behrens,   , and as I write these lines he lies in the stillness of death, at the age of 62, having left instructions that no flowers are to be sent to his funeral and that his remains are to be cremated.

You, who read this column, need not turn away indignantly. I am not going to soar into poetry and describe my friend Mr. Behrens as an angel of light. If you choose you can turn to the cricket news, or the mining notes, or anything else that will not irritate you. I am only going to write some notes on a Man, a man whom I have long respected and admired, and with whom I have exchanged straight words in Talks which can never be repeated, because the lips   are sealed in silence. Let me say, however, that Mr. Behrens and myself have never been associated in any financial or newspaper enterprise. He did not hold a single share in the journals emanating from this office; and once and once only I sat at his table and shared his hospitality. The invitation was always open, but other duties kept

me away from the Cove, ever memorable through the exploits of Harry Carter, the King of Cornish smugglers, a hundred years ago. I exchanged a number of letters with Mr. Behrens and had a few short talks with him.

I began my acquaintance with the deceased landowner by libelling him. Like most other people I am apt to jump at conclusions, and assume that the rich capitalist and landowner is naturally something of a tyrant. The reason is obvious; one's sympathy is always with the Bottom Dog. The village Hampden, especially on paper, is something of a hero. We know there have been some sturdy villagers who have been oppressed by tyrannical landlords, and we are always ready to take the charitable view that the poor man is telling the truth, the whole truth and nothing but the truth; while the rich man, as Saint Basil once wrote, "is a thief." It takes a long time to learn the many-sidedness of human nature; to realise that a poor man can be as unjust, as selfish, as incapable of stating the whole of a case, as full of prejudice and of hatred as the richest Dives that ever lived. And some of us never learn that truth and character do not depend either on poverty or riches; that integrity is not a matter of condition, and that good and evil are found in cot and castle.

PUBLIC AND PRIVATE RIGHTS.

The story   as it came to me seemed so circumstantial that I believed it, and published what I was told were the facts. I knew that in some cases rights-of-way had been illegally filched from the public, and I was ready to believe that here was another case of a rich oppressor riding rough-shod over the legal rights of the poor.

I was invited to investigate the facts for myself. I did so, and came to the conclusion that Mr. Behrens was strictly within the four corners of his rights and that whatever concessions he might make would be an act of grace.

Please remember that I was the first to ventilate in the Press the charges against him; that I started with a prejudice against him; that my sympathies were democratic; that as a youth I had preached Land Nationalisation and Socialism, and have a natural bias in favour of retaining all public rights and resisting all encroachments of private individuals.

To this day I like short cuts across parks and fields, because I loathe the "hard high road," where one is choked with the dust of locomotives and other vehicles, and because I love the woods and the rivulets, and popping rabbits and cows knee deep in grass. I try not to damage hedges or crops, but I hate being confined to a dusty thoroughfare, and I want a law passed giving every Englishman the right to walk around the entire coast and to make the beaches national property.

HOW PRIVILEGES ARE ABUSED AND RIGHTS LOST.

I have also said, and I say it again, that it is rarely that only one party to a dispute is in the wrong. If public rights or privileges are forfeited or cancelled it is often because they have been abused or overstrained. If you can no longer roam at will by day or night, with dogs or without, with packages or without, from Helston to Porthleven, via the Loe Pool, it is partly because some people behaved disgracefully in days long past. The public were punished for the sins of some of their number. It was natural that the pendulum should swing the other way. Apparently the punishment was not merely in excess of the crime, but barriers were erected where they had never been before, and some were smashed by the village Hampdens of twenty years ago. If Captain Rogers had not been ruffled by lawless and destructive people he would probably not have thrown gates across what at one time was open country. On the other hand, if public rights were not challenged by landowners there would be less work for political agitators and less need for lawsuits or for fresh legislation to give the working people of England fresh air, a peep at the country and the breath of the sea. In all these matters tact will go far, and when tact fails and inconsiderateness begins trouble is sure to follow, in little matters as in great. If the public had not abused their privileges at St. Michael's Mount they would now have more than the limited access kindly permitted by Lord St. Levan. If there had been more tact and golden common sense in the conference between Kruger and Milner at Bloemfontein we should have been spared a devastating and futile war. When selfishness and temper enter into human relationships trouble follows as the sparks fly upward.

But to return to Mr. Behrens, who has passed away at a moment when he could have least been spared.

I went   expecting to meet a surly and truculent boor, with the stamp of the money-grubber and land-grabber upon him. I found instead a singularly handsome man, with silvery hair and beard, an old-time cavalier in the garb of a modern squire. Instead of being surly he was high-spirited, accustomed to lead, and in giving courtesy expected it in return; but meeting rudeness would resent it with the strength of a fiery nature.

In his youth he was a soldier. He fought in the Franco-Prussian war (I think he was a native of Austria), and all the comrades who shared his tent left their bones on the battlefield. He alone lived through the war, and a man who faced death in battle was not to be handled as clay in the hands of the potter later in life. He came to England and had a successful business career. He fell in love with   and made it his seaside home. He gave thousands of pounds for land, buying some at above its market value. He experimented with beet-growing, believing that we could grow much of the sugar we import. He planted trees from various parts of the world and tried to acclimatise them. He started a model farm and a laboratory. He believed that waste land should be cultivated. He hated to see broken ginger beer bottles and other litter defacing the cliffs and spoiling the bathing beaches. The West Penwith Rural Council ordered him as owner to attend to a house which was unsafe as a human habitation. He sought to act on his legal rights and made certain offers as compensation to aggrieved persons for disturbance. in order that he might comply with the Council's mandate, and also cultivate the land. The offers were refused. an agitation resulted, litigation followed, and the High Court decided in Mr. Behrens's favour.

You cannot steal the land from its present owners unless you also steal dividends, mines, ships, railroads, and every other form of productive wealth. If you did steal it you would have anarchy among all who had given rein to their predatory instincts. Anarchy would entail bloodshed, and the end of bloodshed would be a new tyranny, not an earthly Paradise. H. G. Wells admits that the weak spot in the Socialist case is the inability of the reformers to guarantee that the administrators of nationalised industries would be any more unselfish and noble people than the rank and file of administrators to-day. If they were not, the return to Individualism would be rapid and inevitable.

I say, therefore, that while I look upon land robbery as a nightmare, and land nationalisation by purchase as a millennial dream, I still think that a nation of more than forty millions of landless people must exercise some control over the land, must use what land is needed for public purposes; must preserve public rights to common land and rights-of-way across private land; that in the public interest no foreshore should be kept as private property and that no landowner should be able to prevent you or me from walking around the entire coast of England, either on the cliffs or the shores, nor be able to prevent the people from our murky cities from migrating to the sea whenever they can escape from the factory-hells which often turn human beings into anæmic and consumptive wrecks when they should be in the heyday of life and health.

All this I told Mr. Behrens, without mincing words; and we remained friends.

MR. BEHRENS WON.

If you try to get by force what you can only expect as an act of grace, you will find an ex-soldier not as pliable as you would wish. Mr. Behrens had given employment to many men at good wages; he had helped the fishermen; had looked after them when they were sick, and was open to give-and-take. Others preferred the test of law and the landowner won. It is easy to say he should have given more; but others might also have demanded less. He knew what his rights were, he wanted them respected, and that concessions should be accepted without resentment and bitterness.

Those who knew Mr. Behrens best respected him most. A Cornish novelist once told me he should like to work this landed tyrant into a book. I said: "Do so, but first go to the Cove, see the man and his work, learn all sides of the right-of-way case, and you will find that the despot is benevolent, and that he is a pioneer and a man worthy of respect, whatever his faults or the faults of his assailants." The novel has never been written.

As in all cases of this kind Mr. Behrens received threats of personal violence. His trees were torn up and fences pulled down. He was intimidated, but would not turn aside. He cared not a rap for public opinion. His private charities remained private. He did good even to some who had fought him. He was interested in the scheme being formulated to promote dairy co-operation in Cornwall, and would have helped it along if he had lived.

Mr. Behrens was more English than many Englishmen. He believed in the gospel of work and in the maintenance of the British Empire. He had a great attachment for England, and Cornwall had an irresistible fascination for him. He was as artistic and intellectual as he could be choleric if crossed and insulted. He could not tolerate political wind-bags, and believed that trade unionism is often tyrannical and a hindrance to trade. With a natural bent for leadership he realised that working men must submit to discipline and must be trained to right methods of work. He hated slackness, and he sent his sons out into the world to hold responsible positions, although he could have given them a measure of luxury and the idleness which is destructive of character. He preached and practised the gospel of work, and was a pioneer who cared nothing for popular applause; was adamant in the face of popular approbrium; and he lived a simple life in an obscure cove, until the sudden development of that fell disease appendicitis, with complications, ended fatally after an operation had been performed.

HELP FOR THE FISHERIES.

Only a few weeks before his death Mr. Behrens wrote me an earnest letter, deploring the collapse of the local fisheries, and expressing a desire to help in rehabilitating this county industry. More than this I have no right to say at present. At this juncture his death is simply deplorable.

In the life of L. W. F. Behrens the little dispute about rights-of-way was a mere speck of dust on the picture. Some people judge a life by an incident of that life. The just man looks at the warp and woof of the whole life; and if we apply that test we shall find much heroism, much chivalry, the qualities of the Spartan, the brightness and energy of the pioneer, and an unusual measure of benevolence beneath a handsome but fierce exterior; in other words he was a Man, with the worth and manliness of a man.

Thinking of his uncompleted schemes, and his desire to greatly help a community which misunderstood and often misrepresented him, I profoundly regret his having passed away beyond that Veil through which he could not see, and I close this little tribute to his memory with lines from Khayyam which he read and marked in the copy he sent to me:

Ah Love! could thou and I with Fate conspire
To grasp this sorry Scheme of Things entire,
    Would not we shatter it to bits—and then
Re-mould it nearer to the Heart's Desire.

Ah, Moon of my Delight who know'st no wane,
The Moon of Heav'n is rising once again:
    How oft hereafter rising shall she look
Through this same Garden after me—in vain!

And when Thyself with shining Foot shall pass
Among the Guests Star-scatter'd on the Grass,
    And in thy joyous Errand reach the Spot
Where I made one—turn down an empty Glass!

HERBERT THOMAS.

George Hotel, Castletown, Isle of Man

16th Sept/23

Dear Brian

I have your letter recalling many memories of byegone days.

Mr Tunstall and his family were good friends to me when I first came to London fifty seven years ago and I have the pleasantest recollections of them since then, excepting only the sad end of your uncle John's life and its effect upon those he loved

I was glad to have the opportunity of seeing your mother in June at Barnet: her severe accident was borne with heroic fortitude and cheerfulness, trusting in God to the end.

Last month I had tea with your Aunt Mabel in her flat. I hope she will be able to retain it in spite of the high rental, for she is happy in it with all its associations and opportunities of relieving her loneliness.

I shall be in London again the first fortnight in November and will write you when there, so that we can meet, all being well.

My son has completed his sea-side residence at Barton on Sea and I spent a fortnight last month with him and his family there.

My kind regards to your wife and to Tancred.

          Yours very sincerely

          George Parker

LXVIII

St Mary's Convent, St Aldhelms Rd, Branksome, Bournmouth

Sep 29th

Dearest Jean,

What a thrilling event is this book of Hilary's. Thank you
so much for sending me a copy. He is such a modest
person, who has never talked of this adventure, which is
truly remarkable. I should think the book would be much
read, a favourite subject with such a large public. I think if
our dear Hilary has any literary career before him, I feel
very proud, & to see the grand old name of Tunstall on
the front page is an extra touch of excitement for me. You
write me dear, such an interesting letter, with all the news.
One is glad to think of Mor & Ken being able to see so
much, – expand their experience. They won't be feeling so
homesick. My admiration for the enterprize of Marigold &
her friends, knows no bounds. You can tell her so. One of
these days you will be going out & we will see you no
more. But it does me good to think of the active & useful
lives you all lead. I shall love to see you dear when you
are able to come. Joy wrote me of the hectic weekend
looking after Simon. I hope he got through all right. His
lively spirits will always help him. I have an appointment
for my eyes on Oct 5th. There is not much wrong with
them. But I try them too much. I manage on many days
to get down to the garden, & walk down to the drive &
crossroads. Where I see the world go by such as it is. I
have not had a subscription to a library since my operation
but Mr Hallett lends me some books, & I read my old
ones with pleasure. The Suez affair is frightful. Were it not
for Russia's backing, we would I think have used force. But
what could we do against the Russian armies? I feel the
glory of our Empire is over. But truly it is a Christian
Empire, & should survive.
My best love & hoping to see you before long

Yours affectionately

Aunt Mabel

Please let me know Hilary's last address.